TREASURY OF Christmas

PUBLICATIONS INTERNATIONAL, LTD.

Front cover photography: Chris Cassidy Photography

Pictured on the front cover *(top to bottom):* Broccoli with Red Pepper and
Shallots *(page 146)*, Glazed Roast Pork Loin with Cranberry Stuffing *(page 94)*
and Eggnog Cheesecake *(page 266)*.

Pictured on the back cover *(clockwise from top):* Tortelloni Wreath with Pesto Dip
(page 14), Roast Turkey with Pan Gravy *(page 108)* and Golden Kolacky
(page 297).

ISBN: 0-7853-2262-0

Library of Congress Catalog Card Number: 97-66764

Manufactured in U.S.A.

8 7 6 5 4 3 2 1

Microwave Cooking: Microwave ovens vary in wattage. Use the cooking times as
guidelines and check for doneness before adding more time.

Contents

Bright Beginnings
TO HOLIDAY COOKING

Cooking takes on special joy during the holiday season. Open houses, intimate dinners, casual gatherings and cookie exchanges all call for the finest holiday foods. The holidays are also a time for remembering special neighbors, teachers, coworkers and friends with tasty homemade gifts from your kitchen. In this holiday treasury you'll find festive recipes for tempting appetizers, savory side dishes, noteworthy main courses, dazzling desserts and irresistible cookies and confections. Make this holiday cooking season your most enjoyable and rewarding ever with the delicious recipes in this wonderful collection.

HOLIDAY ENTERTAINING HOW–TOS
Planning is the most important step for successful holiday entertaining. Following are helpful ways to get started.
• Putting your ideas down on paper is the first step. Doing this helps avoid chaos later on.
• Building a party around the Christmas theme helps coordinate all aspects of the affair. You may want to plan your get-together around holiday activities, such as tree trimming, caroling or sledding. Or coordinate a party to follow an outing to the ballet or theater.
• Keep your budget in mind when deciding on your entertaining style, number of guests, menu selections and party supplies.
• If this will be one of your first company meals, keep it on the small side. It is easier to cook and serve for eight to ten people than for twenty.
• If you are planning a sit-down dinner, do not invite more people than you can comfortably seat at your table. Similarly, for casual get-togethers, do not invite more people than your entertainment area can easily accommodate. Guests may become uncomfortable if they are crowded.
• Not all entertaining requires a full meal. Consider inviting family and friends over for desserts or light snacks.
• Many guests like to contribute to the festivities by bringing a side dish, dessert, appetizer or wine. Be sure to have some recommendations ready so that if you are asked, you may offer suggestions for foods that will complement the rest of the meal.

PLANNING FESTIVE MENUS
Whether you're planning a Christmas dinner with the relatives or a holiday open house, these guidelines for selecting a menu will make the foods you serve more inviting.
• Select the entrée first, then plan the other dishes around it.

• Not every item on the menu needs to be a showstopper. Select one or two involved recipes and let the remainder be foods that are purchased or are easy to prepare.
• Eye appeal is an important consideration when planning a meal. Select foods with a variety of colors. Green or orange vegetables, red cranberry relish or multi-colored salad all add visual interest. A monochromatic meal is not only visually uninteresting, but is usually perceived as less flavorful.
• Pick foods that offer a variety of textures. Crisp-tender broccoli, creamy mashed potatoes and crunchy fruit all complement the firm, chewy texture of meats.
• A balanced meal offers contrasting flavors. The tart flavor of cranberries and the mild flavor of turkey make a perfect combination.
• Choose side dishes with different shapes and sizes. Whole-berry cranberry relish served alongside peas and Brussels sprouts would not be as interesting with a meal as whole-berry cranberry relish served alongside broccoli spears and diagonally sliced carrots.
• When selecting recipes, choose several that can be made ahead of time. This will leave you more time for visiting with your guests.
• Make sure you have enough serving dishes and utensils for the foods you plan to serve. Borrow dishes or utensils from relatives or friends before the party day, if needed.
• Review the recipes you plan to make, then prepare a comprehensive grocery list. Remember to place any special orders well in advance. Nonperishable items can be purchased weeks ahead. More perishable items should be purchased close to the day of your event. Preparing an organized shopping list will prevent those stressful last-minute dashes to the supermarket.

Come for Cocktails
• For a cocktail party or open house where appetizers are the main event, plan a variety of snacks and spreads, including some that are hearty and filling.
• Prepare a balance of hot and cold appetizers that provides a range of flavors and textures, from spicy and rich to light and refreshing.
• Keep in mind that at a large party where

seating is limited, guests appreciate finger food and bite-sized portions with not-too-drippy sauces.
• Remember that the longer the occasion lasts, the more your guests will eat. Plan on a minimum of ten to twelve servings per person for a cocktail party.
• When serving appetizers before a meal, one or two selections should be ample, allowing five to seven servings per person.

MASTERING MEAT AND POULTRY
Selecting the main course is an important first step in the planning of any meal, especially one for the holidays. To please family and friends, consider holiday meal traditions and food preferences. As the host, evaluate your entertaining style (casual to formal) and your monetary and time budgets. When preparing meat and poultry, follow recipe directions closely and make note of the following helpful tips.
• Recommended refrigerator storage time for unopened, prepackaged fresh cuts of meat is generally two to three days; for ground meats, one to two days.
• To prepare beef, pork, lamb or veal roasts, place meat, fat side up, on a rack in a shallow, open roasting pan. Insert a meat thermometer into the thickest part, not resting in fat or on bone. Roasts are usually cooked uncovered in a 325°F oven.
• Standard final temperatures for roast beef, lamb and veal are 140°F for rare, 160°F for medium and 170°F for well done. Pork temperatures should reach 160°F. Fully cooked hams can be warmed to 120° to 140°F. Smoked hams that must be cooked before eating should reach 160°F.
• Thaw frozen poultry in the refrigerator in its original wrapper. Allow 24 hours thawing time for every five pounds. Fresh poultry should be used within two days of purchase.
• Mix stuffing ingredients and stuff the bird immediately before putting it in the oven. Stuff lightly—do not pack.

• To determine when a whole chicken or turkey is cooked and ready to eat, use a meat thermometer inserted in the meatiest part of the thigh, away from bone or fat. For turkey and chicken the thigh temperature should be 180°F; breast temperature 170°F.

• Bone-in chicken pieces are thoroughly cooked when you can insert a fork with ease and the juices run clear, not pink. Boneless chicken pieces are done when the centers are no longer pink.

• The temperatures given in recipes for removing meat and poultry from the oven are 5° to 10°F lower than the standard final temperatures. This is because the temperature continues to rise during the stand time.

• Before serving, allow enough time for cooking the meat, stand time and carving.

The Art of Carving
One of the more formidable tasks when preparing a large meal is carving the roast or bird. To help you carve the main attraction like a pro, follow these general meat preparation guidelines and the special carving instructions for some of the holiday's most popular entrées.

General Guidelines
• After roasting, a stand time of 10 to 20 minutes is recommended for large cuts of meat, such as roasts and turkeys. Stand time allows the meat to finish cooking. It is also easier to carve after standing. If meat is carved right after being removed from the oven, it loses more of its flavorful juices.

• Unless you are planning on carving at the table, place the meat on a large cutting board with a well at one end to hold the juice. (Or, place a cutting board inside a baking sheet. The juice will collect in the baking sheet.) Use a long, sharp carving knife to slice and a long-handled meat fork to steady the meat.

Boneless Cuts
Boneless beef, pork and lamb roasts and boneless hams are easy to carve. Hold the meat steady with a long-handled meat fork. With the knife held perpendicular to the cutting board, cut across the grain into thin, uniform slices. Cut the slices between ¼ and ½ inch thick (illustration 1).

For a thinner cut of meat, such as a beef brisket, follow the preceding directions, but slice the meat diagonally across the grain. This will give a meat slice with a larger surface area.

Standing Beef Rib Roast
For added stability, cut a wedge-shaped slice from the large end of the roast so that the meat will sit flat on the cutting board. Insert a long-handled meat fork below the top rib. Slice across the top of the roast toward the rib bone. This roast can be sliced between ½ and ¾ inch thick (illustration 2).

With the tip of the knife, cut along the rib bone to release the slice of meat (illustration 3).

To remove the meat slice, slide the knife blade under the cut slice of meat. Holding it steady with a meat fork, lift the slice and place it on a platter (illustration 4).

Bone-In Leg of Lamb

For stability, place the roast on its side on the cutting board with the shank bone facing away from you. Cut two or three lengthwise slices from the section of the meat facing you. This will allow the meat to sit flat on the cutting board (illustration 5).

Turn the roast up so that it sits on the cut area. Hold the roast steady with a long-handled meat fork inserted into the meat opposite the shank bone. Holding the knife perpendicular to the cutting board and starting by the shank bone, cut across the grain into uniform, thin slices. Cut the slices between ¼ and ½ inch thick (illustration 6).

When you reach the aitch bone, release the slices by cutting under them along the leg bone (illustration 7). This same technique can be used when carving ham.

Roast Turkey

To remove the leg, hold the drumstick and cut the skin with a carving knife between the thigh and the body of the turkey to the joint. Pull the leg away from the body of the turkey and cut through the joint at the backbone (illustration 8).

To separate the drumstick from the thigh, place the leg on the cutting board skin side up. Cut through at the joint (illustration 9).

At this point, the drumstick may be served as it is or cut into slices. To slice the drumstick, hold the drumstick at an angle, bony side up. Cut down into ¼-inch slices. Rotate the drumstick as you cut. Remove and discard the large tendons (illustration 10).

To cut the thigh into slices, turn the thigh skin side down. Cut along the length of the bone, then turn skin side up and cut the meat across the grain (illustration 11).

To remove the wings, insert a long-handled meat fork into the turkey to hold it steady. Cut down between the wing and the body of the turkey with a carving knife. Pull the wing out and cut through the joint (illustration 12).

To remove the breast meat, insert a long-handled meat fork into the turkey to hold it steady. At the base of the breast meat, make a horizontal cut across the breast to the bone. Cut the slices with straight, even strokes down to the horizontal cut. At that point, the slices will fall free (illustration 13).

SEAFOOD SAVVY

The vast variety of seafood available makes preparing exceptional seafood entrées and appetizers easier than ever. You and your guests will find delicious, nutritious fish and shellfish perfect holiday fare. Following are helpful purchasing and cooking guidelines for successfully preparing the catch of the day.

Purchasing Guidelines

• When buying fresh whole fish, look for bright, clear, protruding eyes and moist, shiny skin. The gills should be red or pink and the flesh firm and elastic. A fresh fish has a fresh, slightly oceanlike, mild odor. If there is a distinctly fishy, sour smell, do not buy it.
• When purchasing fresh fish fillets and steaks, look for cuts with moist flesh that is free from discoloration and skin that is shiny and resilient. If the fillet or steak has an off odor, do not buy it.
• All fresh shellfish should have a fresh, mild, sea-breeze odor. Fresh lobsters and crabs should be purchased live and as close to the time of cooking as possible. Shrimp should feel firm to the touch. Hard-shell clams, mussels and oysters should have tightly closed shells or snap tightly closed when tapped. Freshly shucked oysters are usually creamy white, although the color varies with the variety, and should be surrounded by a clear, slightly milky white or light gray liquid. Freshly shucked clams should be plump, moist and shiny.

Cooking Tips

• Before cooking fish, rinse it under cold running water and pat it dry with paper towels. Fish cooks quickly, so be careful not to overcook it (this makes the fish tough and destroys flavor). Fish is done cooking when the flesh turns opaque and begins to flake easily when tested with a fork.
• When cooking clams, mussels and oysters in the shell, the shell should open. Remove them as they open. Discard any that do not open.
• Shucked shellfish, such as clams, mussels and oysters, become opaque when cooked, and the edges of the oysters will start to curl.
• Raw shrimp turn pink and opaque. Scallops turn milky white or opaque and firm.

BAKING BASICS FOR THE CHRISTMAS KITCHEN

Let the tantalizing aromas of homebaked breads, cakes and pies fill your kitchen during the Christmas season. Ensure successful holiday baking by practicing good cooking techniques.

Getting Started

• Read the entire recipe before beginning your baking to make sure you have all the necessary ingredients and utensils.
• Use the ingredients called for in the recipe. Do not assume that butter, shortening and margarine are interchangeable.

• Adjust oven racks and preheat the oven. Check oven temperature for accuracy with an oven thermometer.
• Do any necessary food preparation before making the recipe (e.g., separating eggs, slicing fruit, toasting nuts, melting chocolate).
• Measure all the ingredients accurately and assemble them in the order in which they are called for in the recipe.
• Use the pan size specified in the recipe. Prepare the pan according to the recipe directions.
• Follow recipe directions and baking times exactly. Check for doneness using the test given in the recipe.

Tips for Melting Chocolate

• Make sure the utensils used for melting chocolate are completely dry. Moisture causes chocolate to become stiff and grainy. If this happens, add ½ teaspoon shortening (not butter) for each ounce of chocolate and stir until smooth. Chocolate scorches easily, and once scorched it cannot be used. Follow one of these three methods for successful melting:

Direct Heat: Place the chocolate in a heavy saucepan and melt over very low heat, stirring constantly. Remove the chocolate from heat as soon as it is melted. Be sure to watch the chocolate carefully because it is easily scorched when using this method.

Double Boiler: This is the safest method because it prevents scorching. Place the chocolate in the top of a double boiler or in a bowl over hot, not boiling, water and stir until smooth. (Make sure that the water remains just below a simmer and is one inch below the bottom of the top pan or bowl.) Be careful that no steam or water gets into the chocolate.

Microwave Oven: Place an unwrapped 1-ounce square or 1 cup of chips in a small microwavable bowl. Microwave on HIGH (100% power) 1 to 1½ minutes, stirring after 1 minute. Stir the chocolate at 30-second intervals until smooth. Be sure to stir microwaved chocolate since it may retain its original shape even after melting.

FILLING THE CHRISTMAS COOKIE JAR

With Santa's arrival, it's time to fill the cookie jar. Adults and kids alike enjoy baking cookies for the yuletide season. Whether you choose to make old-world favorites or quick and easy treats, these tips for preparing, baking and storing your cookies will be helpful.

Preparation Tips

• For cutout cookies, chill cookie dough before rolling for easier handling. Remove only enough dough from the refrigerator to work with at one time.
• For shaped or drop cookies, dough should be portioned in uniform size and shape on cookie sheet.
• Space mounds of dough about 2 inches apart on cookie sheet to allow for spreading unless the recipe directs otherwise.
• Use the pan size called for in the recipe for baking brownies and bar cookies. Substituting a different pan will affect the cookies' cooking time and texture.

Baking Tips

• The best cookie sheets to use are those with no sides or only one or two short sides. These sheets allow the heat to circulate easily during baking and promote even browning.
• For even baking and browning, place only one cookie sheet at a time in the center of the oven. If the cookies begin to brown unevenly, rotate the cookie sheet from front to back halfway through the baking time.
• When baking more than one sheet of cookies at a time, rotate the two sheets from top to bottom and bottom to top halfway through the baking time.
• For best results, use shortening or a nonstick cooking spray to grease cookie sheets. Or, line the cookie sheets with parchment paper.
• Allow cookie sheets to cool between batches, as the dough will spread too quickly if placed on a hot cookie sheet.
• To avoid overbaking the cookies, check them at the minimum baking time. If more time is needed, watch carefully to make sure the cookies don't burn. It is usually better to slightly underbake cookies than to overbake them.

Storing Tips

• Unbaked cookie dough can usually be refrigerated up to one week or frozen up to six weeks before using. Rolls of dough should be sealed tightly in plastic wrap; other doughs should be stored in airtight containers. Label dough with baking information for convenience.

• Store soft and crisp cookies separately at room temperature to prevent changes in texture and flavor. Keep soft cookies in airtight containers. If they begin to dry out, add a piece of apple or bread to the container to help them retain moisture. If crisp cookies become soggy, heat undecorated cookies in a 300°F oven for 3 to 5 minutes or until crisp.

• Store cookies with glazes, icings and fragile decorations in single layers between sheets of waxed paper. Bar cookies and brownies may be stored in their own baking pans; cover with foil or plastic wrap when cool.

• As a rule, crisp cookies freeze better than soft, moist cookies. Rich, buttery bar cookies and brownies are an exception to this rule since they freeze extremely well. Baked cookies can be frozen in airtight containers or plastic food storage bags up to three months. Meringue-based cookies do not freeze well and chocolate-dipped cookies may discolor if frozen. Thaw frozen cookies and brownies, unwrapped, at room temperature.

CANDY MAKING—STEPS TO SWEET SUCCESS

An abundance of irresistible treats is a delicious sign of the Christmas season. Candies are fun to make and a satisfying indulgence for the sweet tooth. The following are tips to ensure successful candy making.

Getting Started

• Read recipes thoroughly before starting. Have all equipment ready and ingredients measured before you begin cooking.

• Do not try to double or halve candy recipes or use ingredient substitutions unless alternates are listed.

• Humidity will affect the preparation of many candies so it's best to choose dry days for candy making.

• Use a heavy saucepan with a flat bottom to prevent candy from scorching during cooking. Pan size is important; pans should be large enough to prevent syrups from boiling and foaming over the rim.

• Using a candy thermometer is the most accurate way to tell the temperature of boiling syrup. Before each use, verify your candy thermometer's accuracy by checking its reading in boiling water. Water normally boils at 212°F at sea level. If the thermometer does not read 212°F, you may not live at sea level or the thermometer may be slightly off. To adjust the temperature given in a recipe, add or subtract the difference from 212°F as needed. For example, if your thermometer reads 210°F in boiling water and the recipe temperature is 240°F, cook the candy to 238°F, or two degrees less than the temperature stated in the recipe.

Cooking Tips

• When making candy, it is necessary to prevent large sugar crystals from forming because they cause candy to become grainy. To prevent large crystals, sugar should be completely dissolved and crystals should be washed down from the side of the pan before a candy thermometer is placed in the pan. To wash down the crystals, use a pastry brush dipped in hot water to gently brush the crystals down into the syrup. Dip the brush frequently in hot water to clean off the bristles.

• It is important to cook candy to the proper temperature. Attach the candy thermometer to the side of the pan after washing down sugar crystals, making sure the thermometer does not touch the bottom of the pan. Be sure the thermometer bulb is completely covered with boiling syrup, not just foam. Read the thermometer at eye level.

• If a candy thermometer is not available, use the cold water test.

Cold Water Test for Candy

Place a small amount of the hot syrup in a cup of cold (but not iced) water. Using your fingers, remove the cooled syrup. If the syrup has not reached the desired ball or thread stage, continue cooking the candy and test again.

Soft-ball stage (234° to 240°F): The syrup can be rolled into a soft ball that flattens when removed from water (photo 1).

Firm-ball stage (244° to 248°F): The syrup can be rolled into a firm ball that does not flatten immediately when removed from water (photo 2).

Hard-ball stage (250° to 266°F): The syrup can be rolled into a firm ball that gives some resistance when pressed (photo 3).

Soft-crack stage (270° to 290°F): The syrup can be stretched into threads that are hard but elastic (photo 4).

Hard-crack stage (300° to 310°F): The syrup forms threads that are thin, hard and brittle and can easily be snapped in half (photo 5).

1

2

3

4

5

TASTY GIFTS—ALWAYS IN GOOD TASTE

Giving a homemade gift from your kitchen is a beautiful way to express warm holiday wishes. And the yuletide season is the perfect time to help a holiday hostess by contributing a favorite appetizer or luscious dessert to the party menu. Here are some tips for festive food gift-giving.

• Buttery cookies, gooey confections, savory breads and fresh-from-the-oven cakes are obvious gift choices. But don't forget homemade soups, heavenly dessert sauces and crispy snack mixes.

• Be sure to label your gifts of food. People like to know what they're eating. Also include any special storage, serving or reheating directions. Some cooks like to include a copy of their recipe, too.

• Festive packaging adds holiday spirit to your homemade specialties. Use baskets, boxes, tins, jars and gift bags as containers. Disposable plates, cups and bakeware come in many delightful holiday designs. Plastic food containers, coffee cans and berry baskets can be recycled into clever packaging.

• It's fun to pair your gifts of food with complementary items: a bottle of wine with your favorite homemade cheese spread, a new wooden bread board with a crusty loaf of homebaked bread or a brightly patterned set of oven mitts with a cheery tin of decorated Christmas cookies.

Mailing Gifts of Food

When sending edible holiday greetings, proper food selection and packaging is important. Moist quick breads and sturdy cookies are ideal choices for mailing, as are many non-fragile confections, such as fudge and caramels. It's best to prepare food just before packing and mailing, and to choose a speedy method of shipment. Foods should be completely cooled before wrapping. For cookies, leave bars uncut and wrap individual cookies in pairs, back-to-back. Use sturdy gift containers and crumpled waxed paper for cushioning. Place containers in sturdy boxes with bubble wrap, foam packing pieces, crumpled tissue or unseasoned, unbuttered popcorn.

Joyous STARTERS

FRENCH–STYLE PIZZA BITES

2 tablespoons olive oil
1 medium onion, thinly sliced
1 medium red bell pepper, cut into
   3-inch-long strips
2 cloves garlic, minced
⅓ cup pitted ripe olives, cut into thin wedges
1 can (10 ounces) refrigerated pizza crust
   dough
¾ cup (3 ounces) finely shredded Swiss or
   Gruyère cheese

Position oven rack to lowest position. Preheat oven to 425°F.
Heat oil in medium skillet over medium heat. Add onion, bell
pepper and garlic. Cook and stir 5 minutes or until vegetables
are crisp-tender. Stir in olives. Remove from heat; set aside. Pat
dough into 16×12-inch rectangle on greased large cookie
sheet. Arrange vegetables over dough. Sprinkle with cheese.
Bake 10 minutes. With long spatula, loosen crust from cookie
sheet. Slide crust onto oven rack. Bake 3 to 5 minutes more or
until golden brown.

Slide cookie sheet under crust; remove crust from rack.
Transfer to cutting board. Cut dough crosswise into eight 1¾-
inch-wide strips. Cut dough diagonally into ten 2-inch-wide
strips, making diamond pieces. Serve immediately.

Makes about 24 servings

TORTELLONI WREATH WITH PESTO DIP

1 (9-ounce) package DIGIORNO® Mushroom Tortelloni
1 (9-ounce) package DIGIORNO® Hot Red Pepper Tortelloni
1 (8-ounce) container PHILADELPHIA BRAND® Soft Cream Cheese
1 (7-ounce) package DIGIORNO® Pesto Sauce
1 teaspoon lemon juice
   Green and red pepper chunks
   Pitted ripe olives

• Add both packages of pasta to 4 quarts boiling water. Boil gently, uncovered, 6 minutes, stirring frequently. Drain; rinse with cold water.

• Mix cream cheese, sauce and juice. Place in small bowl.

• Place bowl in middle of round serving platter. Arrange pasta, peppers and olives around bowl for dipping.   *Makes 24 servings*

PREP TIME: 10 minutes
COOK TIME: 6 minutes

MARINATED MUSHROOMS

1 pint whole, uniformly sized, small white button mushroom caps, washed
½ cup olive oil
3 tablespoons tarragon vinegar
¼ cup finely chopped parsley
1 tablespoon Dijon-style mustard
3 cloves garlic, finely chopped
1 teaspoon sugar
¾ teaspoon dried tarragon leaves, crushed
½ teaspoon salt
   Freshly ground black pepper

Fill 16-ounce jar with mushrooms. Process remaining ingredients in food processor or combine in small bowl with wire whisk. Pour dressing into jar to cover mushrooms completely. Seal jar and marinate overnight at room temperature to blend flavors. Store up to 1 week in refrigerator. Bring to room temperature before serving.
Makes about 6 servings or 3 cups mushrooms

Tortelloni Wreath with Pesto Dip

SPINACH–CHEESE APPETIZERS

¼ cup olive oil

½ cup chopped onion

2 eggs

16 ounces crumbled feta cheese

3 packages (10 ounces each) frozen chopped spinach, thawed and well drained

½ cup minced fresh parsley

1 teaspoon dried oregano leaves, crushed *or* 2 tablespoons fresh oregano, chopped

Freshly grated nutmeg

Salt and black pepper

1 package (16 ounces) frozen phyllo dough, thawed

2 cups margarine, melted

Preheat oven to 375°F. Heat oil over medium-high heat in small skillet. Add onion; cook and stir until translucent. Beat eggs in large bowl; stir in onion, feta cheese, spinach, parsley and oregano. Season with nutmeg, salt and pepper.

Remove phyllo from package; unroll and place on large sheet of waxed paper. Fold phyllo crosswise into thirds. Use scissors to cut along folds into thirds. Cover phyllo with large sheet of plastic wrap and damp clean kitchen towel. Lay 1 strip of phyllo at a time on a flat surface and brush with melted margarine. Fold strip in half lengthwise; brush with margarine again. Place rounded teaspoonful of spinach filling on 1 end of strip; fold over one corner to make triangle. Continue folding end to end, as you would fold a flag, keeping edges straight. Brush top with margarine. Repeat process until all filling is used. Place triangles in a single layer, seam side down, on ungreased baking sheet. Bake 20 minutes or until lightly browned. Serve warm.   *Makes 5 dozen appetizers*

Spinach-Cheese Appetizers

LITTLE CHRISTMAS PIZZAS

⅓ cup olive oil
1 tablespoon TABASCO® pepper sauce
2 large cloves garlic, minced
1 teaspoon dried rosemary, crushed
1 (16-ounce) package hot roll mix with yeast packet
1¼ cups hot water*
All-purpose flour
TOPPINGS
1 large tomato, diced
¼ cup crumbled goat cheese
2 tablespoons chopped fresh parsley
½ cup shredded mozzarella cheese
½ cup sliced pitted green olives
⅓ cup roasted red pepper strips
½ cup chopped artichoke hearts
½ cup cherry tomatoes, sliced into wedges
⅓ cup sliced green onions

In small bowl, combine olive oil, TABASCO sauce, garlic and rosemary. In large bowl, combine hot roll mix, yeast packet, hot water and 2 tablespoons of the TABASCO mixture; stir until dough pulls away from side of bowl. Turn dough onto lightly floured surface; shape dough into a ball. Knead until smooth, adding additional flour as necessary.

Preheat oven to 425°F. Cut dough into quarters; cut each quarter into 10 equal pieces. Roll each piece into a ball. On large cookie sheet, press each ball into 2-inch round. Brush each with remaining TABASCO mixture. Arrange approximately 2 teaspoons toppings on each dough round. Bake 12 minutes or until dough is lightly browned and puffed.
Makes 40 appetizer servings

*Check hot roll mix package directions for temperature of water.

Little Christmas Pizzas, Party Polenta Stars

PARTY POLENTA STARS

3 cups water
2 tablespoons butter or margarine, divided
¾ teaspoon salt
1 cup yellow cornmeal
½ cup grated Parmesan cheese
1 teaspoon TABASCO® pepper sauce
1 tablespoon olive oil
Spicy Tomato Salsa (recipe follows)

Grease jelly-roll pan; set aside. In 2-quart saucepan over high heat, bring water, 1 tablespoon of the butter and salt to a boil. Reduce heat to low; slowly add cornmeal in a thin stream, stirring constantly. Continue to cook, stirring constantly until mixture thickens, about 5 to 10 minutes. Remove from heat; stir in cheese and TABASCO sauce.

Spread cooked cornmeal mixture in prepared jelly-roll pan to a thickness of ½ inch. Refrigerate, uncovered, for 30 minutes.

With a 2½-inch star-shaped cookie cutter, cut cooled polenta mixture into stars. In 12-inch skillet over medium-high heat, heat oil and remaining tablespoon of butter. Add polenta stars; cook 2 minutes on each side or until lightly browned, turning carefully. Repeat with remaining stars, adding oil and butter if necessary. Serve polenta stars with Spicy Tomato Salsa. *Makes 18 stars*

SPICY TOMATO SALSA

8 ounces ripe fresh tomatoes, finely diced (about 1 cup)
3 tablespoons minced green onions
1 tablespoon minced cilantro
1½ teaspoons freshly squeezed lemon juice
½ teaspoon TABASCO® pepper sauce
½ garlic clove, minced
¼ teaspoon ground cumin
⅛ teaspoon salt

Mix all ingredients in small bowl. Cover and refrigerate 1 to 2 hours to blend flavors.
Makes about 1 cup

BAKED ARTICHOKE SQUARES

½ cup plus 3 tablespoons CRISCO® Oil, divided
1 cup chopped mushrooms
¼ cup thinly sliced celery
1 clove garlic, minced
1 can (14 ounces) artichoke hearts, drained, chopped
⅓ cup chopped green onions
½ teaspoon dried marjoram, crushed
¼ teaspoon dried oregano, crushed
¼ teaspoon ground red pepper
1 cup (4 ounces) shredded Cheddar cheese
1 cup (4 ounces) shredded Monterey Jack cheese
2 eggs, slightly beaten
1½ cups all-purpose flour
½ teaspoon salt
¼ cup milk

Heat 3 tablespoons of the Crisco oil in medium skillet over medium-high heat. Cook and stir mushrooms, celery and garlic in hot oil until celery is tender. Remove from heat. Stir in artichoke hearts, onions, marjoram, oregano and ground red pepper. Add cheeses and eggs; mix well. Set aside.

Combine flour and salt in medium bowl. Blend remaining ½ cup Crisco oil and the milk in small bowl. Add to flour mixture. Stir with fork until mixture forms a ball. Press dough in bottom and 1½ inches up sides of 13×9×2-inch pan. Bake in preheated 350°F oven 10 minutes. Spread artichoke mixture on baked crust. Continue baking about 20 minutes more or until center is set. Cool slightly. Cut into 24 squares. Serve warm. *Makes 24 appetizers*

NEUFTY CUPS

2 (18×14-inch) sheets phyllo dough, thawed according to package directions
2 tablespoons butter
1 package (6 ounces) FLEUR DE LAIT® Neufchâtel® cheese, Garden Vegetables variety

Preheat oven to 350°F. Cover phyllo with damp cloth.

Melt butter; brush a small amount onto sides and bottoms of 12 miniature muffin pan cups.

Cut phyllo into 36 (3¼-inch) squares. Place 1 phyllo square into each muffin pan cup with corners pointing upward. Lightly brush phyllo with butter. Top each with another phyllo square, alternating corners; brush with butter. Repeat once more, alternating corners, so that there are 3 phyllo squares arranged in each cup.

Brush all edges of phyllo lightly with melted butter. Bake 8 to 10 minutes or until golden. Remove shells to wire racks; cool completely. Fill with Fleur de Lait®; garnish as desired.

Makes 12 appetizers

CHEDDAR CHEESE PUFFS

PUFFS
1 cup water
6 tablespoons butter, cut into pieces
1 teaspoon salt
   Dash pepper
   Dash ground nutmeg (optional)
1 cup all-purpose flour
5 large eggs, divided
1 cup plus 3 tablespoons finely shredded Cheddar or Swiss cheese, divided
FILLING
1 (11-ounce) jar NEWMAN'S OWN® All Natural Salsa
12 ounces cream cheese, softened

Preheat oven to 425°F. In heavy 2-quart saucepan, bring water, butter, salt, pepper and nutmeg to a full boil over medium heat. Remove from heat. With wooden spoon, beat in flour all at once. (If mixture does not form a ball and leave the sides of pan clean, return to medium heat and beat vigorously for 1 to 2 minutes.) Remove from heat and beat in 4 eggs, 1 at a time, until each egg is thoroughly blended. Beat in 1 cup cheese. Place mixture in pastry bag with ½-inch-diameter round tip. Pipe 1-inch rounds 2 inches apart on 2 greased baking sheets. Beat remaining egg. Brush tops of puffs with beaten egg and sprinkle with remaining 3 tablespoons cheese. Bake 20 to 25 minutes or until golden and crisp; turn off oven. Pierce each puff with knife and return to cooling oven for 10 minutes to dry out. Remove and cool.

Drain approximately ¼ cup liquid from salsa (reserve liquid for another use, if desired). Mix drained salsa with cream cheese. Cut tops off puffs; spoon filling into puffs. Replace tops.

Makes 36 appetizers

Neufty Cups

Elegant Antipasto

ELEGANT ANTIPASTO

1 jar (16 ounces) mild cherry peppers
1 package (9 ounces) frozen artichoke
**   hearts, cooked and drained**
½ pound asparagus spears, cooked
½ cup pitted ripe olives
1 medium red onion, cut into wedges
1 green bell pepper, cut into triangles
1 red bell pepper, cut into triangles
1 bottle (8 ounces) KRAFT® House
**   Italian with Olive Oil Blend Dressing**
1 wedge (4 ounces) KRAFT® Natural
**   Parmesan Cheese, shredded and**
**   divided**
1 package (8 ounces) OSCAR MAYER®
**   Sliced Hard Salami**

• Arrange vegetables in rows in 13×9-inch glass baking dish.

• Pour dressing and ⅓ cup cheese over vegetables; cover. Refrigerate 1 to 2 hours.

• Drain vegetables, reserving marinade. Arrange vegetables and salami on serving platter. Drizzle with marinade; top with remaining cheese.   *Makes 6 servings*

VARIATION: Substitute mushrooms, green beans, cherry tomatoes or broccoli flowerets for any of the vegetables listed.

PREP TIME: 20 minutes plus refrigerating

MINI MISTLETOE TURNOVERS

1 envelope LIPTON® Recipe Secrets®
**   Onion Soup Mix**
2 eggs, beaten
1 package (10 ounces) frozen chopped
**   spinach, cooked and drained**
2 cups (16 ounces) ricotta or creamed
**   cottage cheese**
1 scant cup (about 3 ounces) shredded
**   mozzarella cheese**
3 packages (8 ounces each) refrigerated
**   crescent rolls**

Preheat oven to 375°F.

In large bowl, combine onion soup mix, eggs, spinach and cheeses.

Separate crescent rolls according to package directions; cut each triangle in half (to make 2 smaller triangles) and flatten slightly. Place 1 tablespoon cheese mixture on center of each triangle; fold over and seal edges tightly with fork. Place on ungreased baking sheet; bake 15 minutes or until golden brown.
            Makes 48 turnovers

FREEZING/REHEATING DIRECTIONS:
Tightly wrap turnovers in heavy-duty foil; freeze. To reheat, unwrap and bake as directed for 8 minutes or until heated through.

FESTIVE STUFFED DATES

1 box (8 ounces) DOLE® Whole Pitted Dates
1 package (3 ounces) reduced fat cream cheese, softened
¼ cup powdered sugar
1 tablespoon grated peel of 1 DOLE® Orange

• Make slit in center of each date. Combine cream cheese, powdered sugar and orange peel. Fill centers of dates with cream cheese mixture. Refrigerate.

• Dust with additional powdered sugar just before serving, if desired.

Makes about 27 stuffed dates

PREP TIME: 25 minutes

BRUSCHETTA

1 can (14½ ounces) DEL MONTE® Italian Style Stewed Tomatoes
1 to 2 cloves garlic, crushed
2 tablespoons chopped fresh basil *or*
½ teaspoon dried basil
1 baguette (6 inches) French bread, cut into ½-inch slices
1 tablespoon olive oil

Drain tomatoes, reserving liquid. In small saucepan, boil reserved liquid with garlic, 5 to 6 minutes, stirring occasionally. Remove from heat. Chop tomatoes; combine with garlic mixture and basil. Brush bread with oil. Broil until golden. Top with tomato mixture; serve immediately. Garnish with basil leaves, if desired. *Makes 6 appetizer servings*

STUFFED MUSHROOMS

1 package (6 ounces) STOVE TOP® Stuffing Mix for Chicken
24 large mushrooms (about 1½ pounds)
¼ cup (½ stick) margarine
¼ cup *each* finely chopped red and green pepper
3 tablespoons margarine, melted

Prepare stuffing mix as directed on package, omitting margarine. Remove stems from mushrooms; chop stems. Melt ¼ cup margarine in large skillet on medium heat. Add mushroom caps; cook and stir until lightly browned. Arrange in shallow baking pan. Cook and stir chopped mushroom stems and peppers in skillet until tender; stir into prepared stuffing. Spoon into mushroom caps; drizzle with 3 tablespoons melted margarine. Place under preheated broiler, 3 to 4 inches from heat, 5 minutes or until heated through.

Makes 12 appetizer servings

Bruschetta

EASY VEGETABLE SQUARES

2 (8-ounce) cans refrigerated crescent
    rolls (16 rolls)
1 (8-ounce) package cream cheese,
    softened
1 (3-ounce) package cream cheese,
    softened
⅓ cup mayonnaise or salad dressing
1 teaspoon dried dill weed
1 teaspoon buttermilk salad dressing mix
    (¼ of 0.4-ounce package)
3 cups desired toppings (suggestions
    follow)
1 cup shredded Wisconsin Cheddar,
    Mozzarella, or Monterey Jack cheese

For crust, unroll crescent rolls and pat into
15½×10½×2-inch baking pan. Bake according
to package directions. Cool.

Meanwhile, in a small mixing bowl stir together
cream cheese, mayonnaise, dill weed and
salad dressing mix. Spread evenly over cooled
crust. Sprinkle with desired toppings and
shredded Cheddar, Mozzarella or Monterey
Jack cheese. Cut into squares.

Makes 32 appetizer servings

TOPPING SUGGESTIONS: finely chopped
broccoli, cauliflower or green pepper; seeded
and chopped tomato; thinly sliced green onions,
black olives or celery; *or* shredded carrots.

PREP TIME: 20 minutes

Favorite recipe from **Wisconsin Milk Marketing Board**

MINI SAUSAGE QUICHES

½ cup butter or margarine, softened
3 ounces cream cheese, softened
1 cup all-purpose flour
½ pound BOB EVANS FARMS® Italian
    roll sausage
1 cup (4 ounces) shredded Swiss cheese
1 tablespoon snipped fresh chives
2 eggs
1 cup half-and-half
¼ teaspoon salt
    Dash cayenne pepper

Beat butter and cream cheese in medium bowl
until creamy. Blend in flour; refrigerate 1 hour.
Roll into 24 (1-inch) balls; press each into mini-
muffin cup. Preheat oven to 375°F. To prepare
filling, crumble sausage into small skillet. Cook
over medium heat until browned, stirring
occasionally. Drain off any drippings. Sprinkle
evenly into pastry shells in muffin cups;
sprinkle with Swiss cheese and chives. Whisk
eggs, half-and-half, salt and cayenne until
blended; pour over sausage in pastry shells.
Bake 20 to 30 minutes or until set. Remove
from pans. Serve hot. Refrigerate leftovers.

Makes 24 appetizers

SERVING SUGGESTION: Use standard
2½-inch muffin cups to make larger individual
quiches. Serve for breakfast.

Mini Sausage Quiches

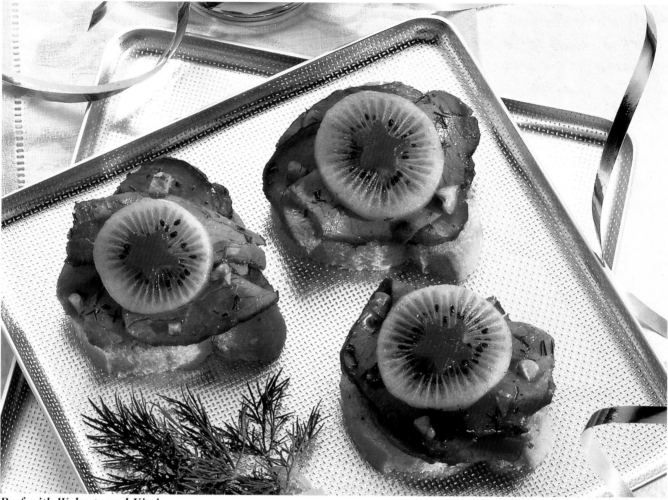

Beef with Walnuts and Kiwi

BEEF WITH WALNUTS AND KIWI

4 ounces sliced rare roast beef, cut into 12 uniform pieces
¼ cup finely chopped walnuts, toasted
1 tablespoon *each* fresh lemon juice, olive oil, wine vinegar and snipped dill
1 small clove garlic, crushed
¼ teaspoon freshly ground black pepper
Dash salt
12 slices French bread, ¼ inch thick
2 kiwi, peeled, cut into 12 slices
Pimiento, cut into small star shapes

Place roast beef slices in glass dish; sprinkle with walnuts. Combine lemon juice, oil, vinegar, dill, garlic, pepper and salt. Pour over beef and walnuts, lifting meat to coat. Cover and marinate 30 minutes. Drain marinade. To assemble, arrange one piece beef with walnuts on bread round. Top with kiwi slice; garnish with pimiento. *Makes 12 appetizer servings*

PREP/MARINATING TIME: 40 minutes
ASSEMBLING TIME: 10 minutes

*Favorite recipe from **National Cattlemen's Beef Association***

HOLIDAY APPETIZER QUICHE

CRUST
    2 cups all-purpose flour
    1 teaspoon salt
    ¾ BUTTER FLAVOR* CRISCO® Stick *or*
        ¾ cup BUTTER FLAVOR CRISCO
        all-vegetable shortening
    5 tablespoons cold water
FILLING
    2 cups (8 ounces) shredded Swiss cheese
    ⅔ cup chopped ham, crumbled cooked
        sausage, diced pepperoni or
        crumbled cooked bacon
    ¾ cup thinly sliced green onions
        (including tops)
    ¼ cup snipped fresh parsley
    1 jar (4 ounces) diced pimientos, well
        drained
    5 eggs
    1 cup whipping cream
    1 cup half-and-half
    1 teaspoon salt
    ¼ teaspoon pepper

1. Heat oven to 400°F.

2. For crust, combine flour and salt in medium bowl. Cut in shortening using pastry blender (or 2 knives) until all flour is blended in to form pea-size chunks. Sprinkle with water, 1 tablespoon at a time. Toss lightly with fork until dough forms ball.

3. Roll out dough to fit 15×10-inch jelly-roll pan. Place dough in greased pan, folding edges under. Flute edges. Prick crust with fork.

4. For filling, sprinkle cheese, ham, onions, parsley and pimientos evenly over crust. Beat eggs, cream, half-and-half, salt and pepper in medium bowl. Pour over filled crust.

5. Bake at 400°F for 25 to 30 minutes or until set. Cool 5 to 10 minutes. Cut into 2×1½-inch pieces. Serve warm.

Makes about 50 appetizers

NOTE: Crust may bubble during baking and need to be pricked with fork again.

*Butter Flavor Crisco® is artificially flavored.

ORANGE MAPLE SAUSAGE BALLS

    1 pound BOB EVANS FARMS® Original
        Recipe roll sausage
    1 small onion, finely chopped
    1 small red or yellow bell pepper, finely
        chopped
    1 egg
    2 tablespoons uncooked wheat farina
        cereal
    ½ cup maple syrup or maple-flavored
        syrup
    3 to 5 tablespoons frozen orange juice
        concentrate to taste, slightly thawed

Combine first 5 ingredients in large bowl until well blended. Shape into ¾-inch balls. Cook in large skillet over medium-high heat until browned on all sides and no longer pink in centers. Drain off any drippings. Add syrup and orange juice concentrate to sausage balls. Cook and stir over medium heat 2 to 3 minutes or until thick, bubbly syrup forms. Serve hot. Refrigerate leftovers.

Makes about 24 appetizers

SERVING SUGGESTIONS: Serve on party picks with sautéed mushrooms and water chestnuts. These meatballs also make an excellent breakfast item; serve with small pancakes.

POTATO WRAPS

4 small new potatoes (1½-inch diameter each)
½ teaspoon LAWRY'S® Seasoned Salt
½ teaspoon LAWRY'S® Seasoned Pepper
¼ teaspoon crushed bay leaves
8 slices bacon, cut in half crosswise

Preheat oven to 400°F. Wash potatoes and cut into quarters. Sprinkle each with a mixture of Seasoned Salt, Seasoned Pepper and bay leaves. Wrap 1 bacon piece around each potato piece. Sprinkle with any remaining seasonings. Place in baking dish and bake uncovered 20 minutes or until bacon is crispy and potatoes are cooked through. Drain on paper towels. Serve with sour cream and chives, if desired.   *Makes 16 appetizers*

MARIACHI DRUMSTICKS

1¼ cups crushed plain tortilla chips
1 package (1.25 ounces) LAWRY'S® Taco Seasoning Mix
18 to 20 chicken drumettes
Salsa

Preheat oven to 350°F. In large plastic bag, combine tortilla chips with Taco Seasoning Mix. Dampen chicken with water and shake off excess. Place a few pieces at a time in plastic bag; shake thoroughly to coat with chips. Arrange chicken in greased shallow baking pan; bake uncovered 30 minutes or until chicken is crispy. Serve with salsa for dipping.
Makes 18 to 20 drumettes

MINI TURKEY EMPANADAS

1 pound ground turkey
1 cup chopped onion
½ cup chopped green pepper
1 clove garlic, minced
1 can (16 ounces) tomatoes, drained and crushed
1 tablespoon dried parsley
1 teaspoon *each* dried cilantro and cumin seed
½ teaspoon *each* dried oregano and red pepper flakes
⅛ teaspoon black pepper
2 packages (15 ounces each) refrigerated pie crusts
Nonstick cooking spray

1. In large nonstick skillet, over medium-high heat, sauté turkey, onion, green pepper and garlic 5 to 6 minutes or until turkey is no longer pink and vegetables are tender. Stir in tomatoes, parsley, cilantro, cumin, oregano, pepper flakes and black pepper. Reduce heat to medium and cook 10 to 15 minutes, stirring constantly, or until any liquid is evaporated. Remove skillet from heat and cool.

2. Using 3-inch round biscuit cutter, cut 12 rounds from each pie crust, rerolling remaining crust to yield 48 rounds.

3. Spoon heaping teaspoonful of filling in center of each round. Fold each pastry in half and pinch edges together to seal. Place mini empanadas on two 15×10-inch cookie sheets lightly coated with nonstick cooking spray. Bake at 400°F 15 to 20 minutes or until mini empanadas are golden brown.
Makes 48 empanadas

Favorite recipe from **National Turkey Federation**

Potato Wraps, Mariachi Drumsticks

GINGERED CHICKEN POT STICKERS

3 cups finely shredded cabbage
1 egg white, lightly beaten
1 tablespoon light soy sauce
¼ teaspoon crushed red pepper
1 tablespoon minced fresh ginger
4 green onions with tops, finely chopped
¼ pound ground chicken breast, cooked
    and drained
24 wonton wrappers, at room temperature
    Cornstarch
½ cup water
1 tablespoon oyster sauce
½ teaspoon honey
⅛ teaspoon crushed red pepper
2 teaspoons grated lemon peel
1 tablespoon peanut oil

Steam cabbage 5 minutes, then cool to room temperature. Squeeze out any excess moisture; set aside. To prepare filling, combine egg white, soy sauce, ¼ teaspoon red pepper, ginger and green onions in large bowl; blend well. Stir in cabbage and chicken.

To prepare pot stickers, place 1 tablespoon filling in center of 1 wonton wrapper. Gather edges around filling, pressing firmly at top to seal. Repeat with remaining wrappers and filling. Place pot stickers on large baking sheet dusted with cornstarch. Refrigerate 1 hour or until cold. Meanwhile, to prepare sauce, combine remaining ingredients except oil in small bowl; mix well. Set aside.

Heat oil in large nonstick skillet over high heat. Add pot stickers and cook until bottoms are golden brown. Pour sauce over top. Cover and cook 3 minutes. Uncover and cook until all liquid is absorbed. Serve warm on tray as finger food or on small plates with chopsticks as first course.   *Makes 8 appetizer servings*

DEVILED SHRIMP

Devil Sauce (recipe follows)
2 eggs, lightly beaten
¼ teaspoon salt
¼ teaspoon TABASCO® pepper sauce
1 quart vegetable oil
1 pound raw shrimp, peeled and cleaned
1 cup dry bread crumbs

Prepare Devil Sauce; set aside. In shallow dish stir together eggs, salt and TABASCO sauce until well blended. Pour oil into heavy 3-quart saucepan or deep-fat fryer, filling no more than ⅓ full. Heat oil over medium heat to 375°F. Dip shrimp into egg mixture, then into bread crumbs; shake off excess. Carefully add shrimp to oil, a few at a time. Cook 1 to 2 minutes or until golden. Drain on paper towels. Just before serving, drizzle Devil Sauce over shrimp.
Makes 4 to 6 appetizer servings

DEVIL SAUCE

2 tablespoons butter or margarine
1 small onion, finely chopped
1 clove garlic, minced
1½ teaspoons dry mustard
½ cup beef consommé
2 tablespoons Worcestershire sauce
2 tablespoons dry white wine
¼ teaspoon TABASCO® pepper sauce
¼ cup lemon juice

In 1-quart saucepan melt butter over medium heat; add onion and garlic. Stirring frequently, cook 3 minutes or until tender. Blend in mustard. Gradually stir in consommé, Worcestershire sauce, wine and TABASCO sauce until well blended. Bring to a boil and simmer 5 minutes. Stir in lemon juice. Serve warm over shrimp or use as a dip.
Makes about 1¼ cups

Gingered Chicken Pot Stickers

TINY SEAFOOD TOSTADAS WITH BLACK BEAN DIP

Nonstick cooking spray
4 (8-inch) whole wheat or flour tortillas
1 cup Black Bean Dip (recipe follows)
1 cup shredded fresh spinach
¾ cup tiny cooked or canned shrimp
¾ cup salsa
½ cup (2 ounces) shredded reduced fat Monterey Jack cheese
¼ cup light sour cream

Preheat oven to 350°F. Spray cooking spray on baking sheet. Cut tortillas with 2½-inch round cookie cutter to make 32 rounds.* Place tortilla rounds evenly on prepared baking sheet. Lightly spray tortilla rounds with cooking spray and bake 10 minutes. Turn over and spray again; bake 3 minutes more. Meanwhile, prepare Black Bean Dip.

To prepare tostadas, spread each toasted tortilla round with 1½ teaspoons Black Bean Dip. Layer each with 1½ teaspoons shredded spinach, 1 teaspoon shrimp, 1 teaspoon salsa, a sprinkle of cheese and a dab of sour cream. Garnish with thin green chili strips or fresh cilantro, if desired. Serve immediately.
Makes 8 appetizer servings

*Tortillas may be cut with cookie cutters into other festive shapes.

BLACK BEAN DIP
1 can (15 ounces) black beans, undrained
1 teaspoon chili powder
¼ teaspoon salt
¼ teaspoon black pepper
¼ teaspoon ground cumin
2 drops hot pepper sauce
¾ cup minced white onion
2 cloves garlic, minced
1 can (4 ounces) chopped green chilies, drained

Drain beans, reserving 2 tablespoons liquid. Combine drained beans, reserved liquid, chili powder, salt, black pepper, cumin and hot pepper sauce in blender or food processor; process until smooth.

Combine onion and garlic in nonstick skillet or saucepan; cover and cook over low heat until onion is soft and translucent. Uncover and cook until slightly browned. Add chilies and cook 3 minutes more. Add bean mixture and mix well.
Makes about 1½ cups

NOTE: Black Bean Dip can be served (hot or cold) as a dip for tortilla chips or cut-up fresh vegetables.

CRAB-STUFFED MUSHROOMS

12 large fresh mushrooms
¼ cup margarine or butter
2 tablespoons finely chopped onion
1 to 4 cloves garlic, finely chopped
1 tablespoon chopped parsley
¼ cup plain dry bread crumbs or cracker crumbs
1 (6-ounce) can HARRIS® or ORLEANS® Crab Meat, drained
Seafood seasonings or seasoned salt, to taste

Preheat oven to 350°F. Remove stems from mushrooms and finely chop. In large skillet, lightly brown mushroom caps in margarine; place in 8- or 9-inch square baking dish. In same skillet, cook chopped mushrooms, onion, garlic and parsley until lightly browned. Stir in crumbs, crab meat and seafood seasonings; fill mushroom caps with crab meat mixture. Bake 8 to 10 minutes or until hot. Serve immediately. Refrigerate leftovers. *Makes 12 appetizers*

Top to bottom: Black Bean Dip, Tiny Seafood Tostadas with Black Bean Dip

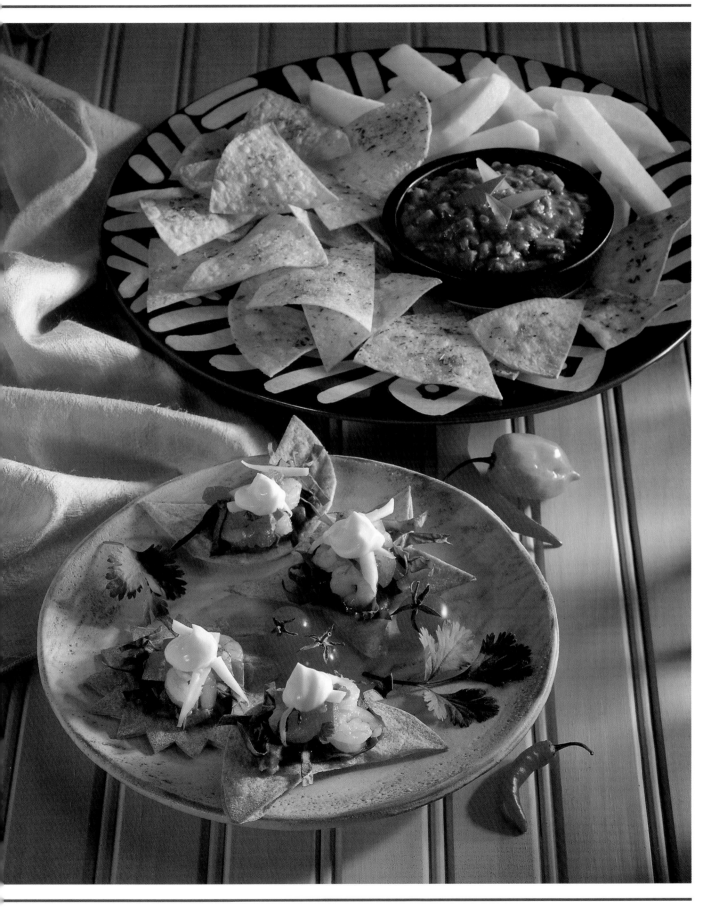

SHRIMP CRESCENTS

    1 can (14 ounces) artichoke hearts,
        drained and chopped
    1 can (4 ounces) diced green chilies,
        drained
    1 cup grated Parmesan cheese
    ¼ cup mayonnaise
    ¼ teaspoon ground red pepper
    ¼ teaspoon garlic powder
    2 cans (8 ounces each) refrigerated
        crescent dinner rolls
    32 cooked small shrimp, peeled and
        deveined

In medium bowl, combine all ingredients except crescent rolls and shrimp. Mix well; set aside.

Unroll crescent rolls and cut each triangle in half lengthwise, forming 32 triangles. Stretch dough to shape and flatten.

Spoon rounded tablespoon of artichoke mixture onto each triangle; place 1 shrimp on top. Roll up, starting at wide end, and place on well-greased baking sheet. (At this point, crescents may be refrigerated until ready to bake and serve.)

Bake at 375°F 12 to 15 minutes or until golden brown. Serve warm.   *Makes 32 appetizers*

Favorite recipe from **Florida Department of Agriculture and Consumer Services Bureau of Seafood and Aquaculture**

Stone Crab Claws with Honey-Mustard Sauce

STONE CRAB CLAWS WITH HONEY–MUSTARD SAUCE

    2½ pounds stone crab claws, cooked,
        cracked
    1 cup mayonnaise
    ⅓ cup half-and-half or light cream
    2 tablespoons honey
    2 tablespoons prepared mustard
    1 teaspoon ground coriander
    Cocktail sauce (optional)

Arrange cracked claws on serving plate.

Combine remaining ingredients except cocktail sauce; stir until well blended. Serve sauces with stone crab claws.
Makes 3 servings crab claws and
1½ cups sauce

Favorite recipe from **Florida Department of Agriculture and Consumer Services Bureau of Seafood and Aquaculture**

BAKED VEGETABLE & SEAFOOD WONTONS

1 envelope LIPTON® Recipe Secrets®
    Vegetable Soup Mix
1 container (15 ounces) ricotta cheese
½ pound imitation crabmeat, chopped
¼ teaspoon garlic powder
⅛ teaspoon pepper
40 refrigerated or thawed frozen wonton
    wrappers
1 tablespoon olive or vegetable oil

Preheat oven to 350°F. In medium bowl,
combine vegetable soup mix, ricotta cheese,
crabmeat, garlic powder and pepper. Place 1
tablespoon ricotta mixture on center of each
wonton. Brush edges with water; fold corners
into centers. Press to seal. Place on lightly
greased cookie sheet; brush with oil. Bake 25
minutes or until crisp and golden brown, turning
once. *Makes 40 wontons*

NOTE: Cover filled wontons with damp cloth
until ready to bake, then brush with oil.

VARIATION: Use 1½ cups chopped cooked
shrimp in place of crabmeat.

GARLIC & HERB DIP

1 cup sour cream
¼ cup mayonnaise
2 tablespoons chopped green onion
1 teaspoon dried basil, crushed
½ teaspoon dried tarragon, crushed
1 clove garlic, minced
¼ teaspoon salt
¼ teaspoon black pepper
    Assorted fresh vegetable dippers or
    pita chips

Combine all ingredients except dippers in
medium bowl until blended. Cover; refrigerate
several hours or overnight. Serve with
dippers. *Makes about 1¼ cups*

Baked Vegetable & Seafood Wontons

TACO DIP

12 ounces cream cheese, softened
½ cup dairy sour cream
2 teaspoons chili powder
1½ teaspoons ground cumin
⅛ teaspoon ground red pepper
½ cup salsa
2 cups shredded lettuce or lettuce leaves
1 cup (4 ounces) shredded Wisconsin
   Cheddar cheese
1 cup (4 ounces) shredded Wisconsin
   Monterey Jack cheese
½ cup diced plum tomatoes
⅓ cup sliced green onions
¼ cup sliced ripe olives
¼ cup sliced pimiento-stuffed green olives
   Tortilla chips and blue corn chips

Combine cream cheese, sour cream, chili powder, cumin and red pepper in large bowl; mix until well blended. Stir in salsa. Spread onto 10-inch serving platter lined with lettuce. Top with cheeses, tomatoes, green onions and olives. Serve with chips.

Makes 10 appetizer servings

Favorite recipe from **Wisconsin Milk Marketing Board**

PICANTE VEGETABLE DIP

⅔ cup sour cream or reduced-fat sour
   cream
½ cup picante sauce
⅓ cup mayonnaise or reduced-fat
   mayonnaise
¼ cup finely chopped green or red bell
   pepper
2 tablespoons finely chopped green onion
¾ teaspoon garlic salt
   Assorted fresh vegetable dippers or
   tortilla chips

Combine all ingredients in medium bowl until well blended. Cover; refrigerate several hours or overnight to allow flavors to blend.

Makes about 1⅔ cups

SPINACH–PARMESAN DIP

1 cup MIRACLE WHIP® Salad Dressing
1 cup BREAKSTONE'S® Sour Cream
1 package (10 ounces) frozen chopped
   spinach, thawed, well drained
½ cup (2 ounces) KRAFT® 100% Natural
   Grated Parmesan Cheese
1 can (8 ounces) water chestnuts,
   drained, chopped
⅛ teaspoon ground red pepper

• Mix all ingredients until well blended. Refrigerate. Serve with assorted crackers.

Makes 4 cups

PREP TIME: 5 minutes plus refrigerating

CLAM DIP

1 package (3 ounces) cream cheese,
   softened
1 cup dairy sour cream
1 can (6½ ounces) minced clams
½ teaspoon LAWRY'S® Seasoned Salt
   Dash LAWRY'S® Seasoned Pepper
2 teaspoons lemon juice
1½ teaspoons Worcestershire sauce

In medium bowl, blend cream cheese and sour cream. Drain clams and reserve 1 tablespoon clam juice. Add to sour cream mixture. Add remaining ingredients and blend well.

Makes 1½ cups

PRESENTATION: Serve with crisp raw vegetables and Johannisberg Riesling.

HINT: For a thinner dip, add more clam juice.

Taco Dip

THREE MUSHROOM RATATOUILLE

1 package (3½ ounces) fresh shiitake
  mushrooms*
1 tablespoon olive oil
1 large onion, chopped
4 cloves garlic, minced
1 package (8 ounces) button mushrooms,
  chopped
1 package (6 ounces) crimini
  mushrooms, chopped
1 cup chicken broth
1 small tomato, chopped
2 tablespoons chopped parsley
2 tablespoons grated Parmesan cheese
3 pita breads (6 inches each)

Remove stems from shiitake mushrooms;
discard stems. Chop caps. Heat oil in large
skillet over medium heat until hot. Add onion
and garlic. Cook 5 minutes, stirring
occasionally. Add all 3 types of mushrooms.
Cook 5 minutes more, stirring often. Add
chicken broth. Bring to a boil. Cook about 10
minutes or until liquid is absorbed. Remove
from heat. Stir in tomato, parsley and cheese.
Spoon into bowl.

Meanwhile, preheat broiler. Split each pita
bread horizontally in half. Stack halves; cut the
stack into 6 wedges. Arrange wedges in single
layer on baking sheet. Broil 4 inches from heat
1 to 3 minutes or until wedges are toasted.
Serve toasted pita bread triangles with warm
dip. Garnish, if desired.

Makes about 2¼ cups

*Or, substitute 1 ounce dried black Chinese
mushrooms. Place dried mushrooms in small
bowl; cover with warm water. Soak 20 minutes
to soften. Drain; squeeze out excess moisture.

MEXICAN TURKEY DIP

1 pound ground turkey
1 package (1¼ ounces) reduced-sodium
  taco seasoning mix
  Nonstick cooking spray
1 cup salsa
3 ounces reduced fat cream cheese,
  softened
½ cup nonfat sour cream
1 cup grated reduced fat Cheddar cheese
2 tablespoons *each* minced green onion
  and sliced black olives
24 no-salt corn chips

1. In large nonstick skillet, over medium-high
heat, sauté turkey 5 to 6 minutes or until turkey
is no longer pink; drain. Stir in seasoning mix.

2. Spread turkey mixture in 9-inch square
baking dish lightly coated with nonstick cooking
spray. Top turkey mixture with salsa.

3. In small bowl combine cream cheese and
sour cream. Spread mixture over salsa and
sprinkle Cheddar cheese over top. Bake at
350°F 25 minutes or until bubbly.

4. Garnish with green onion and olives and
serve with chips.   *Makes 24 servings*

Favorite recipe from **National Turkey Federation**

Three Mushroom Ratatouille

HOT BROCCOLI DIP

1 (1½-pound) round sourdough bread
   loaf
½ cup finely chopped celery
½ cup chopped red pepper
¼ cup finely chopped onion
2 tablespoons margarine
1 pound VELVEETA® Pasteurized
   Process Cheese Spread, cubed
1 (10-ounce) package frozen chopped
   broccoli, thawed, drained
¼ teaspoon dried rosemary leaves,
   crushed

Cut slice from top of bread loaf; remove center,
leaving 1-inch shell. Cut removed bread into
bite-size pieces. Cover shell with top. Place on
cookie sheet with bread pieces. Bake at 350°F,
15 minutes or until hot. In large skillet, sauté
celery, pepper and onion in margarine. Reduce
heat to low. Add process cheese spread; stir
until melted. Stir in remaining ingredients; heat
thoroughly, stirring constantly. Spoon into bread
loaf. Serve hot with toasted bread pieces and
vegetable dippers.   *Makes 6 to 8 servings*

PREP TIME: 15 minutes
BAKE TIME: 15 minutes

Hot Broccoli Dip

MICROWAVE DIRECTIONS: Prepare bread
loaf as directed. Combine celery, pepper, onion
and margarine in 2-quart microwave-safe bowl.
Microwave on HIGH 1 minute. Add remaining
ingredients; microwave on HIGH 5 to 6 minutes
or until hot, stirring after 3 minutes. Spoon into
bread loaf. Serve hot with toasted bread pieces
and vegetable dippers.

PINEAPPLE–ALMOND
CHEESE SPREAD

2 cans (8 ounces each) DOLE® Crushed
   Pineapple
1 package (8 ounces) cream cheese,
   softened
4 cups (16 ounces) shredded sharp
   Cheddar cheese
½ cup mayonnaise
1 tablespoon soy sauce
1 cup DOLE® Chopped Natural Almonds,
   toasted
½ cup finely chopped DOLE® Green Bell
   Pepper
¼ cup minced green onions or chives
   DOLE® Celery stalks or assorted
   breads

• Drain pineapple. In large bowl, beat cream
cheese until smooth; beat in Cheddar cheese,
mayonnaise and soy sauce until smooth. Stir in
pineapple, almonds, green pepper and onions.
Refrigerate, covered. Use to stuff celery stalks
or serve as spread with assorted breads. Serve
at room temperature.   *Makes 4 cups*

Zesty Seafood Vegetable Spread

ZESTY SEAFOOD VEGETABLE SPREAD

    2 (8-ounce) packages cream cheese,
        softened
    1 (8-ounce) container BORDEN® or
        MEADOW GOLD® Sour Cream
    1 (1.7-ounce) package MRS. GRASS®
        Homestyle Vegetable Recipe, Soup
        & Dip Mix
    ¾ cup BENNETT'S® Cocktail or Hot
        Seafood Sauce, chilled
    1 (6-ounce) can ORLEANS® or HARRIS®
        Fancy White Crab Meat, rinsed,
        drained and chilled *or* 1 (4¼-ounce)
        can ORLEANS® Shrimp, rinsed and
        soaked as label directs

In large mixer bowl, beat cream cheese until
fluffy; beat in sour cream and dip mix. On
serving plate, spread cheese mixture into
8-inch circle. Chill at least 1 hour. Just before
serving, top with cocktail sauce, then crab
meat. Garnish as desired. Serve with assorted
crackers. Refrigerate leftovers.

Makes 12 servings

TANGY WISCONSIN BLUE CHEESE WHIP

    1 cup whipping cream
    ½ cup finely crumbled Wisconsin Blue
        cheese (2 ounces)
    1 teaspoon dried basil, crushed
    ¼ teaspoon garlic salt
    ½ cup almonds, toasted and chopped
        Assorted vegetable or fruit dippers

In small mixer bowl combine whipping cream,
Blue cheese, basil, and garlic salt. Beat with
electric mixer on medium speed until slightly
thickened. Gently fold in chopped almonds.
Serve with vegetable or fruit dippers. (Dip can
be made ahead and chilled, covered, up to 2
hours.)   *Makes about 2 cups*

Favorite recipe from **Wisconsin Milk Marketing Board**

FRESH TOMATO EGGPLANT SPREAD

1 medium eggplant
2 large ripe tomatoes, seeded and
    chopped
1 cup minced zucchini
¼ cup chopped green onions with tops
2 tablespoons red wine vinegar
1 tablespoon olive oil
1 teaspoon honey
1 clove garlic, minced
1 tablespoon minced fresh basil
2 teaspoons minced fresh oregano
1 teaspoon minced fresh thyme
⅛ teaspoon ground black pepper
¼ cup pine nuts or slivered almonds
32 melba toast rounds

Preheat oven to 375°F. Poke holes in surface of eggplant with fork. Bake 20 to 25 minutes or until tender. Cool completely; peel and mince. Place in colander; press to release excess water.

Combine eggplant with tomatoes, zucchini, green onions, vinegar, oil, honey, garlic, basil, oregano, thyme and black pepper in large bowl. Mix well. Refrigerate 2 hours to allow flavors to blend. Stir in pine nuts just before serving. Serve with melba toast rounds.

Makes 8 servings

HOLIDAY PATE

1 (8-ounce) package JONES®
    Braunschweiger
1 (3-ounce) package cream cheese,
    softened
1 tablespoon finely chopped onion
1 tablespoon Worcestershire sauce
1 to 2 tablespoons dry sherry
¼ to ½ teaspoon ground nutmeg
    Dash of hot pepper sauce

Blend all ingredients and serve with crackers or cocktail bread. *Makes about 1¼ cups*

BLACK OLIVE TAPANADE

1 can (6 ounces) pitted ripe olives,
    drained
¼ cup chopped red pepper
3 tablespoons olive oil
1 tablespoon lemon juice
1½ teaspoons dried oregano leaves
½ teaspoon minced garlic
½ cup (3 ounces) crumbled ATHENOS®
    Feta Natural Cheese

• Place all ingredients except cheese in blender or food processor container fitted with steel blade; cover. Process until smooth. Stir in cheese.

• Refrigerate several hours or overnight.

• Serve with crackers or French bread chunks. Sprinkle with additional feta cheese, if desired.
Makes 1½ cups

PREP TIME: 15 minutes plus refrigerating

WHIPPED FETA WITH HERBS

1 cup (6 ounces) crumbled ATHENOS®
    Feta Natural Cheese
2 tablespoons sour cream
½ teaspoon lemon juice
¼ teaspoon *each* dried oregano and basil
    leaves, crushed *or* 2 teaspoons *each*
    chopped fresh oregano and basil
Freshly ground black pepper

• Blend all ingredients except pepper in blender or food processor container until smooth. Refrigerate 1 hour. Season with pepper. Serve with pita bread wedges or crackers.
Makes about ½ cup

PREP TIME: 15 minutes plus refrigerating

Fresh Tomato Eggplant Spread

CHEESE PINE CONES

2 cups (8 ounces) shredded Swiss cheese
½ cup butter or margarine, softened
3 tablespoons milk
2 tablespoons dry sherry or milk
⅛ teaspoon ground red pepper
1 cup finely chopped blanched almonds
¾ cup slivered blanched almonds
¾ cup sliced almonds
½ cup whole almonds
   Fresh rosemary sprigs
   Assorted crackers

Beat cheese, butter, milk, sherry and red pepper in medium bowl until smooth; stir in chopped almonds.

Divide mixture into 3 equal portions; shape into tapered ovals to resemble pine cones. Insert slivered, sliced and whole almonds into cones. Cover; refrigerate 2 to 3 hours or until firm.

Arrange Cheese Pine Cones on wooden board or serving plate. Garnish tops with rosemary. Serve with assorted crackers.

Makes 12 to 16 appetizer servings

PESTO CHEESE WREATH

Parsley-Basil Pesto* (page 43)
3 packages (8 ounces each) cream
   cheese, softened
½ cup mayonnaise
¼ cup whipping cream or half-and-half
1 teaspoon sugar
1 teaspoon onion salt
⅓ cup chopped roasted red peppers** or
   pimiento, drained
   Pimiento strips and Italian flat leaf
   parsley leaves (optional)
   Assorted crackers and cut-up
   vegetables

Clockwise from top right: Holiday Appetizer Puffs (page 51), Pesto Cheese Wreath, Cheese Pine Cones

Prepare Parsley-Basil Pesto; set aside. Beat cream cheese and mayonnaise in medium bowl until smooth; beat in whipping cream, sugar and onion salt.

Line 5-cup ring mold with plastic wrap. Spoon half the cheese mixture into prepared mold; spread evenly. Spread Parsley-Basil Pesto evenly over cheese mixture; top with chopped red peppers. Spoon remaining cheese mixture over peppers; spread evenly. Cover; refrigerate until cheese mixture is firm, 8 hours or overnight.

Uncover mold; invert onto serving plate. Carefully remove plastic wrap. Smooth top and sides of wreath with spatula. Garnish with pimiento strips and parsley leaves, if desired. Serve with assorted crackers and vegetables.

Makes 16 to 24 appetizer servings

*½ cup purchased pesto may be substituted for Parsley-Basil Pesto.

**Look for roasted red peppers packed in cans or jars in the Italian food section of the supermarket.

PARSLEY–BASIL PESTO
    2 cups fresh parsley leaves
    ¼ cup pine nuts or slivered almonds
    2 tablespoons grated Parmesan cheese
    2 cloves garlic, peeled
    1 tablespoon dried basil leaves, crushed
    ¼ teaspoon salt
    2 tablespoons olive or vegetable oil

Process all ingredients except oil in food processor or blender until finely chopped. With machine running, add oil gradually, processing until mixture is smooth. *Makes about ½ cup*

CLAM CHEESE BALL

    1 (8-ounce) package cream cheese, softened
    1 (6½-ounce) can SNOW'S® or DOXSEE® Minced Clams, well drained
    ½ teaspoon pepper
    ½ teaspoon garlic powder
    ¼ cup grated Parmesan cheese
    1 tablespoon chopped parsley

In small mixer bowl, beat cream cheese until fluffy. Stir in clams, pepper and garlic powder. Cover; chill about 1 hour. Shape into ball. In small bowl, combine Parmesan cheese and parsley. Roll ball in Parmesan cheese mixture. Cover; chill several hours to blend flavors. Garnish as desired. Serve with assorted crackers. Refrigerate leftovers.

Makes one 3-inch cheese ball

SPICY TURKEY HAM SPREAD

    1 pound turkey ham, cut into chunks
    ¼ cup chopped onion
    ¼ cup Dijon-style mustard
    4 teaspoons Worcestershire sauce
    ¼ teaspoon cayenne pepper

1. In food processor fitted with metal blade, process ham, onion, mustard, Worcestershire sauce and cayenne pepper until smooth.

2. To serve, spoon mixture into red or green bell pepper halves, accompanied with melba toast rounds, if desired. *Makes 2 cups*

*Favorite recipe from **National Turkey Federation***

Pesto-Cheese Logs

Preheat oven to 350°F. To toast walnuts, place on baking sheet. Bake 8 to 10 minutes or until golden brown, stirring frequently; cool. Process walnuts in food processor using on/off pulsing action until walnuts are ground, but not pasty. Remove from food processor; set aside.

Process cream cheese, pesto and feta cheese in food processor until smooth. Spread ¾ cup cheese mixture on waxed paper and form 4-inch log. Wrap waxed paper around cheese log. Repeat with remaining cheese mixture. Refrigerate logs at least 4 hours, until well chilled. Roll each chilled log to form 5-inch log.

Combine walnuts and pepper. Roll 1 log in nut mixture to coat. Combine carrot and parsley. Roll remaining log in carrot mixture to coat. Serve immediately or wrap and refrigerate up to a day before serving. Thinly slice log and serve with crackers. Garnish, if desired.

Makes 2 logs

PESTO–CHEESE LOGS

⅓ cup walnuts
1 package (8 ounces) cream cheese, softened
⅓ cup prepared pesto sauce
⅓ cup crumbled feta cheese
2 teaspoons cracked black pepper
2 tablespoons finely shredded carrot
2 tablespoons chopped fresh parsley
  Assorted crackers
  Carrot slivers, parsley and fresh thyme for garnish

CHEDDAR CHEESE SPREAD

3 ounces *each* white Cheddar, yellow Cheddar and cream cheese, cut into small pieces
6 green onions, white parts only, finely chopped
2 tablespoons butter or margarine, softened
2 tablespoons dry sherry
1 teaspoon Worcestershire sauce
1 teaspoon Dijon-style mustard
¼ teaspoon salt (optional)
  Dash hot pepper sauce (optional)
2 tablespoons finely chopped chives
  Assorted crackers

Place all ingredients except chives and crackers in food processor or blender; process until smooth. Add chives; pulse to mix in. Cover; refrigerate. Allow spread to soften at room temperature before serving. Serve with crackers.   *Makes about 2 cups spread*

BACON AND TWO ONION CHEESECAKE

6 slices bacon, diced
1 large sweet onion, chopped
1 clove garlic, minced
1 container (15 ounces) SARGENTO®
   Light Ricotta Cheese
½ cup half-and-half
2 tablespoons flour
½ teaspoon salt
¼ teaspoon cayenne pepper
2 eggs
½ cup thinly sliced green onions

In 10-inch skillet, cook bacon until crisp; remove to paper towels with slotted spoon. Cook sweet onion and garlic in drippings until tender, about 6 minutes. Drain in strainer; discard bacon drippings. In bowl of electric mixer, combine ricotta cheese, half-and-half, flour, salt and pepper; blend until smooth. Add eggs, one at a time; blend until smooth. Reserve 3 tablespoons of the bacon for garnish. Stir remaining bacon, cooked onion mixture and green onions into ricotta mixture. Lightly grease sides of 8- or 9-inch springform pan; pour batter into pan. Bake at 350°F 40 minutes or until center is just set. Remove to wire cooling rack; cool to room temperature. Remove side of pan. Garnish with reserved bacon; serve with assorted crackers.

Makes 10 appetizer servings

FRUITY CHEESE SPREAD

1 package (8 ounces) cream cheese,
   softened
1 teaspoon grated orange peel
¾ teaspoon almond extract
½ teaspoon ground ginger
1½ cups RALSTON® brand Fruit Muesli
   with Cranberries, crushed to 1 cup,
   divided
Apple and pear slices
Crackers and cookies

Combine cream cheese, orange peel, almond extract and ginger; beat until smooth. Place ½ cup cereal in serving dish; spoon cheese mixture on top. Refrigerate 2 to 3 hours. Just before serving, sprinkle remaining ½ cup cereal over cheese spread. Serve with apple and pear slices, crackers and cookies.

Makes 16 servings

SAVORY PEPPER–HERB CHEESECAKE

CRUST
1¼ cups fresh dark rye or pumpernickel
   bread crumbs (about 2 slices,
   processed in blender or food
   processor)
3 tablespoons melted margarine
FILLING
1 container (15 ounces) SARGENTO®
   Light Ricotta Cheese
½ cup half-and-half
2 tablespoons flour
2 eggs
⅓ cup chopped mixed fresh herbs (such
   as parsley, basil, mint, tarragon,
   rosemary, thyme and oregano)
¼ cup chopped fresh chives or green
   onion tops
1½ teaspoons finely grated lemon peel
¾ teaspoon salt
½ teaspoon cracked black pepper

Lightly grease sides of 8- or 9-inch springform pan. Combine crust ingredients; press evenly over bottom of pan. Chill while preparing filling. In bowl of electric mixer, combine ricotta cheese, half-and-half and flour; blend until smooth. Add eggs, one at a time; blend until smooth. Blend in fresh herbs, chives, lemon peel, salt and pepper. Pour into crust; bake at 350°F 30 to 35 minutes or until center is just set. Remove to wire cooling rack; cool to room temperature. Remove side of pan. Cut into wedges to serve.

Makes 10 appetizer servings

HOT ARTICHOKE SPREAD

1 cup MIRACLE WHIP® Salad Dressing
1 cup (4 ounces) KRAFT® 100% Grated Parmesan Cheese
1 (14-ounce) can artichoke hearts, drained, chopped
1 (4-ounce) can chopped green chilies, drained
1 garlic clove, minced
2 tablespoons green onion slices
2 tablespoons chopped tomato

• Preheat oven to 350°F.

• Mix all ingredients except onion and tomato until well blended.

• Spoon into shallow ovenproof dish or 9-inch pie plate.

• Bake 20 to 25 minutes or until lightly browned. Sprinkle with onion and tomato. Serve with toasted bread cutouts.

Makes 2 cups

PREP TIME: 10 minutes
COOK TIME: 25 minutes

WARM HERB CHEESE SPREAD

3 (8-ounce) packages cream cheese, softened
¼ cup BORDEN® or MEADOW GOLD® Milk
¼ cup REALEMON® Lemon Juice from Concentrate
½ teaspoon *each* dried basil, marjoram, oregano and thyme leaves
¼ teaspoon garlic powder
½ pound cooked shrimp, chopped (1½ cups) (optional)

Preheat oven to 350°F. In large mixer bowl, beat cream cheese just until smooth. Gradually beat in milk then ReaLemon® brand and seasonings. Add shrimp if desired. Spoon into 9-inch quiche dish or pie plate. Cover; bake 15 minutes or until hot. Garnish as desired. Serve warm with crackers, breadsticks and assorted fresh vegetables. Refrigerate leftovers.

Makes about 4 cups

MICROWAVE DIRECTIONS: Prepare cheese mixture as above; spoon into 8- or 9-inch glass pie plate. Cook on 50% power (MEDIUM) 5 to 6 minutes or until hot. Stir before serving. Proceed as above.

MARINATED SHRIMP & VEGETABLES

1 pound raw medium shrimp, peeled, deveined and cooked
1 cup fresh cauliflowerets
4 ounces small whole fresh mushrooms
1 cup sliced zucchini
1 large green bell pepper, seeded and cut into squares
1 large red bell pepper, seeded and cut into squares
¾ cup REALEMON® Lemon Juice from Concentrate
1 tablespoon chopped green onion
2 teaspoons sugar
1 teaspoon salt
¼ to ½ teaspoon dried dill weed
5 drops hot pepper sauce
¾ cup vegetable oil

Place shrimp, cauliflower, mushrooms, zucchini and bell peppers in large shallow dish. In small bowl or jar, combine all remaining ingredients except oil; mix well. Add oil; whisk or shake well. Pour over shrimp mixture. Cover; chill 6 hours or overnight, stirring occasionally. Garnish as desired. Refrigerate leftovers.

Makes 6 to 8 servings

Hot Artichoke Spread

OYSTERS ROMANO

12 oysters, shucked and on the half shell
2 slices bacon, cut into 1-inch pieces
½ cup Italian-seasoned dry bread crumbs
2 tablespoons butter or margarine, melted
½ teaspoon garlic salt
6 tablespoons grated Romano, Parmesan or provolone cheese
Fresh chives for garnish

Preheat oven to 375°F. Place shells with oysters on baking sheet. Top each oyster with 1 piece bacon. Bake 10 minutes or until bacon is crisp. Meanwhile, combine bread crumbs, butter and garlic salt in small bowl. Spoon mixture over oysters; top with cheese. Bake 5 to 10 minutes or until cheese melts. Serve immediately. Garnish with chives, if desired.

Makes 4 appetizer servings

GREEK–STYLE SAUSAGE ROLL

1 pound bulk pork sausage
¼ cup finely chopped onion
1 (10-ounce) package frozen chopped spinach, thawed and drained
¼ pound feta cheese, crumbled
¼ cup finely chopped parsley
⅛ teaspoon white pepper
1 egg, beaten
10 sheets frozen phyllo dough (17×13-inch rectangles), thawed
½ cup butter or margarine, melted

In large skillet, cook sausage and onion over medium-high heat until sausage is done and onion is tender, stirring occasionally. Drain. Stir in spinach, feta cheese, parsley, white pepper and egg. Set aside.

Preheat oven to 350°F. Unfold phyllo dough. Spread 1 sheet flat; top with another sheet of phyllo. Gently brush with some of melted butter.

Top with remaining sheets of phyllo, brushing each with butter. Reserve 1 tablespoon butter for top of pastry.

Spread sausage-spinach mixture lengthwise over bottom third of layered phyllo dough to within 2 inches of ends. Fold ends over. Carefully roll up phyllo. Place roll, seam side down, on lightly greased baking sheet; brush with reserved 1 tablespoon butter. Bake 30 to 35 minutes or until golden. To serve, cut into slices. *Makes 16 appetizer servings*

PREP TIME: 30 minutes
COOK TIME: 30 minutes

*Favorite recipe from **National Pork Producers Council***

FESTIVE PEPPER MEDLEY À LA GRECQUE

1 green bell pepper, cut into thin strips
1 yellow bell pepper, cut into thin strips
1 red bell pepper, cut into thin strips
3 tablespoons olive or vegetable oil
1 tablespoon water
2 teaspoons balsamic or red wine vinegar
1 tablespoon chopped fresh oregano *or* 1 teaspoon dried oregano
Salt and black pepper to taste
¾ cup chopped walnuts
¼ cup olives (Greek or Niçoise)
¼ cup crumbled feta cheese (optional)
Radicchio or spinach leaves for garnish

Arrange bell peppers in microwavable serving dish. In small bowl, combine oil, water, vinegar, oregano, salt and black pepper; pour over bell peppers. Sprinkle with walnuts. Microwave at HIGH (100% power) 5 minutes or until peppers are cooked. Top with olives and cheese. Serve warm or at room temperature. Garnish with radicchio leaves, if desired.

Makes 4 to 6 servings

*Favorite recipe from **Walnut Marketing Board***

Oysters Romano

CHEESE TWISTS

1 cup all-purpose flour
½ teaspoon baking soda
½ teaspoon dry mustard
½ teaspoon salt
⅛ teaspoon ground red pepper (cayenne)
¾ cup grated Parmesan cheese, divided
½ cup butter or margarine, softened
3 egg yolks
2 teaspoons water
1 egg white, slightly beaten
1 tablespoon sesame seeds (optional)

Combine flour, baking soda, mustard, salt and red pepper in large bowl. Reserve 1 tablespoon cheese; stir remaining cheese into flour mixture. Cut in butter with pastry blender or 2 knives until mixture resembles fine crumbs. Add egg yolks and water, mixing until dough forms. Shape into a ball; flatten and wrap in plastic wrap. Refrigerate 2 hours or until firm.

Preheat oven to 400°F. Grease two cookie sheets. Roll out dough on lightly floured surface into 12-inch square (about ⅛ inch thick). Brush surface lightly with egg white and sprinkle with remaining 1 tablespoon cheese and sesame seeds, if desired. Cut dough in half. Cut each half crosswise into ¼-inch strips. Twist 2 strips together. Repeat with remaining strips. Place 1 inch apart on prepared cookie sheets.

Bake 6 to 8 minutes or until light golden brown. Remove from cookie sheets and cool completely on wire racks. Store in airtight container. *Makes about 48 twists*

VARIATION: Prepare dough and cut as directed. Place ¾ of strips on cookie sheets. Form rings with remaining strips; seal edges. Place on cookie sheets. Bake and cool as directed. To serve, arrange 3 to 4 strips to form small stack. Insert stack into ring. Repeat with remaining strips.

Cheese Twists, Deviled Mixed Nuts

DEVILED MIXED NUTS

3 tablespoons vegetable oil
2 cups assorted unsalted nuts, such as
    peanuts, almonds, Brazil nuts or
    walnuts
2 tablespoons sugar
1 teaspoon paprika
½ teaspoon ground chili powder
½ teaspoon curry powder
½ teaspoon ground cumin
½ teaspoon ground coriander
½ teaspoon ground black pepper
¼ teaspoon salt

Heat oil in large skillet over medium heat; cook and stir nuts in hot oil 2 to 3 minutes or until browned. Combine remaining ingredients in small bowl; sprinkle over nuts. Stir to coat evenly. Heat 1 to 2 minutes more. Drain nuts on wire rack lined with paper towels. Serve warm.
Makes 6 to 8 servings or 2 cups nuts

CAJUN-SPICED WALNUTS

Nonstick vegetable cooking spray
2 egg whites, slightly beaten
1 tablespoon garlic salt
2 teaspoons ground cayenne pepper
2 teaspoons mixed dried herbs
2 teaspoons paprika
4 cups (1 pound) walnut halves and
    pieces

Coat large, shallow baking pan with nonstick vegetable cooking spray. Mix egg whites with spices. Stir in walnuts and coat thoroughly. Spread in prepared pan. Bake in 350°F oven 15 to 18 minutes or until dry and crisp. Cool completely before serving.   *Makes 4 cups*

MICROWAVE DIRECTIONS: Prepare ingredients as above. Spread one quarter prepared walnuts in microwavable dish. Microwave on HIGH for 2 to 3 minutes or until dry and crisp. Cool completely. Repeat with remaining walnuts.

NOTE: Cajun-Spiced Walnuts are best if made at least one day ahead. (Flavors intensify overnight.) Store in sealed container.

*Favorite recipe from **Walnut Marketing Board***

HOLIDAY APPETIZER PUFFS

1 sheet frozen puff pastry, thawed (½ of
    17¼-ounce package)
2 tablespoons olive or vegetable oil
    Toppings: grated Parmesan cheese,
    sesame seeds, poppy seeds, dried dill
    weed, dried basil leaves, paprika,
    drained capers, pimiento-stuffed
    green olive slices

Preheat oven to 425°F. Roll pastry on lightly floured surface to 13-inch square. Cut into shapes with cookie cutters (simple-shaped cutters work best). Place on ungreased baking sheets.

Brush cut-outs lightly with oil. Decorate with desired toppings.

Bake 6 to 8 minutes or until golden. Serve warm or at room temperature.
Makes about 1½ dozen appetizers

Merry
SOUPS & SALADS

TOMATO FRENCH ONION SOUP

4 medium onions, chopped
2 tablespoons butter or margarine
1 can (14½ ounces) DEL MONTE® Italian
 Recipe Stewed Tomatoes
2 cups water
1 can (10½ ounces) condensed beef consommé
¼ cup dry sherry
4 slices toasted French bread
1½ cups shredded Swiss cheese
¼ cup grated Parmesan cheese

In large saucepan, cook onions in butter about 10 minutes. Drain tomatoes, reserving liquid. Chop tomatoes. Add tomatoes, reserved liquid, water, consommé and sherry to onions. Bring to a boil, skimming off foam. Reduce heat and simmer 10 minutes. Place soup in four broilerproof bowls; top with bread and cheeses. Broil until cheese is melted and golden.

Makes 4 (1¼-cup) servings

BUTTERNUT BISQUE

1 medium butternut squash (about
    1½ pounds)
1 teaspoon margarine or butter
1 large onion, coarsely chopped (1 cup)
2 cans (about 14 ounces each) reduced-
    sodium or regular chicken broth,
    divided
½ teaspoon ground nutmeg or freshly
    grated nutmeg
⅛ teaspoon ground white pepper
    Plain nonfat yogurt and chives for
    garnish

Peel squash; cut flesh into ½-inch pieces. Set aside. Melt margarine in large saucepan over medium heat. Add onion. Cook and stir 3 minutes. Add squash and 1 can broth. Bring to a boil over high heat. Reduce heat to low. Cover and simmer 20 minutes or until squash is very tender.

Process squash mixture, in 2 batches, in food processor until smooth. Return soup to saucepan; add remaining can of broth, nutmeg and pepper. Simmer, uncovered, 5 minutes, stirring occasionally.*

Ladle soup into soup bowls. Place yogurt in pastry bag fitted with round decorating tip. Pipe yogurt onto soup in decorative design. Garnish with chives, if desired.

Makes about 5 cups, 6 servings

*At this point, soup may be covered and refrigerated up to 2 days before serving. Reheat over medium heat, stirring occasionally.

CREAM OF BUTTERNUT SOUP: Add ½ cup whipping cream or half-and-half with second can of broth. Proceed as directed.

EASY CURRIED CORN CHOWDER

1 can (16 ounces) California cling peach
    slices in juice or extra light syrup
½ pound bacon, cut into 1-inch pieces
1 onion, thinly sliced
½ cup *each* chopped celery, red bell
    pepper and green bell pepper
¼ cup all-purpose flour
2 teaspoons curry powder
1 package (10 ounces) frozen corn,
    thawed
1 large potato, cut into 1-inch cubes
2 (13¾-ounce) cans chicken broth
1 bay leaf
1 cup half-and-half

Drain peaches; cut slices in half and set aside. Cook bacon until crisp in large saucepan over medium heat; remove from pan and drain on paper towels. Reserve. Drain drippings from pan, reserving 2 tablespoons. Cook onion in reserved drippings about 8 minutes or until golden brown.

Stir in celery, bell peppers, flour and curry powder; cook 1 minute. Stir in corn, potato, chicken broth and bay leaf. Bring to a boil, stirring frequently. Cover and simmer 20 minutes or until potatoes are tender. Remove from heat. Remove and discard bay leaf; stir in half-and-half and reserved peaches. Ladle soup into serving bowls. Top with reserved crisp bacon just before serving.

Makes 6 servings

*Favorite recipe from **Canned Fruit Promotion Service***

Butternut Bisque

CARROT CREAM SOUP

¼ cup butter or margarine
¼ cup chopped onion
¼ teaspoon LAWRY'S® Seasoned Salt
½ teaspoon LAWRY'S® Garlic Powder
   with Parsley
2 cups chopped carrots
½ cup all-purpose flour
4½ cups chicken broth
¼ cup whipping cream
   Chopped fresh parsley for garnish

In large saucepan, melt butter and sauté onion, Seasoned Salt and Garlic Powder with Parsley. Add carrots and cook 5 minutes. Stir in flour; blend well. Stirring constantly, add chicken broth; blend well. Bring to a boil; reduce heat, cover and simmer 30 minutes, stirring occasionally. In blender or food processor, purée carrot mixture; return to pan. Stir in cream; heat thoroughly.   *Makes 4 servings*

PRESENTATION: Serve warm soup topped with a sprinkling of parsley. Warm French bread or crackers are welcome accompaniments.

CARROT & CORIANDER SOUP

4 tablespoons butter or margarine
4 cups grated carrots (about 1 pound)
1 cup finely chopped onion
3 cups chicken broth
2 tablespoons fresh lemon juice
1½ teaspoons ground coriander
1½ teaspoons ground cumin
1 clove garlic, finely chopped
2 tablespoons finely chopped fresh
   coriander (cilantro)
   Salt and pepper

Heat butter in medium saucepan over medium-high heat until melted and bubbly. Cook and stir carrots and onion in hot butter 5 minutes or until onion begins to soften. Add broth, lemon juice, ground coriander, cumin and garlic. Bring to a boil over high heat. Reduce heat to low. Cover; simmer 25 to 30 minutes or until vegetables are soft.

Process soup in batches in food processor or blender until smooth. Stir in fresh coriander. Season to taste with salt and pepper. Serve immediately *or* cool and store up to 1 week in refrigerator. Reheat before serving.
   Makes 4 to 6 servings

EASY TOMATO CHEESE BISQUE

1 can (10¾ ounces) condensed Cheddar
   cheese soup
2 cups water
1 cup tomato juice
1 tablespoon margarine
1 tablespoon freeze-dried chopped chives
   (optional)
½ teaspoon salt
½ teaspoon sugar
½ teaspoon dry mustard
½ teaspoon Worcestershire sauce
1 cup MINUTE® Rice, uncooked
¾ cup milk, light cream or evaporated
   milk

Mix soup, water and juice in large saucepan. Add margarine, chives, salt, sugar, mustard and Worcestershire sauce. Bring to a boil over medium heat. Stir in rice and milk. Reduce heat; cover and simmer 10 minutes, stirring occasionally. Garnish with additional chopped chives or popcorn, if desired.
   Makes 5½ cups or 7 servings

Left to right: Italian Vegetable Soup (page 61), Broccoli Cheese Soup

BROCCOLI CHEESE SOUP

½ cup chopped onion
¼ cup margarine or butter
¼ cup unsifted flour
3 cups water
2 (10-ounce) packages frozen chopped broccoli, thawed and well drained
4 teaspoons WYLER'S® or STEERO® Chicken-Flavor Instant Bouillon *or* 4 Chicken-Flavor Bouillon Cubes
1 teaspoon Worcestershire sauce
3 cups (12 ounces) shredded Cheddar cheese
2 cups (1 pint) BORDEN® or MEADOW GOLD® Coffee Cream or Half-and-Half

In large kettle or Dutch oven, cook onion in margarine until tender; stir in flour until smooth. Gradually add water, then broccoli, bouillon and Worcestershire. Over medium heat, cook and stir until thickened and broccoli is tender, about 10 minutes. Add cheese and cream. Cook and stir until cheese melts and soup is hot *(do not boil)*. Refrigerate leftovers.

Makes about 2 quarts

TIP: 6 cups (about 1¼ pounds) chopped fresh broccoli may be substituted for frozen broccoli.

MICROWAVE DIRECTIONS: In 3- to 4-quart microwavable round baking dish, combine onion and margarine; cook covered on 100% power (HIGH) 2 to 3 minutes or until onion is tender. Stir in flour. Gradually stir in water, then broccoli, bouillon and Worcestershire. Cook covered on 100% power (HIGH) 10 to 12 minutes or until mixture is thickened and broccoli is tender. Add cheese and cream; mix well. Cook covered on 100% power (HIGH) 2 to 4 minutes or until heated through.

PUMPKIN ALMOND BISQUE IN A PUMPKIN SHELL

 1 medium-size pumpkin
 3 cups chicken broth, divided
 2 tablespoons butter or margarine
 3 tablespoons chopped celery
 3 tablespoons chopped onion
 2 tablespoons almond paste
 1 tablespoon tomato paste
 1½ cups half-and-half
 3 tablespoons almond-flavored liqueur
 1 teaspoon ground nutmeg
 1 teaspoon black pepper
    Salt to taste
    Toasted Pumpkin Seeds (recipe
    follows)

Cut slice from top of pumpkin. Scoop out seeds and fibers; reserve. Scoop out flesh, leaving shell that can be used for serving. Simmer pumpkin flesh in small amount of the chicken broth until tender. Place cooked pumpkin in food processor or blender container; process until smooth. (There should be 2 cups of pumpkin purée.) Leave purée in food processor.

Melt butter in heavy stockpot. Add celery and onion; cook over low heat 5 minutes. Add celery mixture, almond paste and tomato paste to pumpkin purée; process until smooth. Return contents of food processor to stockpot; add remaining broth and simmer over low heat, 30 minutes. Stir in half-and-half and cook until heated through. Stir in liqueur, nutmeg, pepper and salt. Pour into reserved pumpkin shell. Garnish with Toasted Pumpkin Seeds.

Makes about 8 servings

TOASTED PUMPKIN SEEDS: Preheat oven to 275°F. Carefully separate reserved seeds from fibers. Wash, drain and dry seeds on paper towels. In small bowl, coat seeds with small amount of vegetable oil. Add 2 tablespoons Worcestershire sauce and ½ teaspoon ground red pepper; toss to mix thoroughly. Spread seasoned seeds in single layer on baking sheet. Bake, stirring occasionally, until golden brown.

FRENCH ONION SOUP

 3 medium onions, thinly sliced and
    separated into rings
 2 tablespoons unsalted butter
 1 package (1 ounce) LAWRY'S® Au Jus
    Gravy Mix
 3 cups water
 4 thin slices sourdough French bread
    Unsalted butter, softened
 4 slices Swiss or Gruyère cheese

In large skillet, sauté onions in 2 tablespoons butter until golden. In small bowl, combine Au Jus Gravy Mix and water; add to onions. Bring to a boil. Reduce heat to low; cover and simmer 15 minutes, stirring occasionally. Broil bread on one side until lightly toasted. Turn bread slices over; spread with softened butter. Top with cheese; broil until cheese melts.

Makes 4 servings

PRESENTATION: To serve, pour soup into tureen or individual bowls. Top each serving with toast.

HINT: If using individual, ovenproof bowls, pour soup into bowls; top each with untoasted bread slice. Top with cheese. Place under broiler just until cheese is melted.

Pumpkin Almond Bisque in a Pumpkin Shell

Miami Heat Chili

In Dutch oven or large saucepot, heat 2 teaspoons oil until hot. Add meat, a few pieces at a time; cook and stir until browned on all sides. Remove meat from Dutch oven; repeat until all meat is browned. Set aside. Heat remaining 3 teaspoons oil until hot. Add chili powder, cumin, garlic, oregano, paprika, and red and black peppers; cook and stir 1 minute. Remove from heat. Stir in tomato sauce, beer, water and reserved meat; bring to a boil. Reduce heat and simmer, covered, until meat is tender, about 2 hours, stirring occasionally. Serve with cooked pinto beans, chopped onions, jalapeño peppers and grated Cheddar cheese, if desired.   *Makes 4 to 6 servings*

*Favorite recipe from **American Spice Trade Association***

MIAMI HEAT CHILI

5 teaspoons vegetable oil, divided
1 pound round steak, cut into 1-inch cubes
1 pound boneless chuck steak, cut into 1-inch cubes
3 tablespoons chili powder
1 tablespoon ground cumin
1 tablespoon instant minced garlic
½ teaspoon oregano leaves, crushed
½ teaspoon paprika
⅛ teaspoon ground red pepper
⅛ teaspoon ground black pepper
1 can (15 ounces) tomato sauce
1 can (12 ounces) beer
1½ cups water

ITALIAN-STYLE CHILI

1 pound lean ground beef
¾ cup chopped onion
1 (26-ounce) jar CLASSICO® Di Napoli (Tomato & Basil) Pasta Sauce
1½ cups water
1 (14½-ounce) can whole tomatoes, undrained and broken up
1 (4-ounce) can sliced mushrooms, drained
2 ounces sliced pepperoni (⅓ cup)
1 tablespoon WYLER'S® or STEERO® Beef-Flavor Instant Bouillon *or* 3 Beef-Flavor Bouillon Cubes
1 tablespoon chili powder
2 teaspoons sugar

In large kettle or Dutch oven, brown meat with onion; pour off fat. Add remaining ingredients; bring to a boil. Reduce heat; simmer uncovered 30 minutes, stirring occasionally. Garnish as desired. Refrigerate leftovers.

Makes about 2 quarts

ITALIAN VEGETABLE SOUP

 1 pound bulk Italian sausage
 2 cups chopped onion
 2 cloves garlic, finely chopped
 7 cups water
 4 medium carrots, pared and sliced
 1 (28-ounce) can whole tomatoes,
   undrained and broken up
 2 tablespoons WYLER'S® or STEERO®
   Beef-Flavor Instant Bouillon *or*
   6 Beef-Flavor Bouillon Cubes
 1 teaspoon Italian seasoning
 ¼ teaspoon pepper
 1½ cups coarsely chopped zucchini
 1 (15-ounce) can garbanzo beans,
   drained
 1 cup uncooked CREAMETTE® Rotini or
   Elbow Macaroni

In large kettle or Dutch oven, brown sausage, onion and garlic; pour off fat. Add water, carrots, tomatoes, bouillon, Italian seasoning and pepper; bring to a boil. Reduce heat; cover and simmer 30 minutes. Add zucchini, beans and rotini. Cook 15 to 20 minutes or until rotini is tender, stirring occasionally. Refrigerate leftovers. *Makes about 2½ quarts*

HEAD–'EM–OFF–AT–THE–PASS WHITE CHILI

 ½ cup fresh or frozen chopped onions
 1 tablespoon olive oil
 1½ cups chopped cooked chicken *or*
   2 (5-ounce) cans chopped chicken
 ½ cup chicken broth
 2 (15-ounce) cans cannellini beans,
   undrained
 1 teaspoon dried oregano
 ½ teaspoon celery salt
 1 (11-ounce) jar NEWMAN'S OWN®
   Bandito Salsa*, divided
 1½ cups shredded mozzarella cheese,
   divided

In 2-quart saucepan, cook and stir onions in olive oil until translucent. Add chopped chicken, mixing thoroughly, then add chicken broth. Stir in cannellini beans, oregano, celery salt and ½ cup salsa. Simmer over medium heat 10 minutes, gently stirring occasionally. Just before serving, stir in 1 cup mozzarella cheese. Divide among serving bowls and top each with a portion of remaining mozzarella cheese and salsa. *Makes 4 servings*

*Choose a flavor (mild, medium or hot) that suits your taste.

CREAMY DIJON TURKEY SOUP

 1 cup *each* chopped celery and thinly
   sliced onions
 3 tablespoons margarine
 1 large garlic clove, minced
 3 tablespoons flour
 ½ teaspoon salt
 ¼ teaspoon white pepper
 4 cups skim milk
 ¼ cup Dijon mustard
 2 teaspoons reduced sodium chicken
   bouillon granules
 2 cups cubed cooked turkey (½ to
   ¾-inch cubes)
 French bread (optional)

1. In 3-quart saucepan, over medium-high heat, sauté celery and onions in margarine 5 to 6 minutes or until celery is tender and onions are golden brown. Add garlic and sauté 1 to 2 minutes. Stir in flour, salt and pepper and cook 1 to 2 minutes. Remove pan from heat and slowly add milk, stirring constantly.

2. Return pan to medium-high heat. Stir in mustard and bouillon; cook and stir 5 to 8 minutes or until mixture is thickened and bubbly. Stir in turkey and heat 1 to 2 minutes. Serve with sliced French bread.

Makes 6 servings

*Favorite recipe from **National Turkey Federation***

KALEIDOSCOPE CHOWDER

3 cups water

3 large potatoes, peeled and diced

1 (26-ounce) jar NEWMAN'S OWN®
    Diavolo Sauce

2 large carrots, peeled and thinly sliced

1½ to 2 pounds assorted seafood, such as
    fish fillets, bay scallops, shrimp or
    clams

½ cup dry white wine

2 cups shredded fresh spinach leaves

1 yellow bell pepper, seeded and diced
    Freshly grated Parmesan cheese

In large stockpot, bring water to a boil. Add
potatoes; cook 5 minutes. Stir in Diavolo Sauce
and carrots. Bring to a boil; reduce heat and
simmer 5 minutes.

Cut fish fillets into bite-size pieces. Peel and
devein shrimp. Add seafood and wine to soup.
Cook over medium-high heat, stirring often,
until fish is opaque, 3 to 4 minutes. Add
spinach and pepper; cover. Remove from heat
and let stand until spinach and pepper are
heated through, about 2 minutes. Serve with
Parmesan cheese. *Makes 4 servings*

NOTE: This chowder is also excellent with
diced cooked chicken breast.

QUICK AND ZESTY VEGETABLE SOUP

1 pound lean ground beef

½ cup chopped onion
    Salt and pepper

2 cans (14½ ounces each) DEL MONTE®
    Italian Recipe Stewed Tomatoes

2 cans (13¾ ounces each) beef broth

1 can (17 ounces) DEL MONTE® Mixed
    Vegetables

½ cup uncooked medium egg noodles

½ teaspoon dried oregano

In large pot, brown meat with onion. Cook until
onion is tender; drain. Season to taste with salt
and pepper. Stir in remaining ingredients. Bring
to boil; reduce heat. Cover and simmer 15
minutes or until noodles are tender.
Makes 8 servings

PREP TIME: 5 minutes
COOK TIME: 15 minutes

BULGUR CHILI

1 cup chopped onion

½ cup chopped celery

4 teaspoons sugar

2 tablespoons chili powder

1 tablespoon dried oregano

1 teaspoon ground cumin

1 teaspoon black pepper

2 teaspoons vegetable oil

⅔ cup uncooked bulgur

1½ cups water

1 (14-ounce) can black beans, rinsed and
    drained *or* 2 cups cooked black beans

1 (14-ounce) can cannellini or navy
    beans, rinsed and drained *or* 2 cups
    cooked cannellini or navy beans

1 (28-ounce) can tomatoes, crushed or
    stewed

In 3- to 4-quart saucepan, sauté onion, celery,
sugar and spices in oil 5 minutes. Stir in bulgur
and water. Simmer, covered, over low heat 10
minutes, stirring occasionally. Add beans and
tomatoes. Simmer, covered, over low heat 15 to
20 minutes, stirring occasionally. Serve in
warmed bowls. *Makes 4 servings*

Favorite recipe from **The Sugar Association, Inc.**

Kaleidoscope Chowder

Cobb Salad

COBB SALAD

4 skinless boneless chicken breast
    halves, cooked, cooled
⅔ cup vegetable oil
⅓ cup HEINZ® Distilled White or Apple
    Cider Vinegar
1 clove garlic, minced
2 teaspoons dried dill weed
1½ teaspoons granulated sugar
½ teaspoon salt
¼ teaspoon black pepper
8 cups torn salad greens, chilled
1 large tomato, diced
1 medium green bell pepper, diced
1 small red onion, chopped
¾ cup crumbled blue cheese
6 slices bacon, cooked, crumbled
1 hard-cooked egg, chopped

Shred chicken into bite-size pieces. For
dressing, in jar, combine oil, vinegar, garlic, dill,
sugar, salt and black pepper; cover and shake
vigorously. Pour ½ cup dressing over chicken;
toss well to coat. Toss greens with remaining
dressing. Line each of 4 large individual salad
bowls with greens; mound chicken mixture in
center. Arrange mounds of tomato, green
pepper, onion, cheese, bacon and egg around
chicken. *Makes 4 servings*

HOLIDAY SPLIT PEAS VINAIGRETTE

4 cups green or yellow split peas, washed
2 quarts water
3 pounds cooked smoked sausage, sliced
12 medium (4 pounds) onions, finely
    chopped and steamed or sautéed
2 cups olive oil
¾ cup vinegar
1½ cups chopped fresh parsley
⅓ cup German hot or coarse mustard
    Sugar to taste
    Salt and white pepper to taste
12 medium (4 pounds) tomatoes or red
    bell peppers, coarsely chopped and
    sautéed

1. Combine split peas and water in stockpot.
Bring to a boil; reduce heat and simmer 20
minutes or until peas are tender.

2. Remove from heat; drain, if necessary. Stir
in sausage and onions. Keep warm.

3. Blend together oil, vinegar, parsley, mustard,
sugar, salt and pepper.

4. Pour oil mixture over split pea mixture;
blend.

5. Gently stir in tomatoes. Serve immediately
as warm salad or cassoulet. Cover and
refrigerate several hours for chilled salad.
Makes 24 (1½-cup) servings

Favorite recipe from **USA Dry Pea & Lentil Council**

SMOKED TURKEY & PEPPER PASTA SALAD

¾ cup MIRACLE WHIP® Salad Dressing
1 tablespoon Dijon mustard
½ teaspoon dried thyme leaves
8 ounces fettucini, cooked, drained
1 cup (8 ounces) diced LOUIS RICH®
   Smoked Boneless Turkey Breast
¾ cup zucchini slices, cut into halves
½ cup red bell pepper strips
½ cup yellow bell pepper strips
   Salt and black pepper

Mix salad dressing, mustard and thyme until well blended. Add pasta, turkey and vegetables; mix lightly. Season with salt and black pepper to taste. Chill. Add additional dressing before serving, if desired.

Makes about 6 servings

PREP TIME: 15 minutes plus chilling

Smoked Turkey & Pepper Pasta Salad

SEA BREEZE FISH SALAD

1 pound firm white fish fillets (red snapper, sea bass or orange roughy), about 1 inch thick
1¾ cups water
1 tablespoon grated lemon peel
6 tablespoons lemon juice, divided
3 tablespoons KIKKOMAN® Lite Soy Sauce, divided
6 ounces fresh snow peas, trimmed and cut diagonally into 1-inch pieces
2 tablespoons vegetable oil
1 tablespoon minced onion
½ teaspoon dried thyme, crumbled
¼ teaspoon sugar
½ medium cantaloupe, chunked
1 tablespoon minced fresh cilantro or parsley

Cut fish into 1-inch cubes. Combine water, lemon peel, 4 tablespoons lemon juice and 1 tablespoon lite soy sauce in large skillet. Heat only until mixture starts to simmer. Add fish; simmer, uncovered, 3 minutes, or until fish flakes easily when tested with fork. Remove fish with slotted spoon to plate. Cool slightly; cover and refrigerate 1 hour or until thoroughly chilled. Meanwhile, cook snow peas in boiling water 2 minutes, or until tender-crisp; cool under cold water and drain thoroughly. Chill. Measure remaining 2 tablespoons lemon juice and 2 tablespoons lite soy sauce, oil, onion, thyme and sugar into jar with screw-top lid; cover and shake well. Combine snow peas, cantaloupe and cilantro in large bowl; add dressing and toss to coat all ingredients. Add fish and gently stir to combine. Serve immediately.

Makes 4 servings

CRISP AND CRUNCHY TURKEY SALAD

    1 cup (8 ounces) plain low fat yogurt
    3 tablespoons mayonnaise
    2 teaspoons Dijon-style mustard
    1 clove garlic, minced
    ½ teaspoon salt
    Freshly ground black pepper to taste
  1½ cups chopped cooked turkey
    2 cups shredded red cabbage
    2 cups fresh bean sprouts
    ¼ pound fresh snow peas, trimmed
    ¾ cup celery slices
    ½ cup sliced almonds, toasted
    ¼ cup chopped red onion
    Fresh spinach leaves
    2 hard-cooked eggs, peeled and sliced,
       for garnish

Combine yogurt, mayonnaise, mustard, garlic and seasonings in large bowl. Add turkey, cabbage, bean sprouts, snow peas, celery, almonds and onion; mix lightly. Serve in spinach-lined salad bowl or on spinach-covered salad plates. Garnish with eggs.

Makes 4 servings

SALMON PLATTER SALAD

    1 can (15½ ounces) salmon
    1 pound asparagus
    2 tablespoons oil
    2 tablespoons lemon juice
    ¼ teaspoon dry mustard
    ¼ teaspoon salt
    Dash pepper
    Salad greens
    Tomato wedges
    Cucumber slices
    Pimiento strips
    Radish roses
    ½ cup dairy sour cream
    1 teaspoon dried dill weed

Chill can of salmon. Cook asparagus in boiling salted water until just tender. Drain and place in shallow glass container. Combine oil, lemon juice, mustard, salt and pepper. Pour over asparagus. Marinate for 1 hour. Drain, reserving marinade. Drain salmon and remove from can in one piece. Place salmon and asparagus on platter lined with greens. Garnish with tomato wedges, cucumber slices, pimiento strips and radish roses. Combine reserved marinade with sour cream. Blend in dill weed. Season with additional salt and pepper to taste. Serve with salad. *Makes 4 to 6 servings*

Favorite recipe from **Alaska Seafood Marketing Institute**

CONFETTI CHICKEN SALAD

    ¼ cup white vinegar
    3 tablespoons CHEF PAUL
       PRUDHOMME'S® Poultry Magic®
    1 teaspoon ground allspice
    ½ teaspoon ground bay leaf
    ½ teaspoon salt
    1 cup vegetable oil
    4 cups cooked rice
  12 ounces cooked chicken, cut into bite-
       size pieces
    2 cups small broccoli florets
    2 cups chopped fresh tomatoes
    1 cup shredded carrots
    ½ cup chopped onion
    ½ cup chopped celery
    Lettuce leaves

Make dressing by combining vinegar, Poultry Magic®, allspice, bay leaf and salt in food processor. Process until well mixed. With motor running, add oil in slow steady stream until incorporated and dressing is thick and creamy. Combine remaining measured ingredients in a large mixing bowl. Mix well. Stir in dressing. To serve, line 6 serving plates with lettuce leaves. Divide salad into portions. Mound each portion of salad onto center of lettuce leaf.

Makes 6 servings

Crisp and Crunchy Turkey Salad

Mediterranean Phyllo Twists with Grapes and Cheese

3-GREEN SALAD WITH CRANBERRY VINAIGRETTE

    1 head red leaf lettuce
    1 head romaine
    1 pound (or bag) fresh spinach
    1 cup bottled oil and vinegar dressing
    ½ cup ground cranberries
    1 teaspoon tarragon
    1 clove garlic, crushed
        Red cabbage slivers, cut paper thin, for
          garnish
        Bean sprouts for garnish

Clean greens, removing tough stems or ribs and tearing into bite-sized pieces. Combine greens in large bowl; cover and refrigerate. Mix dressing, cranberries, tarragon and garlic in a covered jar. Allow to steep for at least 2 hours, then toss with greens. Garnish with cabbage and sprouts.   *Makes 6 servings*

Favorite recipe from **Perdue Farms, Incorporated**

MEDITERRANEAN PHYLLO TWISTS WITH GRAPES AND CHEESE

    6 sheets phyllo dough
    2 tablespoons olive oil, divided
    5 to 6 ounces goat cheese
    2 tablespoons chopped fresh basil
    ⅛ teaspoon medium-grind pepper
    2 cups California seedless grapes
    3 quarts mixed greens
        Mustard Vinaigrette (recipe follows)
    12 small California grape clusters

Cut each sheet of phyllo dough into 4 equal (about 6½×8½-inch) pieces and keep under a damp, clean towel to prevent drying. Working with 4 pieces at a time, brush each with oil and stack, alternating directions with each piece to enable the complete covering of filling. Portion ⅙ of cheese in center of dough. Combine basil and pepper; mix well. Top cheese with 1 teaspoon basil mixture and ⅓ cup grapes. Carefully gather dough to enclose filling, twisting dough at top to form small bundle. Brush lightly with oil to prevent drying. Place on greased baking sheet. Repeat with remaining ingredients. Bake at 400°F 10 minutes or until thoroughly heated. Toss mixed greens with Mustard Vinaigrette. Serve each phyllo packet on bed of mixed greens; garnish with grape clusters.   *Makes 6 servings*

MUSTARD VINAIGRETTE: Combine 3 tablespoons balsamic vinegar, 1 tablespoon *each* olive oil and chopped parsley, 1 teaspoon Dijon-style mustard, ½ teaspoon *each* sugar and salt and ¼ teaspoon pepper. Makes ⅓ cup.

Favorite recipe from **California Table Grape Commission**

MANDARIN ORANGE AND RED ONION SALAD

1 cup **BLUE DIAMOND®** Sliced Natural
　　Almonds
1 tablespoon butter
2 tablespoons lemon juice
1 teaspoon Dijon mustard
½ teaspoon sugar
½ teaspoon salt
¼ teaspoon white pepper
½ cup vegetable oil
1 head romaine lettuce, torn into pieces
1 can (11 ounces) mandarin orange
　　segments, drained
1 small red onion, thinly sliced, rings
　　separated

Sauté almonds in butter until golden; reserve.
Combine next 5 ingredients. Whisk in oil.
Combine lettuce, oranges, onion and almonds.
Toss with dressing.　　*Makes 4 to 6 servings*

FRESH SPINACH SALAD WITH RED WINE VINAIGRETTE DRESSING

½ pound spinach leaves, torn into pieces
2 hard-cooked eggs, peeled and chopped
6 bacon slices, cooked and crumbled
2 cups sliced fresh mushrooms
¾ cup **LAWRY'S®** Red Wine Vinaigrette
　　with Cabernet Sauvignon Dressing

In large salad bowl, gently toss together all
ingredients except dressing; chill. Toss with
dressing just before serving.
　　　　　Makes 6 servings

PRESENTATION: Serve on chilled salad
plates with chilled forks, if desired.

Mandarin Orange and Red Onion Salad

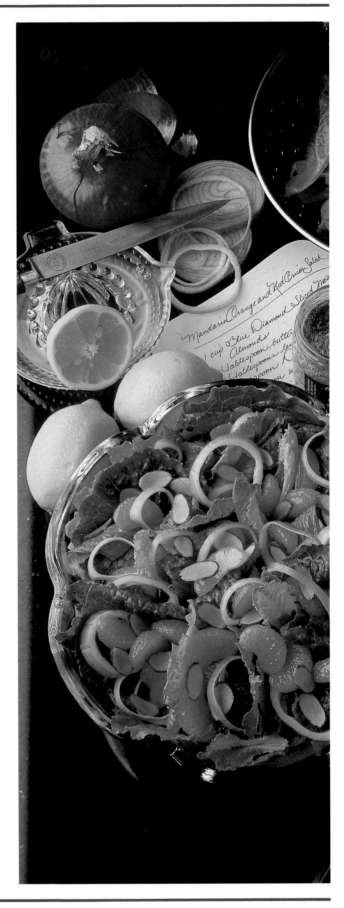

WINTER PEAR AND STILTON SALAD

⅓ cup extra virgin olive oil
1½ tablespoons sherry wine vinegar or white wine vinegar
1 tablespoon Dijon-style mustard
4 teaspoons honey
¼ teaspoon salt
2 ripe Bosc, Bartlett or Anjou pears
    Lemon juice (optional)
5 cups washed and torn assorted gourmet mixed salad greens, such as oakleaf, frisee, watercress, radicchio, arugula or escarole
2 cups washed and torn Boston or Bibb lettuce leaves
6 ounces Stilton or Gorgonzola cheese, crumbled
    Freshly ground black pepper

Place oil, vinegar, mustard, honey and salt in small bowl. Whisk together until combined. Cover and refrigerate up to 2 days.

Quarter and core pears; cut into ½-inch pieces. To help prevent discoloration, brush pear pieces with lemon juice, if desired. Combine greens, pears, cheese and dressing in large bowl. Toss lightly to coat; sprinkle with pepper.

Makes 6 to 8 servings

MARINATED VEGETABLE SPINACH SALAD

Mustard Tarragon Marinade (recipe follows)
8 ounces fresh mushrooms, quartered
2 slices purple onion, separated into rings
16 cherry tomatoes, halved
4 cups fresh spinach leaves, washed and stems removed
3 slices (3 ounces) SARGENTO® Preferred Light® Sliced Mozzarella Cheese, cut into julienne strips
    Freshly ground black pepper

Prepare Mustard Tarragon Marinade. Place mushrooms, onion and tomatoes in bowl. Toss with marinade and let stand 15 minutes. Meanwhile, wash and dry spinach leaves. Arrange on 4 individual serving plates. Divide marinated vegetables among plates and top each salad with ¼ of the cheese. Serve with freshly ground pepper, if desired.

Makes 4 servings

MUSTARD TARRAGON MARINADE

3 tablespoons red wine vinegar
1 tablespoon Dijon mustard
1½ teaspoons dried tarragon
2 tablespoons olive oil

Combine first three ingredients. Slowly whisk oil into mixture until slightly thickened.

Makes ⅓ cup

Winter Pear and Stilton Salad

MIXED GREENS WITH RASPBERRY VINAIGRETTE

  ½ cup walnut pieces
  ⅓ cup vegetable oil
2½ tablespoons raspberry vinegar
  1 tablespoon chopped shallot
  ½ teaspoon salt
  ½ teaspoon sugar
  2 cups washed and torn Romaine lettuce
      leaves
  2 cups washed and torn spinach leaves
  2 cups washed and torn red leaf lettuce
      leaves
  1 cup halved red seedless grapes

Preheat oven to 350°F. To toast walnuts, spread in single layer on baking sheet. Bake 6 to 8 minutes or until lightly golden brown, stirring frequently; cool. Coarsely chop; set aside.

Place oil, vinegar, shallot, salt and sugar in small bowl or small jar with lid. Whisk together or cover and shake jar until mixed. Cover; refrigerate up to 1 week. Combine greens, grapes and chopped walnuts in large bowl. Just before serving, add dressing; toss well to coat.
Makes 6 to 8 servings

CHEESY WALDORF SALAD

  ⅓ cup mayonnaise or reduced-fat
      mayonnaise
  1 tablespoon honey
  1 tablespoon cider vinegar
  4 small or 3 large apples
  4 ounces Provolone cheese
  2 ribs celery, thinly sliced
  ½ cup walnuts or pecans, toasted and
      chopped, divided
      Red leaf lettuce leaves

Combine mayonnaise, honey and vinegar in large bowl until blended. Core apples; cut enough into ½-inch pieces to equal 4 cups. Cut cheese into cubes. Add apples, cheese, celery and ¼ cup walnuts; stir to coat. At this point the salad may be refrigerated, covered with plastic wrap, up to 8 hours. To serve, line individual salad plates with lettuce, then top with salad. Sprinkle remaining ¼ cup walnuts over each serving.
Makes 6 to 8 servings

CREAMY ITALIAN PASTA SALAD

  1 cup HELLMANN'S® or BEST FOODS®
      Real or Low Fat Mayonnaise
      Dressing
  2 tablespoons red wine vinegar
  1 clove garlic, minced
  1 tablespoon chopped fresh basil *or*
      1 teaspoon dried basil
  1 teaspoon salt
  ¼ teaspoon freshly ground black pepper
1½ cups twist or spiral pasta, cooked,
      rinsed with cold water and drained
  1 cup quartered cherry tomatoes
  ½ cup coarsely chopped green pepper
  ½ cup slivered pitted ripe olives

In large bowl combine mayonnaise, vinegar, garlic, basil, salt and pepper. Stir in pasta, cherry tomatoes, green pepper and olives. Cover; chill.
Makes about 6 servings

Mixed Greens with Raspberry Vinaigrette

Christmas Cabbage Slaw

CHRISTMAS CABBAGE SLAW

2 cups finely shredded green cabbage
2 cups finely shredded red cabbage
1 cup jicama strips
¼ cup diced green bell pepper
¼ cup thinly sliced green onions with
    tops
¼ cup vegetable oil
¼ cup lime juice
¾ teaspoon salt
⅛ teaspoon freshly ground black pepper
2 tablespoons coarsely chopped cilantro
    leaves

Combine cabbages, jicama, bell pepper and onions in large bowl. Whisk oil, lime juice, salt and black pepper in small bowl until well blended. Stir in cilantro. Pour over cabbage mixture; toss lightly. Cover; refrigerate 2 to 6 hours for flavors to blend.

Makes 4 to 6 servings

ROASTED TOMATO AND MOZZARELLA PASTA SALAD

3 cups (8 ounces) rotelle (corkscrew)
    pasta, uncooked
    Roasted Fresh Tomatoes (page 75)
1 cup coarsely chopped green bell pepper
4 ounces mozzarella cheese, cut into
    ½-inch cubes
¼ cup chopped sweet red onion
½ teaspoon salt
¼ teaspoon ground black pepper
⅓ cup bottled red wine vinaigrette salad
    dressing

Cook pasta according to package directions; rinse and drain. Place in large bowl. Cut Roasted Fresh Tomatoes into chunks; add to pasta along with green pepper, mozzarella cheese, onion, salt and black pepper. Add salad dressing; toss to coat. Serve garnished with basil leaves, if desired.

Makes 4 servings, 8 cups

ROASTED FRESH TOMATOES

6 large tomatoes (about 3 pounds)
2 tablespoons vegetable oil
½ teaspoon dried basil leaves, crushed
¼ teaspoon dried thyme leaves, crushed
¼ teaspoon salt
¼ teaspoon ground black pepper

Preheat oven to 425°F. Use tomatoes held at room temperature until fully ripe. Core tomatoes; cut in half horizontally. Gently squeeze to remove seeds. Place, cut side up, on rack in broiler pan; set aside. In small bowl combine oil, basil, thyme, salt and black pepper; brush over cut sides of tomatoes. Place tomatoes cut side down. Bake until well browned, about 30 minutes. Remove tomato skins, if desired.

Makes 4 to 6 servings, 3 cups

NOTE: Recipe also may be served hot, warm or chilled as a side dish.

*Favorite recipe from **Florida Tomato Committee***

Roasted Tomato and Mozzarella Pasta Salad

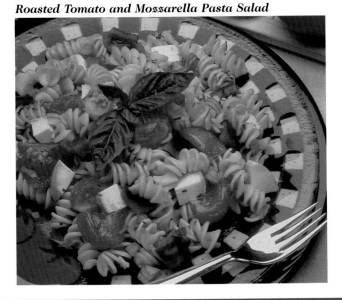

APPLE & DRIED CHERRY CHUTNEY

3 tablespoons vegetable oil
1½ cups chopped red onions
1 tablespoon minced fresh ginger
¼ teaspoon red pepper flakes
⅓ cup dried cherries
1 tablespoon packed dark brown sugar
¼ teaspoon salt
1 cup water
1 Granny Smith apple, cored and finely chopped
1 teaspoon cornstarch, dissolved in 1 tablespoon water
1 teaspoon balsamic vinegar

In large skillet, heat oil over medium heat. Add onions, ginger and pepper flakes; cook and stir 5 minutes. Add dried cherries, brown sugar and salt. Stir in water; cover and cook over medium heat 5 minutes.

Add apple to onion mixture. Cover; cook 6 to 8 minutes or until apple is tender. Stir cornstarch mixture into apple-onion mixture and cook over high heat, stirring constantly, until mixture is thickened and appears glazed, about 1 minute. Remove from heat; stir in vinegar. Cool before serving or storing. Chutney can be refrigerated for one week or frozen for one month.

Makes 2 cups

*Favorite recipe from **Washington Apple Commission***

GINGER PINEAPPLE MOLD

1 can (20 ounces) pineapple chunks in juice*

1½ cups boiling water

1 package (8-serving size) *or* 2 packages (4-serving size) JELL-O® Brand Lime or Apricot Flavor Gelatin

1 cup ginger ale or cold water

¼ teaspoon ground ginger

Drain pineapple, reserving juice. Stir boiling water into gelatin in large bowl 2 minutes or until completely dissolved. Stir in reserved juice, ginger ale and ginger. Refrigerate about 1¼ hours or until slightly thickened (mixture should be consistency of unbeaten egg whites).

Arrange some of the pineapple chunks in 6-cup ring mold or 9×5-inch loaf pan; top with 1 cup of the slightly thickened gelatin. Refrigerate about 10 minutes or until set but not firm (sticks to finger when touched and moves to the side when pan is tilted). Stir remaining pineapple into remaining gelatin; spoon into mold. Refrigerate 4 hours or until firm. Unmold. Garnish as desired. Serve as dessert or salad. *Makes 10 servings*

*Or use 1 can (20 ounces) pineapple slices in juice; reserve 4 slices for garnish and dice remaining slices.

NOTE: Arrangement of pineapple may be omitted; fold all pineapple into thickened gelatin.

Ginger Pineapple Mold

Stir in cranberries, orange and nuts. Spoon into 5-cup mold that has been lightly sprayed with no-stick cooking spray.

Refrigerate about 4 hours or until firm. Unmold. Garnish as desired. Store leftover gelatin mold in refrigerator. *Makes 10 servings*

*Or use 1 can (16 ounces) whole berry cranberry sauce; omit sugar and reduce cold water to ½ cup.

Spiced Cranberry-Orange Mold

SPICED CRANBERRY– ORANGE MOLD

   1 bag (12 ounces) fresh cranberries*
   ½ cup sugar*
   1½ cups boiling water
   1 package (8-serving size) *or* 2 packages (4-serving size) JELL-O® Brand Cranberry, Orange or Lemon Flavor Gelatin
   ¼ teaspoon salt (optional)
   1 cup cold water*
   1 tablespoon lemon juice
   ¼ teaspoon ground cinnamon
   ⅛ teaspoon ground cloves
   1 orange, sectioned, diced
   ½ cup chopped nuts

Finely chop cranberries in food processor; mix with sugar. Set aside.

Stir boiling water into combined gelatin and salt in large bowl 2 minutes or until gelatin is completely dissolved. Stir in cold water, lemon juice, cinnamon and cloves. Refrigerate about 1½ hours or until thickened (spoon drawn through gelatin leaves a definite impression).

HOLIDAY FRUIT SALAD

   3 packages (3 ounces each) strawberry flavor gelatin
   3 cups boiling water
   2 ripe DOLE® Bananas
   1 package (16 ounces) frozen strawberries
   1 can (20 ounces) DOLE® Crushed Pineapple
   1 package (8 ounces) cream cheese, softened
   1 cup dairy sour cream or plain yogurt
   ¼ cup sugar
     Crisp DOLE® Lettuce leaves

• In large bowl, dissolve gelatin in boiling water. Slice bananas into gelatin mixture. Add frozen strawberries and undrained pineapple. Reserve half of the mixture at room temperature. Pour remaining mixture into 13×9-inch pan. Refrigerate 1 hour or until firm.

• In mixer bowl, beat cream cheese with sour cream and sugar; spread over chilled layer. Gently spoon reserved gelatin mixture on top. Refrigerate until firm, about 2 hours.

• Cut into squares; serve on lettuce-lined salad plates. Garnish with additional pineapple and mint leaves, if desired. *Makes 12 servings*

ORANGE–BERRY SALAD

½ cup prepared **HIDDEN VALLEY RANCH®** Original Ranch® salad dressing
2 tablespoons orange juice
1 teaspoon grated orange peel
½ cup heavy cream, whipped
1 (11-ounce) can mandarin orange segments
2 (3-ounce) packages strawberry- or raspberry-flavored gelatin
1 (16-ounce) can whole-berry cranberry sauce
½ cup walnut pieces
   Mint sprigs
   Whole fresh strawberries and raspberries

In large bowl, whisk together salad dressing, orange juice and peel. Fold in whipped cream; cover and refrigerate. Drain oranges, reserving juice. Add water to juice to measure 3 cups; pour into large saucepan and bring to a boil. Remove from heat. Stir in gelatin until dissolved. Cover and refrigerate until partially set. Fold orange segments, cranberry sauce and walnuts into gelatin. Pour into lightly oiled 6-cup ring mold. Cover and refrigerate until firm; unmold. Garnish with mint, fresh strawberries and raspberries. Serve with chilled dressing.   *Makes 8 servings*

RIBBON SQUARES

1 package (4-serving size) **JELL-O®** Brand Lemon Flavor Gelatin
1 package (4-serving size) **JELL-O®** Brand Gelatin, any red flavor
1 package (4-serving size) **JELL-O®** Brand Lime Flavor Gelatin
3 cups boiling water, divided
1 package (8 ounces) **PHILADELPHIA BRAND®** Cream Cheese, softened
1 can (8¼ ounces) crushed pineapple in syrup
1 cup thawed **COOL WHIP®** Whipped Topping*
½ cup **KRAFT®** Real Mayonnaise
1½ cups cold water, divided

Dissolve each flavor of gelatin separately in 1 cup of the boiling water. Gradually add lemon gelatin to cream cheese, mixing until well blended. Stir in pineapple with syrup. Refrigerate about 1¼ hours or until slightly thickened (mixture should be consistency of unbeaten egg whites). Blend in whipped topping and mayonnaise. Refrigerate until thickened (spoon drawn through mixture leaves definite impression).

Meanwhile, add ¾ cup of the cold water to red gelatin. Pour into 9-inch square pan. Refrigerate about 2 hours or until set but not firm. Add the remaining ¾ cup cold water to lime gelatin. Refrigerate about 1¼ hours or until slightly thickened (gelatin should be consistency of unbeaten egg whites).

Spoon lemon gelatin mixture over red gelatin layer in pan. Refrigerate until set but not firm (sticks to finger when touched and moves to side when pan is tilted). Top with lime gelatin. Refrigerate 4 hours or until firm. Unmold. Cut into squares. Garnish with drained, canned, sliced pineapple and celery leaves, if desired.
                    Makes 16 servings

*Or use 1 cup prepared DREAM WHIP® Whipped Topping.

Orange-Berry Salad

HOLIDAY WALDORF SALAD

1½ cups boiling water
1 package (8-serving size) *or* 2 packages
    (4-serving size) JELL-O® Brand
    Strawberry Flavor Gelatin
1 tablespoon lemon juice
1 cup cold water
    Ice cubes
1 medium red apple, diced
½ cup halved seedless grapes
½ cup thinly sliced celery
½ cup chopped walnuts
1 cup KRAFT® Real Mayonnaise

Stir boiling water into gelatin in large bowl 2 minutes or until completely dissolved. Stir in lemon juice. Mix cold water and ice cubes to make 2½ cups. Add to gelatin, stirring until slightly thickened. Remove any remaining ice. Refrigerate about 10 minutes or until thickened (spoon drawn through gelatin leaves definite impression).

Stir apple, grapes, celery and walnuts into gelatin. Measure 1 cup gelatin mixture and set aside. Pour remaining gelatin mixture into 8-cup serving bowl. Refrigerate until set but not firm (sticks to finger when touched and moves to side when bowl is tilted).

Blend mayonnaise into reserved 1 cup gelatin mixture. Spoon over fruited layer. Refrigerate 3 hours or until firm. Garnish with apple slices and grapes, if desired.

Makes about 14 servings

APPLESAUCE CRANBERRY MOLD

2 envelopes unflavored gelatin
½ cup orange or cranberry juice
½ cup boiling water
1 can or jar (16 ounces) whole-berry
    cranberry sauce
1 cup applesauce
1 apple, cored and cut up
1 cup diced celery
½ cup chopped walnuts
1 orange, peeled and diced
2 tablespoons grated orange peel

Soften gelatin in juice. Add boiling water and stir to dissolve; cool. Mix all other ingredients; add to gelatin mixture. Pour into a greased 2-quart mold and refrigerate several hours. Unmold.   *Makes 6 to 8 servings*

Favorite recipe from **New York Apple Association, Inc.**

PINEAPPLE LIME MOLD

1 can (20 ounces) DOLE® Pineapple
    Chunks
2 packages (3 ounces each) lime gelatin
2 cups boiling water
1 cup dairy sour cream
½ cup chopped walnuts
½ cup chopped celery

• Drain pineapple, reserving syrup. Dissolve gelatin in boiling water. Add sour cream and reserved syrup. Chill until slightly thickened. Stir in pineapple, walnuts and celery. Pour into 7-cup mold. Chill until set. Unmold.

Makes 8 servings

CHRISTMAS RIBBON

5 cups boiling water, divided
1 package (8-serving size) *or* 2 packages (4-serving size) JELL-O® Brand Strawberry Flavor Gelatin
⅔ cup BREYER'S® or KNUDSEN® Sour Cream*, divided
1 package (8-serving size) *or* 2 packages (4-serving size) JELL-O® Brand Lime Flavor Gelatin

Stir 2½ cups of the boiling water into strawberry flavor gelatin in large bowl 2 minutes or until completely dissolved. Pour 1½ cups into 6-cup ring mold. Refrigerate about 30 minutes or until set but not firm (should stick to finger when touched and mound). Refrigerate remaining gelatin in bowl until slightly thickened. Gradually stir in ⅓ cup of the sour cream; spoon over gelatin in mold. Refrigerate about 15 minutes or until set but not firm.

Repeat with lime flavor gelatin, remaining 2½ cups boiling water and ⅓ cup sour cream, refrigerating dissolved gelatin before measuring and pouring into mold. Refrigerate 2 hours or until firm. Unmold.

Makes about 12 servings

*Or use BREYER'S® or KNUDSEN® Plain or Vanilla Yogurt.

Christmas Ribbon

Meats

FOR FEASTS

PEPPERED BEEF TIP ROAST WITH CORN PUDDING

1 (3½- to 5-pound) beef tip roast
2 teaspoons *each* **cracked black pepper and**
    dry mustard
½ teaspoon *each* **ground allspice and ground**
    red pepper
1 large clove garlic, minced
1 teaspoon vegetable oil
Corn Pudding (page 153)

Preheat oven to 325°F. Combine black pepper, mustard, allspice, ground red pepper and garlic; stir in oil to form paste.

Spread mixture evenly on surface of beef tip roast. Place roast, fat side up, on rack in open roasting pan. Insert meat thermometer so bulb is centered in thickest part of roast. *Do not add water. Do not cover.* Roast to desired doneness, allowing 30 to 35 minutes per pound. Meanwhile, prepare Corn Pudding. Remove roast when meat thermometer registers 155°F for medium. Allow roast to stand 15 to 20 minutes in a warm place before carving. Roast will continue to rise about 5°F in temperature to reach 160°F. Serve carved roast with Corn Pudding. *Makes 3 to 4 servings per pound*

Favorite recipe from **National Cattlemen's Beef Association**

PRIME RIB WITH YORKSHIRE PUDDING AND HORSERADISH SAUCE

3 cloves garlic, minced
1 teaspoon freshly ground black pepper
1 (3-rib) standing beef roast, trimmed*
  (about 6 to 7 pounds)
  Yorkshire Pudding (recipe follows)
  Horseradish Sauce (recipe follows)

Preheat oven to 450°F. Combine garlic and pepper; rub over roast. Place roast, bone side down, (the bones take the place of a meat rack) in shallow roasting pan. Insert meat thermometer in thickest part of roast, not touching bone or fat. Roast 15 minutes.

Reduce oven temperature to 325°F. Roast 20 minutes per pound or until internal temperature is 120° to 130°F for rare, 135° to 145°F for medium. Meanwhile, prepare Yorkshire Pudding and Horseradish Sauce.

When roast has reached desired temperature, transfer to cutting board; tent with foil. Immediately after roast has been removed from oven, *increase oven temperature to 450°F.* Let roast stand in warm place 20 to 30 minutes to allow for easier carving. Temperature of roast will continue to rise about 10°F during stand time. Reserve ¼ cup drippings from roasting pan. Carve roast. Serve with Yorkshire Pudding and Horseradish Sauce.

Makes 6 to 8 servings

*Ask meat retailer to remove the chine bone for easier carving. Fat should be trimmed to ¼-inch thickness.

YORKSHIRE PUDDING

1 cup milk
2 eggs
½ teaspoon salt
1 cup all-purpose flour
¼ cup reserved drippings from roast or
  unsalted butter

Process milk, eggs and salt in food processor or blender 15 seconds. Add flour; process 2 minutes. Let batter stand in food processor at room temperature 30 minutes to 1 hour. Pour drippings into 9-inch square baking pan. Place in 450°F oven 5 minutes. Process batter another 10 seconds; pour into hot drippings. *Do not stir.* Immediately return pan to oven. Bake 20 minutes. Reduce oven temperature to 350°F; bake 10 minutes or until pudding is golden brown and puffed. Cut into squares.

Makes 6 to 8 servings

HORSERADISH SAUCE

1 cup whipping cream
⅓ cup prepared horseradish, undrained
2 teaspoons balsamic or red wine vinegar
1 teaspoon dry mustard
¼ teaspoon sugar
⅛ teaspoon salt

Beat cream until soft peaks form. *Do not overbeat.* Combine horseradish, vinegar, mustard, sugar and salt in medium bowl. Fold whipped cream into horseradish mixture. Cover and refrigerate at least 1 hour. Sauce may be made up to 8 hours before serving.

Makes 1½ cups

Prime Rib with Yorkshire Pudding
and Horseradish Sauce

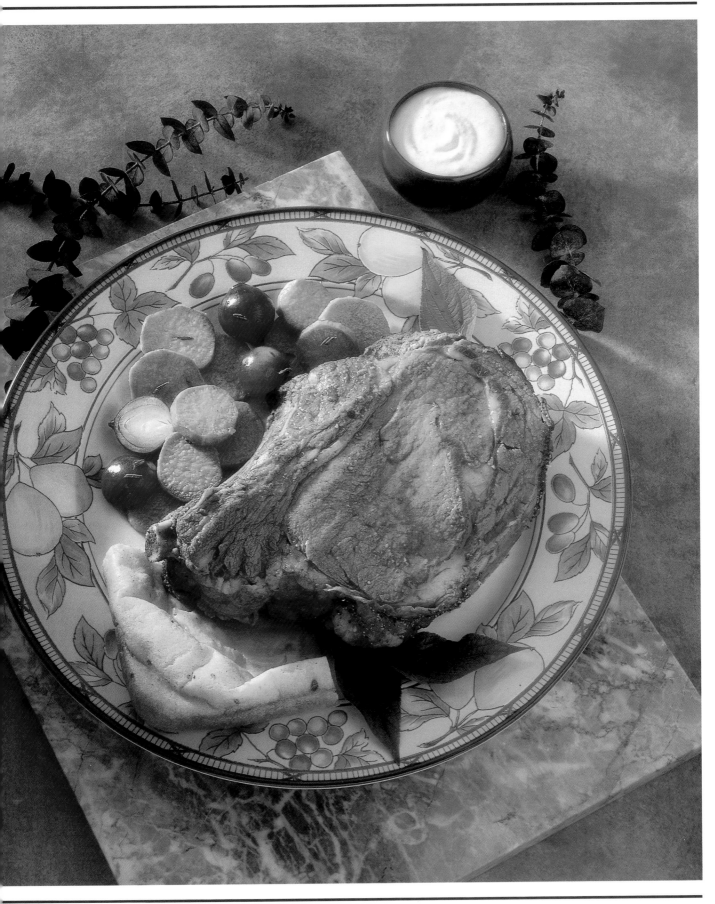

OVEN–BAKED BOURGUIGNONNE

**2 pounds boneless beef chuck, cut into
1-inch cubes**
¼ cup all-purpose flour
1⅓ cups sliced carrots
**1 can (14½ ounces) whole peeled
tomatoes, undrained and chopped**
1 bay leaf
**1 envelope LIPTON® Recipe Secrets®
Onion or Beefy Onion Soup Mix**
½ cup dry red wine
1 cup fresh or canned sliced mushrooms
**1 package (8 ounces) medium or broad
egg noodles**

Preheat oven to 400°F. In 2-quart casserole,
toss beef with flour. Bake uncovered 20
minutes. Add carrots, tomatoes and bay leaf,
then onion soup mix blended with wine. Bake
covered 1½ hours or until beef is tender. Add
mushrooms and bake covered an additional 10
minutes. Remove bay leaf.

Meanwhile, cook noodles according to package
directions. To serve, spoon bourguignonne over
noodles.   *Makes about 8 servings*

MICROWAVE DIRECTIONS: Toss beef with
flour; set aside. In 2-quart casserole, combine
tomatoes, bay leaf and onion soup mix blended
with wine. Heat covered at HIGH (full power)
7 minutes, stirring once. Add beef and carrots.
Heat covered at DEFROST (30% power),
stirring occasionally, 1¼ hours. Add
mushrooms and heat covered at DEFROST
30 minutes or until beef is tender. Remove bay
leaf. Let stand covered 5 minutes. Cook
noodles and serve as above.

FREEZING / REHEATING DIRECTIONS:
Bourguignonne can be baked, then frozen.
Simply wrap covered casserole in heavy-duty
aluminum foil; freeze. To reheat, unwrap and
bake covered at 400°F, stirring occasionally to
separate beef and vegetables, 1 hour. OR,
microwave at HIGH (full power), stirring
occasionally, 20 minutes or until heated
through. Let stand covered 5 minutes.

CHRISTMAS TWO–RIB BEEF ROAST

1 (3-pound) 2-rib beef roast, trimmed
**1 teaspoon *each* dried sage, thyme and
kosher or sea salt**

Preheat oven to 325°F. Place roast, bone side
down, on rack in open roasting pan. Rub
surface with herbs and salt. Do not add water.
Do not cover. Insert meat thermometer in
thickest part, not touching fat or bone. Roast to
desired doneness (about 27 to 30 minutes per
pound for medium). Remove roast when meat
thermometer registers 155°F. Allow roast to
stand tented with foil 10 to 20 minutes before
carving. (Roast temperature will continue to
rise about 5°F.)   *Makes 4 to 6 servings*

PREP TIME: 5 minutes
COOK TIME: 1 to 1½ hours

Favorite recipe from California Beef Council

BRISKET OF BEEF

1 whole well-trimmed beef brisket (about
    5 pounds)
4 cloves garlic, minced
½ teaspoon freshly ground black pepper
2 large onions, cut into ¼-inch-thick
    slices and separated into rings
1 bottle (12 ounces) chili sauce
¾ cup beef broth, beer or water
2 tablespoons Worcestershire sauce
1 tablespoon packed brown sugar

Preheat oven to 350°F. Place brisket, fat side up, in shallow roasting pan. Spread garlic evenly over brisket; sprinkle with pepper. Arrange onions over brisket. Combine chili sauce, broth, Worcestershire sauce and sugar; pour over brisket and onions. Cover with heavy-duty foil or roasting pan lid.

Roast 2 hours. Turn brisket over; stir onions into sauce and spoon over brisket. Cover; roast 1 to 2 hours more or until fork-tender. Transfer brisket to cutting board. Tent with foil; let stand 10 minutes.*

Stir juices in roasting pan. Spoon off and discard fat from juices. (Juices may be thinned to desired consistency with water or thickened by simmering, uncovered, in saucepan.) Carve brisket across grain into thin slices. Spoon juices over brisket.   *Makes 10 to 12 servings*

*At this point, brisket may be covered and refrigerated up to 1 day before serving. To reheat brisket, cut diagonally into thin slices. Place brisket slices and juice in large skillet. Cover and cook over medium-low heat until heated through.

VARIATION: If desired, stir red boiling potatoes or cut carrots, parsnips or turnips into juices during last hour of cooking time.

Brisket of Beef

PEPPERED BEEF TENDERLOIN ROAST

**1 (3- to 4-pound) beef tenderloin, fat
    trimmed**
5 cloves garlic, finely chopped
**2 tablespoons finely chopped fresh
    rosemary**
**1 tablespoon green peppercorns in brine,
    drained and finely chopped**
1 teaspoon freshly ground black pepper
1 teaspoon salt
2 tablespoons olive oil or vegetable oil
1¼ cups beef stock

Place beef on sheet of plastic wrap. Combine remaining ingredients except oil and beef stock; rub over roast. Wrap tightly and refrigerate at least 4 hours and no longer than 48 hours. Return to room temperature before cooking.

Preheat oven to 425°F. In large ovenproof skillet or roasting pan, heat oil over medium-high heat. Place roast in skillet; brown on all sides (about 4 minutes per side). Carefully lift roast with large carving fork and place roasting rack in skillet under roast. Do not cover. Insert meat thermometer in thickest part of roast. Roast until meat thermometer registers 155°F. (Roast temperature will usually increase about 5°F after removal from oven.) Remove to cutting board and let rest in warm place 15 minutes before carving. Place skillet with pan drippings over high heat until hot. Stir in beef stock. Cook, stirring occasionally, until reduced to about ¾ cup. Strain and serve in sauce pitcher.   *Makes 10 to 12 servings*

*Favorite recipe from **California Beef Council***

EASY BEEF STROGANOFF

2 tablespoons oil
2 teaspoons finely chopped garlic
**½ pound boneless sirloin steak, cut into
    thin strips**
¼ cup dry red wine
2 teaspoons Worcestershire sauce
1¼ cups water
½ cup milk
2 tablespoons butter or margarine
**1 package LIPTON® Noodles & Sauce—
    Stroganoff**
½ cup pearl onions

In large skillet, heat oil and cook garlic over medium heat 30 seconds. Add beef and cook over medium-high heat 1 minute or until almost done. Add wine and Worcestershire sauce and cook 30 seconds; remove beef. Into skillet, stir water, milk, butter and noodles & stroganoff sauce. Bring to the boiling point, then continue boiling, stirring occasionally, 7 minutes. Stir in onions and beef, then cook 2 minutes or until noodles are tender. Garnish, if desired, with chopped parsley and paprika.
                    Makes about 2 servings

NOTE: This recipe is also delicious with Lipton® Noodles & Sauce—Beef Flavor.

*Peppered Beef Tenderloin Roast, Baked Mini Acorn
Squash with Peas and Onions (page 146)*

MARVELOUS MARINATED LONDON BROIL

½ cup HELLMANN'S® or BEST FOODS®
   Real or Light Mayonnaise
⅓ cup soy sauce
¼ cup lemon juice
2 tablespoons prepared mustard
1 clove garlic, minced or pressed
½ teaspoon ground ginger
¼ teaspoon freshly ground pepper
1 beef top round steak (3 pounds),
   2 inches thick

In large shallow dish combine mayonnaise, soy sauce, lemon juice, mustard, garlic, ginger and pepper. Add steak, turning to coat. Cover; marinate in refrigerator several hours or overnight. Grill or broil about 6 inches from heat, turning once, 25 to 30 minutes or until desired doneness. To serve, slice diagonally across grain.   *Makes 6 to 8 servings*

HOLIDAY BEEF TIP ROAST

1 (3½- to 5-pound) beef tip roast
1 tablespoon minced fresh ginger
1 large clove garlic, minced
½ teaspoon pepper

Preheat oven to 325°F. Combine ginger, garlic and pepper; rub evenly over surface of beef tip roast. Place roast, fat side up, on rack in open roasting pan. Insert meat thermometer so bulb is centered in thickest part of roast. *Do not add water. Do not cover.*

Roast to desired degree of doneness, allowing 35 to 40 minutes per pound.

Remove roast from oven when meat thermometer registers 155°F (medium). Let roast stand 15 to 20 minutes in warm place before carving.
            Makes 3 to 4 servings per pound

*Favorite recipe from **National Cattlemen's Beef Association***

SPICY CHINESE TORTILLAS

2 tablespoons soy sauce
4 teaspoons sugar
1 tablespoon catsup
1 tablespoon Worcestershire sauce
4 cloves garlic, minced
¼ teaspoon crushed red pepper*
½ pound lean beef, cut into thin strips
1 teaspoon vegetable oil
3 cups thinly sliced green cabbage
2 carrots, peeled and sliced
1 cup well-drained, thawed frozen
   spinach
2 green onions, sliced
12 tortillas, warmed

In small bowl mix soy sauce, sugar, catsup and Worcestershire sauce; set aside. In large skillet sauté garlic, red pepper and beef in oil 5 minutes. Add cabbage, carrots, spinach, onions and reserved soy sauce mixture. Cook covered until vegetables are tender, about 10 minutes. Divide a quarter of the mixture among three tortillas; wrap. Repeat with remaining mixture and tortillas.   *Makes 4 servings*

*This is a spicy dish. If less spice is desired, reduce or eliminate the crushed red pepper.

*Favorite recipe from **The Sugar Association, Inc.***

SPICY–SWEET BRISKET

4 to 5 pounds beef brisket, well trimmed
3 carrots, cut into 2-inch pieces
3 onions, thinly sliced
1 pound fresh whole mushrooms
1 rib celery, cut into 2-inch pieces
1 (26-ounce) jar NEWMAN'S OWN®
   Diavolo Sauce
½ cup water
½ cup packed brown sugar
1 tablespoon garlic powder
½ teaspoon ground black pepper

Heat oven to 350°F. Brown meat in large ungreased skillet. Remove to large Dutch oven. Add vegetables to meat. In separate bowl, combine diavolo sauce, water and brown sugar; pour over meat. Sprinkle with garlic powder and black pepper.

Cover tightly and bake 3 hours. Remove cover; bake 30 minutes more or until meat is fork-tender and slightly browned. Refrigerate meat and sauce mixture overnight to allow flavors to blend. Cut meat in thin slices across the grain. Reheat meat slices and sauce mixture in covered skillet over medium-low heat.

Makes 12 servings

OVERNIGHT CORNBREAD CASSEROLE

1 package (8 ounces) cornbread stuffing mix (about 3½ cups)
2 cups frozen mixed vegetables (any mixture), slightly thawed
1½ cups (about 8 ounces) cubed cooked ham
3 eggs, lightly beaten
2 cups milk
¼ teaspoon salt
¼ teaspoon ground black pepper
½ cup shredded Cheddar cheese

In a 12×8×2-inch microwavable baking dish, stir together stuffing mix, vegetables and ham. In a medium bowl combine eggs, milk, salt and black pepper. Pour over cornbread mixture. Cover with plastic wrap; refrigerate overnight or at least 5 hours. Remove plastic wrap; cover with waxed paper. Microwave on HIGH (100% power) for 6 minutes; rotate ¼ turn. Microwave on MEDIUM-HIGH (80% power) until a knife inserted 1 inch from the center comes out clean, 7 to 9 minutes. Sprinkle with cheese. Let stand, covered, for 10 minutes. Stir gently before serving. *Makes 4 to 6 servings*

Favorite recipe from **National Dairy Board**

Overnight Cornbread Casserole

Creamy Ham and Noodle Dinner

bring to a boil, stirring constantly, until mixture thickens. Cook and stir 1 minute. Stir in ham, noodles and peas. Cook and stir until heated through. *Makes 8 servings*

*Purchase unsliced ham at the deli counter.

*Favorite recipe from **National Dairy Board***

CREAMY HAM AND NOODLE DINNER

¼ cup all-purpose flour
4 cups milk
1½ teaspoons dried dill weed, crushed
1½ teaspoons Dijon-style mustard
2 tablespoons butter
1 cup diced carrots
1 teaspoon minced garlic
1 pound ham, cubed*
1 package (16 ounces) wide egg noodles, cooked according to package directions
1 package (10 ounces) frozen green peas, thawed

In a small bowl combine flour and a small amount of milk until smooth. Add remaining milk, dill and mustard; set aside. In a large saucepan over medium heat melt butter. Add carrots and garlic; cook, stirring occasionally until crisp-tender. Stir in reserved milk mixture;

MEDITERRANEAN BLACK BEAN & RICE SKILLET

2 tablespoons olive oil
1 pound lean boneless pork or chicken, cubed
1 cup chopped onion
4 cloves garlic, minced
1 cup chopped fresh or canned tomatoes
½ cup dry red wine
⅓ cup chopped prunes or chopped raisins
3 cups water
1 (8-ounce) package FARMHOUSE® Spanish Black Beans & Rice
1 teaspoon dried thyme leaves
⅛ teaspoon cayenne pepper
⅓ cup chopped red bell pepper
1 cup frozen peas, thawed
2 tablespoons chopped fresh parsley
1 tablespoon lime or lemon juice
Salt and black pepper to taste

In large skillet, heat olive oil. Brown meat in oil until no longer pink. Add onion and garlic; sauté until tender. Add tomatoes, wine and prunes. Bring to a boil. Cook until liquid has evaporated. Add water; bring to a boil. Add beans & rice, contents of seasoning packet, thyme leaves and cayenne pepper. Reduce heat; cover and simmer 20 minutes. Add red bell pepper; cook 5 minutes longer or until liquid is absorbed. Stir in peas, parsley and lime juice. Season to taste with salt and black pepper. *Makes approximately 6 servings*

HONEY GLAZED HAM

   2 (8-ounce) fully-cooked ham steaks
   ¼ cup honey
   3 tablespoons water
   1½ teaspoons dry mustard
   ½ teaspoon ground ginger
   ¼ teaspoon ground cloves

Pan-fry or broil ham steaks until lightly browned and thoroughly heated. Remove ham from skillet or broiler pan. Combine honey, water and spices; add to pan drippings and bring to a boil. Simmer 1 to 2 minutes. Brush over ham. Serve ham with remaining sauce.

Makes 4 servings

Favorite recipe from **National Honey Board**

PORK TENDERLOIN DIANE

   1 pound pork tenderloin, cut into 8 crosswise pieces
   2 teaspoons lemon pepper
   2 tablespoons butter
   2 tablespoons lemon juice
   1 tablespoon Worcestershire sauce
   1 teaspoon Dijon-style mustard
   1 tablespoon minced fresh parsley or chives

Pound each tenderloin slice with meat mallet to 1-inch thickness; sprinkle with lemon pepper. Heat butter in heavy skillet; cook tenderloin medallions 3 to 4 minutes on each side or until fork-tender. Remove medallions to serving platter; keep warm. Add lemon juice, Worcestershire sauce and mustard to pan juices in skillet. Cook until heated through. Pour sauce over medallions and sprinkle with parsley; serve. *Makes 4 servings*

Favorite recipe from **National Pork Producers Council**

Honey Glazed Ham

GLAZED ROAST PORK LOIN WITH CRANBERRY STUFFING

1¼ cups chopped fresh or partially thawed
  frozen cranberries
2 teaspoons sugar
½ cup butter or margarine
1 cup chopped onion
1 package (8 ounces) herb-seasoned
  stuffing mix
1 cup chicken broth
½ cup peeled and diced orange
1 egg, beaten
½ teaspoon grated orange peel
1 (2½- to 3-pound) boneless center cut
  loin pork roast
¼ cup currant jelly
1 tablespoon cranberry liqueur, cassis or
  cranberry juice

Toss cranberries with sugar in small bowl; set aside. Melt butter in saucepan over medium heat until foamy. Add onion; cook and stir until tender. Remove from heat. Combine stuffing mix, broth, orange, egg and orange peel. Add cranberry mixture and onion; toss lightly.

Preheat oven to 325°F. To butterfly roast, cut lengthwise down roast almost to, but not through bottom. Open like a book. Cover roast with plastic wrap; pound with flat side of meat mallet. Remove plastic wrap; spread roast with stuffing. Tie roast with cotton string at 2-inch intervals. Place leftover stuffing in covered casserole; bake with roast during last 45 minutes of cooking time. Place roast on meat rack in foil-lined roasting pan. Insert meat thermometer in center of stuffing. Roast 30 minutes per pound until temperature registers 155°F.

Combine jelly and liqueur. Brush half of mixture over roast after first 45 minutes in oven. Roast 30 minutes more; brush with remaining jelly mixture. Transfer roast to cutting board; tent with foil. Let stand 10 to 15 minutes. Carve roast crosswise; serve with stuffing.
Makes 8 to 10 servings

PEACH-GLAZED VIRGINIA HAM

GLAZED HAM
1 (8-pound) smoked Virginia ham
½ cup peach preserves
1 tablespoon coarse-grained mustard
¾ teaspoon TABASCO® pepper sauce
⅛ teaspoon ground cloves
PEACH-CORN PICCALILLI
3 large ripe peaches
1 tablespoon vegetable oil
1 medium red bell pepper, diced
¼ cup sliced green onions
1 (17-ounce) can corn, drained
2 tablespoons brown sugar
2 tablespoons cider vinegar
1 teaspoon TABASCO® pepper sauce
¼ teaspoon salt

Heat oven to 325°F. Remove skin from ham; trim off any excess fat. Score fat ¼ inch deep in 1-inch diamonds. Place ham, fat side up, in roasting pan. Insert meat thermometer into thickest part of ham, not touching the bone. Bake 1½ hours until thermometer reaches 135°F.

For glaze, in bowl, mix peach preserves, mustard, TABASCO sauce and cloves. Remove ham from oven, maintaining oven temperature; brush with glaze. Bake 20 minutes or until the temperature reaches 160°F.

Meanwhile, prepare Peach-Corn Piccalilli. Cut peaches in half and remove pits. Chop two of the peach halves; set aside. In 2-quart saucepan heat oil over medium heat. Add red pepper and green onions. Cook 3 minutes, stirring frequently. Add corn, brown sugar, vinegar, TABASCO sauce and salt. Heat to boiling; stir in chopped peaches. Reduce heat to low; cover and simmer 5 minutes or until peaches are just tender.

To serve, arrange ham on a large platter. Fill remaining peach halves with Peach-Corn Piccalilli and arrange around ham on platter.
Makes 8 to 12 servings

Glazed Roast Pork Loin with Cranberry Stuffing

BAKED HAM WITH SWEET AND SPICY GLAZE

1 (8-pound) bone-in smoked half ham
Sweet and Spicy Glaze (recipe follows)

Preheat oven to 325°F. Place ham, fat side up, on rack in roasting pan. Insert meat thermometer with bulb in thickest part away from fat or bone. Roast ham in oven about 3 hours.

Prepare Sweet and Spicy Glaze. Remove ham from oven; do not turn oven off. Generously brush glaze over ham; return to oven 30 minutes longer or until meat thermometer registers internal temperature of 160°F. Remove ham from oven and brush with glaze. Let ham stand about 20 minutes before slicing.
Makes 8 to 10 servings

SWEET AND SPICY GLAZE
   ¾ cup packed brown sugar
   ⅓ cup cider vinegar
   ¼ cup golden raisins
   1 can (8¾ ounces) sliced peaches in heavy syrup, drained, chopped, syrup reserved
   1 tablespoon cornstarch
   ¼ cup orange juice
   1 can (8¼ ounces) crushed pineapple in syrup, undrained
   1 tablespoon grated orange peel
   1 clove garlic, crushed
   ½ teaspoon crushed red pepper flakes
   ½ teaspoon grated fresh ginger

Combine brown sugar, vinegar, raisins and peach syrup in medium saucepan. Bring to a boil over high heat; reduce to low and simmer 8 to 10 minutes. In small bowl, dissolve cornstarch in orange juice; add to brown sugar mixture. Add remaining ingredients; mix well. Cook over medium heat, stirring constantly, until mixture boils and thickens. Remove from heat. *Makes about 2 cups*

HOPPING JOHN

   1 tablespoon vegetable oil
   3 slices bacon, chopped
   1 cup ¼-inch smoked ham cubes
   ½ cup finely chopped onion
   1 tablespoon finely minced garlic
   ½ cup diced red bell pepper
   1 tablespoon chopped fresh parsley
   1 cup FARMHOUSE® Natural Long Grain White Rice
   2 cups canned chicken broth
  1½ teaspoons dried thyme leaves
   ½ teaspoon rubbed sage
   ½ teaspoon salt
   ¼ teaspoon ground red pepper
   ⅛ teaspoon ground black pepper
   1 bay leaf
   1 (15-ounce) can black eyed peas, drained

Heat oil in medium saucepan. Add bacon; cook over medium heat until bacon is crisp. Add ham, onion and garlic; sauté until onion is softened and translucent. Add bell pepper and parsley; sauté 1 minute. Add rice; stir to coat well. Add broth, thyme, sage, salt, ground red pepper, black pepper and bay leaf. Bring to a boil. Reduce heat; cover and simmer 20 to 25 minutes or until liquid is absorbed. Stir in black eyed peas. Remove bay leaf.
Makes approximately 6 (1-cup) servings

Baked Ham with Sweet and Spicy Glaze

Roasted Pork with Apricots and Sweet Spices

ROASTED PORK WITH APRICOTS AND SWEET SPICES

   1 cup plus 2 tablespoons low-sodium chicken broth, divided
   1 tablespoon ground cinnamon
   ½ teaspoon ground cloves
   ⅛ teaspoon ground cumin
   1½ pounds boneless pork loin, rolled and tied
   2 teaspoons olive oil, divided
   ¼ cup chopped onion
   1 teaspoon minced garlic
   1 cup orange juice
   ¼ cup water
   1 tablespoon Worcestershire sauce
   ½ cup julienned California dried apricot halves
   ¼ cup sliced almonds, toasted
   1 teaspoon grated orange peel
   2 tablespoons chopped cilantro
   Salt and pepper to taste

Combine 2 tablespoons chicken broth with cinnamon, cloves and cumin. Rub marinade mixture over pork; cover and refrigerate 4 hours or overnight. (Reserve any remaining marinade mixture.)

Preheat oven to 350°F. Heat 1 teaspoon oil in skillet over high heat; brown pork on all sides. Remove pork to roasting pan. Roast in preheated oven until internal temperature of pork reaches 155°F, about 40 minutes. Transfer pork to cutting board; tent with foil. Let stand 10 minutes.

In same skillet, over medium heat, heat remaining 1 teaspoon oil; cook and stir onion and garlic until tender. Add reserved marinade mixture, juice, remaining 1 cup chicken broth, water and Worcestershire sauce. Bring to a boil; reduce heat and simmer 10 minutes. Add apricots; simmer 5 minutes. Stir in almonds and orange peel; remove from heat. Stir in cilantro; season with salt and pepper. Serve apricot mixture over sliced, roasted pork.

Makes 6 servings

Favorite recipe from **California Apricot Advisory Board**

STRAWBERRY GLAZED HAM

   1 (5- to 7-pound) fully-cooked smoked butt or shank-half ham
   1½ cups SMUCKER'S® Simply Fruit Strawberry
   ⅓ cup prepared mustard
   ¼ cup lemon juice

Trim skin from ham. With sharp knife, score fat surface, making uniform diagonal cuts about ⅛ inch deep and ¾ inch apart. Place ham, fat side up, on a rack in a shallow roasting pan; bake in 325°F oven 1¾ to 2½ hours. Meanwhile, in a small saucepan, combine fruit spread, mustard and lemon juice; cook over low heat, stirring, until blended. During last 20 minutes of baking time, brush ham with about ½ cup strawberry glaze. Let ham stand 10 minutes for easier slicing. Heat remaining glaze and serve as a sauce for the ham.

Makes 8 to 10 servings

APRICOT AND NUT GLAZED HAM

1 (3- to 4-pound) boneless fully cooked
    smoked ham half
½ cup plus 1 teaspoon water
1 teaspoon dry mustard
½ cup apricot preserves
¼ cup chopped pecans
¼ teaspoon ground cloves
    Canned apricot halves and Boston
      lettuce leaves, for garnish

Do not preheat oven. Place smoked ham half (straight from refrigerator) on rack in shallow roasting pan. Add ½ cup water. Insert meat thermometer into thickest part of ham. Cover pan tightly with aluminum foil, leaving thermometer dial exposed. Place in 325°F oven and roast until thermometer registers 135°F, about 19 to 23 minutes per pound.

Meanwhile, stir mustard into 1 teaspoon water; combine with apricot preserves, pecans and cloves. Remove aluminum foil and spread glaze over ham 15 minutes before end of roasting time. When finished roasting, allow ham to stand, covered, about 10 minutes or until thermometer registers 140°F. Garnish with apricot halves and lettuce leaves, if desired.
    Makes 4 to 5 (3-ounce) servings per pound

PREP TIME: 10 minutes
COOK TIME: 1 to 1½ hours

Favorite recipe from **National Cattlemen's Beef Association**

JONES HAM QUICHE

1 cup short strips JONES® Ham
⅓ cup short red bell pepper strips
⅓ cup chopped asparagus
⅓ cup sliced leek
1 cup (4 ounces) shredded Swiss cheese
2 tablespoons all-purpose flour
3 eggs, slightly beaten
2⅓ cups half-and-half or whipping cream
1 (9-inch) pie crust, unbaked

Combine ham, pepper, asparagus, leek, cheese and flour; toss lightly. Gently mix eggs and half-and-half. Add ham mixture to egg mixture, mixing lightly.

Pour mixture into pastry-lined 9-inch quiche dish or pie pan. Bake 10 minutes at 425°F; reduce heat to 325°F. Continue baking 20 minutes or until done.   *Makes 6 to 8 servings*

Apricot and Nut Glazed Ham

GLAZED PORK TENDERLOIN

**2 whole well-trimmed pork tenderloins
(about 1½ pounds total)**
**½ cup currant jelly or canned jellied
cranberry sauce**
**1 tablespoon bottled grated horseradish,
drained**
½ cup chicken broth
**¼ cup Rhine or other sweet white wine
Salt and pepper to taste (optional)**

Preheat oven to 325°F. Place tenderloins on
meat rack in shallow roasting pan. Combine
jelly and horseradish in microwavable dish or
small saucepan. Heat at HIGH 1 minute or over
low heat on rangetop until jelly is melted; stir
well. Brush half of mixture over tenderloins.
Roast 30 minutes; turn tenderloins over. Brush
with remaining jelly mixture. Continue to roast
30 to 40 minutes depending on thickness of
tenderloins or until meat thermometer registers
160°F.*

Transfer tenderloins to cutting board; tent with
foil. Let stand 10 minutes. Remove meat rack
from roasting pan. Pour broth and wine into
pan. Place over burners; cook over medium-
high heat, stirring frequently and scraping up
any browned bits, 4 to 5 minutes or until sauce
is reduced to ½ cup. Strain sauce; season to
taste with salt and pepper. Carve tenderloins
into thin slices. Serve with sauce.

Makes 6 servings

*The most accurate way to measure the
internal temperature of pork tenderloin is with
an instant-read thermometer. Do not leave the
thermometer in the tenderloin during roasting
since it is not ovenproof.

Glazed Pork Tenderloin

FRUITED WINTER PORK CHOPS

1 medium DOLE® Fresh Pineapple
4 (1-inch-thick) pork chops, trimmed
16 DOLE® Pitted Prunes
    Salt and pepper to taste
1 teaspoon vegetable oil
⅓ cup minced onion
    Orange Herb Sauce (recipe follows)
1 DOLE® Orange, peeled and sliced
4 DOLE® Green Onions, sliced

• Twist crown from pineapple. Cut pineapple in half lengthwise. Refrigerate half for another use. Cut fruit from shell, then cut crosswise into slices. Cut fruit into large chunks; set aside.

• Cut slit in side of each pork chop. Stuff each with 2 prunes. Cut remaining prunes into thirds. Season pork chops with salt and pepper. In large nonstick skillet, brown chops in oil. Add cut prunes and onion. Cover, reduce heat and cook 8 minutes. Add Orange Herb Sauce. Cook, stirring, until sauce boils and thickens. Add reserved pineapple, orange and green onions. Heat through.   *Makes 4 servings*

ORANGE HERB SAUCE

½ cup frozen DOLE® Pineapple Orange
    Juice concentrate, thawed
¼ cup water
2 tablespoons white wine vinegar
1 tablespoon grated orange peel
1 teaspoon *each* dried basil and mint
    leaves
1 teaspoon chili powder
1 teaspoon cornstarch
2 large cloves garlic, pressed

Combine all ingredients. Stir until blended.
        Makes about 1 cup

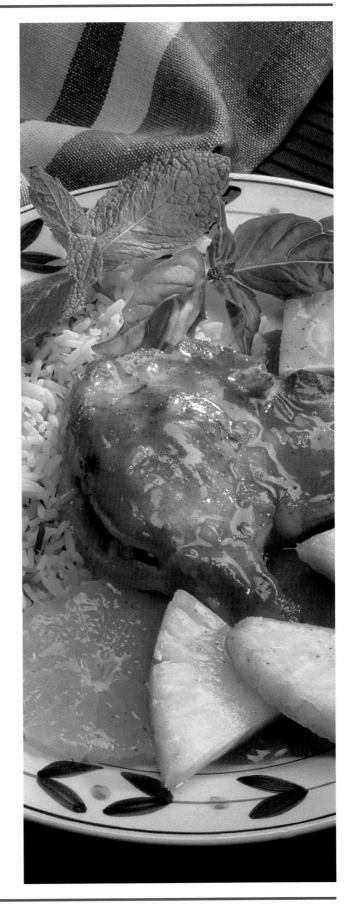

Fruited Winter Pork Chop

PORK CHOPS WITH ALMOND PLUM SAUCE

1 cup water
6 tablespoons lemon juice
6 tablespoons soy sauce
4 cloves garlic, chopped finely
1½ teaspoons cornstarch
½ teaspoon white pepper
¼ teaspoon salt
   Pinch cayenne
4 pork chops, about 1 inch thick
1 tablespoon vegetable oil
⅔ cup plum jam
¼ cup **BLUE DIAMOND®** Sliced Natural
   Almonds, lightly toasted
¼ cup sliced green onion tops, for
   garnish

Combine first 8 ingredients. Marinate pork chops in mixture in refrigerator 1 hour or overnight. Remove pork chops, reserving marinade. Sauté pork chops in oil over high heat 2 to 3 minutes on each side or until golden brown. Remove and reserve. Add marinade and plum jam to pan. Cook over medium heat until mixture thickens and coats the back of a spoon, about 5 minutes. Return pork chops to pan in single layer. Simmer, covered, 5 to 7 minutes. Remove cover and continue cooking 3 to 4 minutes or until pork chops are just cooked through and tender. To serve, remove chops to serving plate; sprinkle 1 tablespoon almonds over each chop. Pour sauce over and sprinkle each chop with 1 tablespoon sliced green onion tops.

Makes 4 servings

LEMON–GINGER–PRUNE– VEAL ROLL

1 cup chopped prunes
1 tablespoon finely shredded lemon peel
1 tablespoon grated fresh ginger
1 (4- to 4½-pound) boneless veal breast
½ teaspoon salt
2 teaspoons vegetable oil
⅔ cup Madeira wine
⅓ cup water
   Lemon wedges

In small bowl, combine prunes, lemon peel and ginger. Unroll boneless veal breast; trim fat. Sprinkle evenly with salt. Distribute prune mixture evenly over surface. Roll up veal breast; tie securely with string. Heat oil in Dutch oven just large enough to hold veal. Brown veal on all sides. Drain excess fat if necessary. Add Madeira and water to pan; cover tightly. Cook in 325°F oven until tender, 2 to 2½ hours. Transfer veal to warm platter; let stand. Skim fat from pan juices. Place Dutch oven over direct heat. Bring pan juices to a boil and cook until reduced by half. Slice veal roll; discard strings. Spoon sauce over each serving. Garnish with lemon wedges.

Makes 10 servings

*Favorite recipe from **National Cattlemen's Beef Association***

Pork Chops with Almond Plum Sauce

LEG OF LAMB WITH APRICOT STUFFING

1 (6-ounce) package dried apricots, snipped
¼ cup apple juice
¼ cup wild rice, rinsed and drained
1½ cups chicken broth
½ cup long-grain rice
¼ cup chutney
¼ cup sliced green onions
2 teaspoons dried basil leaves
½ teaspoon lemon pepper
3 to 3½ pounds American leg of lamb, shank half, boned and butterflied
¼ teaspoon salt
¼ teaspoon ground black pepper

In bowl, combine apricots and apple juice; cover and let stand 20 minutes, stirring occasionally. In saucepan, combine wild rice and broth. Bring to a boil; reduce heat. Cover and simmer 40 minutes. Add long-grain rice. Cover and simmer 15 minutes more. Remove from heat. Let stand, covered, 5 minutes. Stir in apricot mixture, chutney (cut up any large chutney pieces), green onions, basil and lemon pepper.

Trim any fat from lamb. With boned side up, pound meat evenly with a meat mallet to rectangle measuring 20 × 4 inches. Sprinkle lightly with salt and pepper. Spread rice mixture over meat. Roll up, starting with a narrow end; tie securely. Place roast on end, spiral side up, on a rack in a shallow roasting pan. Cover exposed rice mixture with a small piece of foil. Roast at 325°F for 1¾ hours, or to medium doneness (150° to 160°F). Remove from oven. Let stand about 10 minutes. Remove strings; cut into wedges to serve.

Makes 12 servings

*Favorite recipe from **American Lamb Council***

RACK OF LAMB WITH DIJON–MUSTARD SAUCE

1 rack of lamb (3 pounds), all visible fat removed
1 cup finely chopped fresh parsley
½ cup Dijon-style mustard
½ cup soft whole wheat bread crumbs
1 tablespoon chopped fresh rosemary *or* 2 teaspoons dried rosemary
1 teaspoon minced garlic
Fresh rosemary, lemon slices and lemon peel strips (optional)

Preheat oven to 500°F. Place lamb in large baking pan. Combine parsley, mustard, bread crumbs, rosemary and garlic in small bowl. Spread evenly over top of lamb. Place in center of oven; cook 7 minutes for medium-rare. *Turn off oven but do not open door for at least 30 minutes.* Serve 2 to 3 chops on each plate, depending on size and total number of chops. Garnish with additional fresh rosemary, lemon slices and lemon peel strips, if desired.

Makes 6 servings

Rack of Lamb with Dijon-Mustard Sauce

ZESTY ZUCCHINI LASAGNA

    1 pound ground beef
    1 package (1.5 ounces) LAWRY'S®
        Original-Style Spaghetti Sauce
        Spices & Seasonings
    1 can (6 ounces) tomato paste
  1¾ cups water
    2 tablespoons butter or margarine
    ½ teaspoon basil leaves
    ⅛ teaspoon thyme leaves
    2 cups ricotta cheese
    1 egg, slightly beaten
    4 medium zucchini, thinly sliced
        lengthwise
    1 cup shredded mozzarella cheese (about
        4 ounces)

Preheat oven to 350°F. In medium saucepan, brown ground beef until no longer pink; drain. Stir in Spaghetti Sauce Spices & Seasonings, tomato paste, water, butter, basil and thyme. Bring to a boil, then simmer uncovered 10 minutes. In small bowl, combine ricotta cheese with egg; set aside. In medium saucepan, bring 1 quart water to a boil. Add zucchini and cook 2 minutes; remove and rinse under cold running water. In 12×8-inch casserole, layer half the zucchini, ricotta mixture and meat sauce. Repeat layers. Top with mozzarella cheese and bake uncovered 30 minutes or until cheese is melted. *Makes about 6 servings*

SAUSAGE "BRUNCH" CASSEROLE

    6 slices white bread
    2 (12 ounce) packages JONES® All-
        Natural Roll Sausage *or* 1½ pounds
        JONES® Ham, diced
    1 can (8 ounces) chopped mushrooms
    1 pound (16 ounces) Cheddar cheese,
        grated
    6 eggs
    2 cups light cream or milk

Zesty Zucchini Lasagna

Tear bread into bite-size pieces and place in 13×9-inch baking dish. Crumble sausage; cook and drain. Spread over bread. Add mushrooms and top with Cheddar cheese.

Beat eggs; add light cream. Mix well and pour over casserole. Bake uncovered at 350°F 30 to 45 minutes.   *Makes 6 to 8 servings*

JONES SAUSAGE AND WILD RICE

1 cup wild rice
1 (12-ounce) package JONES® All-
     Natural Sausage Links
1 medium onion, chopped
1 rib celery, sliced
1 (10¾-ounce) can condensed cream of
     mushroom soup
1 (4-ounce) can sliced mushrooms,
     drained
½ cup dry white wine

Prepare wild rice according to package directions, omitting salt; do not overcook. Prepare sausage links according to package directions in large skillet; do not overcook. Drain well, leaving 1 tablespoon of fat in pan. Cool sausages slightly and cut into bite-size pieces.

In same pan, sauté onion and celery. Add soup, cooked rice, sausage pieces, mushrooms and wine, stirring carefully to mix. Place in well-greased 12×9-inch baking dish and bake at 350°F 30 minutes.   *Makes 6 servings*

SWEET & SOUR MEATBALLS

1½ pounds lean ground beef
1 (8-ounce) can water chestnuts, drained
     and chopped
2 eggs, slightly beaten
⅓ cup plain dry bread crumbs
4 teaspoons WYLER'S® or STEERO®
     Beef-Flavor Instant Bouillon
1 tablespoon Worcestershire sauce
1 cup water
½ cup firmly packed light brown sugar
½ cup REALEMON® Lemon Juice from
     Concentrate
¼ cup ketchup
2 tablespoons cornstarch
¼ teaspoon salt
1 cup coarsely chopped red and green
     bell peppers
Hot cooked rice

In large bowl, combine meat, water chestnuts, eggs, crumbs, bouillon and Worcestershire; mix well. Shape into 1¼-inch meatballs. In large skillet, brown meatballs. Remove from pan; pour off fat. In same skillet, combine remaining ingredients except peppers and rice; mix well. Over medium heat, cook and stir until sauce thickens. Reduce heat. Add meatballs; simmer uncovered 10 minutes. Add peppers; heat through. Serve with rice. Garnish with parsley, if desired. Refrigerate leftovers.

Makes 6 to 8 servings

Splendid

POULTRY

ROAST TURKEY WITH PAN GRAVY

1 fresh or thawed frozen turkey (12 to 14 pounds), reserve giblets and neck
Sausage-Cornbread Stuffing (page 166) or prepared stuffing (optional)
2 cloves garlic, minced
½ cup butter, melted
Turkey Broth with Giblets (page 110)
1 cup dry white wine or vermouth
3 tablespoons all-purpose flour
Salt and black pepper

Preheat oven to 450°F. Rinse turkey; pat dry with paper towels. Prepare stuffing, if desired. Stuff body and neck cavities loosely with stuffing, if desired. Fold skin over openings and close with skewers. Tie legs together with cotton string or tuck through skin flap, if provided. Tuck wings under turkey. Place turkey on meat rack in shallow roasting pan. Stir garlic into butter. Insert meat thermometer in thickest part of thigh not touching bone. Brush ⅓ of butter mixture evenly over turkey. Place turkey in oven; turn temperature down to 325°F. Roast

continued on page 110

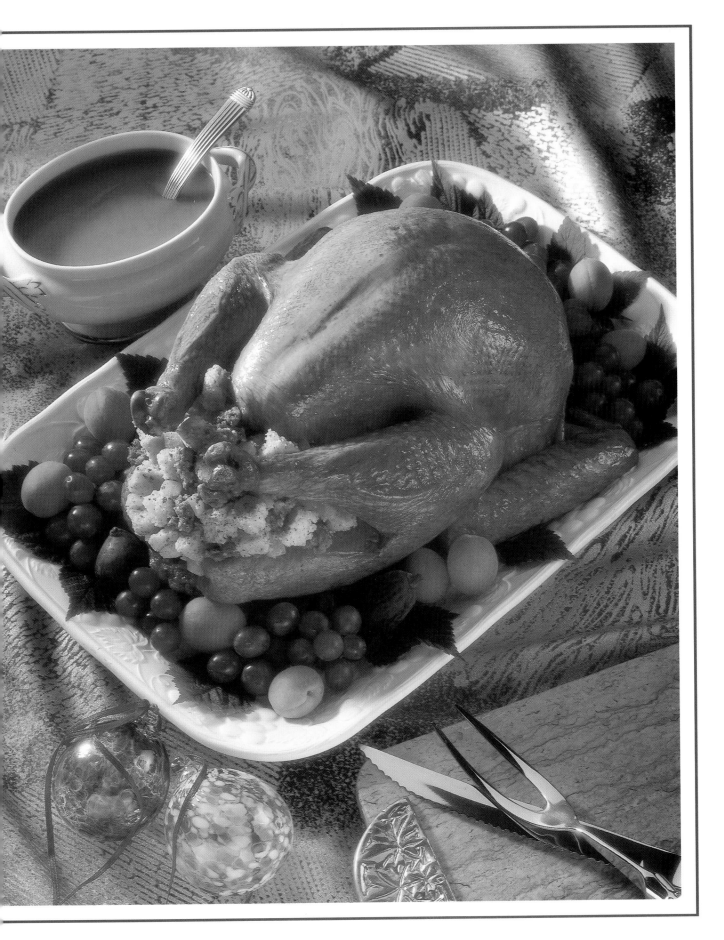

Roast Turkey with Pan Gravy, continued

18 to 20 minutes per pound for unstuffed turkey or 22 to 24 minutes per pound for stuffed turkey, brushing with butter mixture after 1 hour and then after 1½ hours. Baste with pan juices every hour of roasting. (Total roasting time should be 4 to 5 hours.) If turkey is overbrowning, tent with foil. Cook until internal temperature reaches 180°F and legs move easily in sockets. While turkey is roasting, prepare Turkey Broth with Giblets.

Transfer turkey to cutting board; tent with foil. Let stand 15 minutes while preparing gravy. Pour off and reserve juices from roasting pan. To deglaze pan, pour wine into pan. Place over burners and cook over medium-high heat; scrape up browned bits and stir constantly 2 to 3 minutes or until mixture has reduced by about half.

Spoon off ⅓ cup fat from pan drippings; discard remaining fat.* Place ⅓ cup fat in large saucepan. Add flour; cook over medium heat 1 minute, stirring constantly. Slowly stir in 3 cups Turkey Broth, defatted turkey drippings and deglazed wine mixture from roasting pan. Cook over medium heat 10 minutes, stirring occasionally. Stir in reserved chopped giblets; heat through. Season with salt and pepper to taste.

Makes 12 servings and 3½ cups gravy

*Or, substitute ⅓ cup butter or margarine for turkey fat.

CREAMY TURKEY GRAVY: Stir in 1 cup heavy cream with giblets; proceed as recipe directs. Makes 4½ cups gravy.

TURKEY BROTH WITH GIBLETS

Reserved giblets and neck from turkey (discard liver or reserve for another use)
4 cups water
1 can (13¾ ounces) chicken broth
1 medium onion, cut into quarters
2 medium carrots, coarsely chopped
4 large parsley sprigs
1 bay leaf
1 teaspoon dried thyme leaves, crushed
10 whole black peppercorns

For broth, combine giblets and neck, water and chicken broth in 3-quart saucepan. Bring to a boil over high heat; skim off foam. Stir in onion, carrots, parsley, bay leaf, thyme and peppercorns. Reduce heat to low. Simmer, uncovered, 1½ to 2 hours, stirring occasionally. (If liquid evaporates too quickly, add additional ½ cup water.) Cool to room temperature.

Strain broth; set aside. If broth measures less than 3 cups, add water to equal 3 cups liquid. If broth measures more than 3 cups, bring to a boil and heat until liquid is reduced to 3 cups. Remove meat from neck and chop giblets finely; set aside. Broth may be prepared up to 1 day before serving. Cover giblets and broth separately and refrigerate.   *Makes 3 cups*

TURKEY BREAST PROVENÇAL WITH VEGETABLES

1 cup turkey or chicken bouillon
¼ cup white wine
¼ cup lemon juice
1 head garlic, cloves separated, unpeeled
1 bag (10 ounces) frozen onions
2 teaspoons dried rosemary, crushed
1 teaspoon dried thyme leaves, crushed
½ teaspoon salt
¼ teaspoon fennel seeds
¼ teaspoon ground black pepper
6 plum tomatoes, quartered
1 package (9 ounces) frozen artichoke hearts, slightly thawed
1 package (10 ounces) frozen asparagus spears, slightly thawed
1 can (3¼ ounces) pitted ripe olives, drained
1 bone-in (4½-pound) turkey breast

1. Preheat oven to 325°F. In 13×9-inch baking pan combine bouillon, wine, lemon juice, garlic, onions, rosemary, thyme, salt, fennel seeds and black pepper. Cover pan with foil; bake 20 minutes.

2. Remove pan from oven. Add tomatoes, artichoke hearts, asparagus and olives. Place turkey breast on top of vegetables. Cover and bake 1 hour. Remove foil and bake 1 hour or until meat thermometer inserted in thickest part of breast registers 170°F. Baste turkey and vegetables frequently with pan juices.

3. Remove turkey and vegetables to serving platter. Reserve 6 cloves of garlic and pan juices.

4. Remove skin from reserved garlic. Combine garlic with pan juices in food processor; process 30 to 60 seconds until mixture is smooth.

5. Serve sauce with turkey and vegetables.
Makes 12 servings

Favorite recipe from **National Turkey Federation**

Turkey Breast Provençal with Vegetables

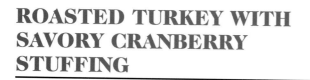

ROASTED TURKEY WITH SAVORY CRANBERRY STUFFING

1 cup chopped celery
1 cup chopped onion
½ cup margarine or butter
1 (16-ounce) can whole-berry cranberry sauce
2 tablespoons WYLER'S® or STEERO® Chicken-Flavor Instant Bouillon *or* 6 Chicken-Flavor Bouillon Cubes
12 cups dry bread cubes (about 16 slices bread)
1 cup chopped pecans
2 teaspoons poultry seasoning
1 teaspoon rubbed sage
3 cups hot water
1 (12- to 14-pound) turkey, thawed if frozen
Vegetable oil
Rich Turkey Gravy (recipe follows)

In large skillet, cook celery and onion in margarine until tender; add cranberry sauce and bouillon. Cook and stir until bouillon dissolves. In large bowl, combine bread cubes, pecans, seasonings and water; add cranberry mixture. Mix well.

Preheat oven to 325°F. Remove neck and giblets from turkey cavities. Rinse turkey; drain well. Stuff neck and body cavities lightly with stuffing. (Place extra stuffing in greased baking dish. Cover baking dish; refrigerate.) Turn wings back to hold neck skin in place. Place turkey, breast side up, on flat rack in open pan. Insert meat thermometer into thickest part of thigh next to body, not touching bone. Brush skin with oil. Place turkey in oven and roast about 4 hours. (Bake extra stuffing with turkey during last 40 minutes or until hot.) When skin is golden brown, shield breast loosely with foil to prevent overbrowning. Check for doneness; thigh temperature should be 180° to 185°F. Let turkey stand 15 to 20 minutes before carving. Serve with Rich Turkey Gravy. Refrigerate leftovers. *Makes 10 to 12 servings*

RICH TURKEY GRAVY: In medium skillet, stir ¼ to ⅓ cup flour into ¼ cup pan drippings; cook and stir until dark brown. Stir in 2 cups hot water and 2 teaspoons WYLER'S® or STEERO® Chicken-Flavor Instant Bouillon or 2 Chicken-Flavor Bouillon Cubes; cook and stir until thickened and bouillon is dissolved. Refrigerate leftovers. Makes about 1½ cups.

TURKEY EN CROÛTE

1 (5-pound) boneless turkey
1 pound fresh mushrooms, chopped
½ cup sliced green onions
2 cloves garlic, minced
¼ cup butter, melted
2 tablespoons dry sherry
¼ cup seasoned dry bread crumbs
2 eggs, divided
½ (17¼-ounce) package frozen puff pastry, thawed

Roast turkey at 350°F for 1 hour until internal temperature on meat thermometer registers 165°F. Cool slightly; remove netting, if present.

Cook mushrooms, onions and garlic in butter until liquid is absorbed. Stir in sherry, bread crumbs and 1 beaten egg. Cut turkey into 1-inch diagonal slices, cutting only ¾ of the way through meat; fill slices with mushroom mixture.

Roll out pastry large enough to enclose turkey. Place turkey, top side down, in center of pastry; wrap pastry around turkey, sealing edges with water. Place enclosed turkey, seam side down, on baking sheet; brush with remaining 1 beaten egg. Prick surface with fork. Bake at 350°F for 1 hour until golden brown; let stand 10 minutes. To serve, cut straight across into slices.
Makes 10 to 12 servings

*Favorite recipe from **National Turkey Federation***

Roasted Turkey with Savory Cranberry Stuffing

TURKEY BREAST WITH SOUTHWESTERN CORN BREAD DRESSING

5 cups coarsely crumbled corn bread
4 English muffins, coarsely crumbled
3 mild green chilies, roasted, peeled, seeded and chopped
1 red bell pepper, roasted, peeled, seeded and chopped
¾ cup pine nuts, toasted
1 tablespoon chopped fresh cilantro
1 tablespoon chopped fresh parsley
1½ teaspoons chopped fresh basil *or*
    1 teaspoon dried basil leaves
1½ teaspoons chopped fresh thyme *or*
    1 teaspoon dried thyme leaves
1½ teaspoons chopped fresh oregano *or*
    1 teaspoon dried oregano leaves
1 pound Italian turkey sausage
3 cups chopped celery
1 cup chopped onion
2 to 4 tablespoons turkey broth or water
1 bone-in turkey breast (5 to 6 pounds)
2 tablespoons minced garlic
½ cup chopped fresh cilantro
    Nonstick cooking spray

1. In large bowl combine corn bread, muffins, chilies, red pepper, pine nuts, 1 tablespoon cilantro, parsley, basil, thyme and oregano; set aside.

2. In large skillet, over medium-high heat, sauté turkey sausage, celery and onion 8 to 10 minutes or until sausage is no longer pink and vegetables are tender. Combine turkey sausage mixture with cornbread mixture. Add broth or water if mixture is too dry; set aside.

3. Loosen skin on both sides of turkey breast, being careful not to tear skin, leaving it connected at breast bone. Spread 1 tablespoon garlic under loosened skin over each breast half. Repeat procedure, spreading ¼ cup cilantro over each breast half.

4. Place turkey breast in 13×9×2-inch roasting pan lightly coated with nonstick cooking spray. Spoon half of stuffing mixture under breast cavity. Spoon remaining stuffing into 2-quart casserole lightly coated with nonstick cooking spray; set aside. Roast turkey breast, uncovered, at 325°F, for 2 to 2½ hours or until meat thermometer registers 170°F in deepest portion of breast. Bake remaining stuffing, uncovered, along with turkey breast during last 45 minutes. *Makes 12 servings*

Favorite recipe from **National Turkey Federation**

ROAST STUFFED TURKEY

2 packages (6 ounces each) STOVE TOP® Stuffing Mix, any variety
½ cup (1 stick) butter or margarine, cut into pieces
3 cups hot water
1 (8- to 12-pound) turkey

Prepare stuffing by placing contents of vegetable/seasoning packets and butter in a large bowl. Add hot water; stir just to partially melt butter. Add stuffing crumbs. Stir just to moisten. *Do not stuff bird until ready to roast.*

Rinse turkey with cold water; pat dry. Do not rub cavities with salt. Lightly stuff neck and body cavities with prepared stuffing. Close openings with skewer and string. Place turkey, breast side up, in roasting pan. Roast at 325°F for 3 to 4 hours or as directed on poultry wrapper. Bake any remaining stuffing at 325°F for 30 minutes. Cover the baking dish for moist stuffing. If drier stuffing is desired, bake uncovered. *Makes 8 to 10 servings*

Stuffed Chicken with Apple Glaze

STUFFED CHICKEN WITH APPLE GLAZE

   1 broiler-fryer chicken (3½ to 4 pounds)
   ½ teaspoon salt
   ¼ teaspoon pepper
   2 tablespoons vegetable oil
   1 package (6 ounces) chicken-flavored stuffing mix, plus ingredients to prepare mix
   1 cup chopped apple
   ¼ cup chopped walnuts
   ¼ cup raisins
   ¼ cup thinly sliced celery
   ½ teaspoon grated lemon peel
   ½ cup apple jelly
   1 tablespoon lemon juice
   ½ teaspoon ground cinnamon

Preheat oven to 350°F. Sprinkle inside of chicken with salt and pepper; rub outside with oil.

Prepare stuffing mix in large bowl according to package directions. Add apple, walnuts, raisins, celery and lemon peel; mix thoroughly. Stuff body cavity loosely with stuffing.* Place chicken in baking pan. Cover loosely with aluminum foil; roast 1 hour.

Meanwhile, combine jelly, lemon juice and cinnamon in small saucepan. Simmer over low heat 3 minutes or until blended. Remove foil from chicken; brush with jelly glaze. Roast chicken, uncovered, brushing frequently with jelly glaze, 30 minutes or until meat thermometer inserted into thickest part of thigh registers 185°F and juices run clear. Let chicken stand 15 minutes before carving.

Makes 4 servings

*Bake any leftover stuffing in covered casserole alongside chicken until heated through.

*Favorite recipe from **Delmarva Poultry Industry, Inc.***

WINE AND HERB ROASTER WITH HAM AND OYSTER STUFFING

1 PERDUE® Oven Stuffer® Roaster
   (5 to 8 pounds)
   Salt
½ teaspoon pepper
¼ cup butter or margarine
¼ cup chopped onion
2 tablespoons chopped celery
½ cup water
6 cooked oysters, diced
3 cups herb stuffing mix (4 ounces)
½ cup diced lean ham
   Wine and Herb Baste (recipe follows)
   Madeira Gravy (recipe follows)

Remove giblets and reserve for gravy. Rinse roaster, if desired; pat dry with paper towel. Season with salt and pepper. In medium skillet, melt butter and sauté onion and celery 5 minutes. Mix in water, oysters, stuffing mix and ham. Stuff roaster and close cavity with skewers or string. Tie legs together and fold wings back.

Place roaster in large roasting pan. Roast at 350°F for 2 to 2¾ hours. After 1 hour, brush with Wine and Herb Baste; repeat occasionally. Roaster is done when Bird-Watcher® thermometer pops up and juices are clear when thigh is pierced. Remove to serving platter and allow to rest 10 minutes while preparing gravy. Serve with Madeira Gravy.

Makes 6 servings

WINE AND HERB BASTE
¼ cup butter
1 clove garlic, minced
1 tablespoon chopped fresh parsley
1 teaspoon dried thyme leaves
½ teaspoon dried rosemary leaves,
   crumbled
¼ cup dry red wine

Combine all ingredients in small saucepan over low heat, stirring until butter is melted.

MADEIRA GRAVY
   Oven Stuffer® Roaster giblets, except
      liver
4 cups water
½ cup Madeira wine
¼ cup flour

While roaster is cooking, place giblets in small saucepan with water and simmer, uncovered, until 2 cups liquid remain. Strain and reserve liquid.

When roaster is done, pour off all but 2 tablespoons drippings. Add reserved liquid from giblets to pan and stir to remove brown bits from bottom of pan. Combine wine and flour to make a smooth paste. Add to pan and cook over medium heat, whisking frequently, until gravy is thickened. Serve with roaster.

HOT & SPICY ARROZ CON POLLO

- **2 tablespoons vegetable oil**
- **1 medium onion, chopped**
- **1 can (14½ ounces) whole tomatoes**
- **1 can (13¾ ounces) chicken broth**
- **1¼ cups long-grain rice**
- **1 teaspoon salt**
- **Pinch saffron threads (optional)**
- **1 jar (4 ounces) chopped pimientos, drained**
- **½ cup sliced pitted ripe olives**
- **1 package (10 ounces) frozen peas, thawed**
- **1 package (12 ounces) PERDUE DONE IT!® Hot & Spicy Wings (about 12 wings)**
- **Water (optional)**

In large deep skillet or Dutch oven over medium-high heat, heat oil. Add onion; cook 3 to 5 minutes or until tender. Stir in tomatoes with their liquid, broth, rice, salt and saffron; bring to a boil. Reduce heat to low; cover and simmer 10 minutes. Stir in pimientos, olives and peas; gently stir in chicken wings. Cover and cook 10 to 15 minutes longer or until all liquid is absorbed, rice is tender and wings are heated through; add ¼ to ½ cup water if mixture becomes too dry. Serve hot.

Makes 4 servings

NOTE: For a larger crowd, recipe may be doubled using PERDUE DONE IT!® Hot & Spicy Wings Party Tray *(24 ounces)*. Double other ingredients and cook in large Dutch oven.

Hot & Spicy Arroz Con Pollo

COUNTRY CAPTAIN JARLSBERG

3½ pounds chicken pieces
1 tablespoon butter or margarine
1 teaspoon salt
¼ teaspoon black pepper
1 small green bell pepper, cut into strips
1 small red bell pepper, cut into strips
2 tablespoons oil
1 large tomato, chopped
1 medium clove garlic, minced
1 teaspoon curry powder
¼ teaspoon ground cumin
1½ cups chicken broth, divided
1 tablespoon cornstarch
¼ cup toasted slivered almonds
¼ cup currants
1½ cups shredded JARLSBERG Cheese

Arrange chicken in shallow baking dish. Dot with butter. Season with salt and black pepper. Bake at 350°F 45 minutes or until tender.

Meanwhile, in large saucepan, sauté bell peppers in oil until just tender. Add tomato, garlic, curry, cumin and 1¼ cups chicken broth. Simmer 10 minutes, stirring occasionally.

Blend cornstarch and remaining ¼ cup chicken broth. Gradually stir into sauce and cook, stirring, until mixture is thickened and smooth. Add almonds and currants. Pour over chicken. Top with cheese. Bake an additional 10 minutes.   *Makes 6 servings*

Favorite recipe from **Norseland, Inc.**

Classic Chicken Curry with Winter Fruit and Walnuts

CLASSIC CHICKEN CURRY WITH WINTER FRUIT AND WALNUTS

¼ cup butter
2 cloves garlic, minced
1 tablespoon curry powder
1 teaspoon paprika
¼ teaspoon ground red pepper (optional)
1 tablespoon cornstarch
1 cup chicken broth
6 chicken breast halves, skinned and boned
2 pears, cored and thickly sliced
¾ cup chopped walnuts
½ cup chopped green onions
¼ cup fresh cranberries or currants
Hot cooked rice or couscous (optional)

MICROWAVE DIRECTIONS: Microwave butter in uncovered 3-quart glass casserole dish 2 minutes at HIGH (100% power). Stir in garlic and spices; microwave 3 minutes. Mix cornstarch with broth and add to garlic mixture; stir. Arrange chicken breast halves in single layer in sauce with thickest pieces toward side of dish. Cover and microwave 6 to 8 minutes, rotating chicken pieces every 2 minutes. Stir in remaining ingredients. Cover and microwave 6 to 8 minutes or until chicken is cooked through. Arrange chicken and pears on serving platter. Pour remaining sauce over chicken; serve with rice or couscous, if desired.

Makes 4 to 6 servings

Favorite recipe from **Walnut Marketing Board**

LOUISIANA CHICKEN

    4 chicken breast halves, skinned and
        boned
    2 cans (14½ ounces each) DEL MONTE®
        Cajun Recipe Stewed Tomatoes
    2 tablespoons cornstarch
    4 slices Monterey Jack cheese
        Parsley
        Hot cooked rice (optional)

Place chicken in baking dish. Cover and bake at 375°F, 30 to 35 minutes; drain. Combine tomatoes and cornstarch in saucepan; stir to dissolve cornstarch. Cook, stirring constantly, until thickened. Remove chicken from baking dish. Pour all but 1 cup sauce into dish. Arrange chicken over sauce in dish; top with remaining sauce. Place 1 slice cheese on each piece of chicken. Bake until cheese melts. Garnish with parsley. Serve with hot cooked rice, if desired. *Makes 4 servings*

CHICKEN VERMOUTH WITH ARTICHOKES

    ½ teaspoon salt, divided
    ⅛ teaspoon black pepper
    2 tablespoons olive oil
    ½ medium red pepper, cut into thin
        strips
    2 whole broiler-fryer chicken breasts,
        halved, boned, skinned
    2 cloves garlic, minced
    1 package (9 ounces) frozen artichoke
        hearts
    ½ cup chicken broth
    ¼ cup dry vermouth
    1 tablespoon lemon juice
    ½ teaspoon dried marjoram

Sprinkle ¼ teaspoon salt and black pepper over chicken. In skillet, place oil and heat to medium-high temperature. Add red pepper strips and cook, stirring, about 2 to 3 minutes or until tender. Remove to small bowl. To drippings in same skillet, add chicken and cook, turning, about 6 minutes or until browned on both sides. Add garlic and cook 1 minute or until translucent. Add artichoke hearts, broth, vermouth, lemon juice, marjoram and remaining ¼ teaspoon salt. Bring to a boil; reduce heat. Cover and cook about 10 minutes or until chicken and artichokes are fork-tender. Arrange chicken and artichokes on serving platter. Top with pan juices. Garnish with red pepper strips. *Makes 4 servings*

Favorite recipe from **Delmarva Poultry Industry, Inc.**

CHICKEN WITH BRANDIED FRUIT SAUCE

**4 broiler-fryer chicken breast halves,
  boned, skinned**
½ teaspoon salt
¼ teaspoon ground nutmeg
2 tablespoons butter or margarine
1 tablespoon cornstarch
¼ teaspoon ground red pepper
  Juice of 1 *each* orange, lemon and lime
⅓ cup orange marmalade
2 tablespoons brandy
1 cup red seedless grapes, halved

With meat mallet or similar flattening utensil, pound chicken to ½-inch thickness. Sprinkle salt and nutmeg over chicken. In skillet, place butter and heat to medium-high temperature. Add chicken and cook, turning, about 8 minutes or until chicken is browned and fork-tender. In small bowl, mix cornstarch and red pepper. Stir in orange, lemon and lime juices; set aside. Remove chicken to serving platter. To juices remaining in same skillet, add marmalade and heat until melted. Stir in juice mixture and cook, stirring, until mixture boils and thickens. Add brandy and grapes. Return chicken to pan; spoon sauce over chicken. Cook over low heat 5 minutes.

Makes 4 servings

Favorite recipe from **Delmarva Poultry Industry, Inc.**

CHICKEN TANDOORI WITH JARLSBERG LITE

8 ounces (1 cup) plain yogurt
**1 tablespoon minced garlic (3 to
  4 cloves)**
**2 teaspoons fresh thyme *or* 1 teaspoon
  dried thyme leaves**
2 teaspoons paprika
2 teaspoons ground cumin
  Pinch ground cloves (optional)
**4 boneless skinless chicken breast
  halves, flattened to ¼ inch (about
  1½ pounds)**
¼ cup seasoned dry bread crumbs
**1 cup (4 ounces) shredded JARLSBERG
  LITE Cheese**

Mix first six ingredients in large glass bowl; reserve ¼ cup. Add chicken to bowl, turning to coat evenly. Marinate in refrigerator 2 hours.

Remove chicken from yogurt mixture; discard yogurt mixture. Mix reserved ¼ cup yogurt mixture, bread crumbs and cheese. Spread one quarter of the cheese mixture on each chicken breast. Roll up from pointed end and secure with wooden picks.

Broil on rack of broiler pan, 10 to 12 inches from heat source, 12 to 15 minutes or until done, turning after 5 minutes.

Makes 4 servings

SERVING SUGGESTION: Serve with brown rice and vinegared cucumbers. Garnish with lemon slices and cilantro, if desired.

Favorite recipe from **Norseland, Inc.**

Chicken with Brandied Fruit Sauce

ALMOND BUTTER CHICKEN

4 boneless skinless chicken breast halves (about 1¼ pounds)
2 tablespoons all-purpose flour
½ teaspoon salt
½ teaspoon pepper
1 egg, beaten
1 package (2¼ ounces) sliced almonds
¼ cup butter
Orange Sauce (recipe follows)

Place each chicken breast half between 2 pieces of plastic wrap. Pound to ¼-inch thickness. Coat chicken with flour. Sprinkle with salt and pepper. Dip one side of each chicken breast into egg; press with almonds. Melt butter in large skillet over medium-high heat. Cook chicken, almond side down, 3 to 5 minutes or until almonds are toasted; turn chicken over. Reduce heat to medium-low; cook 10 to 12 minutes or until chicken is tender and juices run clear. Serve, almond side up, with Orange Sauce. Garnish as desired.

Makes 4 servings

ORANGE SAUCE

1 tablespoon brown sugar
2 teaspoons cornstarch
Juice of 1 orange (about ½ cup)
2 tablespoons butter
1 teaspoon grated orange peel

Combine brown sugar and cornstarch in saucepan. Add juice, butter and orange peel. Cook over medium heat, stirring constantly, until thickened. *Makes ⅔ cup*

*Favorite recipe from **Wisconsin Milk Marketing Board***

PECAN TURKEY SAUTÉ WITH WARM CRANBERRY SAUCE

½ cup unseasoned dry bread crumbs
¼ cup ground pecans
½ teaspoon LAWRY'S® Garlic Powder with Parsley
½ teaspoon LAWRY'S® Seasoned Salt
1 pound turkey cutlets
3 eggs, beaten
3 tablespoons butter or margarine
1 can (8 ounces) jellied cranberry sauce or whole-berry cranberry sauce
⅓ cup French salad dressing
3 tablespoons water
2 tablespoons chopped green onion

In pie plate, combine bread crumbs, pecans and seasonings; mix well. Dip each turkey cutlet in eggs, then coat both sides with crumb mixture. In large skillet, melt butter and brown turkey cutlets 5 minutes on each side or until cooked through. In small saucepan, combine cranberry sauce, salad dressing, water and onion; blend well. Gently heat until warmed through, about 5 minutes. Spoon warm cranberry sauce over cutlets.

Makes 4 servings

PRESENTATION: Serve with mashed potatoes or stuffing.

Almond Butter Chicken

CHICKEN WITH ARTICHOKES AND MUSHROOMS

4 whole broiler-fryer chicken breasts,
    halved, boned, skinned
¾ teaspoon salt, divided
¼ cup butter or margarine, divided
½ pound fresh mushrooms, sliced
¼ cup chopped green onions
3 cloves garlic, minced
1 package (9 ounces) frozen artichoke
    hearts, thawed, drained, cut in half
⅓ cup chicken broth
½ teaspoon dried thyme, crumbled
¼ teaspoon ground red pepper
⅓ cup dry white wine
2 teaspoons cornstarch
    Fresh herbs for garnish

With meat mallet or similar flattening utensil, pound chicken to ¼-inch thickness. Sprinkle ½ teaspoon salt over chicken. In large skillet melt 2 tablespoons butter over medium-high heat. Add chicken, 4 pieces at a time, and cook, turning, about 6 minutes or until browned on both sides. Remove chicken; set aside. To drippings in same skillet, add remaining 2 tablespoons butter and melt over medium heat. Add mushrooms, onions and garlic. Cook, stirring frequently, about 4 minutes or until vegetables are tender. Add artichoke hearts, broth, remaining ¼ teaspoon salt, thyme and red pepper; stir to mix well. In small dish, mix wine and cornstarch. Stir into vegetable mixture and cook, stirring, until slightly thickened. Return chicken to pan, spooning sauce over chicken. Cover and cook about 3 minutes or until chicken is fork-tender and heated through. Garnish with fresh herbs. *Makes 8 servings*

Favorite recipe from **Delmarva Poultry Industry, Inc.**

Chicken with Artichokes and Mushrooms

PÂTÉ STUFFED CHICKEN BREASTS WITH SOUR CREAM

1 (8-ounce) package JONES® Chub
    Braunschweiger
8 boneless skinless chicken breast halves
1 (10¾-ounce) can condensed cream of
    celery soup
3 cups sour cream
½ teaspoon curry powder
½ teaspoon paprika
    Hot cooked rice or mashed potatoes

Cut braunschweiger chub in half crosswise and then cut each half into quarters lengthwise to make 8 strips. Cut pocket in each chicken breast and insert 1 strip in each pocket. Place chicken in 13×9-inch baking pan.

Blend together soup, sour cream, curry powder and paprika; pour over chicken. Cover tightly and bake at 275°F 2 hours. Uncover and continue baking 30 minutes. Serve with hot cooked rice or mashed potatoes, if desired.

Makes 8 servings

APPLE BRANDY CHICKEN

3 whole chicken breasts, halved, boned and skinned
3 tablespoons butter
⅓ cup Calvados or other apple brandy
½ cup minced shallots
1 tablespoon minced parsley
⅛ teaspoon dried thyme
   LAWRY'S® Seasoned Salt to taste
   LAWRY'S® Seasoned Pepper to taste
6 tablespoons apple cider
6 tablespoons whipping cream

In large skillet, brown chicken in butter and continue cooking, over low heat and uncovered, 15 minutes. Add Calvados to skillet and ignite. When flame subsides, add shallots, parsley, thyme, Seasoned Salt, Seasoned Pepper and apple cider. Bring to a boil; reduce heat, cover and simmer about 20 minutes or until chicken is tender. Remove chicken to serving platter and keep warm. Gradually add cream to skillet; heat but do not boil. Season to taste. Pour some of sauce over chicken. Serve remaining sauce in separate bowl.

Makes 4 to 6 servings

CIDER-GLAZED CORNISH HENS

6 PERDUE® fresh Cornish Hens (about 1½ pounds each)
   Salt
   Freshly ground pepper
1 quart apple cider or juice
1 cinnamon stick
2 tablespoons unsalted butter
2 tablespoons honey
1 tablespoon Dijon-style mustard
1 tablespoon red wine vinegar

Preheat oven to 375°F. Wash hens and pat dry with paper towel. Season inside and out with salt and pepper. Tie legs together and fold wings back. For glaze, place cider and cinnamon stick in medium saucepan; boil until volume is reduced to 1 cup. Remove cinnamon stick and stir in butter, honey, mustard and vinegar. Boil until thick, syrupy and translucent.

Place hens in shallow roasting pan. Roast hens, brushing occasionally with glaze, 55 to 60 minutes or until golden and tender.

Makes 6 to 12 servings

BRAISED DUCKLING AND PEARS

1 (4- to 5-pound) frozen duckling, thawed and quartered
1 can (16 ounces) pear halves in heavy syrup
⅓ cup KIKKOMAN® Stir-Fry Sauce
1 cinnamon stick, about 3 inches long

Wash duckling quarters; dry thoroughly with paper towels. Heat large skillet or Dutch oven over medium heat. Add duckling; brown slowly on both sides, about 15 minutes, or until golden. Meanwhile, drain pears; reserve all syrup. Remove ¼ cup pear syrup and combine with stir-fry sauce; set aside. Drain off fat from pan. Pour syrup mixture over duckling; add cinnamon stick. Cover and simmer 40 minutes or until tender, turning quarters over once. Remove duckling to serving platter; keep warm. Remove and discard cinnamon stick. Pour drippings into measuring cup; skim off fat. Combine ½ cup drippings with 2 tablespoons reserved pear syrup; return to pan with pears. Gently bring to boil and cook until pears are heated through, stirring occasionally. Serve duckling with pears and sauce.

Makes 3 to 4 servings

WALNUT TURKEY HASH

4 cups boneless skinless cooked turkey chunks
2 medium baked potatoes, cubed
3 tablespoons butter or margarine
1 cup California walnut pieces
½ cup sliced green onions
1 teaspoon rubbed sage
1 teaspoon dried thyme leaves, crushed
1 cup turkey gravy
Salt and pepper to taste
⅓ cup chopped parsley

Combine turkey and potatoes in food processor. Process until coarsely chopped; set aside. Melt butter in large skillet. Add walnuts; toss over medium-low heat until golden brown. Remove with slotted spoon; set aside. Add onions, sage and thyme to skillet. Cook and stir 2 minutes. Add turkey mixture and gravy. Cook and stir until heated through. Add reserved walnuts, salt and pepper. Spoon onto serving platter; sprinkle with parsley.

Makes 4 to 6 servings

Favorite recipe from **Walnut Marketing Board**

TURKEY CRANBERRY LOAF WEDGES

1 (12-ounce) container cranberry-orange sauce
1½ pounds ground fresh turkey
1½ cups fresh bread crumbs (3 slices)
¼ cup REALEMON® Lemon Juice from Concentrate
1 egg
1 tablespoon WYLER'S® or STEERO® Chicken-Flavor Instant Bouillon or 3 Chicken-Flavor Bouillon Cubes
1 to 2 teaspoons poultry seasoning

Preheat oven to 350°F. Reserve ½ cup cranberry-orange sauce.

In large bowl, combine remaining ingredients; mix well. Press into 9-inch pie plate.

Bake 50 minutes or until set. Top with reserved cranberry-orange sauce. Let stand 5 minutes before serving. Cut into wedges; garnish as desired. Refrigerate leftovers.

Makes 6 servings

QUICK TURKEY TORTELLONI

1 (10-ounce) package DIGIORNO® Alfredo or Four Cheese Sauce
1 (10-ounce) package frozen chopped broccoli, thawed, drained *or* 2 cups broccoli flowerets, cooked tender-crisp
½ pound cooked turkey, cut into strips (about 1½ cups)
1 (2½-ounce) jar sliced mushrooms, drained (optional)
1 (9-ounce) package DIGIORNO® Mushroom or Mozzarella Garlic Tortelloni, cooked, drained
Toasted sliced almonds (optional)

• Mix sauce, broccoli, turkey and mushrooms in saucepan; heat thoroughly.

• Serve over pasta. Top with almonds.

Makes 3 to 4 servings

PREP TIME: 5 minutes
COOK TIME: 10 minutes

Deep-Dish Turkey Pie

DEEP-DISH TURKEY PIE

3 cups cubed cooked turkey or chicken
1 cup sliced cooked carrots
1 cup cubed cooked potatoes
1 cup frozen green peas, thawed
6 tablespoons margarine or butter
⅓ cup unsifted flour
2 tablespoons WYLER'S® or STEERO®
    Chicken-Flavor Instant Bouillon *or*
    6 Chicken-Flavor Bouillon Cubes
¼ teaspoon pepper
4 cups BORDEN® or MEADOW GOLD®
    Milk
2¼ cups biscuit baking mix

Preheat oven to 375°F. In large saucepan, melt margarine; stir in flour, bouillon and pepper. Over medium heat, gradually add milk; cook and stir until bouillon dissolves and mixture thickens. Add remaining ingredients except biscuit mix; mix well. Pour into 2½-quart baking dish. Prepare biscuit mix according to package directions for rolled biscuits. Roll out to cover dish; cut slashes in center of dough. Place on top of dish; crimp edges. Bake 40 minutes or until golden. Refrigerate leftovers.

Makes 6 servings

127

CURRIED TURKEY DINNER

1 package (10 ounces) frozen broccoli spears, cooked and drained
2 cups cubed cooked turkey
1 can (10½ ounces) reduced-sodium cream of mushroom soup
¼ cup reduced-calorie mayonnaise
1½ teaspoons lemon juice
1 teaspoon curry powder
1 cup seasoned croutons

1. Preheat oven to 350°F.

2. In 8-inch square baking dish arrange broccoli; top with turkey.

3. In small bowl combine soup, mayonnaise, lemon juice and curry powder. Pour over turkey and top with croutons.

4. Bake 20 to 25 minutes or until bubbly.

Makes 4 servings

*Favorite recipe from **National Turkey Federation***

HERBED CHICKEN AND BROCCOLI

10 ounces boneless skinless chicken breasts, sliced into ½-inch strips
1 teaspoon Italian herb seasoning
1 cup *undiluted* CARNATION® Lite Evaporated Skimmed Milk
2 tablespoons all-purpose flour
1 clove garlic, crushed
¼ teaspoon salt (optional)
⅛ teaspoon white pepper
½ cup (2 ounces) shredded, reduced-fat Swiss cheese
1 package (10 ounces) frozen broccoli spears, thawed, drained and cut into bite-size pieces
Paprika

Curried Turkey Dinner

Sprinkle chicken with Italian seasoning. Pound between sheets of plastic wrap. Spray nonstick skillet with nonstick cooking spray. Sauté chicken strips just until no longer pink. Keep warm. In small saucepan, whisk small amount of evaporated skimmed milk into flour. Stir in remaining milk, garlic, salt and pepper. Cook over medium heat, stirring constantly, until mixture just comes to a boil and thickens. Add cheese; stir until melted. Spray 10×6×2-inch baking dish with nonstick cooking spray. Spread about ¼ cup sauce in bottom of dish. Arrange broccoli over sauce; top with chicken pieces. Pour remaining sauce over top. Sprinkle with paprika. Cover. Bake in preheated 350°F oven 20 to 25 minutes or until heated through.

Makes 4 servings

TASTY TURKEY POT PIE

½ cup **MIRACLE WHIP®** Salad Dressing
2 tablespoons flour
1 teaspoon instant chicken bouillon
⅛ teaspoon pepper
¾ cup milk
1½ cups chopped cooked turkey or
    chicken
1 (10-ounce) package frozen mixed
    vegetables, thawed, drained
1 (4-ounce) can refrigerated quick
    crescent dinner rolls

Combine salad dressing, flour, bouillon and pepper in medium saucepan. Gradually add milk. Cook, stirring constantly, over low heat until thickened. Add turkey and vegetables; heat thoroughly, stirring occasionally. Spoon into 8-inch square baking dish. Unroll dough into two rectangles. Press perforations together to seal. Place rectangles side-by-side to form square; press edges together to form seam. Cover turkey mixture with dough. Bake at 375°F, 15 to 20 minutes or until browned.

Makes 4 to 6 servings

PREP TIME: 15 minutes
BAKE TIME: 20 minutes

VARIATIONS: Combine 1 egg, beaten, and 1 tablespoon cold water, mixing until well blended. Brush dough with egg mixture just before baking.

Substitute 1 chicken bouillon cube for instant chicken bouillon.

Substitute 10×6-inch baking dish for 8-inch square baking dish.

Substitute 12×8-inch baking dish for 8-inch square dish. Double all ingredients. Assemble recipe as directed, using three dough rectangles to form top crust. Decorate crust with cut-outs from remaining rectangle. Bake as directed.

MICROWAVE TIP: To prepare sauce, combine salad dressing, flour, bouillon and pepper in 1-quart microwave-safe measure or bowl; gradually add milk. Microwave on HIGH 4 to 5 minutes or until thickened, stirring after each minute.

Seafood
TREASURES

BAKED STUFFED SNAPPER

1 red snapper (1½ pounds)
2 cups hot cooked rice
1 can (4 ounces) sliced mushrooms, drained
½ cup diced water chestnuts
¼ cup thinly sliced green onions
¼ cup diced pimiento
2 tablespoons chopped parsley
1 tablespoon finely shredded lemon peel
½ teaspoon salt
⅛ teaspoon ground black pepper
1 tablespoon margarine, melted

Preheat oven to 400°F. Clean and butterfly fish. Combine rice, mushrooms, water chestnuts, onions, pimiento, parsley, lemon peel, salt and pepper; toss lightly. Fill cavity of fish with rice mixture; close with wooden toothpicks soaked in water. Place fish in 13×9-inch baking dish coated with nonstick cooking spray; brush fish with margarine. Bake 18 to 20 minutes or until fish flakes easily when tested with fork. Wrap any remaining rice in foil and bake in oven with fish. *Makes 4 servings*

Favorite recipe from **USA Rice Federation**

Baked Salmon with Almonds and Lime-Parsley Sauce

In food processor or blender, combine garlic, egg yolk, lime juice, cumin, ¼ teaspoon salt and pinch of pepper. With machine running, slowly pour in vegetable oil and 1½ teaspoons olive oil. (To prepare by hand, beat egg yolk until thick and lemon colored. Beat in garlic, lime juice, cumin, ¼ teaspoon salt and pinch of pepper. Combine vegetable oil and 1½ teaspoons olive oil. Whisking constantly, add oil one drop at a time until mixture begins to thicken. Pour remaining oil in a thin, steady stream, whisking constantly.) Mixture will resemble mayonnaise. Fold in chopped parsley. Place salmon in baking dish. Brush with remaining 3 teaspoons olive oil; season with salt and pepper. Spread lime-parsley sauce down center of each fillet. Top with almonds. Bake at 400°F for 8 to 12 minutes or until fish is just firm. *Makes 4 to 6 servings*

BAKED SALMON WITH ALMONDS AND LIME−PARSLEY SAUCE

    1 large clove garlic, finely chopped
    1 egg yolk
    1 teaspoon lime juice
    ½ teaspoon cumin
      Salt
      White pepper
    ½ cup vegetable oil
  4½ teaspoons olive oil, divided
    6 tablespoons chopped parsley
    4 salmon fillets, about 6 ounces each
    ¾ cup BLUE DIAMOND® Sliced Natural Almonds, lightly toasted

BROILED RAINBOW TROUT WITH HERB MAYONNAISE

    6 tablespoons regular or light mayonnaise
    1 clove garlic, minced
    1 tablespoon lemon juice
      Herbs to taste
      Dash pepper
    4 CLEAR SPRINGS® Brand Idaho Rainbow Trout fillets (4 ounces each)

Combine mayonnaise, garlic, lemon juice, herbs and pepper in bowl; mix well. Place trout, skin side down, on rack of broiler pan. Top each fillet with ¼ of mayonnaise mixture. Broil 4 inches from heat source for about 3 to 5 minutes or until fish flakes with a fork and topping is bubbly. *Makes 2 to 4 servings*

SOLEFUL ROULETTES

1 package (6 ounces) long-grain and wild rice mix
1 package (3 ounces) cream cheese, softened
2 tablespoons milk
32 medium fresh spinach leaves, washed
4 sole fillets (about 1 pound)
Salt and coarsely ground black pepper
¼ cup dry white wine
½ cup water

Cook rice mix according to package directions. Place 2 cups cooked rice in large bowl. (Refrigerate remaining rice for another use.) Combine cream cheese and milk in medium bowl. Stir into rice; set aside.

Place spinach in heatproof bowl. Pour very hot water (not boiling) over spinach to wilt leaves slightly. Rinse sole and pat dry with paper towels. Sprinkle both sides of each fillet with salt and pepper. Cover each fillet with spinach leaves. Divide rice mixture evenly and spread over top of each spinach-lined fillet. To roll fillets, begin with thin end of fillet, roll up and secure with wooden toothpicks.

Combine wine and water in large, heavy saucepan. Stand fillets upright on rolled edges in saucepan; cover. Simmer over low heat 10 minutes or until fish flakes easily when tested with fork. *(Do not boil. This will cause fish to break apart.)*   *Makes 4 servings*

Soleful Roulette

TUNA WITH PEPPERCORNS ON A BED OF GREENS

   4 tuna steaks (about 1½ pounds)
     Salt
   2 teaspoons coarsely ground black
       pepper
   1 tablespoon butter or margarine
   1 large onion, thinly sliced
   ¼ cup dry white wine
   ½ pound fresh kale or spinach, washed
   1 tablespoon olive oil
   ½ teaspoon sugar
   ¼ teaspoon black pepper
   12 julienne strips carrot
     Lemon slices and purple kale for
       garnish

Preheat oven to 325°F. Rinse tuna and pat dry with paper towels. Lightly sprinkle fish with salt, then press coarsely ground pepper into both sides of steaks; set aside.

Melt butter in large skillet over medium heat. Add onion; cook and stir 5 minutes or until crisp-tender. Add wine and remove from heat. Spread onion mixture on bottom of 13×9-inch glass baking dish. Top with fish. Bake 15 minutes. Spoon liquid over fish and bake 15 minutes more or until fish flakes easily when tested with fork.

Tuna with Peppercorns on a Bed of Greens

Meanwhile, trim away tough stems from kale; cut leaves into 1-inch strips. Heat oil in medium skillet over medium-high heat. Add kale, sugar and black pepper. Cook and stir 2 to 3 minutes or until tender. Place kale on plates. Top with fish and onion mixture. Top fish with carrot strips. Garnish, if desired. Serve immediately.
Makes 4 servings

BLACKENED SNAPPER WITH RED ONION SALSA

     Cajun Seasoning Mix (recipe follows)
     Red Onion Salsa (page 135)
   4 red snapper fillets (about 6 ounces
       each)
   2 tablespoons butter

Prepare Cajun Seasoning Mix and Red Onion Salsa; set aside. Rinse red snapper and pat dry with paper towels. Sprinkle with Cajun Seasoning Mix. Heat large, heavy skillet over high heat until very hot. Add butter and swirl skillet to coat bottom. When butter no longer bubbles, place fish in pan. Cook fish 6 to 8 minutes or until surface is very brown and fish flakes easily when tested with fork, turning halfway through cooking. Serve with Red Onion Salsa.
Makes 4 servings

CAJUN SEASONING MIX
   2 tablespoons salt
   1 tablespoon paprika
   1½ teaspoons garlic powder
   1 teaspoon onion powder
   1 teaspoon ground red pepper
   ½ teaspoon ground white pepper
   ½ teaspoon ground black pepper
   ½ teaspoon dried thyme leaves, crushed
   ½ teaspoon dried oregano leaves, crushed

Combine all ingredients in small bowl.
Makes about ½ cup

RED ONION SALSA

1 tablespoon vegetable oil
1 large red onion, chopped
1 clove garlic, minced
½ cup Fish Stock (page 136) or chicken
    broth
¼ cup dry red wine or red wine vinegar
¼ teaspoon dried thyme leaves, crushed
    Salt and ground black pepper to taste

Heat oil in small saucepan over medium-high heat. Add onion; cover and cook 5 minutes. Add garlic; cook 1 minute. Add remaining ingredients. Cover and cook about 10 minutes. Uncover and cook until liquid reduces to ¼ cup.

Makes about 1 cup

SAUMON AU FOUR (BAKED SALMON)

5 tablespoons butter, divided
1½ pounds salmon steaks
15 frozen artichoke hearts, cooked, halved
    Juice of 1 large lemon
    Salt and pepper
1 (4-ounce) package ALOUETTE® Garlic
    et Herbes Classique Cheese
1 teaspoon dried basil leaves, crushed

Preheat oven to 375°F. Grease casserole dish with 1 tablespoon butter. Arrange salmon steaks and artichoke hearts in dish; sprinkle with lemon juice. Melt remaining 4 tablespoons butter; pour over salmon and artichokes. Season with salt and pepper.

Spread Alouette® generously over salmon and artichokes; sprinkle with basil. Bake about 20 minutes or until fish flakes easily when tested with fork and cheese is melted.

Makes 4 servings

Favorite recipe from **Bongrain Cheese U.S.A.**

Blackened Snapper with Red Onion Salsa

POACHED SALMON WITH TARRAGON CREAM SAUCE

2 tablespoons butter or margarine
3 tablespoons minced shallot
1 clove garlic, minced
1 cup dry white wine, divided
½ cup clam juice
½ cup heavy cream
1 tablespoon chopped fresh parsley
½ teaspoon dried tarragon leaves,
    crushed
2 salmon steaks, 1 inch thick (about 8
    ounces each)
    Fish Stock (recipe follows), clam juice
    or water
    Fresh tarragon for garnish

To make Tarragon Cream Sauce, melt butter in medium saucepan over medium heat. Add shallot and garlic; reduce heat to low and cook 5 minutes or until shallot is tender. Add ½ cup wine and clam juice. Bring to a simmer. Simmer 10 minutes or until sauce is reduced to ½ cup. Add heavy cream and simmer 5 minutes or until sauce is reduced by half. (The sauce should heavily coat the back of a metal spoon.) Stir in parsley and dried tarragon; keep warm over very low heat.

Rinse salmon and pat dry with paper towels. Place steaks in saucepan just large enough to hold them. Add remaining ½ cup wine and enough Fish Stock to barely cover fish. Bring liquid to a simmer over medium heat. *(Do not boil. This will cause fish to break apart.)* Adjust heat, if necessary, to keep liquid at a simmer. Simmer 10 minutes or until center is no longer red and fish flakes easily when tested with fork. Remove fish with slotted spatula; transfer to serving plates. Top fish with Tarragon Cream Sauce. Garnish, if desired.

Makes 2 servings

FISH STOCK

1¾ pounds fish skeletons and heads from
    lean fish, such as red snapper, cod,
    halibut or flounder
2 medium onions, cut into wedges
3 ribs celery, cut into 2-inch pieces
10 cups cold water
2 slices lemon
¾ teaspoon dried thyme leaves, crushed
8 black peppercorns
3 fresh parsley sprigs
1 bay leaf
1 clove garlic

Rinse fish; cut out gills and discard. Combine fish skeletons and heads, onions and celery in stockpot or Dutch oven. Add remaining ingredients. Bring to a boil over high heat. Reduce heat to medium-low; simmer, uncovered, 30 minutes, skimming foam that rises to the surface. Remove stock from heat and cool slightly. Strain stock through large sieve or colander lined with several layers of dampened cheesecloth, removing all bones, vegetables and seasonings; discard. Use immediately or refrigerate in tightly covered container up to 2 days or freeze stock in freezer containers for several months.

Makes about 10 cups

Poached Salmon with Tarragon Cream Sauce

CAJUN CHRISTMAS GUMBO

10 to 12 chicken thighs (4 to 5 pounds)
¼ cup olive or vegetable oil
1 cup chopped onion
½ cup chopped green bell pepper
⅓ cup all-purpose flour
2 cloves garlic, crushed
1 can (28 ounces) whole peeled tomatoes
2 cups chicken broth or water
½ teaspoon crushed red pepper flakes
½ teaspoon dried thyme leaves, crushed
1 bay leaf
½ package (10 ounces) frozen sliced okra
24 ounces Surimi Seafood, crab flavored, chunk or flake style
½ pint standard oysters
½ cup fresh parsley, finely chopped
   Hot cooked white rice

Preheat oven to 350°F. Place chicken thighs in single layer in shallow baking pan. Bake 45 to 50 minutes or until chicken is no longer pink and juices run clear.

Meanwhile, heat oil in Dutch oven. Add onion and bell pepper; cook over medium-low heat 10 minutes or until onion is translucent, stirring occasionally. Stir in flour; reduce heat to low. Cook 5 minutes, stirring occasionally. Add garlic, tomatoes, chicken broth, red pepper, thyme and bay leaf. Cook, uncovered, stirring constantly, until slightly thickened. Cover; cook over low heat 30 minutes, stirring occasionally to prevent sticking.

Add cooked chicken with pan juices and okra to vegetable mixture. Increase heat to medium-low; simmer 15 to 20 minutes. Stir in Surimi Seafood, oysters and parsley; cook 5 to 10 minutes or until seafood is heated through and oysters begin to curl. Remove and discard bay leaf. Pour gumbo into soup tureen or serving bowl. Ladle gumbo over rice in soup bowls to serve.   *Makes 10 to 12 servings*

Favorite recipe from **National Fisheries Institute**

SEAFOOD OVER ANGEL HAIR PASTA

¼ cup WISH-BONE® Italian Dressing*
¼ cup chopped shallots or onion
1 cup thinly sliced carrots
4 ounces snow peas, thinly sliced (about 1 cup)
1 cup chicken broth
¼ cup dry sherry
½ pound uncooked medium shrimp, cleaned (keep tails on)
½ pound sea scallops
8 mussels, well scrubbed
¼ cup whipping or heavy cream
2 tablespoons all-purpose flour
   Salt and pepper to taste
8 ounces angel hair pasta or capellini, cooked and drained
   Freshly ground black pepper and grated Parmesan cheese (optional)

In 12-inch skillet, heat Italian dressing and cook shallots over medium-high heat 2 minutes. Add carrots and snow peas and cook 2 minutes. Add broth, then sherry. Bring to a boil; add shrimp, scallops and mussels. Simmer covered 3 minutes or until seafood is done and mussel shells open. (Discard any unopened shells.) Stir in cream blended with flour and cook over medium heat, stirring occasionally, 2 minutes or until sauce is slightly thickened. Stir in salt and pepper. Serve over hot pasta and sprinkle, if desired, with freshly ground pepper and grated Parmesan cheese.   *Makes about 4 servings*

*Also terrific with Wish-Bone® Robusto Italian, Italian & Cheese, Herbal Italian, Blended Italian, Classic Dijon Vinaigrette, Olive Oil Vinaigrette or Lite Classic Dijon Vinaigrette Dressing.

Cajun Christmas Gumbo

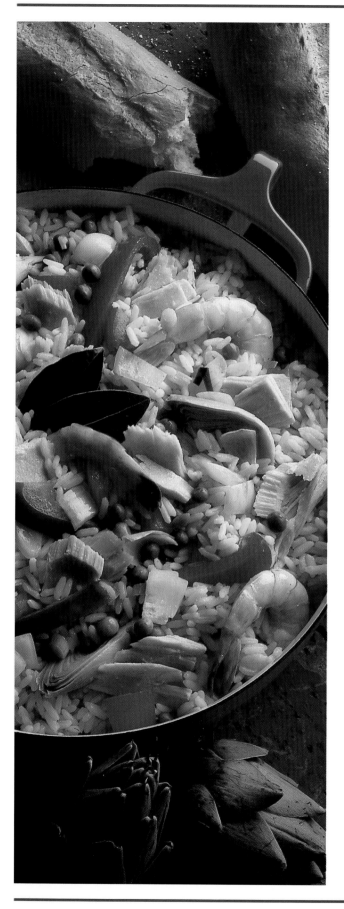

EASY PAELLA

1 medium onion, cut into halves and
    chopped
1 large red or green bell pepper, sliced
1 clove garlic, minced
2 tablespoons vegetable oil
1 can (16 ounces) tomatoes with juice,
    cut up
1 package (9 ounces) frozen artichoke
    hearts, cut into quarters
½ cup dry white wine
½ teaspoon dried thyme, crushed
¼ teaspoon salt
⅛ teaspoon saffron or turmeric
2 cups cooked rice
1 cup frozen peas
½ pound large shrimp, peeled and
    deveined
1 can (6 ounces) STARKIST® Tuna,
    drained and broken into chunks

In a large skillet sauté onion, bell pepper and
garlic in oil for 3 minutes. Stir in tomatoes with
juice, artichoke hearts, wine and seasonings.
Bring to a boil; reduce heat. Simmer for 10
minutes. Stir in rice, peas, shrimp and tuna.
Cook for 3 to 5 minutes more or until shrimp
turn pink and mixture is heated.

Makes 4 servings

PREP TIME: 30 minutes

Easy Paella

CRAB & SHRIMP QUICHE

1 (9-inch) unbaked pastry shell
6 slices BORDEN® Process American
    Cheese Food
2 tablespoons sliced green onion
2 tablespoons chopped pimiento
1 tablespoon flour
1 (6-ounce) can ORLEANS® or HARRIS®
    Crabmeat, drained
1 (4¼-ounce) can ORLEANS® Shrimp,
    drained and soaked as label directs
1½ cups BORDEN® or MEADOW GOLD®
    Half-and-Half
3 eggs, beaten

Place rack in lowest position in oven; preheat oven to 425°F. Cut *4 slices* cheese food into pieces. In large bowl, toss cheese food pieces, onion and pimiento with flour. Add remaining ingredients except pastry shell and cheese food slices. Pour into pastry shell. Bake 20 minutes. Reduce oven temperature to 325°F; bake 20 minutes longer or until set. Arrange remaining *2 slices* cheese food on top of quiche. Let stand 10 minutes before serving. Garnish as desired. Refrigerate leftovers.

Makes one 9-inch quiche

Boiled Whole Lobster with Burned Butter Sauce

BOILED WHOLE LOBSTER WITH BURNED BUTTER SAUCE

½ cup butter
2 tablespoons chopped fresh parsley
1 tablespoon cider vinegar
1 tablespoon capers
2 live lobsters*

Fill 8-quart stockpot with enough water to cover lobsters. Cover stockpot; bring water to a boil over high heat. Meanwhile, to make Burned Butter Sauce, melt butter in medium saucepan over medium heat. Cook and stir butter until it turns dark chocolate brown. Remove from heat. Add parsley, vinegar and capers. Pour into 2 individual ramekins; set aside.

Holding each lobster by its back, submerge head first into boiling water. Cover and continue to heat. When water returns to a boil, cook lobsters from 10 to 18 minutes, according to size:

    1 pound—10 minutes
    1¼ pounds—12 minutes
    1½ pounds—15 minutes
    2 pounds—18 minutes

Transfer to 2 large serving platters. Remove bands restraining claws. Cut through underside of shells with kitchen shears and loosen meat from shells. Provide nutcrackers and seafood forks. Serve lobsters with Burned Butter Sauce.

Makes 2 servings

*Purchase live lobsters as close to time of cooking as possible. Store in refrigerator.

SEAFOOD PAELLA

1 tablespoon olive oil
4 cloves garlic, minced
4½ cups finely chopped onions
2 cups uncooked long-grain white rice
2 cups clam juice
2 cups dry white wine
3 tablespoons fresh lemon juice
½ teaspoon paprika
¼ cup boiling water
½ teaspoon saffron or ground turmeric
1½ cups peeled and diced plum tomatoes
½ cup chopped fresh parsley
1 jar (8 ounces) roasted red peppers, drained, thinly sliced and divided
1 pound bay scallops
1½ cups frozen peas, thawed
10 clams, scrubbed
10 mussels, scrubbed
20 large shrimp (1 pound), shelled and deveined

Preheat oven to 375°F. Heat oil in large ovenproof skillet or paella pan over medium-low heat until hot. Add garlic and cook just until garlic sizzles. Add onions and rice; cook and stir 10 minutes or until onions are soft. Stir in clam juice, wine, lemon juice and paprika; mix well.

Combine boiling water and saffron in small bowl; stir until saffron is dissolved. Stir into onion mixture. Stir in tomatoes, parsley and half the red peppers. Bring to a boil over medium heat. Remove from heat; cover. Place on lowest shelf of oven. Bake 1 hour or until all liquid is absorbed.

Remove from oven; stir in scallops and peas. *Turn oven off;* return paella to oven. Steam clams and mussels 4 to 6 minutes, removing each as shells open. (Discard any unopened clams or mussels.) Steam shrimp 2 to 3 minutes *just* until shrimp turn pink and opaque. Remove paella from oven and arrange clams, mussels and shrimp on top. Garnish with remaining red pepper.   *Makes 10 servings*

SHRIMP PASTA MEDLEY

¼ cup (½ stick) margarine
1 clove garlic, minced
12 ounces medium shrimp, cleaned
1 cup half-and-half
1 cup pea pods, cut in half diagonally
1 red bell pepper, cut into strips
¼ cup dry white wine
¼ teaspoon crushed red pepper
8 ounces linguine, cooked, drained
1 wedge (4 ounces) KRAFT® Natural Parmesan Cheese, shredded, divided

• Melt margarine in large skillet on medium heat. Add garlic; cook and stir until lightly browned.

• Stir in shrimp, half-and-half, pea pods, bell pepper, wine and crushed red pepper. Simmer 3 to 5 minutes or until shrimp turn pink.

• Pour sauce mixture over hot linguine. Sprinkle with ¾ cup of the cheese; toss to coat. Serve with remaining ¼ cup cheese.
Makes 4 servings

PREP TIME: 10 minutes
COOKING TIME: 10 minutes

VARIATION: Substitute 1½ cups chopped cooked chicken for shrimp.

Seafood Paella

Yuletide

ORANGE–GLAZED CARROTS

1 pound fresh or thawed frozen baby carrots
⅓ cup orange marmalade
2 tablespoons butter
2 teaspoons Dijon-style mustard
½ teaspoon grated fresh ginger

To cook carrots, heat 1 inch lightly salted water in 2-quart saucepan over high heat to a boil; immediately add carrots. Return to a boil. Reduce heat to low. Cover and simmer 10 to 12 minutes for fresh carrots (8 to 10 minutes for frozen carrots) or until crisp-tender. Drain well; return carrots to pan. Stir in marmalade, butter, mustard and ginger. Simmer, uncovered, over medium heat 3 minutes or until carrots are glazed, stirring occasionally.*   *Makes 6 servings*

*At this point, carrots may be transferred to a microwavable casserole dish with lid. Cover and refrigerate up to 8 hours before serving. To reheat, microwave at HIGH (100% power) 4 to 5 minutes or until hot.

BROCCOLI WITH RED PEPPER AND SHALLOTS

- 2 bunches fresh broccoli (about 2¼ pounds)
- 2 teaspoons margarine or butter
- 1 large red bell pepper, cut into short thin strips
- 3 large shallots (3 ounces) *or* 1 small onion, thinly sliced
- ½ teaspoon salt
- ¼ teaspoon freshly ground black pepper
- ¼ cup sliced almonds, toasted (optional)

Trim off leaves and tough ends of broccoli stalks. Cut broccoli into flowerets. Peel stalks, then cut into 1-inch pieces. To cook broccoli, heat 2 quarts lightly salted water in 3-quart saucepan over high heat to a boil. Add broccoli and boil, uncovered, 3 to 5 minutes or until bright green and tender. Drain broccoli in colander. Rinse under cold water; drain thoroughly.

Melt margarine in 12-inch nonstick skillet over medium heat. Add bell pepper and shallots. Cook 3 minutes, stirring occasionally. Add broccoli. Cook 4 to 6 minutes, stirring occasionally. Sprinkle with salt and black pepper; mix well. Garnish with almonds, if desired. *Makes 6 cups, 6 to 8 servings*

CHEESY BROCCOLI 'N' MUSHROOM BAKE

- 2 (10-ounce) packages frozen broccoli spears, thawed
- 1 (10¾-ounce) can condensed cream of mushroom soup
- ½ cup MIRACLE WHIP® Salad Dressing
- ½ cup milk
- 1 cup (4 ounces) KRAFT® Natural Shredded Cheddar Cheese
- ½ cup coarsely crushed croutons

Preheat oven to 350°F. Arrange broccoli in 12×8-inch baking dish. Whisk together soup, salad dressing and milk. Pour over broccoli. Sprinkle with cheese and croutons. Bake 30 to 35 minutes or until heated through. Garnish as desired. *Makes 6 to 8 servings*

PREP TIME: 10 minutes
BAKE TIME: 30 to 35 minutes

BAKED MINI ACORN SQUASH WITH PEAS AND ONIONS

- 12 mini acorn squash* (or 1 per person)
- 6 cups frozen peas with pearl onions

Cut 1-inch slit on each side of squash. Preheat oven to 425°F. Bake squash 30 to 40 minutes or until tender. Meanwhile, cook peas and onions until tender; let cool. To serve, remove tops and seeds from squash; spoon about ½ cup peas and onions into each squash. *Makes 12 servings*

*Mini pumpkins may be substituted if mini acorn squash are not available.

*Favorite recipe from **California Beef Council***

Broccoli with Red Pepper and Shallots

GLAZED STIR-FRY HOLIDAY VEGETABLES

  2 tablespoons sugar
  ½ teaspoon grated lemon peel
  3 tablespoons fresh lemon juice
  1 tablespoon low sodium soy sauce
  2 teaspoons cornstarch
  ½ cup water
  4 teaspoons vegetable oil
  3 cups fresh broccoli florets
  1 medium red bell pepper, cut into
       1-inch pieces
  1 cup peeled, julienne-cut jicama
     Lemon zest (slivers of lemon peel)

In small bowl combine sugar, lemon peel, lemon juice, soy sauce and cornstarch. Stir in water; set aside. Heat oil in large nonstick skillet. Add broccoli and pepper; stir-fry over high heat 2 minutes. (If needed, add more oil to skillet.) Add jicama and continue cooking 1 to 2 minutes or until vegetables are crisp-tender. Pour lemon mixture over vegetables and continue cooking just until glaze thickens. Toss vegetables to coat thoroughly with glaze. Garnish with lemon zest.

Makes 6 (½-cup) servings

Favorite recipe from **The Sugar Association, Inc.**

BROCCOLI TIMBALES

  1 pound fresh broccoli
  3 eggs
  1 cup heavy cream
  1 tablespoon lemon juice
  ¼ teaspoon salt
     Dash pepper
  4 cups boiling water
     Chopped tomato and green onion top
        pieces for garnish

Generously butter six 6-ounce ramekins or custard cups; set in 13×9-inch baking pan. Preheat oven to 375°F.

Trim off leaves and tough ends of broccoli stalks. Cut broccoli into flowerets; set aside. Peel stalks with vegetable peeler. Cut into 1-inch pieces, then cut each piece lengthwise in half. Bring ½ inch of water in medium saucepan to a boil over high heat. Reduce heat to medium-low; add broccoli stem pieces. Cover; simmer about 10 minutes or until fork-tender. Transfer cooked stems with slotted spoon to food processor or blender. Add flowerets to same pan. Cover; simmer about 5 minutes or until flowerets turn bright green. Remove flowerets with slotted spoon to cutting board.

Add eggs to stem pieces in food processor; process until smooth. Add cream; pulse to blend. Add lemon juice, salt and pepper; pulse once. Set aside 6 small flowerets for garnish. Chop remaining flowerets; add to food processor. Pulse several times to blend.

Divide mixture evenly into prepared ramekins. Add boiling water to pan so water comes halfway up sides of ramekins. Bake 25 to 30 minutes or until knife inserted in center comes out clean. Top with reserved flowerets. Garnish, if desired. Let stand 5 minutes. Serve in ramekins.   *Makes 6 side-dish servings*

Broccoli Timbales

Savory Lemon Vegetables

SAVORY LEMON VEGETABLES

6 slices bacon, cooked and crumbled, reserving ¼ cup drippings
1 pound carrots, pared and sliced
1 medium head cauliflower, core removed
1 cup finely chopped onion
½ cup REALEMON® Lemon Juice from Concentrate
½ cup water
4 teaspoons sugar
1 teaspoon salt
1 teaspoon dried thyme leaves
Chopped parsley

In large saucepan, cook carrots and cauliflower in small amount of water until tender. Meanwhile, in medium skillet, cook onion in reserved drippings. Add ReaLemon® brand, *½ cup* water, sugar, salt and thyme; bring to a boil. Drain vegetables; arrange on serving dish. Pour warm sauce over vegetables. Garnish with bacon and parsley.   *Makes 8 servings*

MICROWAVE DIRECTIONS: On large microwavable platter with rim, arrange carrots and cauliflower. Cover with plastic wrap; cook on HIGH (100% power) 14 to 16 minutes. In 1-quart glass measure, cook reserved bacon drippings and onion on HIGH 1 minute. Add ReaLemon® brand, water, sugar, salt and thyme. Cook on HIGH 5½ to 6 minutes or until sauce boils. Proceed as directed.

NEW YEAR'S DAY BLACK-EYED PEAS

½ pound dried black-eyed peas, sorted and rinsed
4 cups water
⅓ cup FILIPPO BERIO® Extra Virgin Olive Oil
1 small onion, chopped
2 tablespoons wine vinegar
1 clove garlic, minced
½ teaspoon pepper
1 large bay leaf
⅛ teaspoon dried thyme leaves, crushed
Hot cooked rice (optional)

1. Place peas and water in medium saucepan; bring to a boil over high heat.

2. Reduce heat; stir in olive oil, onion, vinegar, garlic, pepper, bay leaf and thyme. Cover; simmer 1 hour or until peas are tender. Drain peas; remove and discard bay leaf. Serve with rice, if desired.   *Makes 4 servings*

VARIATION: For cold salad, prepare peas as directed in step 1. Stir in *only* the bay leaf; cover and simmer 1 hour or until peas are tender. Drain peas; remove and discard bay leaf. Add onion, garlic, pepper and thyme. In small bowl, whisk together olive oil and vinegar. Pour over pea mixture; stir to combine. Cover; refrigerate at least 2 hours before serving.

PREP TIME: 10 minutes
COOK TIME: 1 hour
CHILL TIME: 2 hours (salad only)

ARABIAN VEGETABLE MEDLEY

2 pounds eggplant, unpeeled, cut into
    1½-inch cubes
2 tablespoons olive oil, divided
4 cups sliced onions
2 teaspoons minced garlic
1 teaspoon salt
½ teaspoon *each* ground cinnamon and
    black pepper
2 cans (16 ounces each) tomatoes,
    undrained and coarsely chopped
1 can (16 ounces) chick peas, rinsed and
    drained

1. In large nonstick skillet, over medium-high heat, sauté eggplant in 1 tablespoon oil 10 to 12 minutes or until lightly browned and crisp-tender. Remove eggplant from pan; set aside.

2. In same skillet, over medium-high heat, sauté onions in remaining 1 tablespoon oil 6 to 8 minutes or until lightly browned and tender. Stir in garlic, salt, cinnamon and pepper and cook 2 to 3 minutes.

3. Stir in eggplant, tomatoes and chick peas; bring to a boil. Reduce heat to low; cover and simmer 30 minutes or until eggplant is tender. Remove cover and cook 15 minutes or until most of liquid is absorbed.

Makes 16 servings

Favorite recipe from **National Turkey Federation**

SAVORY ONION TART

Pastry for 9-inch single-crust pie
¼ cup WISH-BONE® Italian Dressing
2 tablespoons butter or margarine
2 large onions, thinly sliced
1 cup shredded fontina or Gruyère
    cheese (about 4 ounces)
2 eggs
½ cup whipping or heavy cream
2 teaspoons finely chopped fresh sage
    leaves *or* ½ teaspoon dried sage
    leaves, crushed
1 teaspoon dried marjoram leaves,
    crushed
⅛ teaspoon pepper

Preheat oven to 425°F. Roll pastry into 10-inch circle. Press into 9-inch tart pan and crimp edges tightly. Pierce bottom and side with fork. Bake 8 minutes or until lightly golden. Remove to wire rack and cool completely.

Meanwhile, in large skillet, heat Italian dressing and butter over medium heat. Add onions; cook, stirring occasionally, 15 minutes or until onions are tender. Fill prepared tart shell with cheese, then onion mixture. In small bowl, beat eggs, cream, sage, marjoram and pepper; slowly pour over onion mixture. Bake 35 minutes or until golden. To serve, cut into wedges.

Makes about 8 servings

Green Bean Almond Rice

GREEN BEAN ALMOND RICE

1 tablespoon butter or margarine
½ cup slivered almonds
½ cup chopped onion
⅓ cup chopped red bell pepper
3 cups cooked brown rice (cooked in beef broth)
1 package (10 ounces) frozen French-style green beans, thawed
⅛ to ¼ teaspoon ground white pepper
¼ teaspoon dried tarragon leaves, crushed

Melt butter in large skillet over medium-high heat. Add almonds; stir until lightly browned. Add onion and bell pepper; cook 2 minutes or until tender. Add rice, beans, white pepper, and tarragon. Stir until thoroughly heated.

Makes 8 servings

Favorite recipe from **USA Rice Federation**

FESTIVE GREEN BEANS

1 tablespoon olive oil
1 tablespoon butter or margarine
3 medium leeks, well rinsed and sliced
2 large red bell peppers, seeded and cut into thin strips
2 pounds green beans, trimmed
1 large garlic clove, minced
1½ teaspoons salt
1 teaspoon TABASCO® pepper sauce
1 teaspoon grated lemon peel
¼ cup sliced natural almonds, toasted

In 12-inch skillet over medium heat, heat oil and butter; add leeks. Cook 5 minutes, stirring occasionally. Add red peppers; cook 5 minutes longer or until vegetables are tender.

Meanwhile, steam green beans 5 minutes or until crisp-tender. Add beans, garlic, salt, TABASCO sauce and lemon peel to skillet; toss to mix well. Sprinkle with toasted almonds.

Makes 8 servings

DOUBLE ONION QUICHE

3 cups thinly sliced yellow onions
3 tablespoons butter or margarine
1 cup thinly sliced green onions
3 eggs
1 cup heavy cream
½ cup grated Parmesan cheese
¼ teaspoon hot pepper sauce
1 package (1 ounce) HIDDEN VALLEY
   RANCH® Milk Recipe Original
   Ranch® salad dressing mix
1 (9-inch) deep-dish pastry shell, baked
   and cooled
   Fresh oregano sprig

Preheat oven to 350°F. In medium skillet, sauté yellow onions in butter, stirring occasionally, about 10 minutes. Add green onions and cook 5 minutes longer. Remove from heat and let cool.

In large bowl, whisk eggs until frothy. Whisk in cream, cheese, pepper sauce and salad dressing mix. Stir in onion mixture. Pour egg and onion mixture into baked and cooled pastry shell. Bake until top is browned and knife inserted in center comes out clean, 35 to 40 minutes. Cool on wire rack 10 minutes before slicing. Garnish with oregano.

Makes 8 servings

CORN PUDDING

1 bag (20 ounces) frozen whole kernel
   corn, thawed
1 small onion, quartered
2 cups milk
2 eggs, beaten
1 package (8½ ounces) corn muffin mix
½ teaspoon salt
1 cup shredded Cheddar cheese
1 cup thinly sliced romaine lettuce
½ cup julienned radishes

Preheat oven to 325°F. Combine corn and onion in food processor; cover and process using on/off pulse until corn is broken but not puréed, scraping side of bowl as necessary. Add milk and eggs; pulse until just blended. Add muffin mix and salt; pulse only until mixed. Pour mixture into greased 11¾×7½-inch baking dish. Bake 45 to 50 minutes or until outside crust is golden brown. Sprinkle pudding with cheese; place under broiler 3 to 4 inches from heat. Broil until cheese is melted and top is crusty. To serve, top with romaine lettuce and radishes.   *Makes 8 to 10 servings*

*Favorite recipe from **National Cattlemen's Beef Association***

CINNAMON APPLE RINGS

3 large cooking apples
¼ cup lemon juice
1 cup water
½ cup sugar
¼ cup red cinnamon candies

Peel and core apples; cut crosswise into ½-inch-thick rings. Toss with lemon juice to prevent discoloration. Combine water, sugar and candies in large saucepan. Bring to a boil, stirring until sugar and candies are dissolved. Add apple rings and simmer until just tender, about 15 minutes. Let cool in liquid. Drain.

Makes 4 servings

*Favorite recipe from **Perdue Farms Incorporated***

LOW-CALORIE MASHED POTATOES

2 pounds medium red boiling potatoes, peeled and cut into chunks
4 large cloves garlic, peeled
¾ cup cultured buttermilk (1½% fat)
½ teaspoon salt
¼ teaspoon freshly ground black pepper
2 tablespoons chopped chives for garnish

Place potatoes and garlic in large saucepan. Add enough water to cover; bring to a boil over high heat. Reduce heat to medium. Simmer, uncovered, 20 to 30 minutes or until potatoes are fork-tender; drain.

Place potatoes and garlic in medium bowl. Mash with potato masher or beat with electric mixer at medium speed until smooth.* Add buttermilk, salt and pepper. Stir with fork until just combined. Garnish, if desired.

Makes 4 cups, 8 servings

*For a smoother texture, force potatoes through potato ricer or food mill into medium bowl. Proceed as directed.

BUTTERY MASHED POTATOES: Prepare as directed except add 1 tablespoon butter or margarine along with buttermilk, salt and pepper.

CHEESY MASHED POTATOES AND TURNIPS

2 pounds all-purpose potatoes, peeled
1 pound turnips, peeled
¼ cup milk
½ cup shredded Cheddar cheese
¼ cup butter or margarine
1 teaspoon TABASCO® pepper sauce
½ teaspoon salt

In large saucepan over high heat, combine potatoes and turnips with enough water to cover. Bring to a boil and reduce heat to low; cover and simmer 25 to 30 minutes or until vegetables are tender. Drain. Return vegetables to saucepan; heat over high heat for a few seconds to eliminate any excess moisture, shaking saucepan to prevent sticking.

In small saucepan over medium heat, bring milk to a simmer. In large bowl, mash vegetables. Stir in warmed milk, Cheddar cheese, butter, TABASCO sauce and salt.

Makes 8 servings

NOTE: Potatoes may be made up to 2 days in advance and reheated in microwave or double boiler above simmering water.

GOLDEN MASHED POTATOES

2½ cups cubed cooked potatoes, mashed
3 tablespoons milk
2 tablespoons margarine
1 tablespoon chopped fresh chives
½ pound VELVEETA® Pasteurized Process Cheese Spread, cubed, divided
¼ cup (1 ounce) KRAFT® 100% Grated Parmesan Cheese

Combine potatoes, milk, margarine and chives; beat until fluffy. Stir in half of the process cheese spread. Spoon into 1-quart casserole; sprinkle with Parmesan cheese. Bake at 350°F, 20 to 25 minutes or until thoroughly heated. Top with remaining process cheese spread; continue baking until process cheese spread begins to melt. *Makes 4 to 6 servings*

PREP TIME: 20 minutes
BAKE TIME: 30 minutes

Low-Calorie Mashed Potatoes

CINNAMON APPLE SWEET POTATOES

4 medium sweet potatoes
1½ cups finely chopped apples
½ cup orange juice
¼ cup sugar
1½ teaspoons cornstarch
½ teaspoon ground cinnamon
½ teaspoon grated orange peel

Prick potatoes with fork. Place on paper towels and microwave on HIGH 10 to 13 minutes or until tender, turning halfway through cooking. Set aside. In microwavable bowl, combine remaining ingredients. Cover and cook on HIGH 3 minutes; stir. Cook uncovered on HIGH 1½ to 2½ minutes or until sauce is thickened. Slit sweet potatoes and spoon sauce over each.   *Makes 4 servings*

*Favorite recipe from **The Sugar Association, Inc.***

Glazed Stir-Fry Holiday Vegetables (page 148),
Cinnamon Apple Sweet Potatoes

HOT SWEET POTATOES

4 small (4 ounces each) sweet potatoes
2 tablespoons margarine or unsalted butter, softened
½ teaspoon TABASCO® pepper sauce
¼ teaspoon dried savory leaves, crushed

In large saucepan cover potatoes with water. Cover and cook over high heat 20 to 25 minutes or until potatoes are tender. Drain potatoes and cut in half lengthwise.

Preheat broiler. In small bowl, combine margarine and TABASCO sauce. Spread ¾ teaspoon margarine mixture over cut side of each potato half. Season each with pinch of savory. Place on foil-lined broiler pan and broil, watching carefully, about 5 minutes or until lightly browned. Serve hot.

Makes 4 servings

BAKED APPLE & SWEET POTATO CASSEROLE

6 sweet potatoes
3 apples
2 tablespoons butter, divided
½ cup orange juice
¼ cup packed dark brown sugar
⅛ teaspoon ground cinnamon
⅛ teaspoon ground allspice
¼ cup rum

Preheat oven to 350°F. Boil or steam potatoes until tender. Remove skin and cut lengthwise into slices. Peel and core apples; slice into rings. Grease 9×6-inch baking dish with 1 tablespoon butter; alternate potato and apple layers until dish is filled. Pour combined orange juice, sugar, spices, rum and remaining 1 tablespoon butter, melted, over potato mixture. Bake 30 minutes or until potatoes are brown and shiny and liquid is absorbed.

Makes 6 servings

*Favorite recipe from **Michigan Apple Committee***

SWEET POTATO GRATIN

3 pounds sweet potatoes (about 5 large)
½ cup butter or margarine, divided
¼ cup plus 2 tablespoons packed light
    brown sugar, divided
2 eggs
⅔ cup orange juice
2 teaspoons ground cinnamon, divided
½ teaspoon salt
¼ teaspoon ground nutmeg
⅓ cup all-purpose flour
¼ cup uncooked old-fashioned oats
⅓ cup chopped pecans or walnuts

Bake sweet potatoes until tender in preheated 350°F oven 1 hour. Or, pierce sweet potatoes several times with fork and place on microwavable plate. Microwave at HIGH (100% power) 16 to 18 minutes, rotating and turning over after 9 minutes. Let stand 5 minutes. While sweet potatoes are hot, cut lengthwise into halves. Scrape hot pulp from skins into large bowl. Beat ¼ cup butter and 2 tablespoons sugar into sweet potatoes with electric mixer at medium speed until butter is melted. Beat in eggs, orange juice, 1½ teaspoons cinnamon, salt and nutmeg, scraping down side of bowl once. Beat until smooth. Pour mixture into 1½-quart baking dish; smooth top.

For topping, combine flour, oats, remaining ¼ cup sugar and ½ teaspoon cinnamon in medium bowl. Cut in remaining ¼ cup butter with pastry blender or 2 knives until mixture becomes coarse crumbs. Stir in pecans. Sprinkle topping evenly over sweet potatoes.*

Preheat oven to 350°F. Bake 25 to 30 minutes or until sweet potatoes are heated through. For a crisper topping, broil 5 inches from heat 2 to 3 minutes or until golden brown. Garnish, if desired.   *Makes 6 to 8 servings*

*At this point, Sweet Potato Gratin may be covered and refrigerated up to 1 day. Let stand at room temperature 1 hour before baking.

Sweet Potato Gratin

Sherried Mushroom Rice

Melt butter in medium skillet on medium heat. Add garlic; cook and stir 1 minute. Add mushrooms and red pepper; cook and stir 2 minutes.

Add broth, water, sherry, onion flakes and salt. Bring to boil.

Stir in rice; cover. Remove from heat. Let stand 5 minutes or until liquid is absorbed. Stir. Sprinkle with cheese and parsley.

Makes 6 servings

MICROWAVE DIRECTIONS: Mix butter cut into pieces, garlic, mushrooms and red pepper in 2-quart microwavable casserole. Cover. Microwave on HIGH 2 to 3 minutes. Stir in rice, broth, water, sherry, onion flakes and salt. Cover. Microwave on HIGH 4 minutes; stir. Microwave on HIGH 2 to 3 minutes; stir. Let stand 5 minutes or until liquid is absorbed. Sprinkle with cheese and parsley.

SHERRIED MUSHROOM RICE

2 tablespoons butter or margarine
1 clove garlic, minced
2 cups sliced mushrooms
¼ cup chopped red pepper
1 cup chicken broth
¼ cup water
¼ cup dry sherry or water
2 teaspoons onion flakes
¼ teaspoon salt
1½ cups MINUTE® Original Instant
    Enriched Rice, uncooked
2 tablespoons KRAFT® 100% Grated
    Parmesan Cheese
1 tablespoon chopped fresh parsley *or*
    1 teaspoon parsley flakes

FESTIVE RICE

¼ cup oil
2¼ cups MINUTE® Original Instant
    Enriched Rice, uncooked
1 medium green pepper, chopped*
1 envelope GOOD SEASONS® Italian or
    Mild Italian Salad Dressing Mix
2¼ cups water
2 tablespoons chopped pimiento or fresh
    parsley

Heat oil in large skillet on medium heat. Add rice and pepper; cook and stir 2 minutes.

Sprinkle with salad dressing mix. Stir in water; cover. Bring to boil.

Remove from heat. Let stand 5 minutes or until liquid is absorbed. Stir in pimiento.

Makes 6 servings

*Or use ½ medium green pepper, chopped, and ½ cup grated carrot.

FRUITED RICE PILAF

2½ cups water
1 cup uncooked rice
2 tablespoons butter or margarine
1 medium tomato, chopped
⅓ cup minced dried apples
¼ cup minced dried apricots
¼ cup sliced green onions
¾ teaspoon LAWRY'S® Seasoned Salt
¼ teaspoon LAWRY'S® Garlic Powder
  with Parsley
3 tablespoons sliced almonds

In 2-quart saucepan, bring water to a boil; add rice and butter. Return to a boil. Reduce heat; cover and simmer 15 minutes. Add remaining ingredients except almonds; cook 5 to 10 minutes longer or until rice is tender. Stir in almonds. Garnish with apple slices and celery leaves, if desired.   *Makes 4 servings*

PRESENTATION: Serve with baked pork chops, roasted meats or poultry.

HINT: For variety and added flavor, add ¼ teaspoon curry powder to cooked rice.

ORANGE WILD RICE

¾ cup wild rice, rinsed well
1 small onion, chopped
2 tablespoons margarine
  Juice of 1 medium orange plus chicken
    broth to equal 1¼ cups
  Finely grated peel of 1 small orange
½ teaspoon LAWRY'S® Seasoned Pepper
¼ teaspoon LAWRY'S® Garlic Powder
  with Parsley
1 package (10 ounces) frozen peas,
    thawed
⅓ cup chopped pecans
  Mandarin orange sections for garnish

In large saucepan, sauté rice and onion in margarine, stirring frequently. Add combined orange juice and broth, orange peel, Seasoned Pepper and Garlic Powder with Parsley. Bring to a boil; reduce heat, cover and simmer 35 minutes or until liquid is almost absorbed. Stir in peas and pecans; simmer 3 to 5 minutes longer. Garnish with Mandarin orange sections.
          Makes 4 to 6 servings

PRESENTATION: Serve with roast pork.

Fruited Rice Pilaf

HOLIDAY HARVEST RICE

    2 tablespoons margarine
1½ cups MAHATMA®, CAROLINA®,
      RIVER® or WATER MAID® Rice
    ½ teaspoon salt
    2 cups unsweetened apple juice
    1 cup cranberry juice
    2 tablespoons fresh lemon juice
    1 tablespoon chopped raisins
    2 teaspoons light brown sugar
    ½ teaspoon ground cinnamon
    2 small tart apples, peeled, cored and
      chopped
    ½ cup chopped green onions

In saucepan, over medium heat, melt margarine. Stir in rice and salt, stirring to coat rice. Add juices, raisins, sugar and cinnamon. Bring to a boil. Cover and simmer 20 minutes. Stir in apples and green onions.

Makes 6 to 8 servings

APRICOT AND WALNUT BROWN RICE STUFFING

    ½ cup chopped onion
    ½ cup chopped celery
    1 teaspoon margarine
    3 cups cooked brown rice
    ⅔ cup coarsely chopped dried apricots
    ¼ cup coarsely chopped walnuts
    ¼ cup raisins, plumped
    2 tablespoons snipped parsley
    ½ teaspoon dried thyme leaves
    ¼ teaspoon salt
    ¼ teaspoon rubbed sage
    ¼ teaspoon ground black pepper
    ½ cup chicken broth

Cook onion and celery in margarine in large skillet over medium-high heat until tender-crisp. Add rice, apricots, walnuts, raisins, parsley, thyme, salt, sage, pepper and broth; transfer to 2-quart baking dish. Bake in covered baking dish at 375°F for 15 to 20 minutes. (Stuffing may be baked inside poultry.)

Makes 6 servings

TIP: To plump raisins, cover with 1 cup boiling water. Let stand 1 to 2 minutes; drain.

Favorite recipe from **USA Rice Federation**

HERBED RICE

    ¾ cup uncooked long-grain white rice
    ¼ cup uncooked wild rice
    1 chicken-flavor bouillon cube
    2 tablespoons butter
    1 cup finely chopped celery
    ¼ cup finely chopped onion
2½ teaspoons LAWRY'S® Pinch of Herbs
    ½ teaspoon LAWRY'S® Seasoned Salt
    ¼ teaspoon LAWRY'S® Seasoned Pepper
    ½ pound fresh mushrooms, sliced

Cook each rice separately according to package directions, except omitting salt and adding bouillon cube to water for white rice. In large skillet, melt butter; sauté celery and onion until tender. Add Pinch of Herbs, Seasoned Salt, Seasoned Pepper and mushrooms; sauté until mushrooms are tender. Add rice and toss.

Makes 6 side-dish servings or
enough stuffing for 10-pound turkey

PRESENTATION: Serve with broiled chicken, fish or beef.

Holiday Harvest Rice

HOLIDAY GRAPE DRESSING

1 cup brown rice
2 tablespoons olive oil
½ cup *each* chopped onion and sliced
    celery
½ cup *each* chopped rehydrated shiitake*
    and white mushrooms
2 cups chicken broth
½ teaspoon *each* dried thyme and
    oregano leaves, crushed
⅛ teaspoon coarsely ground pepper
2 cups California grapes**
½ cup chopped macadamia nuts or
    almonds
2 tablespoons chopped parsley

Cook and stir rice in oil until browned; remove from skillet and set aside. Cook and stir onion and celery in skillet. Stir in mushrooms, broth, rice and seasonings. Simmer, covered, 25 to 30 minutes or until rice is cooked and liquid is absorbed. Stir in grapes, nuts and parsley; cook about 2 minutes longer or until grapes are thoroughly heated. *Makes 6 servings*

PREPARATION TIME: About 45 minutes

*To rehydrate shiitake mushrooms, cover with warm water and let stand 10 to 14 minutes before slicing.

**Red, green, or blue/black grapes or a combination may be used. Seed grapes if necessary.

*Favorite recipe from **California Table Grape Commission***

Holiday Grape Dressing

PINE NUT DRESSING

1 bag SUCCESS® White or Brown Rice
1 tablespoon reduced-calorie margarine
½ cup chopped onion
½ cup chopped celery
½ cup low sodium chicken broth
¼ cup pine nuts, toasted
1 tablespoon chopped fresh parsley
¾ teaspoon poultry seasoning
¼ teaspoon celery salt
¼ teaspoon pepper

Prepare rice according to package directions.

Melt margarine in large saucepan over medium heat. Add onion and celery; cook and stir until crisp-tender. Stir in rice and remaining ingredients. Reduce heat to low; simmer 10 minutes, stirring occasionally.

Makes 6 servings

SUCCESS WALDORF DRESSING

1 box SUCCESS® Long Grain & Wild
    Rice Mix
3 slices bacon
½ cup chopped celery
1 medium red apple, chopped
1 medium green apple, chopped
½ cup chopped walnuts
½ cup raisins
2 tablespoons honey
2 tablespoons lemon juice

Prepare rice mix according to package directions. Meanwhile, fry bacon in large skillet until crisp. Remove bacon; crumble. Set aside. Add celery to skillet; sauté until tender. Add all remaining ingredients except rice and bacon. Fold in cooked rice. Top with reserved bacon.

Makes 4 to 6 servings

Pine Nut Dressing

APPLE & HERB STUFFING

  2 cups sliced celery
1½ cups chopped onions
  ½ cup margarine or butter
1¾ cups hot water
  1 tablespoon WYLER'S® or STEERO®
      Chicken-Flavor Instant Bouillon *or*
      3 Chicken-Flavor Bouillon Cubes
12 cups dry bread cubes (about 16 slices
      bread)
  3 cups coarsely chopped apples
  1 cup toasted slivered almonds
  1 tablespoon chopped parsley
  2 teaspoons poultry seasoning
  ¼ teaspoon rubbed sage
      Rich Turkey Gravy (page 112,
      optional)

In large skillet, cook celery and onions in margarine until tender. Add water and bouillon; cook until bouillon dissolves. In large bowl, combine remaining ingredients except Rich Turkey Gravy; add bouillon mixture. Mix well. Loosely stuff turkey just before roasting. Place remaining stuffing in greased baking dish. Bake at 350°F for 30 minutes or until hot. Serve with Rich Turkey Gravy, if desired. Refrigerate leftovers.   *Makes about 2½ quarts*

"LITE" APRICOT STUFFING

  1 cup sliced celery
  ¾ cup chopped onion
1½ cups turkey broth or reduced-sodium
      chicken bouillon
16 slices reduced-calorie bread, cubed and
      dried
  2 tablespoons parsley flakes
1½ teaspoons poultry seasoning
  ½ teaspoon salt
  2 egg whites
  ¼ cup dried apricots, chopped

In small saucepan, over medium-high heat, combine celery, onion and turkey broth; bring to a boil. Reduce heat to low; cover and simmer 5 minutes or until vegetables are tender. In large bowl, combine celery mixture, bread cubes, parsley, poultry seasoning, salt, egg whites and apricots. Spoon into lightly greased 2-quart casserole; cover. Bake at 350°F 30 minutes or until heated through.   *Makes 8 servings*

*Favorite recipe from **National Turkey Federation***

CRANBERRY–RAISIN STUFFING

12 slices cinnamon-raisin bread, toasted
  ½ cup butter or margarine
2½ cups chopped onions
  1 teaspoon rubbed sage
  1 bag (12 ounces) fresh or partially
      thawed frozen cranberries, washed,
      picked through, coarsely chopped
  ¼ cup sugar
  ¼ to ½ cup chicken broth*

Cut toast into ½-inch cubes. Place in large bowl; set aside. Melt butter in large skillet; add onions. Cook and stir until tender (about 10 minutes). Add sage; cook 1 minute more. In medium bowl, toss cranberries with sugar; set aside. Add onion mixture and sugared cranberries to bread cubes; mix well. Pour ¼ cup chicken broth over bread cube mixture; mix until evenly moistened. Stuff body and neck of turkey and cook according to instructions given with turkey.   *Makes 7½ cups stuffing*

*If cooking stuffing outside of turkey, use ½ cup chicken broth and bake, covered, at 350°F for 45 minutes or until heated through.

Cranberry-Raisin Stuffing

RAISIN ALMOND STUFFING

**1 package (6 ounces) STOVE TOP®
Stuffing Mix, any flavor**
1⅔ cups water*
½ cup raisins
¼ cup (½ stick) margarine or butter
½ cup slivered almonds

Mix contents of vegetable/seasoning packet, water, raisins and margarine in medium saucepan.

Bring to boil. Reduce heat to low; cover and simmer 5 minutes.

Stir in stuffing crumbs and almonds; cover. Remove from heat. Let stand 5 minutes. Fluff with fork.   *Makes 6 servings*

*For moister stuffing, increase water by 2 tablespoons. For less moist stuffing, decrease water by 2 tablespoons.

EASY OYSTER DRESSING

**1 teaspoon WYLER'S® or STEERO®
Chicken-Flavor Instant Bouillon**
½ cup boiling water
½ cup chopped celery
½ cup margarine or butter
**1 (8-ounce) package herb-seasoned
stuffing mix**
**1 (8-ounce) can ORLEANS® Whole
Oysters, undrained**

Preheat oven to 350°F. Dissolve bouillon in water; set aside. In small skillet, cook celery in margarine until tender. In large bowl, combine all ingredients; mix well. Turn into buttered 1½-quart baking dish. Cover; bake 35 minutes or until hot. Refrigerate leftovers.

Makes 6 to 8 servings

SAUSAGE–CORNBREAD STUFFING

**8 ounces bulk pork sausage (regular or
    spicy)**
½ cup butter or margarine
2 medium onions, chopped
2 cloves garlic, minced
2 teaspoons dried sage
1 teaspoon poultry seasoning
**1 package (16 ounces) prepared dry
    cornbread crumbs**
¾ to 1¼ cups chicken broth
Sage leaves for garnish

Brown sausage in large skillet over medium-high heat until no longer pink, stirring to separate meat. Drain sausage on paper towels; set aside. Wipe skillet with paper towels to remove grease. Melt butter in same skillet over medium heat until foamy. Cook and stir onions and garlic in butter 10 minutes or until onions are softened. Stir in dried sage and poultry seasoning; cook 1 minute more.

Combine cornbread crumbs, sausage and onion mixture in large bowl. *If stuffing is to be cooked in turkey,* drizzle ¾ cup broth over stuffing; toss lightly until evenly moistened. Stuff body and neck cavities loosely with stuffing. Stuffing may be prepared up to 1 day before using. *Do not stuff turkey until just before ready to roast.* Roast according to directions given on page 108 or according to instructions with turkey. *If stuffing is to be cooked separately,* drizzle 1¼ cups broth over stuffing; toss stuffing lightly until evenly moistened. Transfer to 3-quart casserole.

Preheat oven to 350°F. Bake 45 minutes (55 to 60 minutes if refrigerated) or until heated through. For drier stuffing, uncover during last 15 minutes of baking. Garnish, if desired.

Makes 12 cups stuffing

TURKEY PAN GRAVY

Pan drippings from roasted turkey
6 tablespoons all-purpose flour
**4 cups turkey broth, chicken broth, milk
    or water**
LAWRY'S® Seasoned Salt
LAWRY'S® Seasoned Pepper

Pour drippings from turkey into bowl, leaving browned particles on bottom of roasting pan. Let fat rise to top of drippings; skim off fat, reserving 6 tablespoons. Reserve remaining drippings for part of the liquid for gravy, if desired. Return reserved fat to roasting pan. Place roasting pan over low heat; blend in flour and cook, stirring constantly, until bubbly. Add liquid, which should be cool, all at once. Cook, stirring constantly with wire whisk, until thickened. Continue cooking over low heat about 5 minutes, stirring constantly. Season to taste with Seasoned Salt and Seasoned Pepper.

Makes about 4 cups

CREAMED HORSERADISH

1 cup whipping cream
**1 ounce fresh horseradish root, peeled
    and finely grated *or* 1 tablespoon
    prepared horseradish**
1 teaspoon LAWRY'S® Seasoned Salt
2 to 3 drops hot pepper sauce

In medium bowl, whip cream until soft peaks form. Gradually add horseradish, Seasoned Salt and hot pepper sauce to taste. Continue whipping until very stiff. Refrigerate.

Makes 2 cups

PRESENTATION: Serve with prime rib or roast beef.

Sausage-Cornbread Stuffing

FLASH PRIMAVERA

1 pound mostaccioli, ziti or other
    medium pasta shape, uncooked
1 head broccoli or cauliflower, cut into
    small florets
1 tablespoon cornstarch
¼ cup water
1 (13¾-ounce) can low sodium chicken
    broth
3 cloves garlic, minced
1 (10-ounce) package frozen mixed
    vegetables
1 (10-ounce) package frozen chopped
    spinach, thawed
  Salt and pepper
1 cup grated Parmesan cheese

Prepare pasta according to package directions;
3 minutes before pasta is done, stir in broccoli.
Drain pasta and vegetables; transfer to large
bowl. Set aside and keep warm.

Meanwhile, in small bowl dissolve cornstarch in
water; set aside. Simmer broth and garlic in
large saucepan over medium heat 3 minutes.
Whisk in cornstarch mixture. Stir in mixed
vegetables and spinach; cook until hot, about
5 minutes. Toss sauce and vegetables with
pasta. Season to taste with salt and pepper;
sprinkle with Parmesan cheese.

Makes 6 servings

*Favorite recipe from **National Pasta Association***

Flash Primavera

SPINACH–STUFFED MANICOTTI

8 manicotti shells, cooked and drained
1½ teaspoons olive oil
1 teaspoon minced fresh garlic
1½ cups canned or fresh tomatoes, chopped
1 teaspoon dried rosemary leaves, crushed
1 teaspoon dried sage leaves, crushed
1 teaspoon dried oregano leaves, crushed
1 teaspoon dried thyme leaves, crushed
1 package (10 ounces) frozen chopped spinach, cooked, drained and squeezed dry
4 ounces ricotta cheese
1 slice whole wheat bread, torn into coarse crumbs
2 egg whites, slightly beaten

Preheat oven to 350°F. Heat oil in small saucepan over medium heat. Add garlic; cook and stir until lightly browned. Stir in tomatoes, rosemary, sage, oregano and thyme. Reduce heat to low; simmer 10 minutes, stirring occasionally.

Combine spinach, cheese and bread crumbs in medium bowl. Fold in egg whites. Stuff manicotti with spinach mixture. Spoon ⅓ of the sauce into 13×9-inch baking dish. Arrange manicotti over sauce; cover with remaining sauce. Cover with foil. Bake 30 minutes or until hot and bubbly. Garnish as desired.

Makes 4 servings

*Favorite recipe from **National Pasta Association***

Spinach-Stuffed Manicotti

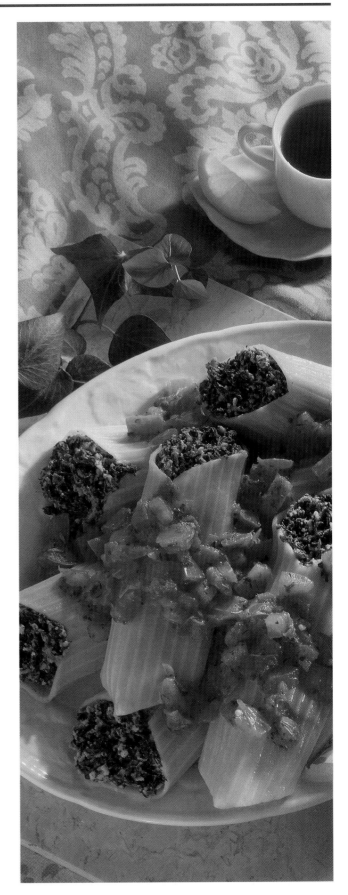

PASTA WITH FRESH VEGETABLES IN GARLIC SAUCE

    3 medium carrots
    2 small zucchini
    ¼ cup butter or margarine
    1 large onion, chopped
    4 cloves garlic, minced
    ½ cup chicken broth
    ½ cup heavy cream
    ½ teaspoon salt
    ½ teaspoon dried tarragon leaves,
        crushed
    ¼ teaspoon pepper
    2 cups hot, cooked, drained pasta
        (fettuccine, ziti or shells)

Cut carrots and zucchini lengthwise into thin slices with vegetable peeler. Bring 1 inch water to a boil in medium saucepan; add carrots and zucchini. Cook until crisp-tender. Remove from saucepan and drain; set aside. Melt butter in same saucepan over medium heat. Add onion and garlic; cook until tender. Gradually stir in broth, cream and seasonings; simmer 5 minutes or until sauce is slightly thickened. Add vegetables; heat thoroughly, stirring occasionally. Add vegetables and sauce to hot cooked pasta; toss lightly.   *Makes 4 servings*

PASTA ROLL-UPS

    1 package (1.5 ounces) LAWRY'S®
        Original-Style Spaghetti Sauce
        Spices & Seasonings
    1 can (6 ounces) tomato paste
  2¼ cups water
    2 tablespoons butter or vegetable oil
    2 cups cottage cheese or ricotta cheese
    1 cup (4 ounces) shredded mozzarella
        cheese
    ¼ cup grated Parmesan cheese
    2 eggs, lightly beaten
    ½ to 1 teaspoon LAWRY'S® Garlic Salt
    ½ teaspoon dried basil, crushed
        (optional)
    8 ounces lasagna noodles, cooked and
        drained

In medium saucepan, prepare Spaghetti Sauce Spices & Seasonings according to package directions using tomato paste, water and butter. In large bowl, combine remaining ingredients except noodles; blend well. Spread ¼ cup cheese mixture on entire length of each lasagna noodle; roll up. Place noodles, seam side down, in microwave-safe baking dish. Cover with vented plastic wrap and microwave on HIGH 6 to 7 minutes or until cheese begins to melt. Pour sauce over rolls and microwave on HIGH 1 minute longer, if necessary, to heat sauce.   *Makes 6 servings*

PRESENTATION: Sprinkle with additional grated Parmesan cheese. Garnish with fresh basil leaves.

HINT: For quick microwavable meals, wrap prepared rolls individually and freeze. Sauce may be frozen in ¼-cup servings.

Pasta with Fresh Vegetables in Garlic Sauce

Mrs. Claus's

BREADS

HOLIDAY STOLLEN

1½ cups unsalted butter, softened
4 egg yolks
½ cup granulated sugar
1 teaspoon salt
   Grated peel from 1 lemon and 1 orange
1 teaspoon vanilla
2½ cups hot milk (120° to 130°F)
8 to 8½ cups all-purpose flour, divided
2 packages active dry yeast
½ cup *each* golden raisins, candied orange
   peel, candied lemon peel, chopped candied
   red cherries, chopped candied green
   cherries and chopped almonds
1 egg, beaten
   Powdered sugar

In large mixer bowl, beat butter, egg yolks, granulated sugar, salt, lemon peel, orange peel and vanilla until light and fluffy. Slowly add milk; mix thoroughly. Add 2 cups flour and yeast; mix well. When mixture is smooth, add enough remaining flour, ½ cup at a time, until dough forms and can be lifted out of bowl. Lightly flour work surface; knead dough until smooth and elastic, about 10 minutes. Mix raisins, candied orange and lemon peels, cherries and almonds in medium bowl; knead fruit mixture into dough.

continued on page 174

Holiday Stollen, continued

Place dough in greased bowl, cover with plastic wrap and let rise in warm place until doubled in bulk, about 1 hour.

Grease 2 large baking sheets. Turn dough out onto floured work surface. Divide dough in half. Place one half back in bowl; cover and set aside. Cut remaining half into thirds. Roll each third into 12-inch rope. Place on prepared baking sheet. Braid ropes together. Repeat procedure with remaining dough.

Brush beaten egg on braids. Let braids stand at room temperature until doubled in bulk, about 1 hour.

Preheat oven to 350°F. Bake braids until golden brown and sound hollow when tapped, about 45 minutes. Remove to wire rack to cool. Sprinkle with powdered sugar before serving.

Makes 2 braided loaves

Chocolate Walnut Coffee Rings

CHOCOLATE WALNUT COFFEE RINGS

6½ to 7 cups all-purpose flour, divided
½ cup granulated sugar
1½ teaspoons salt
1½ teaspoons ground cinnamon
2 packages active dry yeast
1 cup butter or margarine
1 cup milk
½ cup water
2 eggs
2 egg yolks
2 cups (12-ounce package) NESTLÉ®
  Toll House® Semi-Sweet Chocolate
  Morsels
1 cup chopped walnuts
⅓ cup packed brown sugar
  Vegetable oil
  Glaze (recipe page 175)

In large mixer bowl, combine *2 cups* flour, granulated sugar, salt, cinnamon and yeast. In small saucepan over low heat, warm butter, milk and water until very warm (120° to 130°F). On low speed of electric mixer, gradually beat milk mixture into dry ingredients; beat for 2 minutes. Add eggs, egg yolks and *1 cup* flour. Beat on high speed for 2 minutes. Stir in about *2½ cups* flour to make a stiff dough. Cover; let stand for 20 minutes.

In medium bowl, combine morsels, walnuts and brown sugar. Sprinkle work surface with *½ cup* flour. Turn dough onto work surface; sprinkle with additional *½ cup* flour. Knead for 2 to 3 minutes; cut dough in half. On floured surface, roll out one dough half into 16×10-inch rectangle. Sprinkle one half morsel mixture to within ½ inch of edges. Starting at wide end, roll up jelly-roll fashion; pinch seam to seal. Place, seam side down, on large greased baking sheet, joining ends to from a circle. Cut outside edge at 1-inch intervals, two thirds of way through. Turn each slice on its side to overlap. Brush with oil; cover with plastic wrap.

Repeat with remaining dough and filling. Chill for 2 to 24 hours. Let coffee rings stand uncovered at room temperature for 10 minutes. Bake in preheated 375°F oven for 25 to 30 minutes or until golden. Remove from baking sheets; cool on wire racks. Drizzle with Glaze.

Makes 2 coffee rings

GLAZE: In small bowl, combine 1 cup powdered sugar, 5 to 6 teaspoons milk, ½ teaspoon vanilla extract and dash ground cinnamon; blend until smooth.

APPLE CINNAMON COFFEE RING

SWEET DOUGH
 1 package active dry yeast
 ¼ cup warm water (110° to 115°F)
 1 cup milk
 ⅓ cup sugar
 ⅓ cup butter or margarine
 ½ teaspoon salt
 2 eggs
 4½ to 5 cups all-purpose flour
APPLE CINNAMON FILLING
 3 tablespoons butter, divided
 1 cup thinly sliced Golden Delicious
  apples
 ½ cup chopped pecans
 ½ cup firmly packed brown sugar
 1 teaspoon ground cinnamon
 1 teaspoon grated orange peel
GLAZE
 ¾ cup confectioners' sugar
 1 tablespoon orange juice

1. To make Sweet Dough, in small bowl, dissolve yeast in water; set aside until foamy. Meanwhile, heat milk in small saucepan; add sugar, butter and salt. Cool to warm (110°F). In large bowl, combine milk mixture, yeast mixture, eggs and flour, stirring until soft dough forms. Turn out onto lightly floured surface and knead dough 5 minutes or until elastic. Wash, dry, and oil same large bowl; place dough in bowl, cover, and let rise in warm place about 1 hour.

2. Meanwhile, prepare Apple Cinnamon Filling. In skillet, melt 1 tablespoon butter; add apples and sauté until soft. Remove from heat and add pecans, brown sugar, cinnamon and orange peel, mixing well. Set aside.

3. When dough has risen, roll out on lightly floured surface to an 11×9-inch rectangle. Brush with remaining 2 tablespoons melted butter and top with apple mixture, leaving ½-inch border at edges. Fold dough in thirds lengthwise to make 11×3-inch roll. Cut crosswise into 12 equal pieces. Arrange pieces, cut side up, in greased 9-inch springform pan, forming a ring. Cover and let rise 40 minutes.

4. Heat oven to 325°F. Bake coffee ring 30 to 35 minutes or until golden. Cool on wire rack. Remove side of pan. To make Glaze, in small bowl, mix confectioners' sugar and orange juice. Drizzle Glaze over coffee ring and serve.

Makes 12 servings

Favorite recipe from **Washington Apple Commission**

CINNAMON TWISTS

ROLLS
- 1 package DUNCAN HINES® Cinnamon Muffin Mix, divided
- 2 cups all-purpose flour
- 1 package (¼ ounce) quick-rise yeast
- 1 egg, slightly beaten
- 1 cup hot water (120° to 130°F)
- 2 tablespoons butter or margarine, melted
- 1 egg white, slightly beaten
- 1 teaspoon water

TOPPING
- 1½ cups confectioners sugar
- 2½ tablespoons milk

1. Grease 2 large baking sheets.

2. **For rolls,** combine muffin mix, flour and yeast in large bowl; set aside.

3. Combine contents of swirl packet from Mix, egg, hot water and melted butter in medium bowl. Stir until thoroughly blended. Pour into flour mixture; stir until thoroughly blended. Invert onto well-floured surface; let rest for 10 minutes. Knead for 10 minutes or until smooth, adding flour as necessary. Divide dough in half. Cut and shape 24 small ropes from each half. Braid 3 ropes to form small twist and place on greased baking sheet. (Or, join ends of twists to form circles.) Combine egg white and 1 teaspoon water in small bowl. Brush each twist with egg white mixture and sprinkle with contents of topping packet from Mix. Allow twists to rise 1 hour or until doubled in size.

4. Preheat oven to 375°F.

5. Bake at 375°F for 17 to 20 minutes or until deep golden brown. Remove to cooling racks.

6. **For topping,** combine confectioners sugar and milk in small bowl. Stir until smooth. Drizzle over warm rolls. Serve warm or cool completely.   *Makes 16 rolls*

YEASTY CINNAMON LOAVES

- 1 package DUNCAN HINES® Cinnamon Muffin Mix, divided
- 5 cups all-purpose flour
- 2 packages (¼ ounce each) quick-rise yeast
- 2 eggs, slightly beaten
- ¼ cup plus 2 tablespoons butter or margarine, melted, divided
- 2½ cups hot water (120° to 130°F), divided
- Sifted confectioners sugar (optional)

1. Grease two 9×5×3-inch loaf pans.

2. Combine muffin mix, contents of crumb topping from Mix, flour and yeast in large bowl; set aside.

3. Combine contents of swirl packet from Mix, eggs, ¼ cup melted butter and ½ cup hot water in medium bowl. Stir well. Add remaining 2 cups hot water and stir until thoroughly blended. Add liquid ingredients to flour mixture; stir until thoroughly blended. Invert onto well-floured surface; let rest for 10 minutes. Knead for 10 minutes or until smooth, adding flour as necessary. Divide dough in half. Divide each half into 3 sections. Roll each section into 10-inch rope. Braid 3 ropes. Fold ends under. Place in greased pan. Repeat with remaining dough. Let rise 1 hour or until doubled in size.

4. Preheat oven to 375°F.

5. Bake at 375°F for 30 to 35 minutes or until bread is deep golden brown and sounds hollow when tapped. Brush with remaining 2 tablespoons melted butter. Cool in pans 5 minutes. Remove bread from pans to cooling racks. Cool completely. Sprinkle with confectioners sugar, if desired.
          Makes 2 loaves

NOTE: You may also braid loaves and bake free-form on greased baking sheets for 26 to 30 minutes.

Top to bottom: Yeasty Cinnamon Loaf, Cinnamon Twists

HONEY WHEAT BROWN–AND–SERVE ROLLS

2 packages active dry yeast
1 teaspoon sugar
¾ cup warm water (105° to 115°F)
2 cups whole wheat flour
2 to 3 cups all-purpose flour, divided
¼ cup vegetable shortening
¼ cup honey
1 teaspoon salt
1 egg

Sprinkle yeast and sugar over warm water in small bowl; stir until yeast is dissolved. Let stand 5 minutes until mixture is bubbly. Combine whole wheat flour and 2 cups all-purpose flour in medium bowl. Measure 1½ cups flour mixture into large bowl. Add yeast mixture, shortening, honey, salt and egg. Beat with electric mixer at low speed until smooth, scraping down side of bowl once. Increase mixer speed to medium; beat 2 minutes, scraping down side of bowl once. Reduce speed to low; beat in 1 cup flour mixture. Increase mixer speed to medium; beat 2 minutes, scraping down side of bowl once. Stir in remaining flour mixture and enough additional all-purpose flour (about ¼ cup) with wooden spoon to make a soft dough.

Turn dough out onto lightly floured surface. Knead 8 to 10 minutes or until smooth and elastic, adding more flour to prevent sticking, if necessary. Shape dough into a ball; place in large greased bowl. Turn once to grease surface. Cover with clean kitchen towel. Let rise in warm place (80° to 85°F) about 1½ hours or until doubled in bulk. Punch down dough. Turn dough onto lightly floured surface. Knead dough several turns to remove all large air bubbles; cover and let rest 15 minutes. Meanwhile, grease 24 muffin cups.

Honey Wheat Brown-and-Serve Rolls

Divide dough into 24 pieces. Cut each piece into thirds. Roll each third into a ball. Place 3 balls in each muffin cup. Cover and let rise in warm place about 30 minutes until doubled in bulk.

Preheat oven to 275°F.* Bake 20 to 25 minutes or until rolls are set but not brown. Immediately remove rolls from muffin cups and cool completely on wire racks. Store in resealable plastic food storage bags in refrigerator or freezer.

To bake rolls, thaw rolls if frozen. Preheat oven to 400°F. Grease large jelly-roll pan. Place rolls on pan. Bake 8 to 10 minutes or until golden brown.   *Makes 24 rolls*

*To bake rolls immediately, preheat oven to 375°F. Bake 15 to 20 minutes or until golden brown. Immediately remove from pan. Serve warm.

NUT–FILLED CHRISTMAS WREATH

    2 tablespoons warm water (105° to
        115°F)
    1 package active dry yeast
    3 tablespoons sugar, divided
    2 eggs
    ¼ cup butter or margarine, melted,
        cooled
    3 tablespoons milk
    ¾ teaspoon salt
    ½ teaspoon ground cardamom
    2½ to 3 cups all-purpose flour, divided
        Cherry-Nut Filling (recipe follows)
        Almond Icing (recipe follows)

In large bowl, combine water, yeast and 1 tablespoon sugar; stir to dissolve yeast. Let stand until bubbly, about 5 minutes. Add remaining 2 tablespoons sugar, eggs, butter, milk, salt and cardamom; mix well. Stir in 1½ cups flour until smooth. Stir in enough remaining flour to make dough easy to handle. Turn out onto lightly floured surface. Knead 10 minutes or until dough is smooth and elastic, adding as much remaining flour as needed to prevent sticking. Shape dough into ball. Place in large, lightly greased bowl; turn dough once to grease surface. Cover with waxed paper; let rise in warm place (85°F) until doubled, about 1 hour. Meanwhile, prepare Cherry-Nut Filling.

Punch dough down. Roll out dough on floured surface into 24×9-inch rectangle. Sprinkle Cherry-Nut Filling over dough to within 1 inch of edges. Roll up dough, jelly-roll style, beginning on 24-inch side; pinch seam to seal. Using sharp knife, cut roll in half lengthwise; turn each half cut side up. Carefully twist halves together, keeping cut sides up to expose filling. Place dough on greased cookie sheet; shape into a ring. Pinch ends together to seal. Cover; let stand in warm place until almost doubled, about 45 minutes. Bake in preheated 375°F oven 20 minutes or until evenly browned. Remove bread from cookie sheet to wire rack; cool slightly. Prepare Almond Icing; drizzle over warm bread. Serve warm or at room temperature.   *Makes 1 bread ring*

CHERRY–NUT FILLING: In medium bowl, combine ¾ cup chopped nuts (hazelnuts, almonds, walnuts or pecans), ¼ cup *each* all-purpose flour, chopped candied red cherries, chopped candied green cherries and softened butter or margarine, 2 tablespoons brown sugar and ½ teaspoon almond extract; mix well.

ALMOND ICING: In small bowl, combine 1 cup sifted powdered sugar, 1 to 2 tablespoons milk and ¼ teaspoon almond extract; blend until smooth.

APRICOT DATE COFFEE CAKES

1 cup warm milk (105° to 115°F)
2 packages active dry yeast
1 cup butter, softened
½ cup granulated sugar
2 eggs, slightly beaten
1 teaspoon salt
1 teaspoon ground cardamom
5 to 5½ cups all-purpose flour
1 cup prepared apricot filling
½ cup chopped dates
2 cups sifted powdered sugar
3 tablespoons light cream or half-and-half
½ teaspoon vanilla
¼ teaspoon almond extract

In large bowl, combine milk and yeast; stir to dissolve yeast. Stir in next 5 ingredients and 2 cups flour; beat until smooth. Stir in enough remaining flour to make dough easy to handle. Turn out onto lightly floured surface. Knead 10 minutes or until dough is smooth and elastic; add as much remaining flour as needed to prevent sticking. Shape into ball. Place in large, buttered bowl; turn once to coat surface. Cover with waxed paper; let rise in warm place until doubled, about 1½ hours. In small bowl, combine apricot filling and dates; set aside.

Punch dough down; divide into 3 pieces. Roll out one piece on lightly floured surface into 12×10-inch rectangle. Spoon ⅓ apricot mixture down center third of dough. Fold long sides over filling to center; pinch to seal. Pinch ends of rectangle to seal. Place dough, seam side down, on buttered baking sheet. With scissors, snip 1-inch-wide strips almost to center on both long sides of coffee cake. Turn each strip on its side. Repeat with remaining dough and filling. Cover; let rise in warm place until doubled, about 30 minutes. Bake in preheated 375°F oven about 18 minutes or until golden brown. Remove to wire racks to cool. In small bowl, combine remaining ingredients; mix well. Drizzle over cakes.   *Makes 3 coffee cakes*

Favorite recipe from **American Dairy Association**

WHOLESOME WHEAT BREAD

5½ to 6 cups whole wheat flour
2 packages active dry yeast
1 teaspoon salt
1 teaspoon ground cinnamon
1 cup KARO® Dark Corn Syrup
1 cup water
½ cup HELLMANN'S® or BEST FOODS® Real or Low Fat Mayonnaise Dressing
2 eggs

In large mixer bowl, combine 2 cups flour, yeast, salt and cinnamon. In medium saucepan, combine corn syrup, water and mayonnaise; heat mixture over medium heat, stirring occasionally, until very warm (120° to 130°F). Pour hot mixture into flour mixture; beat at medium speed 2 minutes. Reduce speed to low; beat in additional 2 cups flour and the eggs until well mixed. Beat at medium speed 2 minutes. By hand, stir in enough remaining flour to make dough easy to handle. Turn out onto lightly floured surface. Knead 10 minutes or until dough is smooth and elastic, adding as much remaining flour as needed to prevent sticking. Shape dough into a ball. Place in large, greased bowl; turn dough once to grease surface. Cover with towel; let rise in warm place (85°F) until doubled, about 1 hour.

Punch dough down; divide in half. Cover; let rest 10 minutes. Shape each half into 8×4-inch oval. Place on greased, floured large baking sheet. Cut 3 slashes, ¼ inch deep, in top of each loaf. Cover; let rise in warm place until doubled, about 1½ hours. Bake in preheated 350°F oven 30 to 40 minutes or until loaves are browned and sound hollow when tapped. Immediately remove from baking sheet to wire racks to cool.   *Makes 2 loaves*

Clockwise from top right: Apple-Cranberry Muffins (page 196), Wholesome Wheat Bread, Nut-Filled Christmas Wreath (page 179)

CLASSIC BRAN DINNER ROLLS

- 1 cup NABISCO® 100% Bran™
- 1 cup milk
- ½ cup plus 1 tablespoon water
- ½ cup margarine
- 4 to 4½ cups all-purpose flour
- 2 packages FLEISCHMANN'S® RapidRise Yeast
- ⅓ cup sugar
- ¾ teaspoon salt
- 3 eggs
  Poppy, caraway or sesame seed (optional)

Heat bran, milk, ½ cup water and margarine in medium saucepan until very warm (125° to 130°F); let stand 5 minutes.

Meanwhile, in large bowl combine 2 cups flour, undissolved yeast, sugar and salt. Stir warm bran mixture into dry ingredients. Mix in 2 eggs and enough remaining flour to make a soft dough. Grease top of dough. Cover tightly with plastic wrap; refrigerate 2 to 24 hours.

Punch dough down. On lightly floured surface, divide dough in half. Shape as desired (see Shaping Ideas, page 183).

Classic Bran Dinner Rolls

Place rolls about 2 inches apart on greased baking sheets. Cover; let rise in warm place (70° to 80°F) until doubled in size, 20 to 30 minutes.

Beat remaining egg with remaining 1 tablespoon water; brush on rolls. If desired, sprinkle with seed. Bake at 375°F for 15 minutes or until golden brown. Remove from sheets; cool on wire racks.

Makes 1 to 2 dozen rolls

SHAPING IDEAS

Crescents: Roll each half to 14-inch circle; cut each into 12 pie-shaped wedges. Roll up each wedge tightly from wide end. Curve ends slightly to form crescent.

Knots: Divide each half into 12 equal pieces; roll each into 9-inch rope. Loosely tie each rope once.

Coils: Divide each half into 12 equal pieces; roll each into 9-inch rope. Coil each rope, tucking end under coil.

Twists: Divide each half into 12 equal pieces; roll each into 12-inch rope. Fold each rope in half and twist together. Pinch ends to seal.

Sandwich Rolls: Divide each half into 6 equal pieces. Roll each piece into 5-inch round. Roll up tightly as for jelly roll. Pinch seam and ends to seal. Place on greased baking sheets, about 2 inches apart. After rising and brushing with egg wash, carefully make 3 diagonal slashes with sharp knife on each roll. If desired, sprinkle with seed. Bake as directed.

ONION DILL BREAD

  2 cups bread flour
  1 cup whole wheat flour
  ½ cup instant non-fat dry milk
  ½ teaspoon salt
  1 package active dry yeast
  2 tablespoons sugar
1¼ cups water (110° to 115°F)
  1 cup KELLOGG'S® ALL-BRAN® cereal
  2 egg whites
  ¼ cup reduced-calorie margarine
  ¼ cup chopped green onions
  ¼ cup chopped red onion
  1 tablespoon dill weed
  1 tablespoon skim milk
  2 tablespoons finely chopped onion

1. Stir together flours, dry milk and salt.

2. In large electric mixer bowl, combine yeast, sugar and water. Stir in Kellogg's All-Bran cereal; let stand 2 minutes or until cereal is soft.

3. Add egg whites, margarine and half the flour mixture. Beat at medium speed for 2 minutes or about 200 strokes by hand.

4. Mix in green onions, red onion and dill weed. Stir in remaining flour mixture by hand to form stiff, sticky dough. Cover lightly. Let rise in warm place until double in volume (about 1 hour).

5. Stir down dough to original volume. Spoon dough into 2-quart round casserole dish or 9¼×5¼×2¾-inch loaf pan coated with nonstick cooking spray. Brush surface with milk and sprinkle evenly with 2 tablespoons chopped onion.

6. Bake at 350°F about 55 minutes or until loaf is golden brown and sounds hollow when lightly tapped. Place on wire rack; cool.

Makes 1 loaf

SPICY MINCEMEAT BREAD

**6 tablespoons butter or margarine,
softened
1 cup packed light brown sugar
2 eggs
1 teaspoon vanilla
2½ cups all-purpose flour
1½ teaspoons baking soda
1 teaspoon ground cinnamon
¾ teaspoon baking powder
½ teaspoon ground nutmeg
¼ teaspoon salt
¾ cup sour cream
1 cup prepared mincemeat
¾ cup chopped pecans**

Preheat oven to 350°F. Grease 9×5-inch
loaf pan.*

Beat butter and brown sugar in large bowl with
electric mixer on medium speed until light and
fluffy. Beat in eggs and vanilla until blended.
Combine flour, baking soda, cinnamon, baking
powder, nutmeg and salt. Add flour mixture to
butter mixture on low speed alternately with
sour cream, beginning and ending with flour
mixture. Mix well after each addition. Stir in
mincemeat and pecans on low speed until
blended. Spoon into prepared pan.

Bake 55 to 60 minutes or until wooden
toothpick inserted in center comes out clean.
Cool in pan 15 minutes. Remove from pan and
cool completely on wire rack. Store tightly
wrapped in plastic wrap at room temperature.
Makes 1 loaf

*Bread may also be baked in four 5½×3-inch
greased mini-loaf pans. Prepare batter as
directed. Bake at 350°F for 45 to 50 minutes or
until wooden toothpick inserted in centers
comes out clean. Proceed as directed.

LEMON CRANBERRY LOAVES

**1¼ cups finely chopped fresh cranberries
½ cup finely chopped walnuts
¼ cup granulated sugar
1 package DUNCAN HINES® Moist
Deluxe Lemon Supreme Cake Mix
1 package (3 ounces) cream cheese,
softened
¾ cup milk
4 eggs
Confectioners sugar**

Preheat oven to 350°F. Grease and flour two
8½×4½-inch loaf pans.

Stir together cranberries, walnuts and
granulated sugar in large bowl; set aside.

Combine cake mix, cream cheese and milk in
large bowl. Beat at medium speed with electric
mixer for 2 minutes. Add eggs, 1 at a time,
beating for an additional 2 minutes. Fold in
cranberry mixture. Pour into pans. Bake at
350°F for 45 to 50 minutes or until toothpick
inserted in centers comes out clean. Cool in
pans 15 minutes. Loosen loaves from pans.
Invert onto cooling rack. Turn right side up.
Cool completely. Dust with confectioners sugar.
Makes 24 slices

Lemon Cranberry Loaf

WALNUT CHEDDAR APPLE BREAD

½ cup butter or margarine, softened
1 cup packed light brown sugar
2 eggs
1 teaspoon vanilla
2 cups all-purpose flour
2 teaspoons baking powder
1 teaspoon baking soda
¼ teaspoon salt
1 cup sour cream
¼ cup milk
1 cup (4 ounces) shredded Cheddar
   cheese
1 cup diced dried apple
½ cup coarsely chopped walnuts

Preheat oven to 350°F. Grease 9×5-inch loaf pan.

Beat butter and sugar in large bowl with electric mixer on medium speed until light and fluffy. Beat in eggs and vanilla until blended. Combine flour, baking powder, baking soda and salt in small bowl. Add flour mixture to butter mixture on low speed alternately with sour cream and milk, beginning and ending with flour mixture. Mix well after each addition. Stir in cheese, apple and walnuts on low speed until blended. Spoon into prepared pan.

Bake 50 to 55 minutes or until wooden toothpick inserted in center comes out clean. Cool in pan 15 minutes. Remove from pan and cool completely on wire rack. Store tightly wrapped in plastic wrap at room temperature.

Makes 1 loaf

Walnut Cheddar Apple Bread

PIÑA COLADA BREAD

2½ cups flour
½ cup sugar
2 teaspoons baking powder
½ teaspoon baking soda
½ teaspoon salt
2 eggs
½ cup KARO® Light Corn Syrup
⅓ cup MAZOLA® Corn Oil
¼ cup rum
1 can (8 ounces) crushed pineapple in unsweetened juice, undrained
1 cup flaked coconut

Preheat oven to 350°F. Grease and flour 9×5×3-inch loaf pan.

In medium bowl, combine flour, sugar, baking powder, baking soda and salt. In large bowl, with mixer at medium speed, beat eggs, corn syrup, corn oil and rum until blended. Gradually stir in flour mixture just until moistened. Stir in pineapple with juice and coconut. Pour into prepared pan.

Bake 60 to 65 minutes or until toothpick inserted in center comes out clean. Cool in pan 10 minutes. Remove from pan; cool on wire rack. *Makes 1 loaf*

PEANUT BUTTER BREAD

2 cups flour
½ cup sugar
2 teaspoons baking powder
½ teaspoon baking soda
½ teaspoon salt
1 cup SKIPPY SUPER CHUNK® or Creamy Peanut Butter
½ cup KARO® Light or Dark Corn Syrup
2 eggs
1 cup milk

Preheat oven to 350°F. Grease and flour 9×5×3-inch loaf pan.

In medium bowl, combine flour, sugar, baking powder, baking soda and salt. In large bowl, with mixer at medium speed, beat peanut butter and corn syrup until smooth. Beat in eggs, 1 at a time. Gradually beat in milk. Stir in flour mixture just until moistened. Pour into prepared pan.

Bake 50 to 55 minutes or until wooden toothpick inserted in center comes out clean. Cool in pan 10 minutes. Remove from pan; cool on wire rack. *Makes 1 loaf*

BANANA NUT BREAD

2 extra-ripe, large DOLE® Bananas, peeled and cut into chunks
⅓ cup butter
⅔ cup sugar
2 eggs
2 cups all-purpose flour
2 teaspoons baking powder
½ teaspoon baking soda
½ cup buttermilk
¾ cup chopped nuts

• Purée bananas in blender (1¼ cups). Cream butter and sugar until light and fluffy. Beat in bananas and eggs. Combine flour, baking powder and baking soda. Add dry ingredients to banana mixture alternately in thirds with buttermilk, blending well after each addition. Stir in nuts.

• Pour into greased 9×5-inch loaf pan. Bake in 350°F oven 50 to 60 minutes or until wooden toothpick inserted in center comes out clean. Cool in pan on wire rack 10 minutes. Remove from pan and cool completely. *Makes 1 loaf*

Cherry Eggnog Quick Bread

CHERRY EGGNOG QUICK BREAD

2½ cups all-purpose flour
¾ cup sugar
1 tablespoon baking powder
½ teaspoon ground nutmeg
1¼ cups prepared dairy eggnog
6 tablespoons butter or margarine, melted and cooled
2 eggs, slightly beaten
1 teaspoon vanilla
½ cup chopped pecans
½ cup chopped candied red cherries

Preheat oven to 350°F. Grease three 5½×3-inch mini-loaf pans.

Combine flour, sugar, baking powder and nutmeg in large bowl. Stir eggnog, melted butter, eggs and vanilla in medium bowl until well blended. Add eggnog mixture to flour mixture. Mix just until all ingredients are moistened. Stir in pecans and cherries. Spoon into prepared pans.

Bake 35 to 40 minutes or until wooden toothpick inserted in centers comes out clean. Cool in pans 15 minutes. Remove from pans and cool completely on wire rack. Store tightly wrapped in plastic wrap at room temperature.
Makes 3 mini loaves

GOLDEN APPLE BOSTON BROWN BREAD

¼ cup butter or margarine, softened
⅓ cup honey
⅓ cup light molasses
1 cup whole wheat flour
1 cup rye flour
1 cup yellow cornmeal
2 teaspoons baking soda
½ teaspoon salt
2 cups buttermilk
2 cups (2 medium) coarsely chopped
    Golden Delicious apples

In large bowl, cream butter, honey and molasses. In medium bowl, combine flours, cornmeal, baking soda and salt. Add flour mixture to butter mixture alternately with buttermilk, mixing well after each addition. Stir in apples. Pour batter into 2 greased 8½×4½×2½-inch loaf pans. Bake in preheated 350°F oven 1 hour or until wooden pick inserted near centers comes out clean. Let cool in pans on wire racks 10 minutes. Loosen edges; remove from pans. Cool slightly on wire racks; serve warm. *Makes 2 loaves*

VARIATION: To steam brown bread, divide batter evenly between 2 greased 1-pound coffee cans, filling cans about three-fourths full. Cover tops of cans with aluminum foil; tie foil to cans with string. Place rack in large kettle; add boiling water to depth of 1 inch. Place cans on rack; cover kettle. Steam over low heat 3 hours or until wooden pick inserted near centers comes out clean. If necessary, add more boiling water to kettle during steaming. Cool as above.

*Favorite recipe from **Washington Apple Commission***

CHOCOLATE POPOVERS

¾ cup plus 2 tablespoons all-purpose
    flour
¼ cup granulated sugar
2 tablespoons unsweetened cocoa
    powder
¼ teaspoon salt
4 eggs
1 cup milk
2 tablespoons butter or margarine,
    melted
½ teaspoon vanilla
    Powdered sugar

Position rack in lower third of oven. Preheat oven to 375°F. Grease 6-cup popover pan or 6 (6-ounce) custard cups. Set custard cups in jelly-roll pan. Sift flour, granulated sugar, cocoa and salt into medium bowl; set aside. Beat eggs in large bowl with electric mixer at low speed 1 minute. Beat in milk, butter and vanilla. Beat in flour mixture until smooth. Pour batter into prepared pan. Bake 50 minutes. Immediately remove popovers to wire rack. Generously sprinkle powdered sugar over popovers. Serve immediately.
Makes 6 popovers

Chocolate Popovers

TEDDY BEAR GIFT BREAD

Teddy bear baking pan
1½ cups all-purpose flour
¾ cup granulated sugar
½ cup whole wheat flour
½ cup packed brown sugar
1 tablespoon baking powder
1 teaspoon pumpkin pie spice
½ teaspoon salt
½ teaspoon ground cinnamon
¼ teaspoon ground ginger
¼ teaspoon baking soda
1 egg, beaten
1 cup lowfat milk
4½ teaspoons vegetable oil
Candy for decorating

Preheat oven to 350°F. Generously grease baking pan. In food processor or large bowl, combine all dry ingredients. Add egg, milk and oil. Mix just until blended. Spoon batter into prepared pan. Bake 20 to 25 minutes or until toothpick inserted in center comes out clean. Cool completely in pan. Remove from pan onto serving platter.

Use candy to decorate, such as jelly beans for eyes and buttons, nonpareil for nose, red shoestring licorice for mouth and black shoestring licorice for bow tie.

Makes 1 bread loaf

*Favorite recipe from **The Sugar Association, Inc.***

ORANGE MARMALADE BREAD

3 cups all-purpose flour
4 teaspoons baking powder
1 teaspoon salt
½ cup chopped walnuts
2 eggs, lightly beaten
¾ cup SMUCKER'S® Simply Fruit Orange Marmalade
¾ cup milk
¼ cup honey
2 tablespoons vegetable oil

Preheat oven to 350°F. Grease 9×5×3-inch loaf pan. Into large bowl, sift together flour, baking powder and salt. Stir in nuts. In small bowl, combine eggs, marmalade, milk, honey and oil; blend well. Add to flour mixture; stir only until flour is well moistened (batter will be lumpy). Turn batter into prepared pan. Bake 65 to 70 minutes or until lightly browned and wooden toothpick inserted in center comes out clean. Cool in pan on wire rack 10 minutes. Remove from pan; cool completely on rack.

Makes 1 loaf

Orange Marmalade Bread

SWEET POTATO PECAN MUFFINS

MAZOLA® No Stick cooking spray
1¾ cups flour
⅓ cup sugar
2 teaspoons baking powder
1 teaspoon ground cinnamon
½ teaspoon salt
⅛ teaspoon ground nutmeg
¾ cup mashed cooked sweet potatoes
¾ cup KARO® Dark Corn Syrup
⅓ cup MAZOLA® Corn Oil
2 eggs
1 teaspoon vanilla
1 cup chopped pecans

Preheat oven to 400°F. Spray 12 (2½-inch) muffin pan cups with cooking spray.

In medium bowl, combine flour, sugar, baking powder, cinnamon, salt and nutmeg. In large bowl, with mixer at medium speed, beat sweet potatoes, corn syrup, corn oil, eggs and vanilla until blended. Stir in flour mixture until well blended. Stir in pecans. Spoon into prepared muffin pan cups.

Bake 20 minutes or until lightly browned and firm to the touch. Cool in pan on wire rack 5 minutes; remove from pan.

Makes 12 muffins

Cranberry Pecan Muffins

CRANBERRY PECAN MUFFINS

1½ cups fresh or frozen cranberries
¼ cup light corn syrup
1 package DUNCAN HINES® Cinnamon Muffin Mix
1 egg
¾ cup water or milk
½ cup chopped pecans

1. Preheat oven to 400°F. Place 14 (2½-inch) paper liners in muffin cups. Place cranberries and corn syrup in heavy saucepan. Cook on medium heat, stirring occasionally, until cranberries pop and mixture is slightly thickened. Drain cranberries in strainer; set aside.

2. Empty muffin mix into medium bowl. Break up any lumps. Add egg and water. Stir until moistened, about 50 strokes. Stir in cranberries and pecans. Knead swirl packet from Mix for 10 seconds before opening. Cut off 1 end of swirl packet. Squeeze contents over top of batter. Swirl into batter with knife or spatula. *Do not completely mix in.* Spoon batter into muffin cups (see Tip). Sprinkle with contents of topping packet from Mix. Bake at 400°F for 18 to 22 minutes or until toothpick inserted in centers comes out clean. Cool in pans 5 to 10 minutes. Serve warm or cool completely.

Makes 14 muffins

TIP: Fill an equal number of muffin cups in each muffin pan with batter. For more even baking, fill empty muffin cups with ½ inch of water.

PUMPKIN APPLE STREUSEL MUFFINS

   2½ **cups all-purpose flour**
     2 **cups granulated sugar**
     1 **tablespoon pumpkin pie spice**
     1 **teaspoon baking soda**
   ½ **teaspoon salt**
     2 **eggs, lightly beaten**
     1 **cup LIBBY'S® Solid Pack Pumpkin**
   ½ **cup vegetable oil**
     2 **cups peeled, finely chopped apples**
       Streusel Topping (recipe follows)

In large bowl, combine flour, sugar, pumpkin pie spice, baking soda and salt. In medium bowl, combine eggs, pumpkin and oil. Add liquid ingredients to dry ingredients; stir just until moistened. Stir in apples. Spoon batter into greased or paper-lined muffin cups, filling ¾ full. Sprinkle Streusel Topping over batter. Bake in preheated 350°F. oven for 35 to 40 minutes or until wooden pick inserted in centers comes out clean. *Makes 18 muffins*

STREUSEL TOPPING: In small bowl, combine 2 tablespoons all-purpose flour, ¼ cup sugar and ½ teaspoon ground cinnamon. Cut in 4 teaspoons butter until mixture is crumbly.

VARIATION: For 6 giant muffins, follow directions above, increasing baking time to 40 to 45 minutes.

ALMOND CITRUS MUFFINS

   ½ **cup whole natural almonds**
  1¼ **cups all-purpose flour**
    2 **teaspoons baking powder**
   ¼ **teaspoon salt**
    1 **cup shreds of wheat bran cereal**
   ¼ **cup packed brown sugar**
   ¾ **cup milk**
   ¼ **cup orange juice**
    1 **teaspoon grated orange peel**
    1 **egg**
   ¼ **cup vegetable or almond oil**

Spread almonds in single layer on baking sheet. Bake at 350°F, 12 to 15 minutes, stirring occasionally, until lightly toasted. Cool and chop. *Increase oven temperature to 400°F.* In large bowl, combine flour, baking powder and salt. In medium bowl, combine cereal, sugar, milk, orange juice and peel. Let stand 2 minutes or until cereal is softened. Add egg and oil; beat well. Stir in almonds. Add liquid mixture to flour mixture; stir just until moistened. Batter will be lumpy; do not overmix. Spoon batter evenly into 12 greased 2½-inch muffin cups. Bake in preheated 400°F oven 20 minutes or until lightly browned. Remove to wire rack to cool.

Makes 1 dozen muffins

*Favorite recipe from **Almond Board of California***

CRANBERRY ORANGE NUT MUFFINS

    MAZOLA® No Stick cooking spray
1½ cups flour
 ½ cup sugar
 2 teaspoons baking powder
 ½ teaspoon salt
 2 eggs
 ½ cup KARO® Light Corn Syrup
 ½ cup orange juice
 ¼ cup MAZOLA® Corn Oil
 1 teaspoon grated orange peel
 1 cup fresh or frozen cranberries,
    chopped
 ½ cup chopped walnuts

Preheat oven to 400°F. Spray 12 (2½-inch) muffin pan cups with cooking spray.

In medium bowl, combine flour, sugar, baking powder and salt. In large bowl, combine eggs, corn syrup, orange juice, corn oil and orange peel. Stir in flour mixture until well blended. Stir in cranberries and walnuts. Spoon into prepared muffin pan cups.

Bake 18 to 20 minutes or until lightly browned and firm to the touch. Cool in pan on wire rack 5 minutes; remove from pan.

Makes 12 muffins

BANANA SCOTCH MUFFINS

 1 ripe, large DOLE® Banana, peeled and
    cut into chunks
 1 egg, beaten
 ½ cup sugar
 ¼ cup milk
 ¼ cup vegetable oil
 1 teaspoon vanilla
 1 cup all-purpose flour
 1 cup quick-cooking rolled oats
 1 teaspoon baking powder
 ½ teaspoon baking soda
 ½ teaspoon salt
 ½ cup butterscotch chips

• Preheat oven to 400°F. Purée banana in blender (⅔ cup). In medium bowl, combine puréed banana, egg, sugar, milk, oil and vanilla.

• In large bowl, combine flour, oats, baking powder, baking soda and salt. Stir banana mixture and butterscotch chips into dry ingredients just until blended.

• Spoon into well-greased 2½-inch muffin cups. Bake 12 to 15 minutes. Remove from pan.

Makes 12 muffins

CARROT–RAISIN BRAN MUFFINS

    MAZOLA® No Stick cooking spray
 2 cups bran flakes cereal with raisins
 ⅔ cup buttermilk
 ½ cup KARO® Dark Corn Syrup
 1 cup flour
 2 teaspoons baking soda
 1 teaspoon ground cinnamon
 ¼ teaspoon salt
 1 egg, slightly beaten
 ¼ cup sugar
 ¼ cup MAZOLA® Corn Oil
 1 cup shredded carrots

Preheat oven to 400°F. Spray 12 (2½-inch) muffin pan cups with cooking spray.

In large bowl, mix cereal, buttermilk and corn syrup; let stand 5 minutes. In medium bowl, combine flour, baking soda, cinnamon and salt; set aside. Add egg, sugar and corn oil to cereal mixture; mix until blended. Stir in flour mixture until well blended. Stir in carrots. Spoon into prepared muffin pan cups.

Bake 20 minutes or until lightly browned and firm to the touch. Cool in pan on wire rack 5 minutes; remove from pan.

Makes 12 muffins

Clockwise from top: Cranberry Orange Nut Muffins, Carrot-Raisin Bran Muffins, Sweet Potato Pecan Muffins (page 192)

PINEAPPLE CITRUS MUFFINS

⅓ cup honey
¼ cup butter or margarine, softened
1 egg
1 can (8 ounces) DOLE® Crushed
　　Pineapple
1 tablespoon grated orange peel
1 cup all-purpose flour
1 cup whole wheat flour
1½ teaspoons baking powder
¼ teaspoon salt
¼ teaspoon ground nutmeg
1 cup DOLE® Chopped Dates
½ cup chopped walnuts (optional)

• Preheat oven to 375°F. In large mixer bowl, beat together honey and butter 1 minute. Beat in egg, then undrained pineapple and orange peel. In medium bowl, combine remaining ingredients; stir into pineapple mixture until just blended.

Pineapple Citrus Muffins

• Spoon batter into 12 greased muffin cups. Bake in preheated oven 25 minutes or until wooden pick inserted in centers comes out clean. Cool slightly in pan before turning out onto wire rack. Serve warm.

Makes 12 muffins

APPLE–CRANBERRY MUFFINS

1¾ cups plus 2 tablespoons all-purpose
　　flour, divided
½ cup sugar, divided
1½ teaspoons baking powder
½ teaspoon baking soda
½ teaspoon salt
1 egg
¾ cup milk
¾ cup sweetened applesauce
¼ cup butter or margarine, melted
1 cup fresh cranberries, coarsely
　　chopped
½ teaspoon ground cinnamon

In medium bowl, combine 1¾ cups flour, ¼ cup sugar, baking powder, baking soda and salt. In small bowl, combine egg, milk, applesauce and butter; mix well. Add egg mixture to flour mixture; stir just until moistened. Batter will be lumpy; *do not overmix*. In small bowl, toss cranberries with remaining 2 tablespoons flour; fold into batter. Spoon batter evenly into 12 greased 2¾-inch muffin cups. In measuring cup, combine remaining ¼ cup sugar and cinnamon. Sprinkle over tops of muffins. Bake in preheated 400°F oven 20 to 25 minutes or until golden brown. Remove to wire rack to cool.　　　　　*Makes 1 dozen muffins*

*Favorite recipe from **New York Apple Association, Inc.***

Streusel Raspberry Muffins

STREUSEL RASPBERRY MUFFINS

    Pecan Streusel Topping (recipe follows)
1½ cups all-purpose flour
  ½ cup sugar
  2 teaspoons baking powder
  ½ cup milk
  ½ cup butter or margarine, melted and
      cooled
  1 egg, beaten
  1 cup fresh or individually frozen whole
      unsugared raspberries

Preheat oven to 375°F. Grease or paper-line 12 (2½-inch) muffin cups. Prepare Pecan Streusel Topping; set aside.

In large bowl, combine flour, sugar and baking powder. In small bowl, combine milk, butter and egg until blended. Stir into flour mixture just until moistened. Spoon half of batter into muffin cups. Divide raspberries among cups, then top with remaining batter. Sprinkle Pecan Streusel Topping over tops. Bake 25 to 30 minutes or until golden and wooden toothpick inserted in centers comes out clean. Remove from pan. *Makes 12 muffins*

PECAN STREUSEL TOPPING: In small bowl, combine ¼ cup *each* chopped pecans, packed brown sugar and all-purpose flour. Stir in 2 tablespoons melted butter or margarine until mixture resembles moist crumbs.

PEACHY CINNAMON COFFEECAKE

1 can (8¼ ounces) juice-pack sliced yellow cling peaches
1 package DUNCAN HINES® Cinnamon Muffin Mix
1 egg

1. Preheat oven to 400°F. Grease 8-inch square or 9-inch round baking pan.

2. Drain peaches, reserving juice. Add water to reserved juice to equal ¾ cup liquid. Chop peaches.

3. Combine muffin mix, egg and ¾ cup peach liquid in medium bowl; fold in peaches. Pour batter into pan. Knead swirl packet 10 seconds before opening. Squeeze contents on top of batter and swirl with knife. Sprinkle topping over batter. Bake at 400°F for 28 to 33 minutes for 8-inch pan (or 20 to 25 minutes for 9-inch pan) or until golden. Serve warm.

Makes 9 servings

Peachy Cinnamon Coffeecake

CHOCOLATE STREUSEL COFFEE CAKE

Chocolate Streusel (recipe follows)
½ cup butter or margarine, softened
1 cup sugar
3 eggs
1 cup dairy sour cream
1 teaspoon vanilla extract
2 cups all-purpose flour
1 teaspoon baking powder
1 teaspoon baking soda
¼ teaspoon salt

Prepare Chocolate Streusel; set aside. Cream butter and sugar in large mixer bowl until light and fluffy. Add eggs; blend well on low speed. Stir in sour cream and vanilla. Combine flour, baking powder, baking soda and salt; add to batter. Blend well.

Sprinkle 1 cup Chocolate Streusel into greased and floured 12-cup Bundt pan. Spread one third of the batter (about 1⅓ cups) in pan; sprinkle with half the remaining streusel (about 1 cup). Repeat layers, ending with batter on top. Bake at 350°F for 50 to 55 minutes or until cake tester comes out clean. Cool 10 minutes; invert onto serving plate. Cool completely.

Makes 12 to 16 servings

CHOCOLATE STREUSEL
¾ cup packed light brown sugar
¼ cup all-purpose flour
¼ cup butter or margarine, softened
¾ cup chopped nuts
¾ cup HERSHEY'S MINI CHIPS Semi-Sweet Chocolate

Combine brown sugar, flour and butter in medium bowl until crumbly. Stir in nuts and small chocolate chips.

CRANBERRY APPLE STREUSEL COFFEE CAKE

CAKE
> 2 cups any AUNT JEMIMA® Pancake & Waffle Mix (see Note)
> ½ cup granulated sugar
> 1 (8-ounce) carton sour cream
> ¾ cup milk
> 1 egg, beaten
> ¾ cup chopped cranberries
> ¾ cup coarsely chopped, peeled apple

STREUSEL
> ½ cup chopped nuts
> ¼ cup firmly packed brown sugar
> ½ teaspoon ground cinnamon
> 2 tablespoons margarine, melted

GLAZE
> ¾ cup powdered sugar
> 1 tablespoon milk
> ½ teaspoon vanilla

Heat oven to 350°F. Grease 13×9-inch baking pan. Combine pancake mix and granulated sugar. Add sour cream, milk and egg; mix just until dry ingredients are moistened. Spread into pan; top with cranberries and apple. Combine Streusel ingredients; mix until crumbly. Sprinkle over fruit. Bake 30 to 35 minutes or until wooden pick inserted in center comes out clean. Combine Glaze ingredients; drizzle over warm cake. Serve warm. To reheat cooled cake, microwave each serving at HIGH (100% power) about 20 seconds.   *Makes 12 servings*

NOTE: AUNT JEMIMA® Buttermilk Complete, Complete, Original, Whole Wheat or Lite Buttermilk Complete mixes may be used.

NUTTY COCONUT COFFEECAKE

TOPPING
> 2 tablespoons butter, melted
> ⅔ cup flaked coconut
> ⅓ cup packed dark brown sugar
> ⅓ cup coarsely chopped nuts (macadamia nuts, walnuts, almonds or pecans)
> 2 tablespoons *undiluted* CARNATION® Evaporated Milk

BATTER
> 2 cups all-purpose flour
> ½ cup packed brown sugar
> ¼ cup granulated sugar
> 2 teaspoons baking powder
> ½ teaspoon salt
> ¼ cup butter
> 1 cup *undiluted* CARNATION® Evaporated Milk
> 1 egg
> 1 teaspoon vanilla extract

FOR TOPPING:
POUR butter into greased 9-inch round cake pan. Combine coconut, ⅓ cup brown sugar, nuts and 2 tablespoons evaporated milk in small bowl. Sprinkle over butter.

FOR BATTER:
COMBINE flour, ½ cup brown sugar, granulated sugar, baking powder and salt in bowl. Cut in butter. Beat 1 cup evaporated milk, egg and vanilla together in small bowl; stir into flour mixture just until blended. Pour over nut mixture.

BAKE in preheated 350°F. oven for 30 to 35 minutes or until wooden pick inserted in center comes out clean. Cool for 10 minutes on wire rack. Invert onto serving plate.
Makes 1 (9-inch) round cake

BANANA SPICE COFFEE CAKE

     2 extra-ripe, medium DOLE® Bananas,
       peeled and cut into chunks
 ½ cup packed brown sugar
  1 teaspoon ground cinnamon
 ¼ teaspoon ground nutmeg
 ½ cup margarine, divided
 ¾ cup chopped walnuts
  1 cup all-purpose flour
  1 cup whole wheat flour
  1 teaspoon baking powder
  1 teaspoon baking soda
 ½ teaspoon salt
 ½ cup granulated sugar
  3 eggs
  1 teaspoon vanilla
  1 cup DOLE® Raisins

• In food processor or blender, purée bananas (1 cup purée). In small bowl, combine brown sugar, cinnamon and nutmeg. Cut in ¼ cup margarine until mixture resembles coarse crumbs. Stir in walnuts; set aside. In small bowl, combine flours, baking powder, baking soda and salt. In large bowl, beat remaining ¼ cup margarine and granulated sugar until light and fluffy. Beat in eggs and vanilla. Add flour mixture to egg mixture alternately with bananas, ending with flour mixture and beating well after each addition. Stir in raisins.

• Spread half the batter in greased and floured 10-inch tube pan. Sprinkle with half the brown sugar mixture. Repeat layers. Bake in preheated 350°F oven 45 to 50 minutes or until wooden pick inserted in center of cake comes out clean. Let cool in pan on wire rack 10 minutes. Loosen edge; remove from pan. Cool completely on wire rack.

Makes 1 (10-inch) coffee cake

CINNAMON–DATE SCONES

 ¼ cup sugar, divided
 ¼ teaspoon ground cinnamon
  2 cups all-purpose flour
2½ teaspoons baking powder
 ½ teaspoon salt
  5 tablespoons cold butter or margarine
 ½ cup chopped pitted dates
  2 eggs
 ⅓ cup half-and-half or milk

Preheat oven to 425°F. Combine 2 tablespoons sugar and cinnamon in small bowl; set aside. Combine flour, baking powder, salt and remaining 2 tablespoons sugar in medium bowl. Cut in butter with pastry blender or 2 knives until mixture resembles coarse crumbs. Stir in dates.

Beat eggs in another small bowl with fork. Add half-and-half; beat until well combined. Measure 1 tablespoon mixture into small cup; set aside. Stir remaining egg mixture into flour mixture. Stir until mixture forms soft dough that clings together and forms a ball.

Turn out dough onto well-floured surface. Knead dough gently 10 to 12 times. Roll out dough into 9×6-inch rectangle. Cut rectangle into 6 (3-inch) squares. Cut each square diagonally in half. Place triangles 2 inches apart on *ungreased* baking sheets. Brush with reserved egg mixture; sprinkle with reserved sugar mixture. Bake 10 to 12 minutes or until golden brown. Immediately remove from baking sheets; cool on wire racks 10 minutes. Serve warm.

Makes 12 scones

Cinnamon-Date Scones

Mini Morsel Tea Biscuits

MINI MORSEL TEA BISCUITS

4 cups all-purpose flour
⅓ cup sugar
2 tablespoons baking powder
½ teaspoon salt
½ cup cold butter, cut into small pieces
1 cup (6 ounces) NESTLÉ® Toll House®
  Semi-Sweet Chocolate Mini Morsels
4 eggs, divided
1 cup *undiluted* CARNATION®
  Evaporated Milk
1½ teaspoons vanilla extract
2 tablespoons milk

COMBINE flour, sugar, baking powder and salt in large bowl. With pastry blender or two knives, cut in butter until mixture resembles coarse crumbs. Stir in morsels.

BEAT 3 eggs, evaporated milk and vanilla in medium bowl. Add to flour mixture all at once; stir with fork to form a soft dough. Turn dough onto well-floured surface. Knead 6 to 8 times. Pat dough to ¾-inch thickness. Cut with floured 2½-inch biscuit cutter. Transfer to lightly greased baking sheets. Beat remaining egg and milk in small bowl; brush over biscuits.

BAKE in preheated 400°F. oven for 14 to 16 minutes or until golden brown. Remove to wire racks; serve warm.

Makes about 1½ dozen biscuits

FRENCH BREAKFAST PUFFS

1½ **cups unsifted all-purpose flour**
½ **cup confectioners sugar**
1 **teaspoon baking powder**
1 **teaspoon salt**
¾ **teaspoon ground nutmeg**
½ **cup milk**
½ **cup water**
¼ **cup CRISCO® Oil**
1½ **teaspoons grated lemon peel**
3 **eggs**
CRISCO® Oil for frying
Confectioners sugar

Mix flour, ½ cup confectioners sugar, baking powder, salt and nutmeg in small mixing bowl. Set aside. Combine milk, water, Crisco® oil and lemon peel in medium saucepan. Heat to rolling boil over medium-high heat. Add flour mixture all at once. Beat with wooden spoon until mixture pulls away from sides of pan into a ball. Remove from heat; cool slightly. Add eggs, one at a time, beating after each addition.

Heat 2 to 3 inches Crisco® oil in deep-fryer or large saucepan to 350°F.

Drop dough by tablespoonfuls into hot Crisco® oil. Fry 3 or 4 puffs at a time, 4 to 6 minutes, or until golden brown, turning over several times. Drain on paper towels. Sprinkle top of each puff with confectioners sugar.

Makes 32 puffs

FRUITED SCONES

2 **cups unsifted flour**
¼ **cup sugar**
1 **tablespoon baking powder**
½ **teaspoon salt**
½ **cup cold margarine or butter**
1 **egg**
⅓ **cup BORDEN® or MEADOW GOLD® Milk**
1 **(9-ounce) package NONE SUCH® Condensed Mincemeat, crumbled**
1 **egg, beaten (optional)**

Preheat oven to 400°F. In large bowl, combine flour, sugar, baking powder and salt; cut in margarine until crumbly. Stir in *1 egg,* milk and mincemeat; mix well. On floured surface, knead dough lightly 10 times. Roll out to ½-inch thickness; cut into 2-inch circles. Place 1 inch apart on ungreased baking sheets. For a more golden color, brush with beaten egg, if desired. Bake 10 to 12 minutes or until golden. Serve warm. *Makes about 1½ dozen scones*

French Breakfast Puffs

MAPLE FRENCH TOAST

¼ cup CARY'S®, MAPLE ORCHARDS® or
   MACDONALD'S™ Pure Maple Syrup
¼ cup BORDEN® or MEADOW GOLD®
   Milk
 2 eggs, beaten
12 (¾-inch) slices French or Italian bread
   Butter
   Maple Butter (recipe follows)

In medium bowl, combine syrup, milk and eggs.
Dip bread into egg mixture. In large greased
skillet, cook bread in butter until golden brown
on both sides. Serve warm with Maple Butter
and additional syrup.   *Makes 4 to 6 servings*

MAPLE BUTTER: In small mixer bowl, beat
½ cup softened unsalted butter and 2
tablespoons CARY'S®, MAPLE ORCHARDS®
or MACDONALD'S™ Pure Maple Syrup until
light and fluffy. Makes about ⅔ cup.

ONION–HERB BAKED BREAD

1 envelope LIPTON® Recipe Secrets®
   Golden Onion Soup Mix
1 medium clove garlic, finely chopped
1 teaspoon dried basil leaves
1 teaspoon dried oregano leaves
⅛ teaspoon pepper
½ cup butter or margarine, softened
1 loaf Italian or French bread (about
   16 inches long), halved lengthwise

Preheat oven to 375°F. In small bowl,
thoroughly blend all ingredients except bread;
generously spread on bread halves. Arrange
bread, cut side up, on baking sheet. Bake 15
minutes or until golden. Serve warm.
                                    Makes 1 loaf

NOTE: Store any remaining spread, covered,
in refrigerator for future use.

Maple French Toast with Maple Butter

QUICKY STICKY BUNS

3 tablespoons packed brown sugar, divided
¼ cup KARO® Light or Dark Corn Syrup
¼ cup coarsely chopped pecans
2 tablespoons MAZOLA® Margarine, softened, divided
1 can (8 ounces) refrigerated crescent rolls
1 teaspoon ground cinnamon

Preheat oven to 350°F. In small bowl combine 2 tablespoons brown sugar, corn syrup, pecans and 1 tablespoon margarine. Spoon about 2 teaspoons mixture into each of 9 (2½-inch) muffin pan cups. Unroll entire crescent roll dough; pinch seams together to form 1 rectangle. Combine remaining 1 tablespoon brown sugar and cinnamon. Spread dough with remaining 1 tablespoon margarine; sprinkle with cinnamon mixture. Roll up from short end. Cut into 9 slices. Place one slice in each prepared muffin pan cup. Bake 25 minutes or until golden brown. Immediately invert pan onto cookie sheet or tray; cool 10 minutes.

Makes 9 buns

PREPARATION TIME: 15 minutes
BAKE TIME: 25 minutes plus cooling

Quicky Sticky Buns

Festive

CAKES & PIES

CHOCOLATE RASPBERRY AVALANCHE CAKE

2 cups all-purpose flour
2 cups granulated sugar
6 tablespoons unsweetened cocoa
1½ teaspoons baking soda
1 teaspoon salt
1 cup hot coffee
¾ BUTTER FLAVOR CRISCO® Stick *or* ¾ cup
    BUTTER FLAVOR CRISCO all-vegetable
    shortening
½ cup milk
3 eggs
¼ cup raspberry-flavored liqueur
    Confectioners sugar
1 cup fresh raspberries (optional)

1. Heat oven to 350°F. Grease 10-inch (12-cup) Bundt pan with shortening. Flour lightly. Mix flour, granulated sugar, cocoa, baking soda and salt in large bowl. Add coffee and shortening. Beat with mixer at low speed until moistened. Add milk. Beat at medium speed 1½ minutes. Add eggs, 1 at a time, beating well after each addition. Pour into prepared pan.

2. Bake at 350°F for 40 to 45 minutes or until toothpick inserted in center comes out clean. *Do not overbake.* Cool 10 minutes; remove from pan. Cool on wire rack 10 minutes. Brush top and side with liqueur. Cool completely. Dust with confectioners sugar. Serve with raspberries, if desired.
Makes 1 (10-inch) cake (12 to 16 servings)

SNOWMAN CUPCAKES

1 package (18.5 ounces) yellow or white cake mix, plus ingredients to prepare mix
2 (16-ounce) containers vanilla frosting
4 cups flaked coconut
15 large marshmallows
15 miniature chocolate-covered peanut butter cups, unwrapped
Decorations: Pretzel sticks and small red candies
Green and red decorating gels

Preheat oven to 350°F. Line 15 regular-size (2½-inch) muffin pan cups and 15 small (about 1-inch) muffin pan cups with paper muffin cups. Prepare cake mix according to package directions. Spoon batter into muffin cups.

Bake 10 to 15 minutes for small cupcakes and 15 to 20 minutes for regular-size cupcakes or until cupcakes are golden and wooden toothpick inserted in centers comes out clean. Cool in pans on wire racks 10 minutes. Remove from pans to racks; cool completely. Remove paper liners.

Snowman Cupcakes

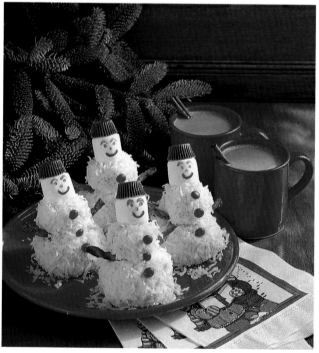

For each snowman, frost bottom and side of 1 regular-size cupcake; coat with coconut. Repeat with 1 small cupcake. Attach small cupcake to regular-size cupcake with frosting to form snowman body. Attach marshmallow to small cupcake with frosting to form snowman head. Attach inverted peanut butter cup to marshmallow with frosting to form snowman hat. Use pretzels for arms and small red candies for buttons. Pipe face with decorating gels. Repeat with remaining cupcakes.

Makes 15 snowmen

CARIBBEAN CHRISTMAS RING

3 tablespoons shortening
2½ cups finely chopped California walnuts, divided
1 cup all-purpose flour
½ cup whole wheat flour
1 teaspoon baking powder
1 teaspoon baking soda
¾ cup butter, softened
1⅓ cups granulated sugar
3 eggs
1 cup sour cream or plain nonfat yogurt
1 ripe banana, mashed
2 tablespoons orange-flavored liqueur
ORANGE SUGAR GLAZE
1 cup powdered sugar, sifted
2 tablespoons orange juice

Caribbean Christmas Ring

WALNUT HOLIDAY CAKE

 2 tablespoons dark rum
 4 single graham cracker squares
 5 eggs, separated
 2 cups powdered sugar
 1 teaspoon grated orange peel
 ¼ teaspoon cream of tartar
 3½ cups finely ground toasted California
     walnuts
 ¼ cup grated semisweet chocolate
 6 squares (1 ounce each) semisweet
     chocolate
 6 tablespoons butter or margarine
 1 tablespoon honey
     California walnut halves for garnish

Grease 9-inch springform pan. Line bottom with waxed paper; grease waxed paper. In small bowl, pour rum over graham crackers. When crackers are softened, mash with fork. In large bowl, beat egg yolks with electric mixer at medium speed until lemon colored. Add sugar and orange peel; beat at high speed until thickened, about 3 minutes. Beat cracker mixture into yolk mixture. In large mixer bowl using clean beaters, beat egg whites and cream of tartar at high speed until stiff, but not dry, peaks form. Gently fold beaten whites, ground walnuts and grated chocolate into yolk mixture. Pour batter into prepared pan. Bake in preheated 350°F oven 45 to 50 minutes or until toothpick inserted in center comes out clean and small crack appears on surface. Let cool completely in pan on wire rack. Remove side of springform pan. Invert cake onto serving plate; remove bottom of pan and waxed paper. Place strips of waxed paper under edge of cake to cover plate.

In top of double boiler, melt chocolate squares and butter over simmering water, stirring to blend. Stir in honey. Pour chocolate mixture over cake; let stand until slightly cool. Spread over top and side of cake. Remove waxed paper strips. Garnish with walnut halves. When firm, cut into thin wedges.

Makes 16 servings

*Favorite recipe from **Walnut Marketing Board***

Thoroughly grease 10- to 12-cup microwave-safe Bundt pan with 3 tablespoons shortening; sprinkle with ½ cup chopped walnuts to coat evenly. Sift flours, baking powder and baking soda into small bowl. In large bowl, beat butter and granulated sugar until fluffy; beat in eggs, one at a time. Stir sour cream, banana and liqueur into egg mixture. Fold flour mixture into banana mixture; stir in remaining 2 cups walnuts. Spoon into prepared pan and place on top of microwave-safe bowl in microwave, raising cake to center of oven. Cook at MEDIUM (50% power) 10 minutes. Continue cooking at HIGH (100% power) 5 to 7 minutes or until cake tests done, turning twice. Let cake stand 15 minutes. Turn out onto serving plate. Let cool.

Mix powdered sugar and orange juice until smooth. Pour glaze evenly over cake and serve.   *Makes 20 to 24 servings*

*Favorite recipe from **Walnut Marketing Board***

Winter Wonderland Cake

WINTER WONDERLAND CAKE

   **1 package DUNCAN HINES® Moist
      Deluxe Cake Mix (any flavor)**
   **2 containers (16 ounces each) DUNCAN
      HINES® Creamy Homestyle Vanilla
      Frosting**
   Green food coloring
   9 ice cream sugar cones
   **½ cup flaked coconut, finely chopped
      Marzipan
      Sliced natural almonds
      Nonpareil decors**

1. Preheat oven to 350°F. Grease and flour
13×9×2-inch baking pan.

2. Prepare, bake and cool cake following
package directions for basic recipe.

3. To assemble, place cake on serving plate.
Frost sides and top with 1 container Vanilla
frosting. Tint remaining container of frosting
with green food coloring to desired color; set
aside. Break off edges of ice cream cones to
form various sized trees. Frost 1 cone with
green frosting. Arrange on cake; sprinkle with
coconut. Repeat for remaining cones. Form
marzipan into bunny shapes. Use almond
slices for ears and nonpareil decors for eyes
and noses. Arrange as desired. Sprinkle
remaining coconut on cake.

Makes 12 to 16 servings

TIP: Marzipan, a cooked mixture of finely
ground almonds, sugar and egg whites, is very
sweet and pliable. It is available in most
supermarkets packaged in cans or in plastic-
wrapped logs.

CHRISTMAS TREE POKE CAKE

2 baked 9-inch square white cake layers, cooled
1 package (4-serving size) JELL-O® Brand Strawberry Flavor Gelatin
1 package (4-serving size) JELL-O® Brand Lime Flavor Gelatin
2 cups boiling water, divided
1 package (7 ounces) BAKER'S® ANGEL FLAKE® Coconut, divided
Green liquid food coloring
1 tub (12 ounces) COOL WHIP® Whipped Topping, thawed
Gumdrops
Peppermint candies
Red string licorice

Place cake layers, top sides up, in two clean 9-inch square cake pans. Pierce cakes with large fork at ½-inch intervals.

Dissolve each flavor of gelatin separately in 1 cup of the boiling water. Carefully pour strawberry flavor gelatin over one cake layer and lime flavor gelatin over second cake layer. Refrigerate 4 hours.

Meanwhile, toast ⅓ cup of the coconut; set aside. Tint remaining coconut with green food coloring.

Dip one cake pan in warm water for 10 seconds; unmold. Place right side up on large cutting board. Cut as shown in illustration 1. Arrange pieces as shown in illustration 2. Top with about 1½ cups of the whipped topping. Unmold second cake layer; cut into pieces as shown in illustration 1. Place pieces on first layer. Frost cake with remaining whipped topping.

Sprinkle trunk of tree with toasted coconut. Sprinkle remaining cake with green coconut. Decorate with gumdrops, peppermint candies and string licorice as desired.

Makes 24 servings

Christmas Tree Poke Cake

ANGEL CAKE

1 (8-inch) round cake layer
Creamy White Frosting (recipe follows)
1 to 2 tablespoons milk
5 tablespoons flaked coconut, divided
Red liquid food coloring
1 teaspoon water
2 small blue or green jelly beans
Silver edible glitter (optional)

With serrated knife, trim top of cake to form flat surface. Cut cake as shown in diagram 1, using ruler as guide. Position cake pieces on covered cake board as shown in diagram 2, connecting with some of the frosting. Thin 1½ cups frosting with milk, adding 1 teaspoon at a time, until frosting is of thin consistency. Frost entire cake with thinned frosting to seal in crumbs. Frost again with remaining Creamy White Frosting.

Place 4 tablespoons coconut in resealable plastic food storage bag. Combine small amount of food coloring with water in small bowl; add to bag. Seal bag; shake until evenly coated. Toast remaining 1 tablespoon coconut in preheated 350°F oven about 5 minutes or until lightly browned, stirring occasionally.

Sprinkle pink coconut on angel's body and toasted coconut on angel's head for hair. Place jelly beans on face for eyes. Sprinkle glitter over angel's wings, if desired.

Makes 8 to 10 servings

CREAMY WHITE FROSTING

½ cup shortening
6 cups sifted powdered sugar, divided
3 tablespoons milk
2 teaspoons clear vanilla extract
Additional milk*

Beat shortening in large bowl with electric mixer at medium speed until fluffy. Gradually beat in 3 cups sugar until well blended and smooth. Carefully beat in 3 tablespoons milk and vanilla. Gradually beat in remaining 3 cups sugar, adding more milk, 1 teaspoon at a time, as needed for good spreading consistency. Store in refrigerator.

*Makes enough to fill and frost
2 (8-inch) round cake layers*

*For thinner frosting, use more milk and for thicker frosting use less milk.

Angel Cake

212

Cassata

CASSATA

2 cups (15 ounces) SARGENTO®
   Part-Skim Ricotta Cheese
¼ cup sugar
3 tablespoons orange-flavored liqueur
⅓ cup finely chopped mixed candied fruit
¼ cup chopped almonds
1¼ cups mini semisweet chocolate chips,
   divided
1 prepared pound cake (10¾ ounces)
1 teaspoon instant coffee dissolved in
   ¼ cup boiling water
6 tablespoons unsalted butter or
   margarine, cut into 8 pieces, chilled
   Chopped almonds, for garnish
   (optional)

In bowl, combine ricotta cheese, sugar and liqueur; beat until light and fluffy, about 3 minutes. Fold in candied fruit, ¼ cup chopped almonds and ¼ cup chocolate chips. Set aside.

Cut pound cake in half horizontally using sharp serrated knife. Cut each half horizontally in half again. Place top layer of pound cake, top side down, on serving platter. Spread one third ricotta mixture evenly over cake. Repeat procedure twice, using two cake layers and remaining ricotta mixture; stack layers. Top with remaining cake layer; press slightly to compact layers. Cover with plastic wrap; chill at least 2 hours.

Meanwhile, combine remaining 1 cup chocolate chips and coffee in top of double boiler over hot, not boiling, water. Stir constantly until chocolate is melted. Add butter pieces, one at a time, stirring constantly, until all butter is added and melted. Remove from heat; chill to spreading consistency, about 2 to 2½ hours. Spread top and sides of cake with frosting. Garnish top with chopped almonds.

Makes 12 servings

TIP: Cake may be made 1 day in advance, covered with plastic wrap and refrigerated. Let stand at room temperature about 30 minutes before slicing.

MOCHA ALMOND ROLL

¾ cups cake flour
1 teaspoon baking powder
¼ teaspoon salt
3 eggs
1 cup granulated sugar
⅓ cup water
1½ teaspoons vanilla extract, divided
½ teaspoon almond extract
   Powdered sugar
1 cup BLUE DIAMOND® Blanched
   Almond Paste
2¾ cups heavy cream, divided
6 ounces semisweet chocolate chips
¾ cups powdered sugar
3 tablespoons coffee-flavored liqueur
   Chocolate curls*

Line a 15½×10½-inch jelly-roll pan with parchment paper or waxed paper; thoroughly grease with shortening.

Combine flour, baking powder and salt in small bowl; set aside. Beat eggs at high speed until foamy, about 3 to 5 minutes. Gradually beat in granulated sugar. On low speed, beat in water, ½ teaspoon vanilla and almond extract. Gradually beat in flour mixture until smooth. Pour evenly into prepared pan.

Bake in 375°F oven 12 to 15 minutes or until toothpick inserted into center comes out clean. Meanwhile, sift powdered sugar onto a clean dishtowel until evenly coated.

When cake is done, immediately turn out from pan onto towel. Peel off parchment. Roll up cake and towel together, starting from narrow end; cool thoroughly on wire rack.

Using rolling pin, spread almond paste between 2 sheets of waxed paper into a 15×10-inch rectangle; set aside.

Heat ¾ cup cream and chocolate chips, whisking until smooth. Remove chocolate mixture from heat and stir occasionally until thickened; set aside and cool completely. Whip remaining 2 cups cream, ¾ cups powdered sugar, liqueur and remaining 1 teaspoon vanilla until soft peaks form. Whisk in ⅓ cup chocolate mixture; beat until stiff peaks form.

Unroll cooled cake. Spread remaining chocolate mixture on cake. Remove waxed paper from one side of almond paste rectangle; turn rectangle, almond paste side down, onto top of chocolate mixture on cake. Peel off remaining waxed paper. Spread 1¼ cups whipped cream mixture over almond paste, leaving 1-inch border at one short edge. Carefully roll up cake from opposite end. Transfer to platter, placing seam side down. Frost cake with remaining whipped cream mixture. Garnish with chocolate curls. Refrigerate until ready to serve.

Makes 8 to 10 servings

*To make chocolate curls: Hold block of chocolate over plate. Draw blade of vegetable peeler or knife down along narrow edge of chocolate block. Chill curls immediately. Place on cake with tip of knife.

Black Forest Cake

BLACK FOREST CAKE

2 cups plus 2 tablespoons all-purpose flour
2 cups granulated sugar
¾ cup unsweetened cocoa powder
1½ teaspoons baking powder
¾ teaspoon baking soda
¾ teaspoon salt
3 eggs
1 cup milk
½ cup vegetable oil
1 tablespoon vanilla
Cherry Topping (page 217)
Frosting (page 217)

Preheat oven to 350°F. Grease and flour two 9-inch round cake pans. Cover bottoms with waxed paper. Combine dry ingredients in large bowl. Add eggs, milk, oil and vanilla; beat until well blended. Pour evenly into prepared pans. Bake 35 minutes or until wooden toothpick inserted in centers comes out clean. Cool layers in pans on wire racks 10 minutes. Loosen edges and remove to racks to cool completely.

While cake is baking, prepare Cherry Topping and Frosting. With long serrated knife, split each cake layer horizontally in half. Tear one split layer into crumbs; set aside. Reserve 1½ cups Frosting for decorating cake; set aside. Gently brush loose crumbs off top and side of each cake layer with pastry brush or hands.

To assemble, place one cake layer on cake plate. Spread with 1 cup Frosting; top with ¾ cup Cherry Topping. Top with second cake layer; repeat layers of Frosting and Cherry Topping. Top with third cake layer. Frost side of cake with remaining Frosting. Pat reserved crumbs onto Frosting on side of cake. Spoon reserved Frosting into pastry bag fitted with star decorator tip. Pipe around top and bottom edges of cake. Spoon remaining Cherry Topping onto top of cake.

Makes 1 (3-layer) cake

CHERRY TOPPING

    2 (20-ounce) cans pitted tart cherries,
        undrained
    1 cup granulated sugar
    ¼ cup cornstarch
    1 teaspoon vanilla

Drain cherries, reserving ½ cup juice. Combine reserved juice, cherries, sugar and cornstarch in 2-quart saucepan. Cook over low heat until thickened, stirring constantly. Stir in 1 teaspoon vanilla. Cool before using.

FROSTING

    3 cups whipping cream
    ⅓ cup powdered sugar

Beat together whipping cream and powdered sugar in chilled medium bowl with electric mixer at high speed until stiff peaks form.

TRIPLE CHOCOLATE CAKE

    ¾ cup butter or margarine, softened
    1½ cups sugar
    1 egg
    1 teaspoon vanilla
    2 cups all-purpose flour
    ⅔ cup unsweetened cocoa powder
    2 teaspoons baking soda
    ¼ teaspoon salt
    1 cup buttermilk
    ¾ cup sour cream
        Light Ganache Filling (recipe follows)
        Dark Chocolate Glaze (recipe follows)

Preheat oven to 350°F. Grease and flour two 9-inch round cake pans. Beat butter and sugar in large bowl with electric mixer at medium speed until light and fluffy. Beat in egg and vanilla until blended. Combine flour, cocoa, baking soda and salt in medium bowl. Add flour mixture to butter mixture, alternately with buttermilk and sour cream, beginning and ending with flour mixture. Beat well after each addition. Divide evenly between prepared pans. Bake 30 to 35 minutes or until wooden toothpick inserted in centers comes out clean. Cool in pans 10 minutes. Remove from pans to wire racks; cool completely.

Meanwhile, prepare Light Ganache Filling. Place one cake layer on serving plate. Spread with Light Ganache Filling. Top with second cake layer. Prepare Dark Chocolate Glaze. Pour over top of cake. Immediately spread glaze over side and top with spatula until smooth. Refrigerate cake at least 30 minutes to set glaze. Garnish as desired. Store tightly covered at room temperature.

Makes 1 (9-inch) layer cake

LIGHT GANACHE FILLING

    4 squares (1 ounce each) semisweet
        chocolate
    1 cup whipping cream
    ½ teaspoon vanilla

Melt chocolate in heavy, small saucepan over low heat, stirring frequently. Pour melted chocolate into small bowl. Wash and dry saucepan. Heat cream in same saucepan over medium heat until hot; *do not boil.* Gradually whisk cream into chocolate. Whisk in vanilla. Let filling stand at room temperature until of spreading consistency. Beat mixture with electric mixer at high speed until light and fluffy.

DARK CHOCOLATE GLAZE

    8 squares (1 ounce each) semisweet
        chocolate
    4 tablespoons butter or margarine
    1 cup whipping cream

Melt chocolate and butter in heavy, small saucepan over low heat, stirring frequently. Pour melted chocolate mixture into medium bowl. Wash and dry saucepan. Heat cream in same saucepan over medium heat until hot; *do not boil.* Gradually whisk cream into chocolate mixture until slightly thickened.

RICH CHOCOLATE TRUFFLE CAKE

2 packages (8 ounces each) semisweet chocolate (16 squares)
1½ cups butter or margarine
1 cup sugar
½ cup light cream
6 large eggs
2 teaspoons vanilla
Chocolate Curls (recipe follows)
Chocolate Glaze (recipe follows)
Sweetened Whipped Cream (recipe follows)
Mint leaves for garnish

Preheat oven to 350°F. Line bottom of 9-inch springform pan with foil, tucking foil edges under bottom. Attach springform side. Bring foil up around outside of pan. Grease foil-lined bottom and side of pan with butter; set aside.

Heat chocolate, butter, sugar and cream in heavy 2-quart saucepan over low heat until chocolate melts and mixture is smooth, stirring frequently. Remove from heat. Beat eggs and vanilla in large bowl with wire whisk until frothy. Slowly whisk in warm chocolate mixture until well blended. *Do not beat mixture vigorously,* as this will incorporate air into the mixture. Pour batter into prepared pan. Bake 45 minutes or until wooden toothpick inserted about 1 inch from edge comes out clean and center is set. Cool cake completely in pan on wire rack.

Prepare Chocolate Curls; refrigerate. When cake is cool, carefully remove side of springform pan. Leave cake on bottom of pan. Wrap cake in foil. Refrigerate until well chilled, at least 4 hours or overnight.

Prepare Chocolate Glaze. Unwrap cake. Turn upside-down on cake plate; remove bottom of pan. Surround cake with waxed paper strips to catch glaze drippings. Spread top and side of cake with warm glaze using metal spatula. Remove waxed paper after glaze sets.

Prepare Sweetened Whipped Cream. Spoon cream mixture into decorating bag with medium star tip. Pipe cream around edge of cake. Garnish piped cream with Chocolate Curls. Refrigerate until serving. Just before serving, garnish with mint leaves.

Makes 16 to 20 servings

CHOCOLATE CURLS

1 square (1 ounce) chocolate, coarsely chopped
1 teaspoon vegetable shortening

Place chocolate and shortening in 1-cup glass measure. Microwave at HIGH (100% power) about 1 minute or until melted, stirring after 30 seconds of cooking. Pour melted chocolate onto back of baking sheet, marble slab or other heat-resistant flat surface. Quickly spread chocolate in very thin layer with metal spatula. Refrigerate about 10 minutes or until firm, but still pliable. Using small straight-edge metal spatula or paring knife, held at 45° angle, push spatula firmly along baking sheet, under chocolate, so chocolate curls as it is pushed. (If chocolate is too firm to curl, let stand a few minutes at room temperature. Refrigerate again if it becomes too soft.) Using small skewer or toothpick, transfer curls to waxed paper. Store in cool, dry place until ready to use.

CHOCOLATE GLAZE

1 cup semisweet chocolate chips
2 tablespoons butter or margarine
3 tablespoons half-and-half
2 tablespoons light corn syrup

Melt chocolate chips and butter in 1-quart saucepan over low heat, stirring frequently. Remove from heat. Stir in half-and-half and corn syrup. *Makes about 1¼ cups*

SWEETENED WHIPPED CREAM

1 cup heavy cream
2 tablespoons powdered sugar
½ teaspoon vanilla

Beat ingredients in bowl until soft peaks form. Refrigerate. *Makes about 2 cups*

Rich Chocolate Truffle Cake

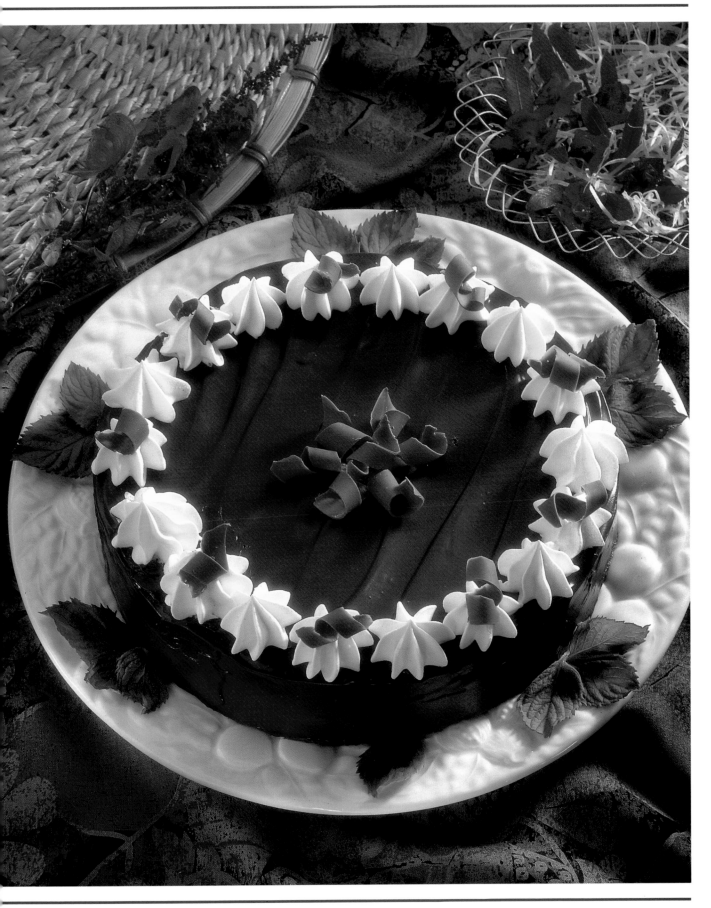

FESTIVE YULE LOG

CAKE
    5 eggs, room temperature, separated
    ⅔ cup granulated sugar
    2 tablespoons all-purpose flour
    3 tablespoons unsweetened cocoa
       Confectioners' sugar

FILLING
    1 bag (7 ounces) Chocolate RIESEN®
       Caramel Candy, unwrapped
    ¼ cup whipping cream
    2 tablespoons rum
    2 cups whipped topping
    ⅓ cup finely chopped pecans

FROSTING
    6 tablespoons butter or margarine,
       softened
    1 cup confectioners' sugar
    ⅓ cup unsweetened cocoa
    2 to 3 tablespoons milk
    ¼ cup finely chopped pecans

Preheat oven to 350°F. For Cake, in large mixing bowl, beat egg yolks at high speed with electric mixer until light and fluffy. Gradually add granulated sugar, beating until mixture is thick and light colored. On low speed add flour and 3 tablespoons cocoa; mix well. In another mixing bowl, using clean beaters, beat egg whites until soft peaks form. Carefully fold egg whites into chocolate mixture. Spread in 15×10×1-inch greased and waxed-paper-lined jelly-roll pan.

Bake 15 minutes or until cake springs back when lightly touched. Cake will fall slightly as it cools. Let cake cool in pan 15 minutes; loosen edges with knife. Turn cake out onto piece of waxed paper dusted with confectioners' sugar. Carefully remove waxed paper lining. Cover cake with dish towel; cool completely.

For Filling, melt caramels with cream in heavy saucepan, stirring constantly, until smooth. Remove from heat and stir in rum. Cool to room temperature. When cool, fold in whipped topping. Spread over cake and sprinkle with ⅓ cup nuts. Roll up, starting from short end. Place in freezer while preparing frosting.

For Frosting, beat butter until fluffy. Alternately add sugar and ⅓ cup cocoa with milk, beating until frosting is smooth and fluffy. Remove cake from freezer. Slice 1-inch piece of cake roll off end of log. Spread frosting on one side of log and press slice, cut side up, in place. (This will resemble stump of log.) Frost entire cake and stump. Swirl ends of log and flat side of stump to resemble cut section of log. Run tines of fork over length of log to resemble bark. Sprinkle with ¼ cup nuts. Refrigerate at least 2 hours before serving.

Makes 8 to 10 servings

ALMOND CHOCOLATE TORTE WITH RASPBERRY SAUCE

    2½ cups BLUE DIAMOND® Blanched
       Whole Almonds, lightly toasted
    9 squares (1 ounce each) semisweet
       chocolate
    ¼ cup butter
    6 eggs, beaten
    ¾ cup sugar
    2 tablespoons flour
    ¼ cup brandy
       Fudge Glaze (page 221)
       Raspberry Sauce (page 221)

In food processor or blender, process 1 cup almonds until finely ground. Generously grease 9-inch round cake pan; sprinkle with 2 tablespoons ground almonds. In top of double boiler, melt chocolate and butter over simmering water, blending thoroughly; cool slightly. In large bowl, beat eggs and sugar. Gradually beat in chocolate mixture. Add flour, remaining ground almonds and brandy; mix well. Pour batter into prepared pan.

Bake in preheated 350°F oven 25 minutes or until toothpick inserted in center comes out almost clean. Let cool in pan on wire rack 10 minutes. Loosen edge; remove from pan. Cool completely on wire rack.

Prepare Fudge Glaze. Place torte on wire rack over sheet of waxed paper. Pour Fudge Glaze over torte, spreading over top and sides with spatula. Carefully transfer torte to serving plate; let glaze set.

Prepare Raspberry Sauce; set aside. Arrange remaining 1½ cups whole almonds, points toward center, in circle around outer edge of torte. Working towards center, repeat circles, overlapping almonds slightly. To serve, pour small amount of Raspberry Sauce on each serving plate; top with slice of torte.

Makes 10 to 12 servings

FUDGE GLAZE: In small saucepan, combine 6 tablespoons water and 3 tablespoons sugar. Simmer over low heat until sugar dissolves. Stir in 3 squares (1 ounce each) semisweet chocolate and 1 tablespoon brandy. Heat, stirring occasionally, until chocolate melts and glaze coats back of spoon.

RASPBERRY SAUCE: In food processor or blender, purée 2 packages (10 ounces each) thawed frozen raspberries. Strain raspberry purée through a fine sieve to remove seeds. Stir in sugar to taste.

Almond Chocolate Torte with Raspberry Sauce

BÛCHE DE NOËL

¾ cup cake flour
½ teaspoon baking powder
½ teaspoon salt
5 eggs, separated
1 cup granulated sugar, divided
1 teaspoon vanilla
½ cup powdered sugar
1 cup semisweet chocolate chips
¾ cup heavy cream
1 tablespoon rum
   Cocoa Frosting (recipe follows)
   White Chocolate Curls (page 224)
2 teaspoons unsweetened cocoa powder
   (optional)

Preheat oven to 375°F. Grease 15½×10½-inch jelly-roll pan; line pan with waxed paper. Grease waxed paper; set pan aside. Place flour, baking powder and salt in small bowl; stir to combine. Beat egg yolks and ⅔ cup granulated sugar in separate small bowl with electric mixer at high speed about 5 minutes or until thick and lemon colored, scraping down side of bowl once. Beat in vanilla; set aside.

Beat egg whites in clean large bowl using clean beaters with electric mixer at high speed until foamy. Gradually beat in remaining ⅓ cup granulated sugar, 1 tablespoon at a time, until stiff peaks form.

Fold flour mixture into egg yolk mixture. Fold flour/egg yolk mixture into egg white mixture until evenly incorporated. Spread mixture into prepared pan. Bake 12 to 15 minutes or until cake springs back when lightly touched with finger. Meanwhile, lightly sift powdered sugar over clean dish towel.

Loosen warm cake from edges of pan with spatula; invert onto prepared towel. Remove pan; carefully peel off waxed paper. Gently roll up cake in towel from short end, jelly-roll style. Let rolled cake cool completely on wire rack.

For chocolate filling, place chocolate chips and cream in heavy, 1-quart saucepan. Heat over low heat until chocolate is melted, stirring frequently. Pour into small bowl; stir in rum. Cover and refrigerate about 1½ hours or until filling is of spreading consistency, stirring occasionally.

Prepare Cocoa Frosting and White Chocolate Curls; refrigerate until ready to use.

Unroll cake; remove towel. Spread cake with chilled chocolate filling to within ½ inch of edge; reroll cake. Spread Cocoa Frosting over cake roll. Garnish with White Chocolate Curls. Sprinkle with cocoa. *Makes 12 servings*

COCOA FROSTING

1 cup heavy cream
2 tablespoons unsweetened Dutch-
   processed* cocoa powder, sifted
½ cup powdered sugar, sifted
1 teaspoon vanilla

Beat cream, cocoa, sugar and vanilla with electric mixer at medium speed until soft peaks form. *Do not overbeat.* Refrigerate until ready to use. *Makes about 2 cups*

*The Dutch-processed, or European-style, cocoa gives this frosting an intense chocolate flavor and a rich color. Other unsweetened cocoas can be substituted, but the flavor may be milder and the color may be lighter.

continued on page 224

Bûche de Noël

Bûche de Noël, continued

WHITE CHOCOLATE CURLS
   **1 package (8 ounces) white chocolate,
      coarsely chopped**
   1 tablespoon vegetable shortening

Place white chocolate and shortening in 2-cup glass measure. Microwave at HIGH (100% power) about 1½ minutes or until melted, stirring after every 30 seconds of cooking. Pour melted white chocolate onto back of baking sheet, marble slab or other heat-resistant flat surface. Quickly spread chocolate into very thin layer with metal spatula. Refrigerate about 10 minutes or until firm, but still pliable. Using small straight-edge metal spatula or paring knife held at 45° angle, push spatula firmly along baking sheet, under chocolate, so chocolate curls as it is pushed. (If chocolate is too firm to curl, let stand a few minutes at room temperature. Refrigerate again if it becomes too soft.) Using small skewer or toothpick, transfer curls to waxed paper. Store in cool, dry place until ready to use.

Chocolate Intensity

CHOCOLATE INTENSITY

CAKE
   **1 package (8 ounces) NESTLÉ®
      Unsweetened Chocolate Baking Bars**
   1½ cups granulated sugar
   ½ cup butter, softened
   3 eggs
   2 teaspoons vanilla extract
   ⅔ cup all-purpose flour
      Sifted powdered sugar (optional)
COFFEE CRÈME ANGLAISE SAUCE
   4 egg yolks
   ⅓ cup granulated sugar
   **1 tablespoon TASTER'S CHOICE®
      Freeze Dried Instant Coffee**
   1½ cups milk
   1 teaspoon vanilla extract

FOR CAKE: In small, heavy saucepan over low heat, melt baking bars, stirring until smooth. Remove from heat; cool to lukewarm. In small mixer bowl, beat granulated sugar, butter, eggs and vanilla for about 4 minutes or until thick and pale yellow. Beat in melted chocolate. Gradually beat in flour. Spread into greased 9-inch springform pan. Bake in preheated 350°F. oven for 25 to 28 minutes. (Wooden pick inserted in center will be moist.) Cool in pan on wire rack for 15 minutes. Remove side of pan; cool completely. Sprinkle with powdered sugar. Cut into 10 to 12 servings. Serve each with 3 to 4 tablespoons sauce.

FOR COFFEE CRÈME ANGLAISE SAUCE: In small bowl, whisk egg yolks. In medium saucepan, combine sugar and instant coffee; stir in milk. Cook over medium heat, stirring constantly, until mixture comes to a simmer. Remove from heat. Gradually whisk ½ of hot milk mixture into yolks; return to saucepan. Continue cooking, stirring constantly for 3 to 4 minutes or until mixture is slightly thickened. Strain into small bowl; stir in vanilla. Cover with plastic wrap; chill.   *Makes 10 to 12 servings*

ALMOND FUDGE BANANA CAKE

3 extra-ripe, medium DOLE® Bananas, peeled
1½ cups sugar
½ cup margarine, softened
3 eggs
3 tablespoons amaretto liqueur *or* ½ to 1 teaspoon almond extract
1 teaspoon vanilla extract
1⅓ cups all-purpose flour
⅓ cup unsweetened cocoa powder
1 teaspoon baking soda
½ teaspoon salt
½ cup DOLE® Chopped Almonds, toasted, ground
Banana Chocolate Glaze (recipe follows)

• Mash bananas; set aside.

• Beat sugar and margarine until light and fluffy. Beat in eggs, liqueur and vanilla.

• Combine dry ingredients. Stir in almonds. Add to sugar mixture alternately with bananas. Beat well.

• Pour batter into greased 10-inch Bundt pan. Bake in preheated 350°F oven 45 to 50 minutes or until toothpick inserted in center comes out almost clean and cake pulls away from side of pan. Cool 10 minutes. Remove cake from pan to wire rack to cool completely. Drizzle glaze over top and down side of cake.

Makes 16 to 20 servings

BANANA CHOCOLATE GLAZE
1 extra-ripe, small DOLE® Banana, puréed
1 square (1 ounce) semisweet chocolate, melted

With wire whisk, beat puréed banana into melted chocolate.

Almond Fudge Banana Cake

CHERRY PECAN POUND CAKE

1 cup butter or margarine, softened
1 cup sugar
4 eggs
1 teaspoon vanilla
½ teaspoon almond extract
½ teaspoon salt
⅛ teaspoon ground nutmeg or mace
1½ cups all-purpose flour
1 jar (6 ounces) maraschino cherries, drained and chopped
¼ cup chopped pecans

In large bowl, beat butter and sugar until light and fluffy. Add eggs, vanilla, almond extract, salt and ground nutmeg; beat until thoroughly blended. Stir in flour, ½ cup at a time, mixing just until blended. Stir in cherries and pecans. Spread batter evenly in greased and floured 9×5×3-inch loaf pan. Bake in preheated 325°F oven 60 to 70 minutes or until toothpick inserted near center comes out clean. Let cool in pan on wire rack 10 minutes. Loosen edges; remove from pan. Cool completely on wire rack.

Makes 1 loaf

*Favorite recipe from **American Egg Board***

RASPBERRY POUND CAKE

1 package DUNCAN HINES® Moist
   Deluxe Raspberry Cake Mix
1 package (4-serving size) vanilla instant
   pudding and pie filling mix
4 eggs
1 cup water
⅓ cup CRISCO® Oil or CRISCO®
   PURITAN® Canola Oil
1 cup miniature semi-sweet chocolate
   chips
⅔ cup DUNCAN HINES® Creamy
   Homestyle Chocolate Buttercream
   Frosting

1. Preheat oven to 350°F. Grease and flour 10-inch Bundt pan.

2. For cake, combine cake mix, pudding mix, eggs, water and oil in large bowl. Beat at low speed with electric mixer until moistened. Beat at medium speed for 2 minutes. Stir in chocolate chips. Pour into pan. Bake at 350°F for 55 to 60 minutes or until toothpick inserted in center comes out clean. Cool in pan 25 minutes. Invert onto cooling rack. Cool completely.

3. For glaze, place frosting in 1-cup glass measuring cup. Microwave at HIGH (100% power) for 10 to 15 seconds. Stir until smooth. Drizzle over top of cooled cake.

Makes 12 to 16 servings

TIP: Store leftover chocolate buttercream frosting covered in refrigerator. Spread frosting between graham crackers for a quick snack.

CHERRY–PINEAPPLE UPSIDE–DOWN CAKE

1¼ cups sifted cake flour
   2 teaspoons baking powder
   ¼ teaspoon salt
   ½ cup (1 stick) butter or margarine,
      softened, divided
   ¾ cup granulated sugar
   1 egg
   ½ cup milk
   1 teaspoon vanilla
   ¾ cup packed brown sugar
   1 (20-ounce) can crushed pineapple, well
      drained
   1 (16-ounce) can pitted tart cherries,
      drained
   Fresh mint leaves for garnish

Preheat oven to 350°F. Combine flour, baking powder and salt in medium bowl; set aside. Beat together ¼ cup butter and granulated sugar in large bowl until light and fluffy. Blend in egg. Add flour mixture alternately with milk, beating well after each addition. Blend in vanilla.

Melt remaining ¼ cup butter in 9-inch ovenproof skillet or 9-inch cake pan. Stir in brown sugar. If necessary, tilt skillet to cover bottom of skillet evenly with brown sugar mixture. Top brown sugar mixture with pineapple. Reserve a few cherries for garnish, if desired. Spoon remaining cherries over pineapple; top with batter. Bake 50 minutes or until wooden toothpick inserted in center comes out clean. Cool cake in pan on wire rack 10 minutes. Loosen edges and turn upside down onto cake plate. Garnish, if desired.

Makes 1 (9-inch) cake

*Favorite recipe from **Illinois State Fair***

Cherry-Pineapple Upside-Down Cake

PUMPKIN JINGLE BARS

¾ cup MIRACLE WHIP® Salad Dressing
1 two-layer spice cake mix
1 (16-ounce) can pumpkin
3 eggs
   Sifted confectioners' sugar
   Vanilla frosting
   Red and green gum drops, sliced

Mix first 4 ingredients in large bowl at medium speed of electric mixer until well blended. Pour into greased 15½×10½×1-inch jelly roll pan. Bake at 350°F, 18 to 20 minutes or until edges pull away from sides of pan. Cool. Sprinkle with sugar. Cut into bars. Decorate with frosting and gum drops.   *Makes about 3 dozen bars*

PREP TIME: 5 minutes
COOK TIME: 20 minutes

JEWELLED FRUITCAKE

2½ cups unsifted flour
1 teaspoon baking soda
2 eggs
1 (27-ounce) jar NONE SUCH® Ready-To-Use Mincemeat (Regular or Brandy & Rum)
1 (14-ounce) can EAGLE® Brand Sweetened Condensed Milk (NOT evaporated milk)
1 (8-ounce) container green candied cherries, halved (1 cup)
1 (8-ounce) container red candied cherries, halved (1 cup)
1 (6-ounce) package dried apricots, chopped (1 cup)
1 (6-ounce) container candied pineapple, chopped (1 cup)
1½ cups chopped pecans

Pumpkin Jingle Bars

Preheat oven to 300°F. Grease and flour 10-inch tube or fluted tube pan. Combine flour and baking soda. In large bowl, beat eggs. Stir in remaining ingredients; blend in flour mixture. Pour batter into prepared pan. Bake 1 hour and 30 to 40 minutes or until wooden pick inserted near center comes out clean. Cool 10 minutes; remove from pan. Cool completely.

Makes 1 (10-inch) cake

TIP: If desired, glaze with heated corn syrup; garnish with candied fruit and dried apricots.

CHERRY FRUIT CAKE

¾ cup flour
½ teaspoon baking powder
½ teaspoon salt
1 (16-ounce) jar whole maraschino
    cherries, well drained
8 ounces diced pitted dates
8 ounces candied pineapple chunks
9 ounces pecan halves
3 eggs
1½ ounces rum
¼ cup light corn syrup

Combine flour, baking powder and salt in large mixing bowl; mix well. Add cherries, dates, pineapple and pecans. Toss together until fruits and nuts are coated with flour mixture. Beat eggs and rum until blended. Pour over coated fruit and mix thoroughly. Grease 9×5×3-inch loaf pan; line with parchment paper and grease again. Turn cake mixture into pan, pressing with spatula to pack tightly. Bake at 300°F 1 hour 45 minutes or until wooden pick inserted near center comes out clean. Cool cake in pan 15 minutes. Remove cake from pan; remove paper. Brush with corn syrup while still warm. Cool completely before serving or storing.

Makes 1 cake

Favorite recipe from **National Cherry Foundation**

GOLDEN APPLE MINCEMEAT CAKE

3 cups flour
4 teaspoons baking powder
1 teaspoon *each* ground allspice and
    cinnamon
½ teaspoon salt
1½ cups vegetable oil
1½ cups packed brown sugar
2 cups grated Golden Delicious apples
1 cup prepared mincemeat
½ cup chopped pecans
1½ teaspoons vanilla
3 eggs
1 to 2 tablespoons sifted powdered sugar
    Hard Sauce (recipe follows, optional)

Preheat oven to 350°F. Combine flour, baking powder, allspice, cinnamon and salt in large bowl; set aside. In large bowl of electric mixer, combine oil and brown sugar; beat well. Add half the flour mixture; mix well. Blend in grated apples, mincemeat, pecans and vanilla. Add remaining flour mixture. Add eggs, 1 at a time; beat well after each addition. Turn into greased 10-inch Bundt pan. Bake 1 hour or until wooden toothpick inserted near center comes out clean. Cool in pan 15 minutes; turn out onto wire rack. When cool, sprinkle with powdered sugar. If desired, cake can be served slightly warm with Hard Sauce.

Makes 16 servings

HARD SAUCE: Beat ½ cup margarine and ⅛ teaspoon salt until light and fluffy. Gradually beat in 1 cup powdered sugar. Stir in 1 tablespoon brandy. Refrigerate 1 hour.

Favorite recipe from **Washington Apple Commission**

SPICY GINGERBREAD WITH CINNAMON PEAR SAUCE

- 2 cups all-purpose flour
- ½ cup packed light brown sugar
- 1 teaspoon baking soda
- 1 teaspoon ground ginger
- 1 teaspoon ground cinnamon
- ¼ teaspoon ground cloves
- ¼ teaspoon salt
- 1 cup light molasses
- ¾ cup buttermilk
- ½ cup butter or margarine, softened
  Cinnamon Pear Sauce (recipe follows)

Preheat oven to 325°F. Grease and lightly flour 9-inch square baking pan.

Combine all ingredients except Cinnamon Pear Sauce in large bowl. Beat with electric mixer at low speed until well blended, scraping side of bowl with rubber spatula frequently. Beat at high speed 2 minutes more. Pour into prepared pan.

Bake 50 to 55 minutes or until wooden toothpick inserted in center comes out clean. Cool in pan on wire rack about 30 minutes. Cut into squares; serve warm with Cinnamon Pear Sauce. *Makes 9 servings*

CINNAMON PEAR SAUCE
- 2 cans (16 ounces each) pear halves in syrup, undrained
- 2 tablespoons granulated sugar
- 1 teaspoon fresh lemon juice
- ½ teaspoon ground cinnamon

Drain pear halves, reserving ¼ cup syrup. Place pears, reserved syrup, granulated sugar, lemon juice and cinnamon in work bowl of food processor or blender; cover. Process until smooth. Just before serving, place pear sauce in medium saucepan; heat until warm. *Makes 2 cups sauce*

LEMON POPPY SEED CAKE

- 6 tablespoons margarine, softened
- ½ cup firmly packed light brown sugar
- ½ cup plain low fat yogurt
- 1 whole egg
- 2 egg whites
- 3 teaspoons fresh lemon juice
- 1¾ cups all-purpose flour
- 1 teaspoon baking powder
- ½ teaspoon baking soda
- ¼ teaspoon salt
- ⅓ cup skim milk
- 2 tablespoons poppy seed
- 1 tablespoon grated lemon peel

LEMON GLAZE
- 1 cup powdered sugar
- 2 tablespoons plus 1½ teaspoons lemon juice
- ½ teaspoon poppy seed

Preheat oven to 350°F. Grease and flour 6-cup Bundt pan. Beat margarine in large bowl with electric mixer until fluffy. Beat in brown sugar, yogurt, whole egg, egg whites and 3 teaspoons lemon juice. Set aside. Combine flour, baking powder, baking soda and salt in medium bowl. Add flour mixture to margarine mixture alternately with milk, beginning and ending with flour mixture. Mix in 2 tablespoons poppy seed and lemon peel. Pour batter into prepared pan.

Bake about 40 minutes or until cake is golden brown and wooden toothpick inserted in center comes out clean. Cool in pan on wire rack 10 minutes. Remove from pan to wire rack; cool completely.

For Lemon Glaze, mix powdered sugar with 2 tablespoons plus 1½ teaspoons lemon juice until of desired consistency. Spoon glaze over cake and sprinkle with ½ teaspoon poppy seed. *Makes 12 servings*

Lemon Poppy Seed Cake

PUMPKIN TART WITH MAPLE CRÈME

1¼ cups all-purpose flour
1 tablespoon granulated sugar
¼ teaspoon salt
⅓ cup cold butter or margarine
3 to 4 tablespoons cold water
1 can (15 ounces) solid-pack pumpkin (not pumpkin pie filling)
½ cup maple syrup
⅓ cup packed light brown sugar
¼ cup half-and-half or cream
2 large eggs
1 teaspoon vanilla extract
1 teaspoon ground cinnamon
½ teaspoon ground ginger
⅛ teaspoon ground nutmeg
    Maple Crème (recipe follows)

For pastry, combine flour, granulated sugar and salt in small bowl. Cut in butter with pastry blender or two knives until mixture resembles coarse crumbs. Stir in water, 1 tablespoon at a time, with fork until dough forms a ball. Wrap dough in plastic wrap; refrigerate 30 minutes.

Roll out dough on lightly floured surface with a lightly floured rolling pin into 12-inch circle. Line 10-inch tart pan with removable bottom with dough; trim excess from edge.

Preheat oven to 400°F. For filling, combine pumpkin, maple syrup, brown sugar, half-and-half, eggs, vanilla, cinnamon, ginger and nutmeg in large bowl; stir until well blended. Pour into tart shell.

Bake 20 minutes. Reduce oven temperature to 350°F. Continue baking 30 to 35 minutes or until filling is set. Cool on wire rack. Prepare Maple Crème; dollop on each piece just before serving.   *Makes 8 servings*

Maple Crème: Beat ½ cup whipping cream in large bowl with electric mixer at high speed until soft peaks form. Beat in 4½ teaspoons maple syrup on low speed, then beat in ¼ cup crème fraîche or sour cream. Cover with plastic wrap. Refrigerate until chilled.

DATE–NUT PUMPKIN PIE

CRUST
1 (9-inch) Classic Crisco® Single Crust (page 233)
DATE–NUT LAYER
1 package (8 ounces) pitted whole dates, chopped
¾ cup water
⅓ cup firmly packed brown sugar
¼ cup butter or margarine
½ cup chopped walnuts
½ teaspoon cinnamon
FILLING
2 eggs
1½ cups mashed cooked pumpkin or canned solid-pack pumpkin (not pumpkin pie filling)
½ cup granulated sugar
½ cup firmly packed brown sugar
1 cup evaporated milk
½ teaspoon cinnamon
½ teaspoon ginger
½ teaspoon nutmeg
¼ teaspoon salt
⅛ teaspoon cloves
GARNISH
Sweetened whipped cream

1. For crust, prepare Classic Crisco® Single Crust. Do not bake. Reserve dough scraps for cutouts, if desired.* Heat oven to 450°F.

2. For date-nut layer, combine dates and water in medium saucepan. Cook on medium heat until mixture comes to a boil and dates have softened. Add ⅓ cup brown sugar and butter. Stir to blend. Remove from heat. Stir in nuts and cinnamon. Cool while preparing filling.

Date-Nut Pumpkin Pie

3. For filling, beat eggs lightly in medium bowl. Add pumpkin, granulated sugar, ½ cup brown sugar, evaporated milk, cinnamon, ginger, nutmeg, salt and cloves. Stir to blend.

4. Spoon date-nut mixture into unbaked pie crust. Pour in filling. Bake at 450°F for 10 minutes. *Reduce oven temperature to 350°F.* Bake 35 minutes or until knife inserted in center comes out clean. Do not overbake. Cool to room temperature before serving.

5. For garnish, spoon whipped cream around outer edge of pie just before serving. Refrigerate leftover pie.   *Makes 1 (9-inch) pie*

*Flute edge or cut small leaves and pumpkins from pastry scraps and press around edge of unbaked pie crust.

CLASSIC CRISCO® SINGLE CRUST
  1⅓ cups all-purpose flour
    ½ teaspoon salt
    ½ CRISCO® Stick *or* ½ cup CRISCO all-vegetable shortening
  3 tablespoons cold water

Spoon flour into measuring cups and level. Combine flour and salt in medium bowl. Cut in shortening using pastry blender (or 2 knives) until all flour is blended to form pea-size chunks. Sprinkle with water, 1 tablespoon at a time. Toss lightly with fork until dough forms a ball. Press dough between hands to form a 5- to 6-inch "pancake." Flour rolling surface and rolling pin lightly. Roll dough into circle. Trim 1 inch larger than upside-down pie plate. Loosen dough carefully. Fold dough into quarters. Unfold and press into pie plate. Fold edge under. Flute.   *Makes 8- to 9-inch single crust*

CLASSIC PUMPKIN PIE WITH CANDIED PECAN TOPPING

CRUST

    1 (9-inch) Classic Crisco® Single Crust
        (page 233)

FILLING

    1 can (16 ounces) solid-pack pumpkin
        (not pumpkin pie filling)
    1 can (12 ounces or 1½ cups)
        evaporated milk
    2 eggs, lightly beaten
    ½ cup granulated sugar
    ¼ cup firmly packed light brown sugar
    1 teaspoon cinnamon
    ½ teaspoon salt
    ½ teaspoon ginger
    ¼ teaspoon nutmeg
    ⅛ teaspoon cloves

TOPPING

    ¼ cup granulated sugar
    ¼ cup water
    2 tablespoons butter or margarine
    1 cup pecan pieces

1. For crust, prepare according to instructions on page 355. Roll and press crust into 9-inch glass pie plate. Do not bake. Heat oven to 350°F.

2. For filling, combine pumpkin, evaporated milk, eggs, granulated sugar, brown sugar, cinnamon, salt, ginger, nutmeg and cloves in large bowl. Mix well. Pour into unbaked pie crust.

3. Bake at 350°F for 1 hour 10 minutes or until knife inserted in center comes out clean. *Do not overbake.* Cool completely.

4. Grease baking sheet lightly with shortening.

5. For topping, combine granulated sugar and water in small saucepan. Cook and stir on medium heat until sugar dissolves. Increase heat. Bring to a boil. Boil 7 to 8 minutes or until mixture becomes light golden brown, stirring frequently. Stir in butter and nuts. Stir briskly. Spread quickly in thin layer on baking sheet. Cool completely. Break into pieces. Sprinkle around edge of pie. (You might not use all of topping. Cover and store any extra for later use.) Refrigerate leftover pie.

Makes 1 (9-inch) pie (8 servings)

PLUM PUDDING PIE

    ⅓ cup plus 2 tablespoons KAHLÚA®
    ½ cup golden raisins
    ½ cup chopped pitted dates
    ⅓ cup chopped candied cherries
    ½ cup chopped walnuts
    ⅓ cup dark corn syrup
    ½ teaspoon pumpkin pie spice
    ¼ cup butter or margarine, softened
    ¼ cup packed brown sugar
    2 tablespoons all-purpose flour
    ¼ teaspoon salt
    2 eggs, slightly beaten
    1 (9-inch) unbaked pie shell
    1 cup whipping cream
      Maraschino cherries (optional)

In medium bowl, combine ⅓ cup Kahlúa®, raisins, dates and cherries; mix well. Cover; let stand 1 to 4 hours. Stir in walnuts, corn syrup and spice. In large bowl, cream butter, sugar, flour and salt. Stir in eggs. Add fruit mixture; blend well. Pour into unbaked pie shell. Bake in preheated 350°F oven 35 minutes or until filling is firm and crust is golden. Cool completely on wire rack. When ready to serve, in small bowl, beat whipping cream with remaining 2 tablespoons Kahlúa® just until soft peaks form. Spoon whipped cream into pastry bag fitted with large star tip and pipe decoratively on top. If desired, garnish with maraschino cherries.

Makes 8 servings

Classic Pumpkin Pie with Candied Pecan Topping

TRADITIONAL PUMPKIN PIE

- 1 (9-inch) unbaked pastry shell
- 1 (16-ounce) can solid-pack pumpkin (2 cups)
- 1 (14-ounce) can EAGLE® Brand Sweetened Condensed Milk (NOT evaporated milk)
- 2 eggs
- 1 teaspoon ground cinnamon
- ½ teaspoon ground ginger
- ½ teaspoon ground nutmeg
- ½ teaspoon salt

Place rack in lowest position in oven; preheat oven to 425°F. In large mixer bowl, combine all ingredients except pastry shell; mix well. Pour into pastry shell. Bake 15 minutes. *Reduce oven temperature to 350°F;* bake 35 to 40 minutes longer or until knife inserted near edge comes out clean. Cool. Garnish as desired. Refrigerate leftovers.   *Makes 1 (9-inch) pie*

OPTIONAL TOPPINGS

Sour Cream Topping: In medium bowl, combine 1½ cups Borden® or Meadow Gold® Sour Cream, 2 tablespoons sugar and 1 teaspoon vanilla extract. After reducing oven temperature to 350°F and baking pie for 30 minutes, spread topping evenly over pie; bake 10 minutes longer. Garnish as desired.

Traditional Pumpkin Pie

Streusel Topping: In medium bowl, combine ½ cup firmly packed light brown sugar and ½ cup unsifted flour; cut in ¼ cup cold margarine or butter until crumbly. Stir in ¼ cup chopped nuts. After reducing oven temperature to 350°F and baking pie for 30 minutes, spread topping evenly over pie; bake 10 minutes longer.

FESTIVE MINCEMEAT TARTLETS

- Pastry for double pie crust
- 1½ cups prepared mincemeat
- ½ cup chopped, peeled tart apple
- ⅓ cup golden raisins
- ⅓ cup chopped walnuts
- 3 tablespoons brandy or frozen apple juice concentrate, thawed
- 1 tablespoon grated lemon peel

Preheat oven to 400°F. Divide pastry in half. Refrigerate one half. Roll remaining half on lightly floured surface to form 13-inch circle. Cut six 4-inch rounds. Fit each pastry round into 2¾-inch muffin cup. Prick inside of crust with fork; set aside. Repeat with remaining pastry.

Bake unfilled pastry crusts 8 minutes. Meanwhile, combine mincemeat, apple, raisins, walnuts, brandy and lemon peel in medium bowl until well blended. Remove crusts from oven; fill each with rounded tablespoonful of mincemeat mixture. Press lightly into crust with back of spoon.

Bake 18 to 20 minutes more or until crust edges are golden. Cool in pan 5 minutes. Carefully remove from pan to wire rack. Serve warm or cool completely.   *Makes 12 tartlets*

Apple Streusel Mince Pie

APPLE STREUSEL MINCE PIE

3 all-purpose apples, pared and thinly
    sliced
½ cup plus 3 tablespoons unsifted flour
2 tablespoons margarine or butter,
    melted
1 (9-inch) unbaked pastry shell
1 jar NONE SUCH® Ready-to-Use
    Mincemeat (Regular or Brandy &
    Rum)
¼ cup firmly packed light brown sugar
1 teaspoon ground cinnamon
⅓ cup cold margarine or butter
¼ cup chopped nuts

In large bowl, toss apples with *3 tablespoons*
flour and melted margarine; arrange in pastry
shell. Top with mincemeat. In medium bowl,
combine remaining *½ cup* flour, sugar and
cinnamon; cut in cold margarine until crumbly.
Add nuts; sprinkle over mincemeat. Bake in
lower half of 425°F oven 10 minutes. *Reduce
oven temperature to 375°F;* bake 25 minutes
longer or until golden. Cool. Garnish as
desired. *Makes 1 (9-inch) pie*

SWEET POTATO CUSTARD PIE

Pecan Crust (recipe follows)
3 eggs
1 can (16 ounces) vacuum-packed sweet
    potatoes, drained, mashed
½ cup packed brown sugar
1½ teaspoons ground cinnamon
1 teaspoon ground allspice
½ teaspoon salt
1 can (12 ounces) evaporated milk
Whipped cream (optional)
Pecan halves (optional)

Prepare Pecan Crust. In large bowl, beat eggs,
sweet potatoes, sugar, spices and salt. In small
saucepan, heat evaporated milk over medium
heat until hot; gradually stir into sweet potato
mixture. Pour into unbaked pie shell. Bake in
lower third of preheated 400°F oven 40 to 45
minutes or until knife inserted near center
comes out clean. Cool completely on wire rack.
If desired, garnish with whipped cream and
pecan halves. *Makes 1 (9-inch) pie*

PECAN CRUST

1½ cups all-purpose flour
¼ cup ground pecans
½ teaspoon salt
½ cup shortening
1 egg yolk
4 to 5 tablespoons ice water
2 teaspoons lemon juice

In large bowl, combine flour, ground pecans
and salt. Cut in shortening until mixture
resembles coarse crumbs. In small bowl, blend
egg yolk, 4 tablespoons water and lemon juice.
Add to flour mixture, mixing lightly with fork just
until dough sticks together. Add more water, if
necessary. Press into ball. Roll out on lightly
floured surface into 10-inch circle. Carefully fit
into 9-inch pie plate. Trim edge; flute as
desired. Prick bottom and side of pastry with
fork.

*Favorite recipe from **American Egg Board***

CLASSIC PECAN PIE

3 eggs
1 cup sugar
1 cup KARO® Light or Dark Corn Syrup
2 tablespoons MAZOLA® Margarine,
    melted
1 teaspoon vanilla
1½ cups pecan halves
    Easy-As-Pie Crust (recipe follows) *or* 1
    (9-inch) frozen deep-dish pie crust*

Preheat oven to 350°F. In medium bowl beat eggs slightly. Add sugar, corn syrup, margarine and vanilla; stir until well blended. Stir in pecans. Pour into pie crust. Bake 50 to 55 minutes or until knife inserted halfway between center and edge comes out clean. Cool on wire rack.   *Makes 8 servings*

*To use prepared frozen pie crust, do not thaw crust. Preheat oven and a cookie sheet. Pour filling into frozen crust; bake pie as directed on cookie sheet.

PREP TIME: 10 minutes
BAKE TIME: 55 minutes, plus cooling

CALIFORNIA PECAN PIE: Stir ¼ cup sour cream into eggs until blended.

KENTUCKY BOURBON PECAN PIE: Add up to 2 tablespoons bourbon to filling.

CHOCOLATE PECAN PIE: Reduce sugar to ⅓ cup. Melt 4 squares (1 ounce each) semisweet chocolate with margarine.

EASY–AS–PIE CRUST

1¼ cups flour
⅛ teaspoon salt
½ cup MAZOLA® Margarine
2 tablespoons cold water

In medium bowl mix flour and salt. With pastry blender or 2 knives, cut in margarine until mixture resembles fine crumbs. Sprinkle water over flour mixture while tossing with fork to blend well. Press dough firmly into ball. On lightly floured surface roll out to 12-inch circle. Fit loosely into 9-inch pie plate. Trim and flute edge. Fill and bake according to recipe.
                    Makes 1 (9-inch) pie crust

PREP TIME: 15 minutes

ORANGE PECAN PIE

3 eggs
½ cup GRANDMA'S® MOLASSES
    Unsulphured
½ cup light corn syrup
¼ cup orange juice
1 teaspoon grated orange peel
1 teaspoon vanilla
1½ cups whole pecans
1 (9-inch) unbaked pie shell

Heat oven to 350°F. In large bowl, beat eggs. Add molasses, corn syrup, orange juice, orange peel and vanilla; beat until well blended. Stir in pecans. Pour into unbaked pie shell. Bake at 350°F. for 40 to 50 minutes or until filling is set. Cool. Serve with whipped cream, if desired.
                            Makes 8 servings

Classic Pecan Pie

RICE PUDDING PEAR TART

½ (15-ounce) package refrigerated pie
    crust
2 cups dry red wine
1 teaspoon ground cinnamon
2 large pears, peeled, halved, and cored
2 cups cooked rice
2 cups half-and-half
½ cup sugar
2 tablespoons butter or margarine
¼ teaspoon salt
2 eggs, beaten
1 teaspoon vanilla extract
1 tablespoon sugar

Preheat oven to 450°F. Prepare pie crust according to package directions. Place in 10-inch tart pan. Bake 8 to 10 minutes or until lightly browned; set aside. *Reduce oven temperature to 350°F.*

Place wine and cinnamon in 10-inch skillet; bring to a boil. Add pears; reduce heat, cover and poach 10 minutes. Carefully turn pears in liquid; poach 5 to 10 minutes or until tender. Remove from wine; set aside.

Combine rice, half-and-half, ½ cup sugar, butter, and salt in 3-quart saucepan. Cook over medium heat 12 to 15 minutes or until slightly thickened. Gradually stir ¼ of hot rice pudding mixture into eggs; return mixture to saucepan, stirring constantly. Continue to cook 1 to 2 minutes. Stir in vanilla. Pour rice pudding mixture into prepared crust. Place pears, cut sides down, on cutting surface. Cut thin lengthwise slices into each pear one third of the way down from stem end. Fan pears over pudding mixture.

Bake 30 minutes or until pudding is set. Remove from oven; sprinkle with 1 tablespoon sugar. Place tart in oven about 4 to 5 inches from heat; broil 1 to 2 minutes or until top is browned. Cool before serving. Garnish as desired. Tart can be made ahead, if desired.
Makes 1 (10-inch) tart

*Favorite recipe from **USA Rice Federation***

Rice Pudding Pear Tart

BRANDIED FRUIT PIE

**1 KEEBLER® Ready-Crust® Graham
  Cracker Pie Crust
2 packages (8 ounces each) mixed, pitted
  dried fruit
¾ cup plus 1 tablespoon water
¼ cup plus 1 tablespoon brandy or
  cognac
5 thin lemon slices
¾ cup packed brown sugar
1 teaspoon ground cinnamon
¼ teaspoon ground nutmeg
¼ teaspoon ground cloves
¼ teaspoon salt
½ cup graham cracker crumbs
¼ cup butter or margarine, melted
  Hard sauce or whipped cream
    (optional)
  Lemon slices for garnish**

In medium saucepan, combine dried fruit, ¾
cup of the water, ¼ cup of the brandy and the
5 lemon slices. Simmer over low heat 10
minutes or until liquid is absorbed. Remove and
discard lemon slices. Stir in sugar, spices, salt,
remaining 1 tablespoon water and remaining 1
tablespoon brandy; pour into pie crust. Sprinkle
graham cracker crumbs evenly over top of pie.
Drizzle melted butter over crumbs. Bake in
preheated 350°F oven 30 minutes. Cool on
wire rack. Serve warm or at room temperature.
If desired, serve with hard sauce or whipped
cream; garnish with lemon slices.

Makes 8 servings

Brandied Fruit Pie

PREMIER WHITE FRUIT TART

Pastry for single-crust, 9-inch pie
⅓ cup granulated sugar
¼ cup all-purpose flour
3 egg yolks
1 cup milk
1 package (6 ounces) NESTLÉ® Premier
   White Baking Bars, chopped
1 teaspoon vanilla extract
¼ cup apricot jam, warmed
2 kiwifruit, peeled and sliced
1 cup raspberries
   Premier White Leaves (page 243),
   optional

LINE 9-inch tart pan with pastry; trim edges. Prick pastry with fork. Bake in preheated 425°F. oven for 10 to 12 minutes until crust is lightly browned. Cool to room temperature.

COMBINE sugar and flour in small saucepan; stir in egg yolks and milk. Cook over medium heat, stirring constantly, until mixture comes to a boil. Reduce heat. Simmer, stirring constantly, for 3 minutes until mixture is thickened and smooth. Remove from heat.

ADD baking bars and vanilla; stir until smooth. Press plastic wrap directly on surface of filling; chill completely.

REMOVE tart shell from pan. Brush jam over bottom; let stand 5 minutes. Spread with filling. Arrange fruit on top. Chill. Garnish with Premier White Leaves, if desired.

Makes 6 to 8 servings

Premier White Fruit Tart

PREMIER WHITE LEAVES: Wash and dry very well about 6 non-toxic leaves, such as lemon leaves, grape leaves, rose leaves, violet leaves or nasturtium leaves;* set aside.

Melt 4 ounces NESTLÉ® Premier White Baking Bars. Onto the back side of each leaf, spoon or brush melted Premier White mixture about 1⁄16 inch thick. If Premier White mixture runs over edge of leaf, wipe off edge of leaf with fingertip. Place coated leaves on plate or cookie sheet; refrigerate about 30 minutes or until firm. Gently peel leaf from firm Premier White mixture. Arrange white leaves on dessert, as desired.

Makes about 6 large leaves

*These non-toxic leaves are available in florist shops.

PEPPERMINT FUDGE PIE

1 KEEBLER® Ready Crust® Chocolate Flavored Pie Crust
1 packaged (6 ounces) semisweet chocolate chips
2 cups miniature marshmallows
¼ cup milk or cream
2 tablespoons chocolate-mint liqueur
3 cups whipped cream, divided
2 tablespoons crushed peppermint candies or candy canes

In microwave-safe bowl, combine chocolate chips, marshmallows and milk. Cook at MEDIUM (50% power) 2 to 3 minutes, stirring twice, until smooth. Stir in liqueur. Cool at room temperature. Fold in 1½ cups whipped cream. Spoon into pie shell. Fold crushed candies into remaining 1½ cups whipped cream. Spread over chocolate layer. Cover and freeze until firm, about 3 hours. Pie may be made and frozen several weeks ahead. Remove pie from freezer and slice. Let stand 3 to 5 minutes before serving. Store leftovers in freezer.

Makes 8 servings

CHOCOLATE TRUFFLE TART

CRUST
⅔ cup all-purpose flour
½ cup powdered sugar
½ cup ground walnuts
6 tablespoons butter or margarine, softened
⅓ cup NESTLÉ® Toll House® Baking Cocoa

FILLING
1¼ cups heavy whipping cream
¼ cup granulated sugar
2 cups (12-ounce package) NESTLÉ® Toll House® Semi-Sweet Chocolate Morsels
2 tablespoons seedless raspberry jam
Sweetened whipped cream (optional)
Fresh raspberries (optional)

FOR CRUST:
BEAT flour, powdered sugar, walnuts, butter and cocoa in large mixer bowl until a soft dough forms. Press dough onto bottom and side of ungreased 9- or 9½-inch fluted tart pan with removable bottom.

BAKE in preheated 350°F. oven for 12 to 14 minutes or until puffed. Cool completely on wire rack.

FOR FILLING:
HEAT cream and granulated sugar in medium saucepan just until boiling, stirring occasionally. Remove from heat. Stir in morsels and jam; let stand for 5 minutes. Whisk until chocolate mixture is smooth. Transfer to small mixer bowl. Cover; chill for 45 to 60 minutes or until mixture is cool and slightly thickened.

BEAT for 20 to 30 seconds, just until color lightens slightly. Spoon into crust. Chill until firm. Remove rim of pan; garnish with whipped cream and raspberries. *Makes 1 (9-inch) tart*

NOTE: This tart may be made in 9-inch pie plate following above directions.

GINGER & PEAR TART

30 gingersnap cookies
½ cup chopped pecans
⅓ cup butter, melted
1 cup sour cream
¾ cup half-and-half
1 package (4-serving size) vanilla instant
  pudding mix
2 tablespoons apricot brandy
4 ripe pears*
⅓ cup packed dark brown sugar
½ teaspoon ground ginger

Preheat oven to 350°F. Combine cookies and pecans in food processor or blender container; process until finely crushed. Combine crumb mixture and butter in medium bowl. Press firmly onto bottom and up side of 10-inch quiche dish or 9-inch pie plate. Bake 7 minutes; cool completely on wire rack.

Combine sour cream and half-and-half in large bowl. Mix until smooth. Whisk in pudding mix. Add apricot brandy. Whisk until smooth. Pour into prepared crust. Cover; refrigerate several hours or overnight.

Just before serving, preheat broiler. Peel pears. Cut into thin slices. Arrange in overlapping circles on top of pudding mixture. Combine brown sugar and ginger in small bowl. Sprinkle evenly over pears. Broil 4 to 6 minutes or until sugar is melted and bubbly. (Watch carefully so sugar does not burn.) Serve immediately.

Makes 6 to 8 servings

*Or, substitute 1 (16-ounce) can pear halves, drained and thinly sliced.

MARGARITA SOUFFLÉ PIE

PRETZEL CRUST
½ cup margarine
1¼ cups finely crushed pretzels
¼ cup sugar
FILLING
½ cup plus 2 tablespoons sugar
½ teaspoon grated lime peel
½ cup fresh lime juice
½ teaspoon salt
4 eggs, beaten
1 envelope unflavored gelatin
¼ cup tequila
¼ cup Triple Sec
3 drops green food coloring
1 container (4 ounces) frozen whipped
  topping, thawed

1. In 9-inch glass pie plate, melt margarine in microwave oven at HIGH (100% power) 1 to 1½ minutes. Add pretzels and sugar; mix well. Press mixture firmly in bottom and up side of pie plate. Refrigerate crust while preparing filling.

2. In 4-cup glass measure combine sugar, lime peel, lime juice and salt. Cook in microwave oven at HIGH (100% power) 1 to 1½ minutes or until sugar dissolves, stirring once. Slowly add eggs to lime juice mixture, whisking constantly. Cook at HIGH 30 seconds; stir mixture. Continue cooking at HIGH until mixture thickens, stirring every 15 seconds.

3. In 1-cup glass measure sprinkle gelatin over combined tequila and Triple Sec. Let stand 1 minute to soften. Cook gelatin mixture at HIGH 45 seconds or until gelatin dissolves. Add gelatin mixture and food coloring to lime mixture. Refrigerate 1 hour or until mixture is cool and slightly thickened. Fold in whipped topping and pour into prepared pretzel crust. Chill several hours or until set.

Makes 8 servings

*Favorite recipe from **National Turkey Federation***

Ginger & Pear Tart

Holiday

DESSERTS

FRUITED MERINGUE HEARTS MELBA

6 egg whites
¼ teaspoon cream of tartar
¼ teaspoon ground allspice
1½ cups sugar
   Melba Sauce (page 248)
3 cups assorted fruit (melon balls; sliced
      kiwifruit, peaches and strawberries; whole
      blackberries, blueberries, raspberries and
      grapes; pitted cherries)
   Mint sprigs (optional)

Line large cookie sheet with parchment paper; draw 6 hearts
(3×3 inches) on paper. Beat egg whites in large bowl with
electric mixer until foamy. Add cream of tartar; beat until soft
peaks form. Add allspice. Add sugar, 1 tablespoon at a time,
beating at high speed until stiff peaks form, about 5 minutes.

Preheat oven to 250°F. Spoon meringue into large pastry bag
fitted with medium star tip; pipe heart outlines on parchment
paper. Fill in heart shapes with meringue. Pipe second row on
top of first row of meringue around outside edges of hearts to
form rims. Bake 1 hour or until meringues are firm and crisp to
the touch. Turn off oven; leave meringues in oven with door
closed at least 2 hours.

Prepare Melba Sauce. Set aside. Fill meringue hearts with fruit.
Spoon about ¼ cup sauce onto each dessert plate and place
filled hearts on sauce. Garnish with mint sprig, if desired.
Makes 6 servings

continued on page 248

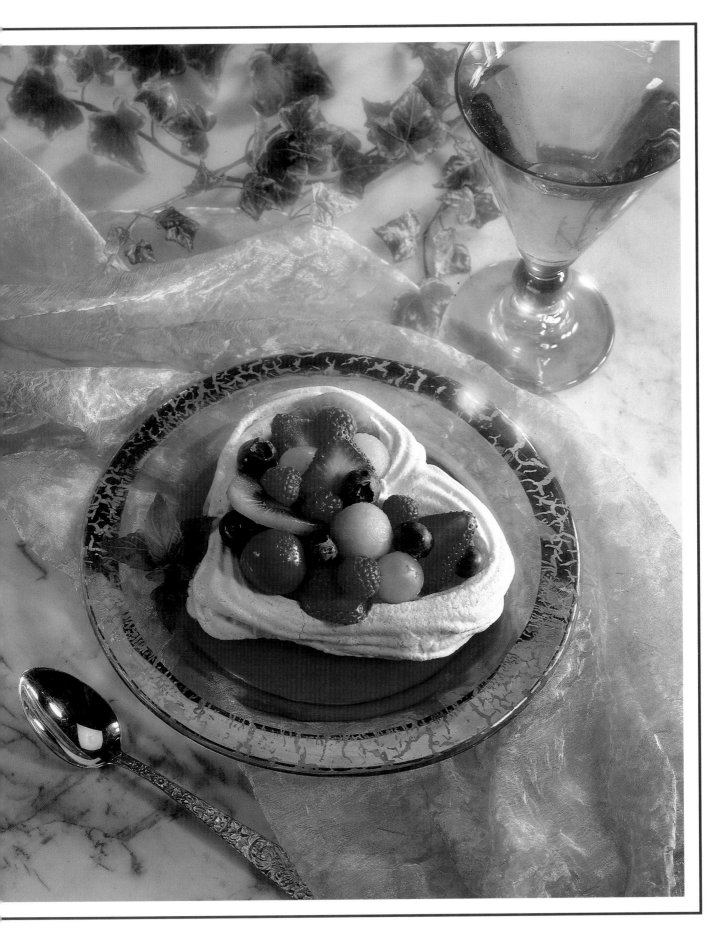

Fruited Meringue Hearts Melba, continued

MELBA SAUCE
 1 package (16 ounces) frozen
    unsweetened raspberries, thawed,
    drained
 ¼ cup sugar

Place raspberries and sugar in food processor or blender; process until smooth. Strain and discard seeds.   *Makes 1½ cups*

AMBROSIAL FRUIT DESSERT

 1 medium DOLE® Fresh Pineapple
 1 medium DOLE® Orange, peeled, sliced
 1 red DOLE® Apple, cored, sliced
 1 cup seedless DOLE® Grapes
   Fruit Glaze (recipe follows)
 4 teaspoons flaked coconut

• Twist crown from pineapple. Cut pineapple in half lengthwise. Refrigerate one half for another use, such as fruit salad. Cut fruit from shell. Cut fruit crosswise into thin slices.

• Arrange fruits on 4 dessert plates. Drizzle with Fruit Glaze. Sprinkle with coconut.
                    Makes 4 servings

FRUIT GLAZE
 ¾ cup DOLE® Pineapple Orange Juice
 2 tablespoons orange marmalade
 1 tablespoon cornstarch
 1 teaspoon rum extract
 2 teaspoons grated lime peel

Combine all ingredients except lime peel in saucepan. Cook, stirring, until sauce boils and thickens. Cool. Stir in lime peel.

MICROWAVE BAKED APPLES WITH RUM RAISIN SAUCE

 4 Rome Beauty apples (7 to 8 ounces
    each)
   Spiced Lemon Baste (recipe follows)
 ½ cup raisins
 3 tablespoons light rum*
 ¾ cup butter or margarine
 ¾ cup sugar
 ⅓ cup half-and-half
 1 egg, beaten
 ¾ teaspoon ground cinnamon
 ¾ teaspoon grated lemon peel

Core apples; peel skin from top third of each apple. Place apples in microwave-safe baking dish or custard cups. Pour Spiced Lemon Baste over apples. Cover with vented plastic wrap. Microwave at HIGH (100% power) 7 to 10 minutes or until apples are tender yet firm, rotating dish ¼ turn and basting apples after 4 minutes. Let stand while preparing sauce.

Microwave raisins and rum, covered, in microwave-safe container at HIGH 1 minute; set aside. Combine butter and sugar in microwave-safe container; microwave at HIGH 1½ minutes or until butter melts. Stir in half-and-half; microwave at HIGH 2 minutes or until just boiling. Stir small amount of hot sugar mixture into egg; return to remaining hot sugar mixture. Microwave at MEDIUM (50% power) 2½ to 3 minutes or until thickened, stirring after every minute. Stir in raisin mixture, cinnamon and lemon peel. Spoon over apples.
                    Makes 4 apples and 2½ cups sauce

*3 tablespoons water and ¼ teaspoon rum extract may be substituted for rum.

SPICED LEMON BASTE: Combine ¼ cup water or apple juice, 2 tablespoons lemon juice and ½ teaspoon ground cinnamon; stir to blend. Makes about ⅓ cup.

*Favorite recipe from **Washington Apple Commission***

ALL–AMERICAN PINEAPPLE & FRUIT TRIFLE

1 DOLE® Fresh Pineapple
1 cup frozen sliced peaches, thawed
1 cup frozen strawberries, thawed, sliced
1 cup frozen raspberries, thawed
1 (10-inch) angel food cake
1 package (4-serving size) vanilla flavor
   sugar free instant pudding and pie
   filling mix
⅓ cup cream sherry
½ cup thawed frozen whipped topping

• Twist crown from pineapple. Cut pineapple in half lengthwise. Refrigerate one half for another use, such as fruit salad. Cut fruit from shell. Cut fruit into thin wedges. Reserve 3 wedges for garnish; combine remaining pineapple with peaches and berries.

• Cut cake in half. Freeze one half for another use. Tear remaining cake into chunks.

• Prepare mix according to package directions.

• In 2-quart glass serving bowl, arrange half of cake chunks; sprinkle with half of sherry. Top with half each fruit mixture and pudding. Repeat layers. Cover; chill 1 hour or overnight.

• Just before serving, garnish with whipped topping and reserved pineapple wedges.
Makes 8 to 10 servings

All-American Pineapple & Fruit Trifle

PEARS EN CROÛTE (BAKED PEARS IN PASTRY)

  2 teaspoons granulated sugar
  ¼ teaspoon ground cinnamon
  1 egg white, slightly beaten
     Cold water
  ¼ cup golden raisins
  ¼ cup chopped walnuts
  2 tablespoons brown sugar
  1 package DUNCAN HINES® Cinnamon
     Muffin Mix
  8 small ripe pears
  1 cup all-purpose flour
  ½ BUTTER FLAVOR* CRISCO® Stick *or*
     ½ cup BUTTER FLAVOR CRISCO
     all-vegetable shortening
     Cinnamon sticks or vanilla beans, for
     garnish
     Caramel flavor topping, at room
     temperature or warmed

1. Preheat oven to 375°F. Grease 13×9×2-inch baking pan.

2. Combine granulated sugar and cinnamon in small bowl; set aside. Combine beaten egg white and 1 teaspoon water in small bowl; set aside.

3. Combine raisins, walnuts, brown sugar, contents of cinnamon swirl packet from Mix and contents of crumb topping packet from Mix in medium bowl; set aside.

4. Core and peel pears; set aside.

5. Combine muffin mix and flour in medium bowl. Cut in shortening with pastry blender or 2 knives until flour is blended to form pea-size chunks. Sprinkle 5 tablespoons *cold* water, 1 tablespoon at a time, over flour mixture. Toss lightly with fork until dough forms ball. Divide in half. Wrap one half with plastic wrap; reserve. Roll remaining dough on well-floured surface to form 13-inch square. Cut square into four 6½-inch squares. Repeat using reserved dough ball.

6. To assemble, fill pear centers with 1½ tablespoons raisin mixture. Cover each pear with square of pastry. Mold with palm of hand to shape, folding corners under pear bottom. Place pears ¾ inch apart in greased pan. Brush with egg white mixture. Sprinkle ¼ teaspoon cinnamon-sugar mixture over each pear.

7. Bake at 375°F for 33 to 35 minutes or until golden brown and pears are tender. Cool in pan for 5 minutes. Remove to serving dish. Insert cinnamon stick or piece of vanilla bean on top of pear to form stem. Drizzle caramel topping over pear, as desired. Serve warm or at room temperature. Refrigerate leftovers.

Makes 8 servings

*Butter Flavor Crisco® is artificially flavored.

QUICK RUMTOPF

  1 can (16 ounces) DEL MONTE® Yellow
     Cling Sliced Peaches
  1 can (16 ounces) DEL MONTE® Bartlett
     Pear Halves
  1 can (15½ ounces) DEL MONTE®
     Pineapple Chunks
  1 can (11 ounces) DEL MONTE®
     Mandarin Oranges
  1 cup rum
  1 cinnamon stick
  ½ cup DEL MONTE® Seedless Raisins

Drain fruit reserving syrup in medium saucepan. Add rum and cinnamon stick to reserved syrup. Bring to a boil, stirring occasionally. Cool. Layer fruit and raisins in rumtopf pot or large jars. Pour syrup mixture over fruit. Refrigerate. Allow 1 week to mellow. Serve as fruit compote or on ice cream or pound cake.

Makes 2 quarts

Pear en Croûte

CALIFORNIA KIWIFRUIT HOLIDAY FROZEN YOGURT WITH RED RASPBERRY SAUCE

2 California kiwifruit, peeled and
   coarsely chopped
1 tablespoon honey
1 pint frozen lowfat or nonfat vanilla
   yogurt, softened
1 to 2 drops green food coloring
   (optional)
1 package (10 ounces) frozen red
   raspberries in syrup, thawed
2 tablespoons triple sec or other orange-
   flavored liqueur
2 teaspoons cornstarch
3 California kiwifruit, ends trimmed and
   sliced lengthwise
  Fresh mint leaves (optional)
  Fresh or frozen whole raspberries
   (optional)

In food processor or blender, purée chopped kiwifruit; stir in honey. Place in freezer and freeze until slushy (about 45 minutes). In stainless steel bowl, quickly combine softened yogurt, kiwifruit mixture and food coloring; refreeze in bowl. With small ice cream scoop (about 2 tablespoons) form 12 balls frozen yogurt mixture and place on waxed-paper-lined tray; refreeze.

Meanwhile, to make sauce, in food processor or blender purée thawed raspberries. Over saucepan, strain berries through a fine sieve, pressing with back of spoon. Discard seeds. Stir in triple sec and cornstarch. Bring to boil, stirring constantly until slightly thickened. Cool; cover and chill. To assemble, spoon about 2 tablespoons sauce on each of 6 dessert plates or shallow bowls. Arrange kiwifruit slices and frozen yogurt balls on sauce. Garnish with mint and whole raspberries. *Makes 6 servings*

*Favorite recipe from **California Kiwifruit Commission***

California Kiwifruit Holiday Frozen Yogurt with Red Raspberry Sauce

HAZELNUT MERINGUE WITH POACHED PEARS

POACHED PEARS
3 Bosc pears, peeled and cored
2 cups NEWMAN'S OWN® Lemonade
¾ cup sugar
1 vanilla bean
1 cinnamon stick
  Water
MERINGUE
4 egg whites
1½ cups granulated sugar
1 teaspoon vanilla
½ teaspoon white vinegar
1 cup (4½ ounces) ground hazelnuts
1 cup whipping cream, whipped*
  Powdered sugar
  Chocolate Sauce (page 253)

In medium saucepan place pears, lemonade, sugar, vanilla bean and cinnamon stick. Add enough water to cover pears. Bring to a boil and simmer slowly until just tender, 10 to 20 minutes. Let pears cool in liquid. Drain and slice.

Preheat oven to 375°F. Grease and flour two 9-inch springform pans. Line bottom of each pan with parchment paper; grease paper. Beat egg whites until stiff. Gradually add granulated sugar while beating continuously until mixture is very stiff and stands in peaks. Beat in vanilla and vinegar. Fold in ground nuts. Spread in prepared pans, smoothing tops. Bake 30 to 40 minutes. Tops should be crisp but insides should be soft. Remove from pans and cool on wire racks.

At least 3 hours before serving, arrange sliced pears on one meringue; spread with whipped cream. Top with second meringue, flat side up. Sprinkle with powdered sugar. Refrigerate for 3 hours. Serve with Chocolate Sauce.

Makes 6 servings

*Add 1 tablespoon granulated sugar and 1 teaspoon vanilla to whipped cream, if desired.

CHOCOLATE SAUCE
    1 cup light cream
    4 ounces semi-sweet chocolate
    3 tablespoons sugar
    4 egg yolks**
    2 teaspoons vanilla
    2 tablespoons orange-flavored liqueur
        (optional)

In small saucepan heat cream and chocolate over low heat. Meanwhile, beat sugar and yolks until light. Stir into chocolate-cream mixture and stir over low heat for 2 to 3 minutes or until rich and smooth. Do not bring to a boil. Let cool slightly and add flavorings. *Makes 1½ cups*

**Use clean, uncracked eggs.

COUNTRY HOLIDAY CRISP

    6 cups sliced peeled apples
    ¼ cup orange juice
    2 cups RALSTON® brand Fruit Muesli
        with Cranberries
    ½ cup all-purpose flour
    ⅓ cup sugar
    ¼ cup (½ stick) margarine or butter,
        softened
    1 teaspoon ground cinnamon
        Vanilla ice cream (optional)

Preheat oven to 375°F. In ungreased 2-quart baking dish place apples and orange juice; toss lightly. In medium bowl place cereal, flour, sugar, margarine and cinnamon; blend together. Sprinkle cereal mixture over apples. Bake, covered, 30 to 35 minutes or until apples are tender. Remove cover and bake an additional 10 minutes. Serve with vanilla ice cream, if desired. *Makes 8 servings*

MICROWAVE DIRECTIONS: In ungreased 2-quart microwave-safe baking dish place apples and orange juice; toss lightly. In medium bowl place cereal, flour, sugar, margarine and cinnamon; blend together. Sprinkle cereal mixture over apples. Microwave on HIGH (100% power) 10 to 12 minutes or until apples are tender. Serve with vanilla ice cream, if desired.

TEMPTING APPLE TRIFLES

- ½ cup skim milk
- 1½ teaspoons cornstarch
- 4½ teaspoons dark brown sugar
- 1 egg white
- ½ teaspoon canola oil
- ½ teaspoon vanilla extract
- ½ teaspoon rum extract, divided
- ¼ cup unsweetened apple cider, divided
- 2 tablespoons raisins
- ½ teaspoon ground cinnamon
- 1 cup peeled and chopped Golden Delicious apple
- 1 cup ½-inch angel food cake cubes, divided

To prepare custard, combine milk and cornstarch in small, heavy saucepan; stir until cornstarch is completely dissolved. Add brown sugar, egg white and oil; blend well. Slowly bring to a boil over medium-low heat until thickened, stirring constantly with whisk. Remove from heat; stir in vanilla and ¼ teaspoon rum extract. Set aside; cool completely.

Combine 2 tablespoons cider, raisins and cinnamon in medium saucepan; bring to a boil over medium-low heat. Add apple and cook until apple is fork-tender and all liquid has been absorbed, stirring frequently. Remove from heat; set aside to cool.

To assemble, place ¼ cup cake cubes in bottom of 2 small trifle or dessert dishes. Combine remaining 2 tablespoons cider and ¼ teaspoon rum extract in small bowl; mix well. Spoon 1½ teaspoons cider mixture over cake in each dish. Top each with ¼ of custard mixture and ¼ cup cooked apple mixture. Repeat layers. Serve immediately. Garnish with fresh mint, if desired. *Makes 2 servings*

WINTERFRUIT COBBLER

FILLING
- 2 cups SUN-MAID® Raisins
- 2 cups fresh or frozen cranberries
- ¾ cup sugar
- 2 teaspoons cornstarch
- ½ teaspoon ground allspice
- 1 cup orange juice

TOPPING
- 1 cup all-purpose flour
- 2 tablespoons sugar
- 2 teaspoons baking powder
- ¼ teaspoon salt
- ¼ cup butter or margarine
- ½ cup milk
  - Sugar
  - Ground cinnamon

TO PREPARE FILLING: In medium saucepan, combine raisins, cranberries, sugar, cornstarch and allspice. Gradually stir in orange juice. Bring to boil over high heat; reduce heat to low and simmer, stirring until cranberries begin to pop and mixture thickens slightly. Pour into shallow 1½-quart baking dish.

TO PREPARE TOPPING: In small bowl, combine flour, sugar, baking powder and salt. Cut in butter until mixture resembles coarse crumbs. Mix in milk lightly with fork. Drop spoonfuls of batter over filling; sprinkle lightly with additional sugar mixed with a little cinnamon. Bake in preheated 400°F oven about 25 minutes or until golden. Serve warm with ice cream or whipping cream. *Makes 6 servings*

Tempting Apple Trifles

MOCHA FRUITY TORTE

1⅓ cups plus ¼ cup sugar, divided
1 cup all-purpose flour
3 tablespoons unsweetened cocoa
1 tablespoon espresso powder or instant coffee
1 teaspoon baking soda
¼ teaspoon salt
½ cup sour cream
½ cup butter or margarine, softened
2 eggs
1 teaspoon vanilla
1 package (3 ounces) cream cheese, softened
1 cup whipping cream
1 can (11 ounces) mandarin orange segments, drained
2 kiwifruit, peeled, halved lengthwise and sliced
3 or 4 strawberries, sliced
1 slice star fruit (optional)

Preheat oven to 350°F. Grease and flour 9-inch round pan. Combine 1⅓ cups sugar, flour, cocoa, espresso powder, baking soda and salt in large bowl. Add sour cream, butter, eggs and vanilla. Beat at low speed until combined. Beat at medium speed 3 minutes or until fluffy. Pour into pan. Bake 40 minutes or until set. Cool in pan on wire rack 10 minutes. Remove from pan; cool on wire rack.

Process cream cheese and remaining ¼ cup sugar in food processor until light and fluffy. Beat whipping cream in bowl until soft peaks form. Beat cream cheese mixture into whipped cream.

To serve, carefully cut cake horizontally in half to make two layers. Place bottom half of cake on plate. Spread with half the filling. Top with remaining cake layer. Spread with remaining filling. Arrange fruit over top.

Makes 10 servings

CINNAMON CRISP PLUM PUDDING

2 cups KEEBLER® Cinnamon Crisp Graham Cracker crumbs (about 15 large crackers)
1¼ teaspoons baking soda
½ teaspoon salt
¼ teaspoon ground ginger
¼ teaspoon ground cloves
½ cup shortening
½ cup packed brown sugar
2 eggs
½ cup water
1 can (16 ounces) purple plums in heavy syrup, drained, pitted and chopped (syrup reserved)
1 cup golden raisins
½ cup chopped walnuts
Plum Sauce (recipe follows)

Stir together Cinnamon Crisp Graham Cracker crumbs, baking soda, salt, ginger and cloves; set aside. Cream shortening with brown sugar until fluffy. Beat in eggs, 1 at a time. Add crumb mixture alternately with water to sugar mixture, beating well after each addition. Stir in chopped plums, raisins and walnuts. If mixture is dry, stir in more water 1 tablespoon at a time. Pour batter into well-greased 5- to 6-cup kugelhopf or Bundt pan. Bake in preheated 375°F oven 40 to 50 minutes or until wooden pick inserted near center comes out clean. Loosen edges of plum pudding; immediately turn out of pan onto serving platter. Spoon Plum Sauce over slices of pudding.   *Makes 8 to 10 servings*

PLUM SAUCE: Combine plum syrup (about 1 cup), ¼ cup granulated sugar and 2 tablespoons cornstarch in small saucepan. Cook over medium heat, stirring constantly, until thickened, about 5 minutes. Stir in 1 tablespoon lemon juice or brandy.

Mocha Fruity Torte

CHOCOLATE/ESPRESSO DREAM LAYERS

½ gallon DREYER'S or EDY'S Chocolate
    Brownie Chunk Frozen Yogurt
1 quart DREYER'S or EDY'S GRAND
    Espresso Chip Ice Cream
½ gallon DREYER'S or EDY'S GRAND
    Mocha Almond Fudge Ice Cream or
    Light Ice Cream
Chocolate Espresso Sauce (recipe
    follows)

• Slightly soften frozen yogurt and ice creams at room temperature for 10 minutes.

• Press alternating layers of frozen yogurt and ice cream flavors into 6-cup ring mold, fluted mold or springform pan. Freeze until firm (about 30 minutes).

• To unmold, briefly dip mold in hot water to loosen sides, then turn out onto serving plate. Slice and serve with warm Chocolate Espresso Sauce.   *Makes 8 servings*

CHOCOLATE ESPRESSO SAUCE

1 cup sugar
½ cup water
2 tablespoons unsalted butter
4 ounces unsweetened chocolate,
    chopped
1 teaspoon instant espresso or coffee
    granules

• Combine sugar, water and butter in heavy saucepan. Bring to a simmer, stirring until sugar dissolves. Remove from heat.

• Add chocolate and coffee. Stir until melted and smooth.   *Makes about 1½ cups*

NOTE: Sauce may be made ahead and reheated.

TIRAMISU

2 packages (8 ounces each) cream
    cheese, softened
⅔ cup sugar
¼ cup Marsala wine
2 teaspoons vanilla extract
2 cups whipping cream, whipped
1 cup strong coffee or espresso, chilled
2 tablespoons almond liqueur *or*
    1 teaspoon almond extract
2 packages (3 ounces each) ladyfingers
    (24 ladyfingers)
1 cup HEATH® Bits

In mixing bowl, beat cream cheese and sugar until light. Blend in wine and vanilla. Fold in whipped cream. In small bowl or measuring cup, combine coffee and liqueur. To assemble, split each ladyfinger in half horizontally and vertically. Place four pieces in each of eight footed dessert or wine glasses. Drizzle ladyfingers with coffee mixture. Top with about ¼ cup cream mixture and several teaspoons Heath® Bits. Repeat for two more layers, ending with Heath® Bits. Cover; refrigerate at least 2 hours before serving.

Makes 8 servings

Tiramisu

Linzer Torte

LINZER TORTE

½ cup whole almonds, toasted
1½ cups all-purpose flour
1 teaspoon ground cinnamon
¼ teaspoon salt
¾ cup granulated sugar
½ cup butter or margarine, softened
½ teaspoon grated lemon peel
1 egg
¾ cup raspberry or apricot jam
Sifted powdered sugar

Process almonds in food processor until ground, but not pasty. Preheat oven to 375°F. Combine flour, almonds, cinnamon and salt in medium bowl; set aside. Beat granulated sugar, butter and lemon peel in large bowl with electric mixer at medium speed about 5 minutes or until light and fluffy, scraping down side of bowl once. Beat in egg until well blended. Beat in flour mixture at low speed until well blended.

Spoon ⅔ of dough onto bottom of 10-inch tart pan with removable bottom. Pat dough evenly over bottom and up side of pan. Spread jam over bottom of dough. Roll remaining ⅓ of dough on lightly floured surface into 10×5-inch rectangle. Cut dough into ten ½-inch-wide strips using pizza wheel or sharp knife.

Arrange 4 or 5 strips of dough lengthwise across jam. Arrange another 4 or 5 strips of dough crosswise across top. Trim and press ends of dough strips into edge of crust. Bake 25 to 35 minutes or until crust is golden brown. Cool completely in pan on wire rack. Remove torte from pan. Sprinkle with powdered sugar. Cut into wedges. Store, tightly covered, at room temperature 1 to 2 days.   *Makes 12 servings*

CHARLOTTE RUSSE

2 cups boiling water
1 package (8-serving size) *or* 2 packages
    (4-serving size) JELL-O® Brand
    Black Cherry, Orange or Black
    Raspberry Flavor Gelatin
1 quart vanilla ice cream, softened
12 ladyfingers, split*
    COOL WHIP® Whipped Topping,
    thawed

Stir boiling water into gelatin in medium bowl 2 minutes or until dissolved. Spoon in ice cream, stirring until melted and smooth. Refrigerate until thickened (or when spoon drawn through mixture leaves definite impression.)

Meanwhile, trim about 1 inch off one end of each split ladyfinger. Place ladyfingers, cut ends down, around side of 8-inch springform pan. Spoon gelatin mixture into pan. Refrigerate 4 hours or until firm. Remove side of pan. Garnish with whipped topping. Decorate as desired. *Makes 10 servings*

*Or use thin strips of sponge cake.

PREP TIME: 20 minutes
CHILL TIME: 4 hours

Charlotte Russe

CHOCOLATE TRUFFLE LOAF WITH SWEET RASPBERRY SAUCE

    2 cups heavy cream, divided
    3 egg yolks
    16 squares (1 ounce each) semisweet
        chocolate
    ½ cup KARO® Light or Dark Corn Syrup
    ½ cup MAZOLA® Margarine
    ¼ cup confectioners' sugar
    1 teaspoon vanilla
        Sweet Raspberry Sauce (recipe
        follows)

Line 9¼×5¼×2¾-inch loaf pan with plastic wrap. In small bowl mix ½ cup cream with egg yolks. In large saucepan combine chocolate, corn syrup and margarine; stir over medium heat until melted. Add egg mixture. Cook 3 minutes over medium heat, stirring constantly. Cool to room temperature. In small bowl with mixer at medium speed, beat remaining 1½ cups cream, sugar and vanilla until soft peaks form. Gently fold into chocolate mixture just until combined. Pour into prepared pan; cover with plastic wrap. Refrigerate overnight or chill in freezer 3 hours. Slice and serve with Sweet Raspberry Sauce. Garnish with fresh raspberries, if desired.   *Makes 12 servings*

Chocolate Truffle Loaf with Sweet Raspberry Sauce

SWEET RASPBERRY SAUCE: In blender or food processor purée 1 package (10 ounces) frozen raspberries, thawed; strain to remove seeds. Stir in ⅓ cup KARO® Light Corn Syrup.

PREP TIME: 30 minutes, plus chilling

MICROWAVE DIRECTIONS: Prepare pan and egg mixture as above. In 3-quart microwavable bowl mix chocolate, corn syrup and margarine. Microwave on HIGH (100% power) 2 to 2½ minutes or until melted, stirring twice. Stir in egg mixture. Microwave on HIGH 3 minutes, stirring twice. Continue as above.

PUMPKIN GINGERBREAD SURPRISE

    2 tablespoons butter
    ½ (6¼-ounce) bag miniature
        marshmallows
    1 cup gingersnaps
    1 quart DREYER'S or EDY'S GRAND
        Pumpkin Ice Cream*
        Pumpkin pie spice or ground nutmeg

• Melt butter in saucepan over low heat; slowly add marshmallows, stirring constantly until melted.

• Divide gingersnaps among 4 serving bowls or dessert plates; top each serving with 1 scoop Dreyer's or Edy's Grand Pumpkin Ice Cream.

• Spoon marshmallow mixture over ice cream; sprinkle with pumpkin pie spice.
                                    Makes 4 servings

*Available September through December.

Tiramisu

TIRAMISU

6 egg yolks
½ cup sugar
⅓ cup cognac or brandy
2 cups (15 ounces) SARGENTO® Old
    Fashioned Ricotta Cheese
1 cup whipping cream, whipped
32 ladyfingers, split in half
3 teaspoons instant coffee dissolved in
    ¾ cup boiling water
1 tablespoon unsweetened cocoa
  Chocolate Curls (recipe follows),
    optional

In top of double boiler, whisk together egg yolks, sugar and cognac. Place pan over simmering water. Cook, whisking constantly, until mixture is thickened, about 2 to 3 minutes. Cool. In large bowl of electric mixer, beat yolk mixture and Ricotta cheese on medium speed until blended. Fold in whipped cream.

Place 32 ladyfinger halves in bottom of 13×9-inch pan, cut side up. Brush with half of coffee; spread with half of Ricotta mixture. Repeat layers. Chill 2 hours. Just before serving, dust with cocoa; cut into squares. Garnish with Chocolate Curls. *Makes 16 servings*

CHOCOLATE CURLS: Combine ½ cup semisweet chocolate chips and 2 teaspoons shortening in small microwavable bowl. Microwave at HIGH (100% power) 1 minute. Stir until chocolate is melted. Spread evenly in thin layer on small cookie sheet. Cool. Hold small pancake turner upside-down at a 45° angle to cookie sheet. Run pancake turner across chocolate, allowing chocolate to curl.

Peppermint Cheesecake

Lightly grease sides of 8- or 9-inch springform pan. Combine crust ingredients; mix well. Press evenly over bottom of pan. Chill while preparing filling. In bowl of electric mixer, combine Ricotta cheese, sugar, half-and-half, flour, vanilla and salt; beat until smooth. Add eggs, one at a time; beat until smooth. Place candies in heavy plastic bag. Crush with meat mallet or hammer. Reserve ¼ cup large pieces for garnish; stir remaining crushed candies into batter. Pour batter over crust. Bake at 350°F 1 hour or until center is just set. Turn off oven; cool in oven with door propped open 30 minutes. Remove to wire cooling rack; loosen cake from rim of pan with metal spatula. Cool completely; chill at least 4 hours. Just before serving, garnish cake around top edge with reserved crushed candies and mint leaves, if desired.

Makes 8 servings

PEPPERMINT CHEESECAKE

CRUST
  1¼ cups vanilla wafer crumbs
  3 tablespoons melted margarine
FILLING
  4 cups (30 ounces) SARGENTO® Light
    Ricotta Cheese
  ½ cup sugar
  ½ cup half-and-half
  ¼ cup all-purpose flour
  1 teaspoon vanilla
  ¼ teaspoon salt
  3 eggs
  16 peppermint candies
    Fresh mint leaves (optional)

RASPBERRY PEAR CHEESECAKE

  1 (10-ounce) package frozen raspberries
    in syrup, thawed
  2 teaspoons cornstarch
  1 (6½- to 8-inch diameter) prepared
    plain cheesecake
    Canned Pears (page 265)
    Fresh raspberries (optional)
  ½ ounce semi-sweet chocolate
  ½ teaspoon shortening

Combine raspberries in syrup and cornstarch in small saucepan. Stir to dissolve cornstarch. Over medium heat, bring to a boil and cook just until clear and thickened, stirring constantly. Cool for 10 minutes. Spoon ⅓ cup raspberry sauce on top of cheesecake. Cut 3 or 4 Canned Pear halves in half lengthwise. Arrange pears spoke-fashion on top of sauce. Garnish with fresh raspberries, if desired. Melt chocolate with shortening. Drizzle over pears. Cut into wedges and serve with remaining raspberry sauce. *Makes 6 to 8 servings*

CANNED PEARS

- **4 pounds pears**
- **3½ cups water**
- **1¾ cups sugar**
- **3 tablespoons bottled lemon juice**
- **6 KERR® pint jars *or* 3 KERR® quart jars (with bands and lids)**

Peel, core and halve pears lengthwise. In 6- to 8-quart saucepan, combine water, sugar and lemon juice. Over medium-high heat, bring to a boil. Add pears and return to a boil. Remove from heat. Immediately fill jars with pears and syrup, leaving ½-inch headspace. Carefully run a non-metallic utensil down inside of jars to remove trapped air bubbles. Wipe jar tops and threads clean. Place hot lids on jars and screw bands on firmly. Process in boiling water canner 20 minutes for pint jars, 25 minutes for quart jars.   *Makes 6 pints or 3 quarts*

NOTES: For smaller yield, halve ingredients. Processing times and other directions remain the same.

Processing times must be increased for altitudes higher than 1000 feet. For altitudes between 1001-3000 feet, add 5 minutes; 3001-6000 feet, add 10 minutes; 6001-8000 feet, add 15 minutes; 8001-10,000 feet, add 20 minutes.

Raspberry Pear Cheesecake

EGGNOG CHEESECAKE

2 packages (5½ ounces each) chocolate-laced pirouette cookies
⅓ cup graham cracker crumbs
3 tablespoons margarine, melted
2 packages (8 ounces each) PHILADELPHIA BRAND® Cream Cheese, softened
2 cups canned or dairy eggnog
1 cup milk
2 packages (4-serving size each) JELL-O® French Vanilla or Vanilla Flavor Instant Pudding & Pie Filling
1 tablespoon light rum
⅛ teaspoon ground nutmeg
COOL WHIP® Whipped Topping, thawed (optional)

Cut 1 inch crosswise off each cookie. Crush short pieces; set aside long pieces for garnish.

Combine cookie crumbs, graham cracker crumbs and margarine until well mixed. Press firmly into bottom of 9-inch springform pan.

Beat cream cheese in large bowl with electric mixer on medium speed until well blended. Gradually add 1 cup of the eggnog, blending until smooth. Add remaining 1 cup eggnog, milk, pudding mix, rum and nutmeg. Beat until well blended, about 1 minute. Pour into prepared pan. Refrigerate 3 hours or until firm.

Run a small knife or spatula around side of pan to loosen cheesecake; remove side of pan. Press reserved cookie pieces, cut sides down, into side of cake. Garnish with whipped topping and additional cookies, if desired.

Makes 12 servings

CHOCOLATE TURTLE CHEESECAKE

24 chocolate sandwich cookies, ground (about 2¾ cups)
2 tablespoons butter or margarine, melted
2 packages (8 ounces each) cream cheese, softened
⅓ cup sugar
¼ cup sour cream
2 eggs
1 teaspoon vanilla
½ cup prepared caramel sauce
½ cup prepared fudge sauce
½ cup pecan halves

Preheat oven to 350°F. Combine ground cookies and butter in medium bowl; pat evenly on bottom and 1 inch up side of 9-inch springform pan. Place in freezer while preparing filling.

Beat cream cheese in large bowl with electric mixer at medium speed until fluffy. Beat in sugar, sour cream, eggs and vanilla until smooth. Pour mixture into prepared crust.

Bake cheesecake 30 to 35 minutes or until almost set in center. Loosen cheesecake from side of pan by running a spatula between cheesecake and pan. Cool on wire rack. Refrigerate, loosely covered, 8 hours or up to 3 days.

Remove side of springform pan from cheesecake, then place on a serving plate. Drizzle caramel and fudge sauces over cheesecake. Top each serving with 2 or 3 pecan halves.
Makes 12 servings

Chocolate Turtle Cheesecake

Chilled Raspberry Cheesecake

CHILLED RASPBERRY CHEESECAKE

1½ cups vanilla wafer crumbs (about 45 wafers, crushed)
⅓ cup HERSHEY'S Cocoa
⅓ cup powdered sugar
⅓ cup butter or margarine, melted
1 package (10 ounces) frozen raspberries, thawed
1 envelope unflavored gelatin
½ cup cold water
½ cup boiling water
2 packages (8 ounces each) cream cheese, softened
½ cup granulated sugar
1 teaspoon vanilla extract
3 tablespoons seedless red raspberry preserves
Chocolate Whipped Cream (recipe follows)

Heat oven to 350°F. In medium bowl stir together crumbs, cocoa and powdered sugar; stir in melted butter. Press mixture onto bottom and 1½ inches up side of 9-inch springform pan. Bake 10 minutes; cool completely. Purée and strain raspberries; set aside. In small bowl sprinkle gelatin over cold water; let stand several minutes to soften. Add boiling water; stir until gelatin dissolves completely and mixture is clear. In large mixer bowl beat cream cheese, granulated sugar and vanilla, blending well. Gradually add raspberry purée and gelatin, mixing thoroughly; pour into prepared crust. Refrigerate several hours or overnight; remove rim of pan. Spread raspberry preserves over top. Garnish with Chocolate Whipped Cream. Cover leftovers; refrigerate.
Makes 10 to 12 servings

CHOCOLATE WHIPPED CREAM: In small mixer bowl stir together ½ cup powdered sugar and ¼ cup HERSHEY'S Cocoa. Add 1 cup chilled whipping cream and 1 teaspoon vanilla extract; beat until stiff.

RASPBERRY CHOCOLATE CHEESECAKE

1 KEEBLER® Chocolate-Flavored Ready-
   Crust Pie Crust
12 ounces cream cheese, softened
½ cup sugar
1 teaspoon vanilla extract
2 eggs
½ cup frozen raspberries, well drained

GLAZE

1 ounce unsweetened chocolate
¼ cup powdered sugar
1 tablespoon evaporated milk
2 teaspoons boiling water
1 teaspoon butter
1 teaspoon dark corn syrup
½ teaspoon vanilla

Preheat oven to 325°F. Beat cream cheese in large mixer bowl until fluffy; beat in sugar and vanilla. Add eggs, one at a time, beating after each addition until well blended.

Fold in raspberries, reserving a few for garnish. Pour mixture into crust. Bake 30 to 35 minutes. Cool completely; refrigerate.

To make Glaze, combine all ingredients except vanilla in saucepan. Stir constantly over low heat until smooth. Remove from heat; add vanilla. Pour over chilled cheesecake and refrigerate at least 3 hours. Use reserved raspberries for garnish when serving.

Makes 8 servings

HEATH® BAR CHEESECAKE

CRUST

1¾ cups vanilla wafer crumbs
2 tablespoons sugar
⅓ cup margarine, melted

FILLING

3 (8-ounce) packages cream cheese,
   softened
1 cup sugar
3 eggs
1 cup sour cream
1½ teaspoons vanilla
5 (1.2-ounce) HEATH® Bars, crushed

Preheat oven to 350°F. Combine crust ingredients; press into bottom and 1½ inches up side of 9-inch springform pan. Refrigerate.

In large mixer bowl, beat cream cheese with sugar at medium speed until fluffy. Add eggs, 1 at a time, beating well after each addition. Beat in sour cream and vanilla; blend until smooth. Spoon half of filling over prepared crust. Sprinkle half of Heath® Bars over filling; cover with remaining filling. Bake 1 hour or until cheesecake is just firm when pan is tapped gently. Cool completely in pan on wire rack. Sprinkle remaining Heath® Bars over top. Refrigerate until chilled.

Makes 10 to 12 servings

INDIVIDUAL ORANGE SOUFFLÉS

    Nonstick cooking spray
3 oranges
**1 tablespoon plus 1½ teaspoons
    cornstarch**
3 tablespoons orange-flavored liqueur
6 egg whites
⅛ teaspoon salt
6 tablespoons granulated sugar
1½ tablespoons sliced almonds (optional)
1½ tablespoons powdered sugar (optional)

Preheat oven to 450°F. Spray 6 individual soufflé dishes (8 to 10 ounces each) with cooking spray. Place dishes on jelly-roll pan; set aside.

Grate enough orange peel to equal 1½ teaspoons; set aside. Cut peel and membrane from oranges; section oranges over 1-quart saucepan. Dice oranges; add to saucepan. (There will be 1½ cups juice and pulp.) Stir in cornstarch until smooth. Cook and stir over medium heat until mixture comes to a boil and thickens slightly. Remove from heat. Stir in liqueur and reserved orange peel.

Beat egg whites and salt with electric mixer at high speed in large bowl until soft peaks form. Gradually beat in granulated sugar, 1 tablespoon at a time, until stiff peaks form and sugar is dissolved. Fold ¼ of egg white mixture into orange mixture, using rubber spatula or wire whisk. Fold all of orange mixture into remaining egg white mixture. Spoon into prepared dishes. Sprinkle with almonds, if desired. Immediately bake 12 to 15 minutes or until soufflés are puffed and browned. Sprinkle with powdered sugar, if desired. Serve immediately. *Makes 6 servings*

CHOCOLATE MOUSSE

1 teaspoon unflavored gelatin
1 tablespoon cold water
2 tablespoons boiling water
½ cup sugar
¼ cup HERSHEY'S Cocoa
1 cup chilled whipping cream
1 teaspoon vanilla extract

In small bowl sprinkle gelatin over cold water; let stand 1 minute to soften. Add boiling water; stir until gelatin is completely dissolved and mixture is clear. Cool slightly. In small mixer bowl stir together sugar and cocoa; add whipping cream and vanilla. Beat at medium speed, scraping bottom of bowl occasionally, until mixture is stiff; pour in gelatin mixture and beat until well blended. Spoon into serving dishes. Refrigerate about 30 minutes.
Makes four ½-cup servings

TROPICAL RICE PUDDING

**1 cup FARMHOUSE® Original Quick
    Brown Rice**
1½ cups water
⅛ teaspoon salt
2 cups milk
**1 (8-ounce) can crushed pineapple in
    juice, undrained**
**1 (3½-ounce) package instant vanilla
    pudding mix**
**1 (3½-ounce) can *or* 1⅓ cups shredded
    sweetened coconut**
⅔ cup coarsely chopped walnuts, toasted
2 tablespoons brown sugar

In medium saucepan, prepare rice according to package directions using water and salt. Meanwhile, combine remaining ingredients; add cooked rice to pudding mixture, stirring to combine. Serve warm or chilled.
Makes 5 cups

Individual Orange Soufflés

Apple Pumpkin Dessert

Heat oven to 400°F. Spoon apple filling into 8 to 10 custard cups. In large mixer bowl, beat pumpkin, sweetened condensed milk, eggs, cinnamon, nutmeg and salt; spoon over apple filling. Combine crumbs and margarine. Sprinkle over pumpkin mixture. Place cups on 15×10-inch baking pan. Bake 10 minutes. *Reduce oven temperature to 350°F; bake 15 minutes or until set. Cool. Garnish with whipped cream, if desired. Refrigerate leftovers.*   *Makes 8 to 10 servings*

PREP TIME: 20 minutes
TOTAL TIME: 1 hour

APPLE PUMPKIN DESSERTS

  1 (21-ounce) can COMSTOCK® Brand Apple Filling or Topping
  1 (16-ounce) can COMSTOCK® Brand Pumpkin (about 2 cups)
  1 (14-ounce) can EAGLE® Brand Sweetened Condensed Milk (NOT evaporated milk)
  2 eggs
  1 teaspoon ground cinnamon
  ½ teaspoon ground nutmeg
  ½ teaspoon salt
  1 cup gingersnap crumbs (about 18 cookies)
  2 tablespoons margarine or butter, melted

CRANBERRY 'N' BARLEY PUDDING

  2 cups cooked barley
  ½ cup chopped dried cranberries
  1⅓ cups milk
  ½ cup packed brown sugar
  2 eggs, beaten
  1 tablespoon butter or margarine, melted
  1 teaspoon vanilla
  ½ teaspoon ground cinnamon

Combine cooked barley and cranberries; set aside. In large bowl, combine remaining ingredients; beat well. Stir in barley mixture. Pour into greased 2-quart casserole. Bake at 325°F 50 minutes or until set. Serve hot or cold with cream or your favorite topping.
                              Makes 6 to 8 servings

Favorite recipe from **North Dakota Barley Council**

RICE PUDDING WITH DRIED FRUITS AND NUTMEG

⅔ cup CAROLINA®, MAHATMA®,
 RIVER®, or WATER MAID® Rice
⅛ teaspoon salt
4 cups water
3 large eggs *or* 3 ounces egg substitute
2 cups whole milk or 2% lowfat milk
¾ cup sugar
2 teaspoons vanilla
½ teaspoon freshly grated nutmeg
1 package unflavored gelatin
¼ cup cold water
1 cup combined raisins and chopped
 dried apricots, peaches and other
 dried fruit
1 cup whipping cream
 Fresh fruit (optional)
 Toasted coconut (optional)

In large saucepan, combine rice and salt with 4 cups water; bring to a boil. Reduce heat; simmer until most of the water has been absorbed, stirring occasionally. In bowl, whisk together eggs, milk, sugar, vanilla and nutmeg. Stir egg mixture into rice mixture and cook on low heat until thickened. *Do not boil.* In small bowl, sprinkle gelatin over ¼ cup cold water and let soften 10 minutes. Add gelatin mixture to rice mixture. Stir. Add dried fruit. Cover and refrigerate, stirring occasionally.

Whip cream until soft peaks form; fold into rice mixture. Refrigerate 2 to 3 hours. Garnish with additional freshly grated nutmeg, fresh fruit and coconut. *Makes 8 servings*

VARIATION: Substitute 1 cup light sour cream or lowfat vanilla yogurt for whipped cream.

Rice Pudding with Dried Fruits and Nutmeg

OLD–FASHIONED BREAD PUDDING

1 package (4-serving size) JELL-O®
    Vanilla Flavor Pudding & Pie Filling
4 tablespoons sugar, divided
3 cups milk, divided
¼ cup raisins
2 tablespoons grated lemon peel
    (optional)
1 tablespoon margarine
½ teaspoon vanilla
6 slices day-old white bread, cut into
    cubes
¼ teaspoon cinnamon
⅛ teaspoon ground nutmeg

Mix pudding mix and 2 tablespoons of the sugar in large saucepan. Gradually stir in 2 cups of the milk. Add raisins and lemon peel. Stirring constantly, cook on medium heat until mixture comes to full boil. Remove from heat; stir in margarine and vanilla.

Pour remaining 1 cup milk over bread cubes in large bowl to moisten. Stir in pudding mixture. Pour into 1-quart baking dish. Combine remaining 2 tablespoons sugar with cinnamon and nutmeg. Sprinkle over pudding. Heat broiler. Broil 2 to 3 inches from heat 4 minutes or until sugar mixture is lightly browned and bubbly. Serve warm or chilled.

Makes about 6 servings

MOCHA PARFAIT

1½ tablespoons margarine
⅓ cup unsweetened cocoa powder
1 cup boiling water
½ cup sugar
1 tablespoon instant coffee granules
1 teaspoon vanilla
1 pint coffee-flavored nonfat frozen
    yogurt
12 whole coffee beans (optional)

Melt margarine in heavy saucepan over low heat. Add cocoa; cook and stir 3 minutes. Add boiling water, sugar and coffee; cook and stir until thickened. Remove from heat; stir in vanilla. Cool.

Place 2 tablespoons frozen yogurt in bottom of each of 4 parfait glasses. Top each with 1 tablespoon sauce. Top sauce with another 2 tablespoons frozen yogurt; top frozen yogurt with 2 tablespoons sauce. Repeat layering of 2 tablespoons frozen yogurt and 2 tablespoons sauce twice more. Top each parfait with 3 coffee beans, if desired. *Makes 4 servings*

Mocha Parfaits

CRÈME CARAMEL

½ cup sugar, divided
1 tablespoon hot water
2 cups skim milk
⅛ teaspoon salt
½ cup cholesterol free egg substitute
½ teaspoon vanilla
⅛ teaspoon maple extract

Heat ¼ cup sugar in heavy saucepan over low heat, stirring constantly until melted and straw colored. Remove from heat; stir in water. Return to heat; stir 5 minutes or until mixture is dark caramel color. Divide melted sugar evenly among 6 custard cups. Set aside.

Preheat oven to 350°F. Combine milk, remaining ¼ cup sugar and salt in medium bowl. Add egg substitute, vanilla and maple extract; mix well. Pour ½ cup mixture into each custard cup. Place cups in heavy baking pan and pour 1 to 2 inches hot water into pan.

Bake 40 to 45 minutes or until knife inserted near edge of each cup comes out clean. Cool on wire rack. Refrigerate 4 hours or overnight. Before serving, run knife around edge of custard cup. Invert custard onto serving plate; remove cup.   *Makes 6 servings*

MAPLE SUNDAE

½ gallon DREYER'S or EDY'S GRAND
    Eggnog Ice Cream
½ cup maple syrup
    Ground cinnamon
    Toasted chopped pecans

• Place 1 scoop Dreyer's or Edy's Grand Eggnog Ice Cream in each of 8 dessert dishes.

• Heat maple syrup and drizzle small amount over each scoop.

• Dust lightly with cinnamon and sprinkle with pecans.   *Makes 8 servings*

CREAMY CARAMEL SAUCE

1 cup granulated sugar
1 cup whipping cream
½ cup packed light brown sugar
⅓ cup corn syrup
1 teaspoon vanilla extract

Place granulated sugar, cream, brown sugar and corn syrup in heavy 2-quart saucepan. Stir over low heat until mixture boils. Carefully clip candy thermometer to side of pan (do not let bulb touch bottom of pan). Cook, stirring occasionally, about 20 minutes or until thermometer registers 238°F. Immediately remove from heat. Stir in vanilla. Cool about 15 minutes. Serve warm or pour into clean glass jars and seal tightly. Store up to 6 months in refrigerator. Reheat sauce over low heat before serving.   *Makes about 2 cups sauce*

Crème Caramel

Honey Turtle Sauce, Honey Caramel Sauce, Honey Chocolate Sauce

HONEY CARAMEL SAUCE

1 cup honey
1 cup evaporated skim milk
½ cup butter or margarine

Combine honey, milk and butter in medium saucepan; mix well. Cook and stir until mixture comes to a boil. Cook over medium heat 8 to 10 minutes longer or until mixture thickens and becomes caramel colored. Pour into sterilized gift jars. Keep refrigerated.   *Makes 2 cups*

Favorite recipe from **National Honey Board**

HONEY CHOCOLATE SAUCE

1½ cups honey
1½ cups unsweetened cocoa
2 tablespoons butter or margarine

Combine all ingredients; mix well. Cover with waxed paper and microwave at HIGH (100% power) 2 to 2½ minutes, stirring after 1 minute. Pour into sterilized gift jars. Keep refrigerated.
Makes 2½ cups

Favorite recipe from **National Honey Board**

HONEY TURTLE SAUCE

2 cups Honey Caramel Sauce (page 278)
1 cup Honey Chocolate Sauce (page 278)
½ to 1 cup broken pecans

Combine Honey Caramel Sauce, Honey Chocolate Sauce and pecans; mix well. Pour into sterilized gift jars. Keep refrigerated.

Makes 3 cups

*Favorite recipe from **National Honey Board***

HOT FUDGE SAUCE

1 (6-ounce) package semi-sweet chocolate chips *or* 4 (1-ounce) squares semi-sweet chocolate
2 tablespoons margarine or butter
1 (14-ounce) can EAGLE® Brand Sweetened Condensed Milk (NOT evaporated milk)
2 tablespoons water
1 teaspoon vanilla extract

In heavy saucepan, over medium heat, melt chips and margarine with sweetened condensed milk and water. Cook and stir constantly until thickened, about 5 minutes. Add vanilla. Serve warm over ice cream or as a fruit dipping sauce. Refrigerate leftovers.

Makes about 2 cups

MICROWAVE DIRECTIONS: In 1-quart glass measure, combine ingredients. Cook on HIGH (100% power) 3 to 3½ minutes, stirring after each minute. Proceed as above.

TO REHEAT: In small heavy saucepan, combine desired amount of sauce with small amount of water. Over low heat, stir constantly until heated through.

VARIATIONS
Mocha: Add 1 teaspoon instant coffee with water. Proceed as directed.

Toasted Almond: Omit vanilla extract. Add ½ teaspoon almond extract. When sauce is thickened, stir in ½ cup chopped toasted almonds.

Choco-Mint: Omit vanilla extract. Add ½ to 1 teaspoon peppermint extract.

Spirited: Add ⅓ cup almond-, coffee-, mint- or orange-flavored liqueur after mixture has thickened.

Mexican: Omit water. Add 2 tablespoons coffee-flavored liqueur *or* 1 teaspoon instant coffee dissolved in 2 tablespoons water and 1 teaspoon ground cinnamon after mixture has thickened.

GOOEY HOT FUDGE SAUCE

2 cups (12 ounces) semisweet chocolate chips
2 tablespoons butter
½ cup half-and-half
1 tablespoon corn syrup
⅛ teaspoon salt
½ teaspoon vanilla extract

Melt chocolate and butter with half-and-half, corn syrup and salt in heavy 2-quart saucepan over low heat, stirring until smooth. Remove from heat; let stand 10 minutes. Stir in vanilla. Serve warm or pour into clean glass jars and seal tightly. Store up to 6 months in refrigerator. Reheat sauce in double-boiler over hot (not boiling) water before serving, if desired.

Makes about 1½ cups sauce

Santa Pleasin'

COOKIES

PINWHEELS

1 package DUNCAN HINES® Golden Sugar
    Cookie Mix
1 egg
¼ cup CRISCO® Oil or CRISCO® PURITAN®
    Canola Oil
4½ teaspoons water
1 egg white, lightly beaten
    Coarse decorating sugar
18 candied maraschino cherries, halved

1. Preheat oven to 375°F.

2. Combine cookie mix, egg, oil and water in large bowl. Stir until thoroughly blended. Roll dough to ⅛-inch thickness on lightly floured surface. Cut into 2½-inch squares. Place squares 1 inch apart on ungreased baking sheets. Cut 1-inch slits diagonally from each corner towards center. Fold every other corner tip towards center. Brush tops with egg white. Sprinkle with sugar. Place cherry half on center of each pinwheel. Bake at 375°F for 8 to 9 minutes or until edges are light golden brown. Remove to cooling racks. Cool completely. Store between layers of waxed paper in airtight containers.

Makes 3 dozen cookies

TIP: You may substitute granulated sugar for coarse decorating sugar, if desired.

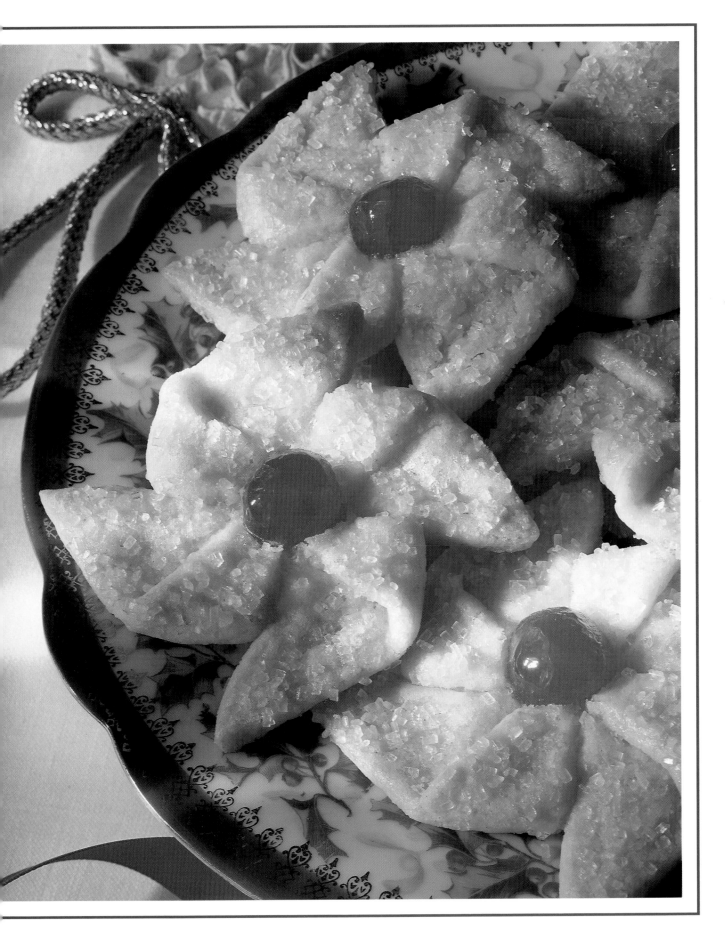

CHRISTMAS ORNAMENT COOKIES

2¼ cups all-purpose flour
¼ teaspoon salt
1 cup granulated sugar
¾ cup butter or margarine, softened
1 large egg
1 teaspoon vanilla
1 teaspoon almond extract
Icing (recipe follows)
Assorted candies or decors

Place flour and salt in medium bowl; stir to combine. Beat sugar and butter in large bowl with electric mixer at medium speed until light and fluffy. Beat in egg, vanilla and almond extract. Gradually add flour mixture. Beat at low speed until well blended. Divide dough in half; cover and refrigerate 30 minutes or until firm.

Preheat oven to 350°F. Working with 1 portion at a time, roll out dough on lightly floured surface to ¼-inch thickness. Cut dough into desired shapes with assorted floured cookie cutters. Reroll trimmings and cut out more cookies. Place cutouts on *ungreased* cookie sheets. Using drinking straw or tip of sharp knife, cut a hole near top of each cookie to allow for piece of ribbon or string to be inserted for hanger. Bake 10 to 12 minutes or until edges are golden brown. Let cookies stand on cookie sheets 1 minute. Remove cookies to wire racks; cool completely.

Prepare Icing. Spoon Icing into small resealable plastic food storage bag. Cut off very tiny corner of bag; pipe Icing decoratively onto cookies. Decorate with candies as desired. Let stand at room temperature 40 minutes or until set. Thread ribbon through each cookie hole to hang as Christmas tree ornament.   *Makes about 2 dozen cookies*

ICING
2 cups powdered sugar
2 tablespoons milk or lemon juice
Food coloring (optional)

Place powdered sugar and milk in small bowl; stir with spoon until smooth. (Icing will be very thick. If it is too thick, stir in 1 teaspoon additional milk.) Divide into small bowls and tint with food coloring, if desired.

DUTCH ST. NICHOLAS COOKIES

½ cup whole natural almonds
¾ cup butter or margarine, softened
½ cup packed brown sugar
2 tablespoons milk
1½ teaspoons ground cinnamon
¼ teaspoon ground nutmeg
¼ teaspoon ground ginger
¼ teaspoon ground cloves
2 cups sifted all-purpose flour
1½ teaspoons baking powder
½ teaspoon salt
¼ cup coarsely chopped citron

Spread almonds in single layer on baking sheet. Bake at 375°F, 10 to 12 minutes, stirring occasionally, until lightly toasted. Cool. Chop finely. In large bowl, cream butter, sugar, milk and spices. In small bowl, combine flour, baking powder and salt. Add flour mixture to creamed mixture; blend well. Stir in almonds and citron. Knead dough slightly to make ball. Cover; refrigerate until firm. Roll out dough ¼ inch thick on lightly floured surface. Cut out with cookie cutters. Place 2 inches apart on greased cookie sheets. Bake at 375°F, 7 to 10 minutes, until lightly browned. Remove to wire racks to cool.

Makes about 3½ dozen cookies

*Favorite recipe from **Almond Board of California***

Christmas Ornament Cookies

CHRISTMAS STAINED GLASS COOKIES

Colored hard candy
¾ cup butter or margarine, softened
¾ cup granulated sugar
2 eggs
1 teaspoon vanilla extract
3 cups all-purpose flour
1 teaspoon baking powder
Frosting (optional)
Small decorative candies (optional)

Separate colors of hard candy into resealable plastic freezer bags. Crush with mallet or hammer to equal about ⅓ cup crushed candy; set aside. In mixing bowl, cream butter and sugar. Beat in eggs and vanilla. In another bowl, sift together flour and baking powder. Gradually stir flour mixture into butter mixture until dough is very stiff. Wrap in plastic wrap and chill about 3 hours.

Preheat oven to 375°F. Roll out dough to ⅛-inch thickness on lightly floured surface. Additional flour may be added to dough if necessary. Cut out cookies using large Christmas cookie cutters. Transfer cookies to foil-lined baking sheets. Using small Christmas cookie cutter of the same shape as large one, cut out and remove dough from center of each cookie.* Fill cut out sections with crushed candy. If using cookies as hanging ornaments, make holes near tops of cookies for string with drinking straw or chopstick. Bake 7 to 9 minutes or until cookies are lightly browned and candy is melted. Slide foil off baking sheets. When cool, carefully loosen cookies from foil. Use frosting and candy for additional decorations, if desired.
Makes about 2½ dozen medium-sized cookies

*For different designs, other cookie cutter shapes can be used to cut out centers of cookies (i.e., small circle and star-shaped cutters can be used to cut out ornament designs on large Christmas tree cookies).

*Favorite recipe from **The Sugar Association, Inc.***

APPLE SAUCE GINGERBREAD COOKIES

4 cups all-purpose flour
2 teaspoons ground ginger
2 teaspoons ground cinnamon
1 teaspoon baking soda
½ teaspoon salt
¼ teaspoon ground nutmeg
½ cup margarine, softened
1 cup sugar
⅓ cup light (gold label) molasses
1 cup MOTT'S® Natural Apple Sauce
Decorator Icing (recipe follows)

Sift together flour, ginger, cinnamon, baking soda, salt and nutmeg; set aside. In bowl, with electric mixer at high speed, beat margarine, sugar and molasses until creamy. Alternately blend in dry ingredients and apple sauce. Cover and chill dough for several hours or overnight.

Preheat oven to 375°F. On floured surface, roll dough out to ⅛-inch thickness with lightly floured rolling pin. Cut with floured gingerbread man cutter or other shapes. Place on greased baking sheet. Bake 12 minutes or until done. Remove from sheet; cool on wire rack. Frost with Decorator Icing as desired. After icing dries, store in airtight container.
Makes 2½ dozen (5½-inch) cookies

DECORATOR ICING: Mix 2 cups confectioners' sugar and 1 tablespoon water. Add more water, 1 teaspoon at a time, until icing holds its shape and can be piped through a decorating tube.

Christmas Stained Glass Cookies, Teddy Bear Gift Bread (page 190)

Gingerbread Bears

GINGERBREAD BEARS

3½ cups all-purpose flour
  2 teaspoons ground cinnamon
1½ teaspoons ground ginger
  1 teaspoon salt
  1 teaspoon baking soda
  1 teaspoon ground allspice
  1 cup butter or margarine, softened
  1 cup firmly packed brown sugar
  1 teaspoon vanilla
  ⅓ cup molasses
  2 eggs
    Assorted cookie nonpareils (optional)
    Ornamental Frosting (page 287) or
      prepared creamy or gel-type frostings
      in tubes (optional)
    Colored sugar, assorted candies and
      grated chocolate (optional)

Place flour, cinnamon, ginger, salt, baking soda and allspice in medium bowl; stir to combine. Set aside. Beat butter, sugar and vanilla in large bowl with electric mixer at medium speed about 5 minutes or until light and fluffy. Beat in molasses and eggs until well blended. Beat in flour mixture at low speed until well blended. Divide dough into 3 equal portions; cover and refrigerate at least 2 hours or up to 24 hours.

Preheat oven to 350°F. Grease large cookie sheets; set aside. Working with 1 portion at a time, roll out dough on lightly floured surface to ⅛-inch thickness. Cut out dough with 3-inch bear-shaped cookie cutters. Place cookies 1 inch apart on prepared cookie sheets. Roll dough scraps into balls and ropes to make eyes and noses and to decorate bears. Decorate bears with nonpareils, if desired. Bake 10 minutes or until bottoms of cookies are golden brown. Let stand on cookie sheets 1 minute. Remove cookies to wire racks; cool completely.

Prepare Ornamental Frosting, if desired. Pipe or spread frosting on cooled cookies to decorate. Decorate with assorted nonpareils, colored sugar, assorted candies and/or grated chocolate, if desired. Store tightly covered at room temperature.

Makes about 3½ dozen cookies

ORNAMENTAL FROSTING

    ½ cup butter or margarine, softened
    1 teaspoon vanilla
    1 package (16 ounces) powdered sugar, sifted
    2 tablespoons milk

Beat butter and vanilla in large bowl with electric mixer at medium speed. Beat in powdered sugar and enough milk at low speed until frosting is of desired spreading consistency. *Makes about 2 cups*

KRINGLE'S CUTOUTS

    1¼ cups granulated sugar
    1 BUTTER FLAVOR* CRISCO® Stick *or*
        1 cup BUTTER FLAVOR CRISCO all-vegetable shortening
    2 eggs
    ¼ cup light corn syrup or regular pancake syrup
    1 teaspoon vanilla
    3 cups plus 4 tablespoons all-purpose flour, divided
    ¾ teaspoon baking powder
    ½ teaspoon baking soda
    ½ teaspoon salt
        Colored sugar, decors and prepared frosting (optional)

1. Combine sugar and shortening in large bowl. Beat at medium speed of electric mixer until well blended. Add eggs, syrup and vanilla. Beat until well blended and fluffy.

2. Combine 3 cups flour, baking powder, baking soda and salt. Add gradually to creamed mixture at low speed. Mix until well blended.

3. Divide dough into 4 quarters. Cover and refrigerate at least two hours or overnight.

4. Heat oven to 375°F. Place sheets of foil on countertop for cooling cookies.

5. Spread 1 tablespoon flour on large sheet of waxed paper. Place one quarter of dough on floured paper. Flatten slightly with hands. Turn dough over. Cover with another large sheet of waxed paper. Roll dough to ¼-inch thickness. Remove top layer of waxed paper. Cut out dough with seasonal cookie cutters. Place cutouts 2 inches apart on ungreased baking sheets. Roll and cut out remaining dough. Sprinkle with colored sugar and decors or leave plain to frost when cool.

6. Bake at 375°F for 5 to 9 minutes, depending on size of cookies. (Bake small, thin cookies about 5 minutes; larger cookies about 9 minutes.) *Do not overbake.* Cool 2 minutes on baking sheets. Remove cookies to foil sheets to cool completely.

Makes 3 to 4 dozen cookies
(depending on size and shape)

*Butter Flavor Crisco® is artificially flavored.

LINZER SANDWICH COOKIES

1⅓ cups all-purpose flour
¼ teaspoon baking powder
¼ teaspoon salt
¾ cup granulated sugar
½ cup butter, softened
1 large egg
1 teaspoon vanilla
   Powdered sugar (optional)
   Seedless raspberry jam

Place flour, baking powder and salt in small bowl; stir to combine. Beat granulated sugar and butter in medium bowl with electric mixer at medium speed until light and fluffy. Beat in egg and vanilla. Gradually add flour mixture. Beat at low speed until dough forms. Divide dough in half; cover and refrigerate 2 hours or until firm.

Preheat oven to 375°F. Working with 1 portion at a time, roll out dough on lightly floured surface to ³⁄₁₆-inch thickness. Cut dough into desired shapes with floured cookie cutters. Cut out equal numbers of each shape. (If dough becomes too soft, refrigerate several minutes before continuing.) Cut 1-inch centers out of half the cookies of each shape. Reroll trimmings and cut out more cookies. Place cookies 1½ to 2 inches apart on *ungreased* cookie sheets. Bake 7 to 9 minutes or until edges are lightly browned. Let cookies stand on cookie sheets 1 to 2 minutes. Remove cookies to wire racks; cool completely.

Sprinkle cookies with holes with powdered sugar, if desired. Spread 1 teaspoon jam on flat side of whole cookies, spreading almost to edges. Place cookies with holes, flat side down, over jam. Store tightly covered at room temperature or freeze up to 3 months.
Makes about 2 dozen cookies

OLD-FASHIONED MOLASSES COOKIES

4 cups sifted all-purpose flour
2 teaspoons ARM & HAMMER® Pure
   Baking Soda
1½ teaspoons ground ginger
½ teaspoon ground cinnamon
⅛ teaspoon salt
1½ cups molasses
½ cup shortening, melted
¼ cup butter or margarine, melted
⅓ cup boiling water
   Sugar

In medium bowl, combine flour, baking soda, spices and salt. In large bowl, mix molasses, shortening, butter and water. Add flour mixture to molasses mixture; blend well. Cover; refrigerate until firm, about 2 hours. Roll out dough ¼ inch thick on well-floured surface. Cut out with 3½-inch cookie cutters; sprinkle with sugar. Place 2 inches apart on ungreased cookie sheets. Bake in preheated 375°F oven about 12 minutes. Remove to wire racks to cool.
Makes about 3 dozen cookies

Linzer Sandwich Cookies

SUGAR-DUSTED SNOWFLAKES

½ cup Florida orange juice
⅓ cup milk
1 tablespoon butter or margarine
1 cinnamon stick, 3 inches long
2 cups unsifted all-purpose flour
1½ teaspoons grated orange peel
⅛ teaspoon baking powder
Vegetable oil for frying
Confectioners' sugar

In small saucepan, combine orange juice, milk, butter and cinnamon stick. (Mixture will curdle.) Bring to a boil over high heat. Remove from heat; let stand 15 minutes. Remove and discard cinnamon stick.

In large bowl, mix flour, orange peel and baking powder; make well in center. Add warm milk mixture all at once; stir, gradually incorporating flour mixture, until dry ingredients are moistened.

Turn out onto well-floured surface; knead 2 or 3 times until smooth. Cover; let stand 20 minutes to allow dough to cool and become less sticky.

Divide dough in half; roll half on well-floured surface to ⅛-inch thickness. Using floured 3-inch star or round cookie cutter, cut dough into shapes. Place on paper towel and let dry 10 minutes or until top is dry to the touch. Repeat with remaining dough, rolling scraps together. Cut out small designs in each cookie with canapé cutters, so cookie resembles snowflake.

Pour 1 inch of oil in medium skillet; heat to 350°F. Fry cookies, 2 or 3 at a time, turning once until very lightly browned. Drain on paper towels. Cool; sprinkle liberally with confectioners' sugar.   *Makes 3 dozen cookies*

Favorite recipe from **Florida Department of Citrus**

GLAZED SUGAR COOKIES

COOKIES
1 package DUNCAN HINES® Golden Sugar Cookie Mix
1 egg
¼ cup CRISCO® Oil or CRISCO® PURITAN® Canola Oil
1 teaspoon water
GLAZE
1½ cups sifted confectioners sugar
2 to 3 tablespoons water or milk
¾ teaspoon vanilla extract
Food coloring (optional)
Red and green sugar crystals, nonpareils or cinnamon candies

1. Preheat oven to 375°F.

2. For Cookies, combine cookie mix, egg, oil and water in large bowl. Stir until thoroughly blended. Roll dough to ¼-inch thickness on lightly floured surface. Cut dough into desired shapes using floured cookie cutters. Place cookies 2 inches apart on ungreased baking sheets. Bake at 375°F for 7 to 8 minutes or until edges are light golden brown. Cool 1 minute on baking sheets. Remove to cooling racks. Cool completely.

3. For Glaze, combine confectioners sugar, water and vanilla extract in medium bowl. Beat until smooth. Tint glaze with food coloring, if desired. Brush glaze on each cookie with clean pastry brush. Sprinkle cookies with sugar crystals, nonpareils or cinnamon candies before glaze sets. Allow glaze to set before storing between layers of waxed paper in airtight containers.   *Makes 4 dozen cookies*

TIP: Use DUNCAN HINES® Creamy Homestyle Vanilla Frosting for a quick glaze. Heat frosting in opened container in microwave oven at HIGH (100% power) for 10 to 15 seconds. Stir well. Spread on cookies and decorate as desired before frosting sets.

Top to bottom: Bavarian Cookie Wreaths (page 297),
Sugar-Dusted Snowflakes

PINWHEELS AND CHECKERBOARDS

2 cups flour
1 teaspoon CALUMET® Baking Powder
½ teaspoon salt
⅔ cup margarine or butter
1 cup sugar
1 egg
1 teaspoon vanilla
2 squares BAKER'S® Unsweetened
  Chocolate, melted

Mix flour, baking powder and salt in medium bowl. Beat margarine in large bowl with electric mixer on medium speed to soften. Gradually add sugar, beating until light and fluffy. Beat in egg and vanilla. Stir in flour mixture until well blended. Divide dough into two equal portions; blend chocolate into one portion. Use prepared doughs to make Pinwheels or Checkerboards.

Makes about 4½ to 5 dozen cookies

PINWHEELS: Roll out chocolate and plain doughs separately between sheets of waxed paper into 12×8-inch rectangles. Remove top sheets of paper. Invert plain dough onto chocolate dough and remove remaining paper. Roll up as for jelly roll; wrap in waxed paper. Refrigerate 3 hours or overnight. (Or, freeze 1 hour.) Heat oven to 375°F. Slice dough into ¼-inch-thick slices. Place on ungreased cookie sheets. Bake 10 minutes or until cookies just begin to brown around edges. Cool on racks.

CHECKERBOARDS: Roll out chocolate and plain doughs separately between sheets of waxed paper into 9×4½-inch rectangles. Brush chocolate dough lightly with milk and top with plain dough. Using a long, sharp knife, cut lengthwise into 3 equal strips, 1½ inches wide. Stack strips, alternating colors and brushing each layer with milk. Cut lengthwise again into 3 equal sections, ½ inch wide. Invert middle section so that colors are alternated; press together lightly. Carefully wrap in waxed paper; refrigerate overnight or freeze until firm enough to slice. Heat oven to 375°F. Slice dough into ⅛-inch-thick slices. Place on ungreased cookie sheets. Bake 8 minutes or just until white portions begin to brown. Cool on racks.

NOTES: If dough softens while handling, refrigerate until firm. To hang on Christmas tree, poke holes in unbaked cookies near edges, using a straw or wooden pick. Insert red string licorice through holes in cooled, baked cookies and tie.

CHOCO-COCO PECAN CRISPS

½ cup butter or margarine, softened
1 cup packed light brown sugar
1 egg
1 teaspoon vanilla
1½ cups all-purpose flour
1 cup chopped pecans
⅓ cup unsweetened cocoa
½ teaspoon baking soda
1 cup flaked coconut

Left to right: Choco-Coco Pecan Crisps,
Holiday Fruit Drops (page 304)

Cream butter and sugar in large bowl until light and fluffy. Beat in egg and vanilla. Combine flour, pecans, cocoa and baking soda in small bowl until well blended. Add to creamed mixture, blending until stiff dough is formed. Sprinkle coconut on work surface. Divide dough into 4 parts. Shape each part into a roll about 1½ inches in diameter; roll in coconut until thickly coated. Wrap in plastic wrap; refrigerate until firm, at least 1 hour or up to 2 weeks. (For longer storage, wrap in foil and freeze up to 6 weeks.)

Preheat oven to 350°F. Cut rolls into ⅛-inch-thick slices. Place 2 inches apart on ungreased cookie sheets. Bake 10 to 13 minutes or until firm, but not overly browned. Remove to wire racks to cool.   *Makes about 6 dozen cookies*

AUSTRIAN TEA COOKIES

1½ cups sugar, divided
½ cup (1 stick) butter, softened
½ cup vegetable shortening
1 egg, beaten
½ teaspoon vanilla extract
2 cups all-purpose flour
2 cups ALMOND DELIGHT® brand cereal, crushed to 1 cup
½ teaspoon baking powder
¼ teaspoon ground cinnamon
14 ounces almond paste
2 egg whites
5 tablespoons raspberry or apricot jam, warmed
¼ cup sliced almonds (optional)

In large bowl cream 1 cup sugar, butter and shortening. Add egg and vanilla; mix well. Stir in flour, cereal, baking powder and cinnamon until well combined. Chill 1 to 2 hours or until firm.

Preheat oven to 350°F. Roll dough on lightly floured surface to ¼-inch thickness. Cut into 2-inch circles and place on ungreased cookie sheet; set aside. In small bowl beat almond paste, egg whites and remaining ½ cup sugar until smooth. With pastry tube, pipe almond paste mixture ½ inch thick on top of each cookie along outside edge. Place ¼ teaspoon jam in center of each cookie, spreading out to paste. Place 1 sliced almond on top of jam. Bake 8 to 10 minutes or until lightly browned. Let stand 1 minute before removing from cookie sheet. Cool on wire rack.
Makes 3½ dozen cookies

BASIC HOLIDAY RAISIN COOKIES

½ cup butter or margarine, softened
⅓ cup sugar
1 egg yolk
⅛ teaspoon salt
1 cup all-purpose flour
½ cup raisins
   Semisweet or white chocolate
   Colored sprinkles, raisins, nuts or
      candied fruit pieces, for decoration

Cream butter and sugar; beat in egg yolk and salt. Add flour just to blend thoroughly. Mix in raisins. On lightly floured surface, roll into 12-inch log. Wrap securely and refrigerate at least 1 hour or up to 1 week.

Preheat oven to 350°F. With sharp knife, slice cookies ⅓ inch thick; place 1 inch apart on ungreased baking sheets. Bake 15 to 20 minutes until cookies are set and bottoms are lightly browned. Remove to racks to cool completely. Decorate as desired with melted semisweet or white chocolate and top with colored sprinkles, raisins, nuts or candied fruit pieces. Cool; store between sheets of waxed paper in airtight container.

Makes 3 dozen cookies

*Favorite recipe from **California Raisin Advisory Board***

CHOCOLATE SPRITZ COOKIES

1 package DUNCAN HINES® Golden
     Sugar Cookie Mix
⅓ cup unsweetened cocoa
1 egg
⅓ cup CRISCO® Oil or CRISCO®
     PURITAN® Canola Oil
2 tablespoons water

1. Preheat oven to 375°F.

2. Combine cookie mix and cocoa in large mixing bowl. Stir until blended. Add egg, oil and water. Stir until thoroughly blended.

3. Fill cookie press with dough. Press desired shapes 2 inches apart onto ungreased cookie sheets. Bake at 375°F for 6 to 8 minutes or until set. Cool 1 minute on cookie sheets. Remove to cooling racks. Cool completely.
Makes 5 to 6 dozen cookies

NOTE: For a delicious, no-cholesterol variation, substitute 2 egg whites for whole egg.

TIP: For festive cookies, decorate before baking with assorted decors or after baking with melted milk chocolate or semi-sweet chocolate, or white chocolate and chopped nuts.

Chocolate Spritz Cookies

294

DANISH COOKIE RINGS
(VANILLEKRANSER)

½ cup blanched almonds
2 cups all-purpose flour
¾ cup sugar
¼ teaspoon baking powder
1 cup butter, cut into small pieces
1 large egg
1 tablespoon milk
1 tablespoon vanilla
8 candied red cherries
16 candied green cherries

Grease cookie sheets; set aside. Process almonds in food processor until ground, but not pasty. Place almonds, flour, sugar and baking powder in large bowl. Cut butter into flour mixture with pastry blender or 2 knives until mixture is crumbly.

Beat egg, milk and vanilla in small bowl with fork until well blended. Add egg mixture to flour mixture; stir until soft dough forms.

Spoon dough into pastry bag fitted with medium star tip. Pipe 3-inch rings 2 inches apart onto prepared cookie sheets. Refrigerate 15 minutes or until firm.

Preheat oven to 375°F. Cut cherries into halves. Cut each red cherry half into quarters; cut each green cherry half into 4 slivers. Press red cherry quarter onto each ring where ends meet. Arrange 2 green cherry slivers on either side of red cherry to form leaves. Bake 8 to 10 minutes or until golden. Remove cookies to wire racks; cool completely. Store tightly covered at room temperature or freeze up to 3 months. *Makes about 5 dozen cookies*

Danish Cookie Rings

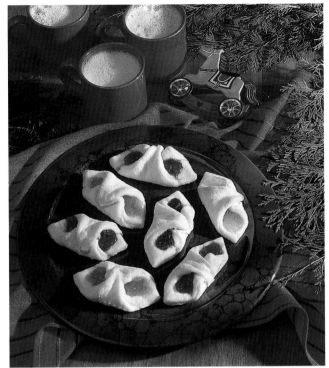

Golden Kolacky

GOLDEN KOLACKY

½ cup butter, softened
4 ounces cream cheese, softened
1 cup all-purpose flour
   Fruit preserves

Combine butter and cream cheese in large bowl; beat until smooth and creamy. Gradually add flour to butter mixture, blending until mixture forms soft dough. Divide dough in half; cover and refrigerate until firm.

Preheat oven to 375°F. Roll out dough, ½ at a time, on floured surface to ⅛-inch thickness. Cut into 3-inch squares. Spoon 1 teaspoon preserves in center of each square. Bring two opposite corners to center; pinch together tightly to seal. Fold sealed tip to one side; pinch to seal. Place 1 inch apart on *ungreased* cookie sheets. Bake 10 to 15 minutes or until lightly browned. Remove to cooling racks; cool completely.   *Makes about 2½ dozen cookies*

BAVARIAN COOKIE WREATHS

3½ cups unsifted all-purpose flour
1 cup sugar, divided
3 teaspoons grated orange peel, divided
¼ teaspoon salt
1⅓ cups butter or margarine
¼ cup Florida orange juice
⅓ cup finely chopped blanched almonds
1 egg white beaten with 1 teaspoon water
   Prepared frosting (optional)

Preheat oven to 400°F. In large bowl, mix flour, ¾ cup sugar, 2 teaspoons orange peel and salt. Using pastry blender, cut in butter and orange juice until mixture holds together. Knead a few times and press into a ball.

Shape dough into ¾-inch balls. On lightly floured surface, roll each ball into a 6-inch rope. Using two ropes, twist together to form one rope. Pinch ends of rope together to make a wreath; place on lightly greased baking sheets.

In shallow dish, mix almonds, remaining ¼ cup sugar and 1 teaspoon orange peel. Brush top of each wreath with egg white mixture and sprinkle with sugar-almond mixture.

Bake 8 to 10 minutes or until lightly browned. Remove to wire racks; cool completely. Frost if desired.   *Makes 5 dozen cookies*

*Favorite recipe from **Florida Department of Citrus***

Pfeffernusse

PFEFFERNUSSE

3½ cups all-purpose flour

2 teaspoons baking powder

1½ teaspoons ground cinnamon

1 teaspoon ground ginger

½ teaspoon baking soda

½ teaspoon salt

½ teaspoon ground cloves

½ teaspoon ground cardamom

¼ teaspoon freshly ground black pepper

1 cup butter, softened

1 cup granulated sugar

¼ cup dark molasses

1 large egg

Sifted powdered sugar

Grease cookie sheets; set aside. Place flour, baking powder, cinnamon, ginger, baking soda, salt, cloves, cardamom and pepper in large bowl; stir to combine. Beat butter and granulated sugar in large bowl with electric mixer at medium speed until light and fluffy. Beat in molasses and egg. Gradually add flour mixture. Beat at low speed until dough forms. Cover dough and refrigerate until firm, 30 minutes or up to 3 days.

Preheat oven to 350°F. Roll dough into 1-inch balls. Place balls 2 inches apart on prepared cookie sheets. Bake 12 to 14 minutes or until golden brown. Remove cookies to wire racks; dust with sifted powdered sugar. Cool completely. Store tightly covered at room temperature or freeze up to 3 months.

Makes about 5 dozen cookies

ALMOND CRESCENTS

1 cup butter or margarine, softened
⅓ cup granulated sugar
1¾ cups all-purpose flour
¼ cup cornstarch
1 teaspoon vanilla extract
1½ cups ground almonds, toasted*
    Chocolate Glaze (recipe follows) or
        powdered sugar

Preheat oven to 325°F. Beat butter and granulated sugar in large bowl until creamy. Mix in flour, cornstarch and vanilla. Stir in almonds. Shape tablespoonfuls of dough into crescents. Place 2 inches apart on *ungreased* cookie sheets. Bake 22 to 25 minutes or until light brown. Cool 1 minute. Remove to wire racks; cool completely. Drizzle with Chocolate Glaze, if desired. Allow chocolate to set, then store cookies in airtight container. Or, before serving, sprinkle with powdered sugar.

Makes about 3 dozen cookies

Top to bottom: Scottish Shortbread (page 308), Almond Crescents

CHOCOLATE GLAZE: Place ½ cup semisweet chocolate chips and 1 tablespoon butter or margarine in small resealable plastic bag. Place bag in bowl of hot water for 2 to 3 minutes or until chocolate is softened. Dry with paper towel. Knead until chocolate mixture is smooth. Cut off very tiny corner of bag. Drizzle chocolate mixture over cookies.

*To toast almonds, spread on cookie sheet. Bake at 325°F for 4 minutes or until almonds are fragrant and golden.

RASPBERRY JEWELS

1 package DUNCAN HINES® Moist
    Deluxe Raspberry Cake Mix
¾ cup butter or margarine, softened
2 eggs, separated
    Chopped pecans
    Seedless raspberry jam

1. Preheat oven to 350°F.

2. Combine cake mix, butter and egg yolks in large bowl. Beat at low speed with electric mixer until dough forms. Shape dough into 1-inch balls. Dip into egg whites, then into chopped pecans. Place, pecan side up, 2 inches apart on ungreased baking sheets. Make indentation in center of each ball with thumb or handle of wooden spoon. Fill with ¼ teaspoon jam.

3. Bake at 350°F for 10 to 12 minutes or until light golden brown. Cool 1 minute on baking sheets. Remove to cooling racks. Cool completely.

Makes 4½ dozen cookies

CHRISTMAS SPRITZ COOKIES

2¼ cups all-purpose flour
¼ teaspoon salt
1¼ cups powdered sugar
1 cup butter, softened
1 large egg
1 teaspoon vanilla
1 teaspoon almond extract
Green food coloring (optional)
Candied red and green cherries and
assorted decorative candies
(optional)
Icing (recipe follows), optional

Preheat oven to 375°F. Place flour and salt in medium bowl; stir to combine. Beat powdered sugar and butter in large bowl with electric mixer until light and fluffy. Beat in egg, vanilla and almond extract. Gradually add flour mixture. Beat at low speed until well blended.

Divide dough in half. If desired, tint half of dough with green food coloring. Fit cookie press with desired plate (or change plates for different shapes after first batch). Fill press with dough; press dough 1 inch apart onto *ungreased* cookie sheets. Decorate cookies with cherries and assorted candies, if desired.

Bake 10 to 12 minutes or until just set. Remove cookies to wire racks; cool completely.

Prepare Icing, if desired. Pipe or drizzle onto cooled cookies. Decorate with cherries and assorted candies, if desired. Store tightly covered at room temperature or freeze up to 3 months.   *Makes about 5 dozen cookies*

ICING
1½ cups powdered sugar
2 tablespoons milk plus 1 teaspoon
additional, if needed
⅛ teaspoon almond extract

Place all ingredients in medium bowl; stir with spoon until thick, but spreadable. (If Icing is too thick, stir in 1 teaspoon additional milk.)

Christmas Spritz Cookies

CALIFORNIA APRICOT PISTACHIO BISCOTTI

1¼ cups all-purpose flour
½ cup whole-wheat flour
1 cup sugar
½ teaspoon baking powder
¼ teaspoon salt
5 tablespoons cold unsalted butter, cut into pieces
¾ teaspoon vanilla extract
2 eggs, slightly beaten
⅔ cup coarsely chopped California dried apricots
1 cup shelled natural California pistachios
1 teaspoon sugar

Preheat oven to 350°F. Lightly grease large baking sheet.

In food processor or blender, process flours, 1 cup sugar, baking powder and salt until blended. Add butter and vanilla; process until mixture resembles coarse crumbs. Add eggs; process until blended. Add apricots and pistachios; process just until dough is evenly moistened.

Remove dough from food processor; form into 2 balls. On prepared baking sheet, shape each half of dough into a 12-inch log. With hands, flatten each log to a width of 2 inches. Sprinkle each log with ½ teaspoon sugar. Bake 25 minutes or until golden brown. Remove logs to cooling rack; cool 10 minutes. *Do not turn oven off.* With serrated knife, carefully cut logs diagonally into ½-inch slices. Place on baking sheet with cut sides up; return to oven and bake 7 minutes or until very lightly browned. Transfer to wire rack; cool completely.
Makes 4 dozen cookies

Favorite recipe from California Apricot Advisory Board

LEMONY SPRITZ STICKS

1 cup butter or margarine, softened
1 cup confectioners' sugar
¼ cup REALEMON® Lemon Juice from Concentrate
2½ cups unsifted flour
¼ teaspoon salt
Chocolate Glaze (recipe follows)
Finely chopped nuts

Preheat oven to 375°F. In large mixer bowl, beat butter and sugar until fluffy. Add ReaLemon® brand; beat well. Stir in flour and salt; mix well. Place dough in cookie press with star-shaped plate. Press dough onto greased baking sheets into 3-inch strips. Bake 5 to 6 minutes or until lightly browned on edges. Cool 1 to 2 minutes; remove from baking sheets. Cool completely. Dip ends of cookies in Chocolate Glaze, then into nuts.
Makes about 8½ dozen cookies

CHOCOLATE GLAZE: In small saucepan, melt 3 ounces semisweet chocolate and 2 tablespoons margarine or butter. Makes about ⅓ cup.

TIP: When using electric cookie gun, use decorator tip. Press dough onto greased baking sheets into 3×½-inch strips. Bake 8 to 10 minutes or until lightly browned on edges.

MINI MINCE LEMON TARTS

1⅓ cups (½ of 27-ounce jar) NONE SUCH®
   Ready-to-Use Mincemeat (Regular or
   Brandy & Rum)
1½ teaspoons grated lemon peel
1 (15-ounce) package refrigerated pie
   crusts

Preheat oven to 375°F. In small bowl, combine mincemeat and peel; mix well. Cut pastry into 24 (2¼-inch) circles; press each circle into 1¾-inch muffin cup. Fill with mincemeat mixture. From pastry scraps, cut out small designs; top tarts with cutouts. Bake 20 to 25 minutes or until lightly browned. Cool. Remove from pans. Store loosely covered at room temperature.   *Makes 2 dozen tarts*

ORANGE–CASHEW COOKIES

½ cup butter or margarine, softened
⅔ cup sugar
1 egg
1 teaspoon grated orange peel
3 tablespoons orange juice
2 cups all-purpose flour
1 teaspoon baking soda
¼ teaspoon salt
1 cup chopped cashews

Preheat oven to 350°F. Beat butter and sugar in large bowl until creamy. Beat in egg, orange peel and juice until light and fluffy. Mix in flour, baking soda and salt until well blended. Stir in cashews. Drop tablespoonfuls of dough 2 inches apart onto ungreased cookie sheets.

Bake 9 minutes or until lightly browned. Remove to wire racks; cool completely. Store in airtight container.
        Makes about 1½ dozen cookies

MILK CHOCOLATE FLORENTINE COOKIES

⅔ cup butter
2 cups quick oats, uncooked
1 cup granulated sugar
⅔ cup all-purpose flour
¼ cup corn syrup
¼ cup milk
1 teaspoon vanilla extract
¼ teaspoon salt
2 cups (11½-ounce package) NESTLÉ®
   Toll House® Milk Chocolate Morsels

In medium saucepan, melt butter; remove from heat. Stir in oats, sugar, flour, corn syrup, milk, vanilla and salt; mix well. Drop by level teaspoonfuls, about 3 inches apart, onto foil-lined baking sheets. With rubber spatula, spread thinly. Bake in preheated 375°F. oven for 6 to 8 minutes, until golden brown; cool. Peel foil from cookies. Over hot (not boiling) water, melt morsels, stirring until smooth. Spread thin layer of melted chocolate on flat side of half the cookies. Top with remaining cookies.
        Makes about 3½ dozen sandwich cookies

Milk Chocolate Florentine Cookies

ANGEL PILLOWS

½ BUTTER FLAVOR* CRISCO® Stick *or*
  ½ cup BUTTER FLAVOR CRISCO
  all-vegetable shortening
1 package (3 ounces) cream cheese,
  softened
1 tablespoon milk
¼ cup firmly packed brown sugar
½ cup apricot preserves
1¼ cups all-purpose flour
1½ teaspoons baking powder
1½ teaspoons ground cinnamon
¼ teaspoon salt
½ cup coarsely chopped pecans or flake
  coconut

FROSTING

1 cup confectioners' sugar
¼ cup apricot preserves
1 tablespoon BUTTER FLAVOR*
  CRISCO® Stick *or* 1 tablespoon
  BUTTER FLAVOR CRISCO all-
  vegetable shortening
Flake coconut or finely chopped
  pecans (optional)

Angel Pillow

Heat oven to 350°F. Grease baking sheets with shortening. Place sheets of foil on countertop for cooling cookies. Cream shortening, cream cheese and milk at medium speed of electric mixer until well blended. Beat in brown sugar. Beat in preserves. Combine flour, baking powder, cinnamon and salt. Mix into creamed mixture. Stir in nuts. Drop 2 level measuring tablespoons of dough into a mound to form each cookie. Place 2 inches apart on baking sheets.

Bake one baking sheet at a time at 350°F for 14 minutes. *Do not overbake.* Cool on baking sheet one minute. Remove cookies to foil to cool completely.

For frosting, combine confectioners' sugar, preserves and shortening in small mixing bowl. Beat with electric mixer until well blended. Frost cooled cookies. Sprinkle coconut over frosting, if desired.   *Makes 1½ dozen cookies*

TIP: Try peach or pineapple preserves in place of apricot.

*Butter Flavor Crisco® is artificially flavored.

PREP TIME: 25 minutes
BAKE TIME: 14 minutes

HOLIDAY FRUIT DROPS

½ cup butter, softened
¾ cup packed brown sugar
1 egg
1¼ cups all-purpose flour
1 teaspoon vanilla
½ teaspoon baking soda
½ teaspoon ground cinnamon
   Pinch salt
1 cup (8 ounces) diced candied
   pineapple
1 cup (8 ounces) whole red and green
   candied cherries
8 ounces chopped pitted dates
1 cup (6 ounces) semisweet chocolate
   chips
½ cup whole hazelnuts
½ cup pecan halves
½ cup coarsely chopped walnuts

Preheat oven to 325°F. Lightly grease cookie sheets or line with parchment paper. Cream butter and sugar in large bowl. Beat in egg until light and fluffy. Mix in flour, vanilla, baking soda, cinnamon and salt. Stir in pineapple, cherries, dates, chocolate chips, hazelnuts, pecans and walnuts. Drop dough by rounded teaspoonfuls 2 inches apart onto prepared cookie sheets.

Bake 15 to 20 minutes or until firm and lightly browned around edges. Remove to wire racks to cool completely.

Makes about 8 dozen cookies

NOTE: The cherries, hazelnuts and pecan halves are not chopped, but left whole.

CAPPUCCINO BON BONS

1 package DUNCAN HINES® Chocolate
   Lovers' Fudge Brownie Mix, Family
   Size
2 eggs
⅓ cup water
⅓ cup CRISCO® Oil or CRISCO®
   PURITAN® Canola Oil
1½ tablespoons FOLGERS® Instant Coffee
1 teaspoon ground cinnamon
   Whipped topping
   Ground cinnamon

1. Preheat oven to 350°F. Place 40 (2-inch) foil cupcake liners on cookie sheet.

2. Combine brownie mix, eggs, water, oil, instant coffee and 1 teaspoon cinnamon. Stir with spoon until well blended, about 50 strokes. Fill each cupcake liner with 1 measuring tablespoonful batter. Bake at 350°F for 12 to 15 minutes or until toothpick inserted in center comes out clean. Cool completely. Garnish with whipped topping and a dash of cinnamon. Refrigerate until ready to serve.

Makes 40 bon bons

Cappuccino Bon Bons

HOLIDAY LAYER BARS

½ cup butter
1⅔ cups graham cracker crumbs
2⅔ cups flaked coconut
1¼ cups sweetened condensed milk
1 cup strawberry preserves or jam
⅓ cup finely chopped toasted pecans
½ cup semisweet chocolate chips, melted
¼ cup white chocolate chips, melted

Preheat oven to 350°F.

Place butter in bottom of 13×9-inch baking pan; melt in oven. Pour cracker crumbs evenly over melted butter; press down firmly to form crust. Combine coconut and milk in small bowl; pour evenly over crust. Bake 20 to 25 minutes or until lightly browned; cool. Spread preserves evenly over coconut; chill in refrigerator 3 to 4 hours. Sprinkle with pecans. Drizzle melted chocolates over top; chill. Cut into bars.

Makes 24 bar cookies

COCONUT MACAROONS

2 (7-ounce) packages flaked coconut
    (5⅓ cups)
1 (14-ounce) can EAGLE® Brand
    Sweetened Condensed Milk (NOT
    evaporated milk)
2 teaspoons vanilla extract
1½ teaspoons almond extract

Preheat oven to 350°F. In large bowl, combine coconut, sweetened condensed milk and extracts; mix well. Drop by rounded teaspoonfuls onto baking sheets lined with generously greased aluminum foil. Bake 8 to 10 minutes or until lightly browned around edges. *Immediately* remove from baking sheets (macaroons will stick if allowed to cool). Store loosely covered at room temperature.

Makes about 4 dozen cookies

WALNUT MACAROONS

2⅔ cups flaked coconut
1¼ cups coarsely chopped California
        walnuts
⅓ cup flour
½ teaspoon ground cinnamon
¼ teaspoon salt
4 egg whites
1 teaspoon grated lemon peel
2 (1-ounce) squares semisweet chocolate

Combine coconut, walnuts, flour, cinnamon and salt. Add egg whites and lemon peel; mix well.

Drop teaspoonfuls of walnut mixture onto lightly greased baking sheets. Bake in 325°F oven 20 minutes or until golden brown. Remove from baking sheets immediately.

Place chocolate in microwavable bowl. Microwave on HIGH (100% power) until melted, about 2½ minutes; stir. Dip macaroon bottoms in chocolate. Place on waxed paper. Let stand until chocolate is set.

Makes about 3 dozen cookies

*Favorite recipe from **Walnut Marketing Board***

Top to bottom: Walnut Macaroons, Walnut Brandy Shortbread (page 314), Chocolate Walnut Truffles (page 339)

OATMEAL MACAROONS

1¼ cups all-purpose flour
1 teaspoon baking soda
1 cup margarine, softened
1 cup packed brown sugar
2 eggs
½ teaspoon almond extract
3 cups QUAKER® Oats (quick or old-fashioned), uncooked
1 package (4 ounces) flaked or shredded coconut

In medium bowl, combine flour and baking soda. In large bowl, cream margarine and sugar until light and fluffy. Blend in eggs and almond extract. Add flour mixture; mix well. Stir in oats and coconut. Drop dough by rounded teaspoonfuls onto greased cookie sheets. Bake in preheated 350°F oven 10 minutes or until light golden brown. Let cookies cool 1 minute before removing from cookie sheets to wire racks.   *Makes 4½ dozen cookies*

BUTTER DROP-INS

½ BUTTER FLAVOR* CRISCO® Stick *or*
    ½ cup BUTTER FLAVOR CRISCO
    all-vegetable shortening
¾ cup granulated sugar
1 tablespoon milk
1 egg
½ teaspoon vanilla
1¼ cups all-purpose flour
¼ teaspoon salt
¼ teaspoon baking powder
FROSTING
½ BUTTER FLAVOR* CRISCO Stick *or*
    ½ cup BUTTER FLAVOR CRISCO
    all-vegetable shortening
1 pound (4 cups) confectioners' sugar
⅓ cup milk
1 teaspoon vanilla

Heat oven to 375°F. Grease baking sheets with shortening. Place sheets of foil on countertop for cooling cookies. Combine shortening, granulated sugar and milk in medium bowl at medium speed of electric mixer until well blended. Beat in egg and vanilla. Combine flour, salt and baking powder. Mix into creamed mixture. Drop level measuring tablespoonfuls 2 inches apart onto baking sheet. Bake one baking sheet at a time at 375°F for 7 to 9 minutes. Remove cookies to foil to cool completely.

For frosting, combine shortening, confectioners' sugar, milk and vanilla in small mixing bowl. Beat at low speed of electric mixer for 15 seconds. Scrape bowl. Beat at high speed for 2 minutes, or until smooth and creamy. Frost cookies.   *Makes 1½ to 2 dozen cookies*

*Butter Flavor Crisco® is artificially flavored.

NOTE: Frosting can be tinted with food coloring and piped decoratively onto cookies, if desired.

PREP TIME: 20 minutes
BAKE TIME: 7 to 9 minutes

GOOEY CARAMEL CHOCOLATE BARS

2 cups all-purpose flour
1 cup granulated sugar
¼ teaspoon salt
2 cups (4 sticks) butter or margarine, divided
1 cup packed light brown sugar
⅓ cup light corn syrup
1 cup (6 ounces) semisweet chocolate chips

Preheat oven to 350°F. Line 13×9-inch baking pan with foil. Combine flour, granulated sugar and salt in medium bowl; stir until blended. Cut in 14 tablespoons (1¾ sticks) butter until mixture resembles coarse crumbs. Press into bottom of prepared pan.

Bake 18 to 20 minutes or until lightly browned around edges. Remove pan to wire rack; cool completely.

Combine 1 cup (2 sticks) butter, brown sugar and corn syrup in heavy medium saucepan. Cook over medium heat 5 to 8 minutes or until mixture boils, stirring frequently. Boil gently 2 minutes, without stirring. Immediately pour over cooled base; spread evenly to edges of pan with metal spatula. Cool completely.

Melt chocolate in double boiler over hot (not simmering) water. Stir in remaining 2 tablespoons butter. Pour over cooled caramel layer and spread evenly to edges of pan with metal spatula. Refrigerate 10 to 15 minutes or until chocolate begins to set. Remove pan from refrigerator; cool completely. Cut into bars.
Makes 3 dozen bars

OAT-Y NUT BARS

½ cup butter or margarine
½ cup honey
¼ cup corn syrup
¼ cup packed brown sugar
2¾ cups uncooked quick oats
⅔ cup raisins
½ cup salted peanuts

Preheat oven to 300°F. Grease 9-inch square baking pan. Melt butter with honey, corn syrup and brown sugar in medium saucepan over medium heat, stirring constantly. Bring to a boil; boil 8 minutes until mixture thickens slightly. Stir in oats, raisins and peanuts until well blended. Press evenly into prepared pan.

Bake 45 to 50 minutes or until golden brown. Place pan on wire rack; score top into approximately 2-inch squares. Cool completely. Cut into bars.
Makes 16 bars

SCOTTISH SHORTBREAD

5 cups all-purpose flour
1 cup rice flour
2 cups butter or margarine, softened
1 cup sugar
Candied fruit (optional)

Preheat oven to 325°F. Sift together flours. Beat butter and sugar in large bowl with electric mixer until creamy. Blend in ¾ of flour until mixture resembles fine crumbs. Stir in remaining flour by hand. Press dough firmly into ungreased 15½×10½×1-inch jelly-roll pan or two 9-inch fluted tart pans; crimp and flute edges, if desired. Bake 40 to 45 minutes or until light brown. Place pan on wire rack. Cut into bars or wedges while warm. Decorate with candied fruit, if desired. Cool completely. Store in airtight containers.
Makes about 4 dozen bars or 24 wedges

Top to bottom: Oat-y Nut Bars,
Gooey Caramel Chocolate Bars

Santa's Favorite Brownies

Bake 25 to 30 minutes or until wooden toothpick inserted in center comes out clean. Place pan on wire rack; cool completely. Frost with Buttercream Frosting, if desired. Cut into squares. Decorate with jelly beans, icing gels and colored sugar, if desired. Store in airtight container. *Makes 16 brownies*

BUTTERCREAM FROSTING
>   3 cups powdered sugar, sifted
>   ½ cup butter or margarine, softened
>   3 to 4 tablespoons milk, divided
>   ½ teaspoon vanilla extract

Combine powdered sugar, butter, 2 tablespoons milk and vanilla in large bowl. Beat with electric mixer on low speed until blended. Beat on high speed until light and fluffy, adding more milk, 1 teaspoon at a time, as needed for good spreading consistency.
Makes about 1½ cups frosting

SANTA'S FAVORITE BROWNIES

>   1 cup (6 ounces) milk chocolate chips
>   ½ cup butter or margarine
>   ¾ cup granulated sugar
>   2 eggs
>   1 teaspoon vanilla extract
> 1¼ cups all-purpose flour
>   3 tablespoons unsweetened cocoa
>   1 teaspoon baking powder
>   ½ teaspoon salt
>   ½ cup chopped walnuts
>   Buttercream Frosting (recipe follows), optional
>   Small jelly beans, icing gels and colored sugar for decoration (optional)

Preheat oven to 350°F. Grease 9-inch square baking pan. Melt chocolate and butter with granulated sugar in medium saucepan over low heat, stirring constantly. Pour into large bowl; add eggs and vanilla. Beat with electric mixer until well blended. Stir in flour, cocoa, baking powder and salt; blend well. Fold in walnuts. Spread into prepared pan.

SPICED DATE BARS

>   ½ cup margarine, softened
>   1 cup packed brown sugar
>   2 eggs
>   ¾ cup light sour cream
>   2 cups all-purpose flour
>   1 teaspoon baking soda
>   1 teaspoon ground cinnamon
>   ½ teaspoon ground nutmeg
>   1 package (8 or 10 ounces) DOLE®
>   Chopped Dates or Pitted Dates, chopped
>   Powdered sugar (optional)

• Beat margarine and brown sugar until light and fluffy. Beat in eggs, one at a time. Stir in sour cream.

• Combine dry ingredients. Beat into sour cream mixture; stir in dates. Spread batter evenly into greased 13×9-inch baking pan.

• Bake at 350°F 25 to 30 minutes or until toothpick inserted in center comes out clean. Cool completely in pan on wire rack. Cut into bars. Dust with powdered sugar.

Makes 24 bars

PREP TIME: 15 minutes
BAKE TIME: 30 minutes

CHOCONUT FINGER COOKIES

> 1 package (8 ounces) PHILADELPHIA BRAND® Cream Cheese, softened
> ½ cup margarine, softened
> ¾ cup sugar
> 1 teaspoon vanilla
> 2 cups flour
> ½ teaspoon CALUMET® Baking Powder
> 1 cup BAKER'S® Semi-Sweet Real Chocolate Chips
> ½ cup BAKER'S® ANGEL FLAKE® Coconut, toasted
> ½ cup butterscotch chips
> ½ cup chopped pecans, toasted

• Heat oven to 375°F.

• Beat cream cheese, margarine, sugar and vanilla in large mixing bowl at medium speed with electric mixer until well blended. Add flour and baking powder; mix well. Spread mixture into ungreased 13×9-inch baking pan.

• Bake 15 minutes. Immediately sprinkle chocolate chips over crust; let stand about 5 minutes or until chocolate chips are slightly softened. Spread chocolate over crust. Sprinkle with remaining ingredients. Cool. Cut into bars.

Makes 2 dozen cookies

PREP TIME: 10 minutes
COOK TIME: 15 minutes

CRANBERRY ALMOND SQUARES

> 3 cups cranberries
> 1 cup raisins
> 1 cup chopped peeled apple
> 1 cup unsweetened apple juice
> 1 tablespoon granulated sugar
> 1½ cups whole wheat flour
> 1 cup regular oats, uncooked
> ⅓ cup firmly packed brown sugar
> 1 teaspoon ground cinnamon
> ⅛ teaspoon salt
> ½ cup molasses
> ¼ cup CRISCO® Oil
> 2 tablespoons slivered almonds, toasted, chopped

Heat oven to 350°F. Lightly oil 13×9-inch baking pan. Combine cranberries, raisins, apple, apple juice and granulated sugar in saucepan. Bring to a boil. Cook 5 minutes or until cranberry skins pop, stirring occasionally. Reduce heat and simmer, uncovered, 10 minutes. Stir occasionally. Cool.

Combine flour, oats, brown sugar, cinnamon and salt in medium bowl. Combine molasses and Crisco® Oil; add to flour mixture. Toss with fork until mixture resembles coarse meal.

Press 2 cups flour mixture in bottom of prepared pan. Top with cranberry mixture. Spread evenly. Combine remaining flour mixture and almonds. Sprinkle over cranberry mixture. Press lightly.

Bake at 350°F for 35 minutes or until golden. Cool. Cut into squares. Store loosely covered.

Makes 24 servings

GERMAN HONEY BARS
(LEBKUCHEN)

2¾ cups all-purpose flour
2 teaspoons ground cinnamon
1 teaspoon baking powder
½ teaspoon baking soda
½ teaspoon salt
½ teaspoon ground cardamom
½ teaspoon ground ginger
½ cup honey
½ cup dark molasses
¾ cup packed brown sugar
3 tablespoons butter, melted
1 large egg
½ cup chopped toasted almonds
 (optional)
Glaze (recipe follows)

Preheat oven to 350°F. Grease 15×10-inch jelly-roll pan; set aside. Place flour, cinnamon, baking powder, baking soda, salt, cardamom and ginger in medium bowl; stir to combine. Combine honey and molasses in medium saucepan; bring to a boil over medium heat. Remove from heat; cool 10 minutes. Stir in brown sugar, butter and egg.

Place brown sugar mixture in large bowl. Gradually add flour mixture. Beat at low speed until dough forms. Stir in almonds with spoon. (Dough will be slightly sticky.) Spread evenly into prepared pan. Bake 20 to 22 minutes or until golden brown and set. Remove pan to wire rack; cool completely.

Prepare Glaze. Spread over cooled bar cookies. Let stand until set, about 30 minutes. Cut into 2×1-inch bars. Store tightly covered at room temperature or freeze up to 3 months.
Makes about 6 dozen bars

GLAZE
1¼ cups powdered sugar
1 teaspoon grated lemon peel
3 tablespoons fresh lemon juice

Place all ingredients in medium bowl; stir with spoon until smooth.

KAHLÚA® PUMPKIN SQUARES WITH PRALINE TOPPING

1 cup flour
¼ cup powdered sugar
½ cup unsalted butter
1 cup LIBBY'S® Solid Pack Pumpkin
1 (8-ounce) package cream cheese, cut
 up and softened
2 eggs
¼ cup granulated sugar
¼ cup KAHLÚA®
1 cup chopped walnuts or pecans
¾ cup firmly packed brown sugar
¼ cup unsalted butter, melted

In bowl, combine flour and powdered sugar. Using 2 knives or pastry blender, cut in ½ cup butter until mixture forms fine crumbs. Press mixture into bottom of 8-inch square broilerproof baking dish. Bake at 350°F for 15 to 18 minutes or until golden.

Meanwhile, in food processor or blender, process pumpkin, cream cheese, eggs, granulated sugar and Kahlúa® until smooth. Pour pumpkin filling over warm baked crust; return to oven and bake about 20 minutes or until set. Cool in dish on rack. Cover; refrigerate.

In small bowl, combine nuts, brown sugar and melted butter. Just before serving, sprinkle topping over pumpkin filling.

Broil, watching carefully, just until topping begins to brown. Cut into 2-inch squares.
Makes 16 squares

German Honey Bars

Pear Mince Oatmeal Bars

PEAR MINCE OATMEAL BARS

¾ cup butter or margarine, softened
¾ cup packed brown sugar
1½ cups all-purpose flour
1¼ cups quick-cooking oats
½ cup chopped walnuts
½ teaspoon salt
½ teaspoon baking soda
2 USA Anjou pears, cored and chopped
1 cup prepared mincemeat
1 teaspoon lemon juice
½ teaspoon grated lemon peel

Preheat oven to 375°F. Cream butter and sugar. Stir in flour, oats, nuts, salt and baking soda until crumbly. Press ⅔ of flour mixture into ungreased 13×9-inch baking pan.

Combine pears, mincemeat, lemon juice and peel; spread over crumb crust. Top with remaining crumb mixture; pat lightly. Bake 25 to 30 minutes or until crust is golden. Cut into bars.   *Makes 30 to 35 bars*

Favorite recipe from **Oregon Washington California Pear Bureau**

WALNUT BRANDY SHORTBREAD

1 cup butter, softened
½ cup packed brown sugar
⅛ teaspoon salt
2 tablespoons brandy
1 cup all-purpose flour
1 cup finely chopped toasted California walnuts
Granulated sugar

Cream butter with brown sugar and salt; mix in brandy. Gradually add flour; stir in walnuts. Spread in ungreased 9-inch square baking pan. Refrigerate 30 minutes.

Prick dough all over using fork. Bake at 325°F about 55 minutes or until dark golden brown. If dough puffs up during baking, prick again. Sprinkle lightly with granulated sugar; cool. Cut into fingers or squares with sharp knife.
Makes 36 shortbreads

NOTE: Shortbread may be stored in airtight container at room temperature 1 to 2 months.

Favorite recipe from **Walnut Marketing Board**

YULETIDE TOFFEE SQUARES

4½ cups quick or old-fashioned oats, uncooked
1 cup packed brown sugar
¾ cup (1½ sticks) butter or margarine, melted
½ cup light corn syrup
1 tablespoon vanilla extract
½ teaspoon salt
2 cups (12-ounce package) NESTLÉ® Toll House® Semi-Sweet Chocolate Morsels
⅔ cup chopped nuts

COMBINE oats, brown sugar, butter, corn syrup, vanilla and salt in large bowl; mix well. Firmly press mixture into greased 15×10-inch jelly-roll pan.

BAKE in preheated 400°F. oven for about 18 minutes or until mixture is brown and bubbly. Remove from oven. Immediately sprinkle chocolate morsels evenly over toffee. Let stand for 10 minutes.

SPREAD chocolate evenly over toffee; sprinkle with nuts. Cool completely; cut into squares. Store tightly covered in cool, dry place.

Makes about 6 dozen squares

PEANUT BUTTER PAISLEY BROWNIES

½ cup butter or margarine, softened
¼ cup peanut butter
1 cup granulated sugar
1 cup packed light brown sugar
3 eggs
1 teaspoon vanilla extract
2 cups all-purpose flour
2 teaspoons baking powder
¼ teaspoon salt
½ cup (5.5-ounce can) HERSHEY®S Syrup

Blend butter and peanut butter in large mixer bowl. Add granulated sugar and brown sugar; beat well. Add eggs, one at a time, beating well after each addition. Blend in vanilla. Combine flour, baking powder and salt; add to peanut butter mixture.

Spread half the batter in greased 13×9-inch baking pan. Spoon syrup over top. Carefully spread with remaining batter. Swirl with spatula or knife for marbled effect. Bake at 350°F for 35 to 40 minutes or until lightly browned. Cool; cut into squares.

Makes about 3 dozen brownies

BANANA CARAMEL BARS

2½ cups all-purpose flour
1 cup sugar
1 teaspoon baking powder
1 cup margarine, cut up
1 large egg, beaten
2 extra-ripe, medium DOLE® Bananas, peeled
½ cup caramel topping

• Combine flour, sugar and baking powder in large bowl. Cut in margarine with pastry blender until mixture resembles coarse meal. Slowly stir in egg, mixing with a fork until crumbly. Pat half of mixture into 13×9-inch baking pan to form crust.

• For filling, mash bananas. Blend bananas with caramel topping. Spread evenly over crust.

• Sprinkle remaining crumb mixture over filling. Pat gently. Bake in 375°F oven 35 minutes or until golden brown. Cool pan on wire rack. Cut into bars when cooled. *Makes 24 bars*

Banana Caramel Bars

SWIRL OF CHOCOLATE CHEESECAKE TRIANGLES

CRUST
  2 cups graham cracker crumbs
  ½ cup (1 stick) butter or margarine, melted
  ⅓ cup granulated sugar
FILLING
  2 packages (8 ounces each) cream cheese, softened
  1 cup granulated sugar
  ¼ cup all-purpose flour
  1½ cups (12-fluid-ounce can) *undiluted* CARNATION® Evaporated Milk
  2 eggs
  1 tablespoon vanilla extract
  1 cup (6 ounces) NESTLÉ® Toll House® Semi-Sweet Chocolate Morsels

FOR CRUST:
COMBINE crumbs, butter and sugar in medium bowl; press onto bottom of ungreased 13×9-inch baking pan.

FOR FILLING:
BEAT cream cheese, sugar and flour in large mixer bowl until smooth. Gradually beat in evaporated milk, eggs and vanilla.

MICROWAVE morsels in medium, microwave-safe bowl on HIGH (100% power) for 1 minute; stir. Microwave at additional 10 to 20 second intervals, stirring until smooth. Stir 1 cup cream cheese mixture into chocolate. Pour remaining cheese mixture over crust. Pour chocolate mixture over cheese mixture; swirl with spoon to create marble effect.

BAKE in preheated 325°F. oven for 40 to 45 minutes or until set. Cool to room temperature; chill until firm. Cut into triangles.
Makes about 2½ dozen triangles

CINNAMONY APPLE STREUSEL BARS

  1¼ cups graham cracker crumbs
  1¼ cups all-purpose flour
  ¾ cup packed brown sugar, divided
  ¼ cup granulated sugar
  1 teaspoon ground cinnamon
  ¾ cup butter or margarine, melted
  2 cups chopped apples (2 medium apples, cored and peeled)
  Glaze (recipe follows)

Preheat oven to 350°F. Grease 13×9-inch baking pan. Combine graham cracker crumbs, flour, ½ cup brown sugar, granulated sugar, cinnamon and melted butter in large bowl until well blended; reserve 1 cup. Press remaining crumb mixture into bottom of prepared pan.

Bake 8 minutes. Remove from oven; set aside. Toss apples with remaining ¼ cup brown sugar in medium bowl until brown sugar is dissolved; arrange apples over baked crust. Sprinkle reserved 1 cup crumb mixture over filling. Bake 30 to 35 minutes more or until apples are tender. Remove pan to wire rack; cool completely. Drizzle with Glaze. Cut into bars.
Makes 3 dozen bars

GLAZE: Combine ½ cup powdered sugar and 1 tablespoon milk in small bowl until well blended.

Cinnamony Apple Streusel Bars

Sugarplum

GERMAN CHOCOLATE
NO-COOK FUDGE

3 (4-ounce) packages German sweet chocolate,
   broken into pieces
1 cup (6 ounces) semisweet chocolate chips
1 can (14 ounces) sweetened condensed milk
1 cup chopped pecans
2 teaspoons vanilla
36 pecan halves (optional)

Butter 8-inch square pan; set aside. Melt chocolate and chips
in heavy, small saucepan over very low heat, stirring constantly.
Remove from heat. Stir in condensed milk, chopped pecans
and vanilla until combined. Spread in prepared pan. Arrange
pecan halves on fudge. Score fudge into squares with knife.
Refrigerate until firm.

Cut into squares. Store in refrigerator. Bring to room
temperature before serving.	*Makes about 2 pounds*

EGGNOG GIFT FUDGE

¾ cup prepared eggnog
2 tablespoons light corn syrup
2 tablespoons butter or margarine
2 cups sugar
1 teaspoon vanilla

Butter 8-inch square pan. Lightly butter inside of heavy, medium saucepan. Combine eggnog, corn syrup, butter and sugar in prepared saucepan. Cook over medium heat, stirring constantly, until sugar dissolves and mixture comes to a boil. Wash down side of pan with pastry brush frequently dipped in hot water to remove sugar crystals. Add candy thermometer. Continue to cook until mixture reaches 238°F (soft-ball stage). Pour into large heatproof bowl. Cool to lukewarm (about 110°F). Add vanilla; beat with heavy-duty electric mixer until thick. Spread in prepared pan. Score fudge into 36 squares with knife. Refrigerate until firm. Cut into squares. Wrap individual pieces in plastic wrap and decorate with fabric or paper bows.

Makes 36 pieces

Left to right: Cherry Merry Christmas Crunch (page 342), Eggnog Gift Fudge

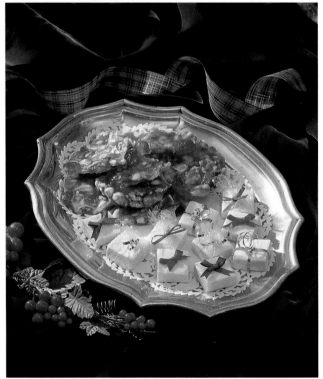

CREAMY WHITE FUDGE

1½ pounds white confectioners' coating*
1 (14-ounce) can EAGLE® Brand Sweetened Condensed Milk (NOT evaporated milk)
⅛ teaspoon salt
¾ to 1 cup chopped nuts
1½ teaspoons vanilla extract

In heavy saucepan, over low heat, melt confectioners' coating with sweetened condensed milk and salt. Remove from heat; stir in nuts and vanilla. Spread evenly into wax paper-lined 8- or 9-inch square pan. Chill 2 hours or until firm. Turn out fudge onto cutting board; peel off paper and cut into squares. Store tightly covered at room temperature.

Makes about 2¼ pounds

MICROWAVE DIRECTIONS: In 2-quart glass measure, combine coating, sweetened condensed milk and salt. Microwave on full power (HIGH) 3 to 5 minutes or until coating melts, stirring after 3 minutes. Stir in nuts and vanilla. Proceed as above.

*If white confectioners' coating is not available at your grocery store it can be purchased in candy specialty stores.

PRALINE FUDGE: Omit vanilla. Add 1 teaspoon maple flavoring and 1 cup chopped pecans. Proceed as above.

CONFETTI FUDGE: Omit nuts. Add 1 cup chopped mixed candied fruit. Proceed as above.

RUM RAISIN FUDGE: Omit vanilla. Add 1½ teaspoons white vinegar, 1 teaspoon rum flavoring and ¾ cup raisins. Proceed as above.

CHERRY FUDGE: Omit nuts. Add 1 cup chopped candied cherries. Proceed as above.

Cherries 'n Chocolate Fudge

CHERRIES 'N CHOCOLATE FUDGE

    1 can (14 ounces) sweetened condensed milk
    2 cups (12-ounce package) HERSHEY'S Semi-Sweet Chocolate Chips
    ½ cup coarsely chopped almonds
    ½ cup chopped candied cherries
    1 teaspoon almond extract
    Candied cherry halves and pecan halves

MICROWAVE DIRECTIONS: Line 8-inch square pan with foil; set aside. In medium microwave-safe bowl, combine sweetened condensed milk and chocolate chips; stir lightly. Microwave at HIGH (100% power) 1½ to 2 minutes or until chips are melted and mixture is smooth when stirred. Stir in almonds, cherries and almond extract. Spread evenly in prepared pan. Place cherry and pecan halves over fudge. Cover; refrigerate until firm. Cut into 1-inch squares. Cover; store in refrigerator.

Makes about 5 dozen squares

CHRISTMAS FUDGE

    3 cups sugar
    1 cup PET® Evaporated Milk
    ½ cup butter
    2 cups semisweet chocolate chips
    1 jar (7 to 7½ ounces) marshmallow creme
    1 teaspoon vanilla extract
    1 cup crushed peppermint candies

1. Butter 13×9×2-inch pan; set aside.

2. In heavy 3-quart saucepan, combine sugar, evaporated milk and butter. Bring to a full rolling boil over high heat, stirring constantly.

3. Reduce heat to medium and boil 6 minutes (234°F), stirring constantly.

4. Remove from heat and stir in chocolate chips, marshmallow creme and vanilla.

5. Stir in peppermint candies.

6. Pour into prepared pan. Cool until firm. Cut into 1-inch squares.

Makes 117 (1-inch) pieces

EASY ROCKY ROAD

    2 cups (12-ounce package) HERSHEY'S Semi-Sweet Chocolate Chips
    ¼ cup butter or margarine
    2 tablespoons shortening
    3 cups miniature marshmallows
    ½ cup coarsely chopped nuts

Butter 8-inch square pan. In large microwave-safe bowl, place chocolate chips, butter and shortening. Microwave at HIGH (100% power) 1 to 1½ minutes or just until chocolate chips are melted and mixture is smooth when stirred. Add marshmallows and nuts; blend well. Spread evenly in prepared pan. Cover; refrigerate until firm. Cut into 2-inch squares.

Makes 16 squares

Coffee Liqueur Pecan Fudge

COFFEE LIQUEUR PECAN FUDGE

   3 cups miniature marshmallows
   **2 cups (12-ounce package) NESTLÉ®
      Toll House® Semi-Sweet Chocolate
      Morsels**
   **2 ounces NESTLÉ® Unsweetened
      Chocolate Baking Bars, coarsely
      chopped**
  **⅔ cup *undiluted* CARNATION®
      Evaporated Milk**
1⅓ cups granulated sugar
  ¼ cup butter
   1 cup coarsely chopped pecans
  ¼ cup coffee liqueur

In large bowl, combine marshmallows, morsels and unsweetened chocolate. In heavy 2-quart saucepan, combine evaporated milk, sugar and butter. Bring to a boil over medium heat, stirring frequently; boil for 6 minutes, stirring constantly. Pour over marshmallow mixture; stir until marshmallows and chocolate are completely melted and mixture is smooth. Stir in nuts and liqueur. Pour into buttered 8-inch square baking pan; cool. Chill until firm. Cut into 36 squares.

Makes 2½ pounds

TRADITIONAL CHRISTMAS FUDGE

2 tablespoons butter or margarine
⅔ cup *undiluted* CARNATION®
  Evaporated Milk
1½ cups granulated sugar
¼ teaspoon salt
2 cups (4 ounces) miniature
  marshmallows
1½ cups (9 ounces) NESTLÉ® Toll House®
  Semi-Sweet Chocolate Morsels
½ cup chopped pecans or walnuts
1 teaspoon vanilla extract

COMBINE butter, evaporated milk, sugar and salt in medium, heavy saucepan. Bring to a boil over medium heat, stirring constantly. Boil for 4 to 5 minutes, stirring constantly. Remove from heat.

STIR in marshmallows, morsels, nuts and vanilla. Stir vigorously for 1 minute or until marshmallows are melted. Pour into foil-lined 8-inch square baking pan. Sprinkle with additional pecans if desired. Chill until firm. Cut into pieces.   *Makes about 2 pounds*

VARIATIONS

Milk Chocolate Fudge: Substitute 2 cups (11½-ounce package) NESTLÉ® Toll House® Milk Chocolate Morsels for Semi-Sweet Morsels.

Butterscotch Fudge: Substitute 2 cups (12-ounce package) NESTLÉ® Toll House® Butterscotch Flavored Morsels for Semi-Sweet Morsels.

Mint Chocolate Fudge: Substitute 1½ cups (10-ounce package) NESTLÉ® Toll House® Mint-Chocolate Morsels for Semi-Sweet Morsels.

HONEY NUT WHITE FUDGE

2 tablespoons butter or margarine
⅔ cup *undiluted* CARNATION®
  Evaporated Milk
1½ cups granulated sugar
2 cups (4 ounces) miniature
  marshmallows
2 cups (12-ounce package) NESTLÉ®
  Toll House® Premier White Morsels
1½ cups honey roasted peanuts, divided
2 teaspoons vanilla extract

COMBINE butter, evaporated milk and sugar in medium, heavy saucepan. Bring to a *full rolling boil* over medium heat, stirring constantly. Boil for 4½ to 5 minutes, stirring constantly. Remove from heat.

STIR in marshmallows, morsels, *1 cup* peanuts and vanilla. Stir vigorously for 1 minute or until marshmallows are melted. Pour into foil-lined 9-inch square baking pan. Coarsely chop *remaining* peanuts; sprinkle over fudge and press lightly. Chill until firm. Remove fudge from pan by lifting edges of foil. Remove foil and cut fudge into squares.
          Makes about 1¾ pounds fudge

CHOCOLATE-NUT SQUARES

1 cup (6 ounces) semisweet chocolate
  chips
1 cup milk chocolate chips
1 tablespoon shortening
1 package (14 ounces) caramels
2 tablespoons butter or margarine
3 tablespoons milk
2 cups coarsely chopped pecans

Line 8-inch square pan with buttered foil; set aside. Melt both kinds of chips with shortening in heavy, small saucepan over very low heat, stirring constantly. Spoon half the chocolate mixture into prepared pan, spreading evenly over bottom and ¼ inch up sides of pan. Refrigerate until firm.

Meanwhile, combine caramels, butter and milk in heavy, medium saucepan. Cook over medium heat, stirring constantly. When mixture is smooth, stir in pecans. Cool to lukewarm. Spread caramel mixture evenly over chocolate in pan. Melt remaining chocolate mixture again over very low heat, stirring constantly; spread over caramel layer. Refrigerate until almost firm. Cut into squares. Store in refrigerator.

Makes about 2 pounds

HINT: Squares are easier to cut without breaking if chocolate is not completely firm.

CHOCOLATE PEPPERMINTS

1 cup (6 ounces) semisweet chocolate
  chips
1 cup milk chocolate chips
¼ teaspoon peppermint extract
½ cup crushed peppermint candy

Line baking sheet with buttered waxed paper; set aside. Melt both kinds of chips in heavy, medium saucepan over low heat, stirring constantly. Stir in peppermint extract. Spread mixture in rectangle about ¼ inch thick on prepared baking sheet. Sprinkle with candy; press into chocolate. Refrigerate until almost firm. Cut into squares. Refrigerate until firm before removing from paper.

Makes about 100 mints

HINT: Squares are easier to cut without breaking if chocolate is not completely firm.

TRIPLE CHOCOLATE SQUARES

1½ cups BLUE DIAMOND® Blanched
  Almond Paste, divided
8 ounces semisweet chocolate, melted
¾ cup softened butter, divided
8 ounces milk chocolate, melted
8 ounces white chocolate, melted

Line bottom and sides of 8-inch square pan with aluminum foil. Beat ½ cup almond paste with semisweet chocolate. Beat in ¼ cup butter. Spread evenly in bottom of prepared pan. Chill to harden. Beat ½ cup almond paste with milk chocolate. Beat in ¼ cup butter. Spread mixture evenly over chilled semisweet chocolate layer. Chill to harden. Beat remaining ½ cup almond paste with white chocolate. Beat in remaining ¼ cup butter. Spread mixture evenly over chilled milk chocolate layer. Chill. Remove candy from pan by lifting edges of foil. Peel off foil and cut candy into 1-inch squares.

Makes 64 squares

Chocolate-Nut Squares, Chocolate Peppermints

LOUISIANA CREAM PRALINES

2⅓ cups packed brown sugar
¾ cup PET® Evaporated Milk
1 tablespoon butter
⅛ teaspoon salt
2 cups pecan halves
1 teaspoon vanilla extract

1. Grease baking sheet; set aside.

2. In heavy 2-quart saucepan, combine sugar, evaporated milk, butter and salt. Cook and stir over low heat until sugar is dissolved.

3. Add pecans. Cook over medium heat to 234°F (approximately 9 minutes), stirring constantly.

4. Remove from heat; add vanilla. Cool 5 minutes without stirring.

5. Stir vigorously until mixture thickens and loses its gloss; about 5 minutes.

6. Drop quickly by tablespoonfuls onto prepared baking sheet. Cool. Store in covered container. *Makes 2½ to 3 dozen*

PECAN ROLLS

¼ cup corn syrup
¼ cup water
1¼ cups sugar
1 egg white
⅛ teaspoon cream of tartar
1 teaspoon vanilla
1 package (14 ounces) caramels
3 tablespoons water
2 cups coarsely chopped pecans

Line 9×5-inch loaf pan with buttered waxed paper; set aside. Combine corn syrup, ¼ cup water and sugar in heavy, small saucepan. Cook over medium heat, stirring constantly, until sugar dissolves and mixture comes to a boil. Wash down side of pan frequently with pastry brush dipped in hot water to remove sugar crystals. Carefully clip candy thermometer to side of pan (do not let bulb touch bottom of pan). Continue to cook until mixture reaches the hard-ball stage (255°F).

Meanwhile, beat egg white and cream of tartar with heavy-duty electric mixer until stiff but not dry. Slowly pour hot syrup into egg white mixture, beating constantly. Add vanilla; beat until candy forms soft peaks and starts to lose its gloss. Spoon mixture into prepared pan. Cut into 3 strips lengthwise, then crosswise in center. Freeze until firm.

Line baking sheet with waxed paper; set aside. Melt caramels with 3 tablespoons water in heavy, small saucepan over low heat, stirring occasionally. Arrange pecans on waxed paper. Working quickly, drop 1 piece of frozen candy mixture into melted caramels to coat. Roll in pecans to coat completely. Place on prepared baking sheet to set. Repeat with remaining candy pieces, reheating caramels if mixture becomes too thick.

Cut logs into ½-inch slices. Store in refrigerator in airtight container between layers of waxed paper or freeze up to 3 months. *Makes 6 (5-inch) rolls*

HINT: For perfect slices, freeze finished rolls before cutting.

Pecan Rolls

ELEGANT CREAM CHEESE MINTS

  Chocolate Topping (recipe follows),
    optional
1 package (3 ounces) cream cheese,
    softened
3 tablespoons butter or margarine,
    softened
½ teaspoon vanilla extract
¼ to ½ teaspoon desired food coloring
¼ teaspoon peppermint extract
1 pound powdered sugar (3½ to 4 cups)
⅓ cup granulated sugar

Line large cookie sheet with waxed paper. Prepare Chocolate Topping, if desired; keep warm.

Beat cream cheese, butter, vanilla, food coloring and peppermint extract in large bowl with electric mixer on medium speed until smooth. Gradually beat in powdered sugar on low speed until well combined. (If necessary, stir in remaining powdered sugar with wooden spoon or knead candy on work surface that has been lightly sprinkled with powdered sugar.)

Place granulated sugar in shallow bowl. Roll 2 teaspoons cream cheese mixture into a ball. Roll ball in granulated sugar until coated. Flatten ball with fingers or fork to make a patty. Place patty on prepared cookie sheet. Repeat with remaining cream cheese mixture and granulated sugar. Drizzle patties with topping, if desired. Refrigerate until firm. Store in airtight container in refrigerator.
  Makes about 1½ pounds or 40 (1-inch) mints

CHOCOLATE TOPPING: Place ½ cup semisweet chocolate chips and 1 tablespoon shortening in 1-cup glass measuring cup. Microwave on HIGH (100% power) about 2 minutes or until melted, stirring after 1½ minutes.

Citrus Candied Nuts (page 526),
Elegant Cream Cheese Mints

PEANUT BUTTER LOGS

1 (12-ounce) package peanut butter flavored chips
1 (14-ounce) can EAGLE® Brand Sweetened Condensed Milk (NOT evaporated milk)
1 cup CAMPFIRE® Miniature Marshmallows
1 cup chopped peanuts

In heavy saucepan, over low heat, melt chips with sweetened condensed milk. Add marshmallows; stir until melted. Remove from heat; cool 20 minutes. Divide in half; place each portion on a 20-inch piece of wax paper. Shape each portion into 12-inch log. Roll in nuts. Wrap tightly; chill 2 hours or until firm. Remove paper; cut into ¼-inch slices.

Makes 2 (12-inch) logs

MICROWAVE DIRECTIONS: In 2-quart glass measure, microwave chips, sweetened condensed milk and marshmallows on full power (HIGH) 4 minutes or until melted, stirring after 2 minutes. Let stand at room temperature 1 hour. Proceed as above.

PEANUT BUTTER FUDGE: Stir peanuts into hot mixture. Spread into wax paper-lined 8- or 9-inch square pan. Chill 2 hours or until firm. Turn out fudge onto cutting board; peel off paper and cut into squares.

COAL CANDY

2 cups sugar
¾ cup light corn syrup
½ cup water
1 teaspoon anise extract
½ teaspoon black paste food coloring

Line 8-inch square baking pan with foil, extending edges over sides of pan. Lightly grease foil with butter; set aside. Measure sugar, corn syrup and water into heavy 2-quart saucepan. Stir over medium-low heat until sugar is dissolved and mixture comes to a boil, being careful not to splash sugar mixture on side of pan. Carefully clip candy thermometer to side of pan (do not let bulb touch bottom of pan). Cook about 15 minutes, without stirring, until thermometer registers 290°F. Immediately remove from heat. Stir in anise extract and food coloring. Pour mixture into prepared pan. Cool completely.

Lift candy out of pan using foil; remove foil. Place candy between 2 layers of heavy-duty foil. Pound with mallet to break candy into 1- to 2-inch pieces. *Makes about 1½ pounds*

CHIPPER PEANUT CANDY

1 cup semi-sweet chocolate chips or butterscotch-flavored chips
1 (14-ounce) can EAGLE® Brand Sweetened Condensed Milk (NOT evaporated milk)
1 cup peanut butter
2 cups crushed potato chips
1 cup coarsely chopped peanuts

In large heavy saucepan, over low heat, melt chocolate chips with sweetened condensed milk and peanut butter; stir until well blended. Remove from heat. Add potato chips and peanuts; mix well. Press into aluminum foil-lined 8- or 9-inch square pan. Chill 2 hours or until firm. Turn out onto cutting board; peel off foil and cut into squares. Store loosely covered at room temperature.

Makes about 2 pounds

MICROWAVE DIRECTIONS: In 2-quart glass measure, combine chocolate chips, sweetened condensed milk and peanut butter. Cook on 100% power (HIGH) 4 minutes, stirring after each 2 minutes. Proceed as directed.

GOOD LUCK MERINGUE MUSHROOMS

  2 egg whites
  Pinch cream of tartar
½ cup sugar
½ cup semisweet chocolate chips, melted
  Unsweetened cocoa

Preheat oven to 250°F. Beat egg whites in small bowl until foamy. Add cream of tartar and beat until soft peaks form. Add sugar, 2 tablespoons at a time, beating until stiff and glossy. Line baking sheets with parchment paper. Spoon mixture into pastry bag fitted with large writing tip. Pipe 1-inch rounds to make mushroom caps. Smooth tops with wet fingertips. Pipe 1-inch-high cones to make stems. (Pipe an equal number of caps and cones.) Bake about 30 minutes or until firm. Turn oven off; let stand in oven 1 hour. Remove from oven; cool completely. Make small hole in center of flat side of each cap with sharp knife. Fill hole with melted chocolate. Insert stem into hole. Set aside until chocolate sets. Sift cocoa through fine-mesh sieve over mushroom caps.

Makes about 2½ dozen

NOTE: These confections may be made ahead and stored, loosely covered, at room temperature for up to 1 week. Avoid making on humid days as the candy may become moist and sticky.

DREAMY DIVINITY

3½ cups DOMINO® Granulated Sugar
  ⅔ cup water
  ⅔ cup light corn syrup
  ⅓ teaspoon salt
  3 egg whites, beaten until stiff
1½ teaspoons vanilla extract
    Food coloring, candied cherries and
    chopped nuts (optional)

Combine sugar, water, corn syrup and salt in saucepan. Heat, stirring occasionally, until sugar dissolves. Wipe down sugar crystals from side of pan as necessary with pastry brush dipped in water. Boil syrup mixture, without stirring, until mixture reaches 265°F or hard-ball stage on candy thermometer.

Gradually beat hot syrup into beaten egg whites. Add vanilla. Tint with food coloring, if desired. Continue beating until candy holds shape. Drop by teaspoonfuls onto buttered baking sheet or plate. Garnish with cherries and nuts as desired. When firm, store in airtight container. *Makes 50 pieces (1½ pounds)*

CHOCOLATE BRITTLE DROPS

½ package (4 squares) BAKER'S® Semi-
    Sweet Chocolate
1½ cups (½ pound) coarsely crushed
    peanut brittle

Place unwrapped chocolate in heavy saucepan on very low heat; stir constantly until just melted. Remove from heat; stir in peanut brittle. Drop by teaspoonfuls onto wax paper-lined cookie sheet. Let stand at room temperature or refrigerate until chocolate is firm.

Makes about 2 dozen

COCONUT RUM BALLS

1 (12-ounce) package vanilla wafer
    cookies, finely crushed (about 3 cups
    crumbs)
1 (3½-ounce) can flaked coconut
    (1⅓ cups)
1 cup finely chopped nuts
1 (14-ounce) can EAGLE® Brand
    Sweetened Condensed Milk (NOT
    evaporated milk)
¼ cup rum
    Additional flaked coconut or
    confectioners' sugar

In large mixing bowl, combine crumbs, coconut
and nuts. Add sweetened condensed milk and
rum; mix well. Chill 4 hours. Shape into 1-inch
balls. Roll in coconut. Store tightly covered in
refrigerator.   *Makes about 8 dozen*

TIPS: The flavor of these candies improves
after 24 hours. They may be made ahead and
stored in refrigerator for several weeks.

FRUIT BON BONS

1 (14-ounce) can EAGLE® Brand
    Sweetened Condensed Milk (NOT
    evaporated milk)
2 (7-ounce) packages flaked coconut
    (5⅓ cups)
1 (6-ounce) package fruit flavor gelatin,
    any flavor
1 cup ground blanched almonds
1 teaspoon almond extract
    Food coloring (optional)

In large mixing bowl, combine sweetened
condensed milk, coconut, ⅓ cup gelatin,
almonds, extract and enough food coloring to
tint mixture desired shade. Chill 1 hour or until
firm enough to handle. Using about ½
tablespoon mixture for each, shape into 1-inch
balls. Sprinkle remaining gelatin on wax paper;
roll each ball in gelatin to coat. Place on wax
paper-lined baking sheets; chill. Store covered
at room temperature or in refrigerator.
Makes about 5 dozen

MILK CHOCOLATE BOURBON BALLS

1 (12-ounce) package vanilla wafer
    cookies, finely crushed (about 3 cups
    crumbs)
5 tablespoons bourbon or brandy
1 (11½-ounce) package milk chocolate
    chips
1 (14-ounce) can EAGLE® Brand
    Sweetened Condensed Milk (NOT
    evaporated milk)
    Finely chopped nuts

In medium mixing bowl, combine crumbs and
bourbon. In heavy large saucepan, over low
heat, melt chips. Remove from heat; add
sweetened condensed milk. Gradually add
crumb mixture; mix well. Let stand at room
temperature 30 minutes or chill. Shape into
1-inch balls; roll in nuts. Store tightly covered.
Makes about 5½ dozen

TIP: The flavor of these candies improves after
24 hours. They may be made ahead and stored
in freezer. Thaw before serving.

RICH CHOCOLATE PUMPKIN TRUFFLES

2½ cups crushed vanilla wafers
1 cup toasted ground almonds
¾ cup sifted powdered sugar, divided
2 teaspoons ground cinnamon
1 cup (6 ounces) NESTLÉ® Toll House®
  Semi-Sweet Chocolate Morsels,
  melted
½ cup LIBBY'S® Solid Pack Pumpkin
⅓ cup coffee liqueur or apple juice

In medium bowl, combine vanilla wafer crumbs, ground almonds, *½ cup* powdered sugar and cinnamon. Blend in melted chocolate, pumpkin and coffee liqueur. Form into 1-inch balls. Chill. Dust with *remaining ¼ cup* powdered sugar just before serving. *Makes 4 dozen*

HOLIDAY ALMOND TREATS

2½ cups crushed vanilla wafers
1¾ cups toasted ground almonds, divided
½ cup sifted powdered sugar
½ teaspoon ground cinnamon
1 cup LIBBY'S® Pumpkin Pie Mix
⅓ cup almond liqueur or apple juice

In medium bowl, blend vanilla wafer crumbs, *1 cup* ground almonds, powdered sugar and cinnamon. Stir in pumpkin pie mix and almond liqueur. Form into 1-inch balls. Roll in *remaining ¾ cup* ground almonds. Chill.

Makes 4 dozen

Left to right: Rich Chocolate Pumpkin Truffles, Holiday Almond Treats

MINT TRUFFLES

1 package (10 ounces) mint chocolate chips
⅓ cup whipping cream
¼ cup butter or margarine
1 container (3½ ounces) chocolate sprinkles

Line baking sheet with waxed paper; set aside. Melt chips with whipping cream and butter in heavy, medium saucepan over low heat, stirring occasionally. Pour into pie pan. Refrigerate until mixture is fudgy, but soft, about 2 hours.

Shape about 1 tablespoonful of mixture into 1¼-inch ball. To shape, roll mixture between palms. Repeat procedure with remaining mixture. Place balls on waxed paper.

Place sprinkles in shallow bowl; roll balls in sprinkles. Place truffles in petit four or candy cups. (If sprinkles won't stick because truffle has set, roll truffle between palms until outside is soft.) Truffles may be refrigerated 2 to 3 days or frozen several weeks.

Makes about 24 truffles

HINT: Truffles can be coated with unsweetened cocoa, powdered sugar, chopped nuts, sprinkles or cookie crumbs to add flavor and prevent the truffle from melting in your fingers.

Mint Truffles

CHOCOLATE TRUFFLES

**3 (6-ounce) packages semi-sweet
   chocolate chips
1 (14-ounce) can EAGLE® Brand
   Sweetened Condensed Milk (NOT
   evaporated milk)
1 tablespoon vanilla extract
   Finely chopped nuts, flaked coconut,
   chocolate sprinkles, colored
   sprinkles, unsweetened cocoa,
   colored sugar or confectioners' sugar**

In heavy saucepan, over low heat, melt chips with sweetened condensed milk. Remove from heat; stir in vanilla. Chill 2 hours or until firm. Shape mixture into 1-inch balls; roll in any of the above coatings. Chill 1 hour or until firm. Store covered at room temperature.

Makes about 6 dozen

MICROWAVE DIRECTIONS: In 1-quart glass measure, combine chips and sweetened condensed milk. Microwave on full power (HIGH) 3 minutes, stirring after 1½ minutes. Stir until smooth. Proceed as directed.

AMARETTO: Omit vanilla. Add 3 tablespoons amaretto or other almond-flavored liqueur and ½ teaspoon almond extract. Roll in finely chopped toasted almonds.

ORANGE: Omit vanilla. Add 3 tablespoons orange-flavored liqueur. Roll in finely chopped toasted almonds mixed with finely grated orange peel.

RUM: Omit vanilla. Add ¼ cup dark rum. Roll in flaked coconut.

BOURBON: Omit vanilla. Add 3 tablespoons bourbon. Roll in finely chopped toasted nuts.

Chocolate Truffles

BOURBON FRUIT BALLS

1 (9-ounce) package NONE SUCH® Condensed Mincemeat, finely crumbled
2 cups vanilla wafer crumbs (about 56 wafers)
1 cup flaked coconut
1 cup confectioners' sugar
¼ cup bourbon or rum
3 tablespoons light corn syrup
2 tablespoons water
  Additional confectioners' sugar

In large bowl, combine all ingredients except additional confectioners' sugar until well blended. Cover; chill 4 hours or overnight. Dip hands in confectioners' sugar; shape mixture into 1-inch balls. (Chill again if mixture becomes too soft.) Roll balls in additional confectioners' sugar. Place on wax paper-lined baking sheets; chill 2 hours or until firm. Store tightly covered at room temperature. Reroll in additional confectioners' sugar before serving, if desired. Store tightly covered.

Makes 50 to 55 balls

TIP: These candies can be made ahead and frozen for several weeks. Reroll in additional confectioners' sugar before serving, if desired.

CHAMPAGNE COCOA TRUFFLES

¾ cup unsalted butter
¾ cup HERSHEY'S Cocoa
1 can (14 ounces) sweetened condensed milk
1 teaspoon vanilla extract
2 to 3 tablespoons champagne
  Cocoa or powdered sugar

In heavy, medium saucepan over low heat, melt butter. Add cocoa; stir until smooth. Blend in sweetened condensed milk; stir constantly until mixture is thick, smooth and glossy, about 4 minutes. Remove from heat; stir in vanilla. Pour mixture into medium bowl; cool to room temperature. Stir in champagne. Cover and refrigerate until firm, 4 to 5 hours. Taking small amount of mixture at a time, form into 1¼-inch balls; roll in cocoa or powdered sugar. Place balls on wax paper-lined tray; refrigerate until firm, 1 to 2 hours. Store, covered, in refrigerator. *Makes about 2½ dozen candies*

FUDGE RUM BALLS

1 package DUNCAN HINES® Moist Deluxe Butter Recipe Fudge Cake Mix
1 cup finely chopped pecans or walnuts
1 tablespoon rum extract
2 cups sifted confectioners sugar
¼ cup unsweetened cocoa
  Pecans or walnuts, finely chopped

1. Preheat oven to 375°F. Grease and flour 13×9×2-inch baking pan. Prepare, bake and cool cake following package directions.

2. Crumble cake into large bowl. Stir with fork until crumbs are fine and uniform in size. Add 1 cup nuts, rum extract, confectioners sugar and cocoa. Stir until well blended.

3. Shape heaping tablespoonfuls of mixture into balls. Garnish by rolling balls in finely chopped nuts. Press firmly to adhere nuts to balls. *Makes 6 dozen*

TIP: Substitute rum for rum extract.

Fudge Rum Balls

Chocolate Peanut Butter Balls, Crisp Chocolate Truffles

In top of double boiler, over hot water, melt chocolate coating and shortening. Dip each peanut butter ball in coating and place on waxed-paper-lined baking sheet. Drizzle with melted white coating, if desired. Refrigerate until firm. Place in small candy paper cups to serve. *Makes 4½ dozen*

NOTE: One package (12 ounces) semi-sweet chocolate morsels may be used in place of chocolate candy coating.

CHOCOLATE PEANUT BUTTER BALLS

1 cup crunchy peanut butter
¼ cup margarine or butter, softened
2 cups KELLOGG'S® RICE KRISPIES® cereal
1 cup confectioners sugar
1 package (14 ounces) chocolate candy coating
2 tablespoons shortening
White candy coating, melted (optional)

In large bowl, combine peanut butter and margarine. Add Kellogg's® Rice Krispies® cereal and sugar, mixing until evenly combined. Portion cereal mixture using a rounded measuring teaspoon. Roll into balls; set aside.

CRISP CHOCOLATE TRUFFLES

1 jar (7 ounces) marshmallow creme
2 tablespoons margarine or butter
1 package (6 ounces) semi-sweet chocolate morsels (1 cup)
2 cups KELLOGG'S® RICE KRISPIES® cereal
1 package (14 ounces) white candy coating
2 tablespoons shortening
Multicolored sprinkles (optional)

In heavy 2-quart saucepan, combine marshmallow creme, margarine and chocolate morsels. Cook over low heat, stirring constantly, until chocolate is melted and mixture is smooth; remove from heat. Stir Kellogg's® Rice Krispies® cereal into hot chocolate mixture, mixing until thoroughly combined. Drop by rounded measuring teaspoonfuls onto waxed-paper-lined baking sheet. Refrigerate until firm, about 1 hour.

In top of double boiler, over hot water, melt white coating and shortening. Dip each chocolate ball in coating and place on waxed-paper-lined baking sheet. Decorate with sprinkles, if desired. Refrigerate until firm. Place in small candy paper cups to serve.
Makes 4½ dozen

BUCKEYES

    2 (3-ounce) packages cream cheese,
       softened
    1 (14-ounce) can EAGLE® Brand
       Sweetened Condensed Milk (NOT
       evaporated milk)
    2 (12-ounce) packages peanut butter
       flavored chips
    1 cup finely chopped peanuts
    ½ pound chocolate confectioners'
       coating*

In large mixer bowl, beat cheese until fluffy. Gradually beat in sweetened condensed milk until smooth. In heavy saucepan, over low heat, melt peanut butter chips; stir into cheese mixture. Add peanuts. Chill 2 to 3 hours; shape mixture into 1-inch balls. In small heavy saucepan, over low heat, melt confectioners' coating. With wooden pick, dip each peanut ball into melted coating, not covering completely. Place on wax paper-lined baking sheets until firm. Store covered at room temperature or in refrigerator.

Makes about 7 dozen

*If chocolate confectioners' coating is not available at your grocery store it can be purchased in candy specialty stores.

CHOCOLATE WALNUT TRUFFLES

    1 cup heavy cream
    16 ounces semisweet chocolate, cut into
       small pieces
    2 tablespoons butter
    1 cup finely chopped California walnuts
    4 tablespoons coffee liqueur
      Grated chocolate, shredded coconut
       and finely chopped California
       walnuts

Bring cream to a boil in saucepan over medium heat; add chocolate pieces. Stir with wooden spoon until mixture is smooth and thickened. Add butter; stir until melted. Pour mixture into large bowl; cool slightly. Stir in 1 cup walnuts and liqueur. Refrigerate until firm. Form mixture into walnut-sized balls and roll in chocolate, coconut or walnuts. Chill to set. Store in airtight container in refrigerator.

Makes 3½ dozen truffles

*Favorite recipe from **Walnut Marketing Board***

WHITE TRUFFLES

    2 pounds EAGLE™ Brand Vanilla-
       Flavored Candy Coating
    1 (14-ounce) can EAGLE® Brand
       Sweetened Condensed Milk (NOT
       evaporated milk)
    1 tablespoon vanilla extract
    1 pound EAGLE™ Brand Chocolate-
       Flavored Candy Coating, melted *or*
    ¾ cup unsweetened cocoa

In large, heavy saucepan, over low heat, melt vanilla candy coating with sweetened condensed milk, stirring frequently until smooth. Remove from heat; stir in vanilla. Cool. Shape into 1-inch balls. With wooden pick, partially dip each ball into melted chocolate candy coating or roll in cocoa. Place on wax paper-lined baking sheets until firm. Store covered at room temperature or in refrigerator.

Makes about 8 dozen

MICROWAVE DIRECTIONS: In 2-quart glass measure with handle, combine vanilla candy coating and sweetened condensed milk. Cook on 100% power (HIGH) 3 to 3½ minutes or until coating melts, stirring after each 1½ minutes. Proceed as directed.

CHOCOLATE–DIPPED MORSELS

1 package (4 ounces) BAKER'S®
   GERMAN'S® Sweet Chocolate *or* 6 to
   8 squares BAKER'S® Semi-Sweet
   Chocolate*
Assorted centers (suggestions follow)

Microwave chocolate in small microwavable bowl on HIGH 1½ to 2 minutes, stirring halfway through heating time. Stir until chocolate is completely melted.**

Insert toothpicks into food to be dipped. Dip, 1 at a time, into chocolate, covering at least half; let excess chocolate drip off. (To dip pretzels or nuts, stir into chocolate to coat; then remove with fork.)

Let stand at room temperature or refrigerate on wax paper-lined cookie sheet 30 minutes or until chocolate is firm. Store fresh fruit in refrigerator up to 2 days. Store dried fruit, cookies, nuts and pretzels in airtight container for up to 1 month.   *Makes about 2 dozen*

SUGGESTED CENTERS:
Fruit: Firm strawberries, ½-inch banana slices, fresh pineapple wedges or drained canned pineapple chunks, peeled orange slices or orange sections, well-drained stemmed maraschino cherries, dried figs, dried apricots or dates.
Cake: Cut into 1-inch squares.
Peanut Butter and Jelly Sandwich on White Bread: Cut into 1-inch squares.
Large Marshmallows
Nuts: Walnut or pecan halves, or whole almonds or Brazil nuts.
Fruitcake Fingers: Coat only half of cake.
Pretzels

*Or use 1 package (6 squares) BAKER'S® Premium White Chocolate.

****TOP OF STOVE PREPARATION:** Melt chocolate in heavy saucepan on very low heat; stir constantly until just melted. Remove from heat. Continue as above.

MARZIPAN FRUITS

1¾ cups BAKER'S® ANGEL FLAKE®
   Coconut, finely chopped
1 package (4-serving size) JELL-O®
   Brand Gelatin, any flavor
1 cup ground blanched almonds
⅔ cup sweetened condensed milk
1½ teaspoons sugar
1 teaspoon almond extract
Food coloring (optional)

Mix all ingredients in large bowl until well combined. Shape by hand into small fruits, vegetables, hearts, Easter eggs or other forms. (Or use small candy molds.) If desired, use food coloring to paint details on fruit; add whole cloves and citron or angelica for stems and blossom ends. Refrigerate until dry. Store at room temperature in airtight container.
   Makes about 3 cups or 2 to 3 dozen pieces

FOR FRUITS: Use the appropriate flavors and/or colors: strawberry flavor gelatin for strawberries; lemon flavor gelatin for bananas, grapefruit, lemons and Bartlett pears; lime flavor gelatin for green apples, pears, leaves, stems and limes; orange flavor gelatin for tangerines and oranges; cherry or black cherry flavor gelatin for cherries; grape flavor gelatin for grapes.

WALNUT–GRANOLA CLUSTERS

¼ cup butter
1 (10½-ounce) package miniature
   marshmallows
½ teaspoon ground cinnamon
3 cups rolled oats
2 cups chopped California walnuts
1 cup flaked coconut
2 (1-ounce) squares semi-sweet
   chocolate

Microwave butter in large microwavable mixing bowl at HIGH (100% power) 40 seconds or until melted. Stir in marshmallows and cinnamon. Microwave 1½ minutes or until melted, stirring halfway through cooking time. Quickly stir in oats, walnuts and coconut. With wet hands, form mixture into small balls and place on wax paper-lined baking sheets.

Microwave chocolate in glass measuring cup at HIGH 2½ minutes or until melted; stir. Lightly drizzle chocolate over clusters. Clusters may be stored at room temperature, uncovered, 4 to 5 days. *Makes 5 dozen*

Favorite recipe from **Walnut Marketing Board**

ALMOND BUTTER CRUNCH

1 cup BLUE DIAMOND® Blanched Slivered Almonds
½ cup butter
½ cup sugar
1 tablespoon light corn syrup

Line bottom and sides of 8- or 9-inch cake pan with aluminum foil (*not* plastic wrap or wax paper). Butter foil heavily; set aside. Combine almonds, butter, sugar and corn syrup in 10-inch skillet. Bring to a boil over medium heat, stirring constantly. Boil, stirring constantly, until mixture turns golden brown, about 5 to 6 minutes. Working quickly, spread candy in prepared pan. Cool about 15 minutes or until firm. Remove candy from pan by lifting edges of foil. Peel off foil. Cool thoroughly. Break into pieces. *Makes about ¾ pound*

Almond Butter Crunch

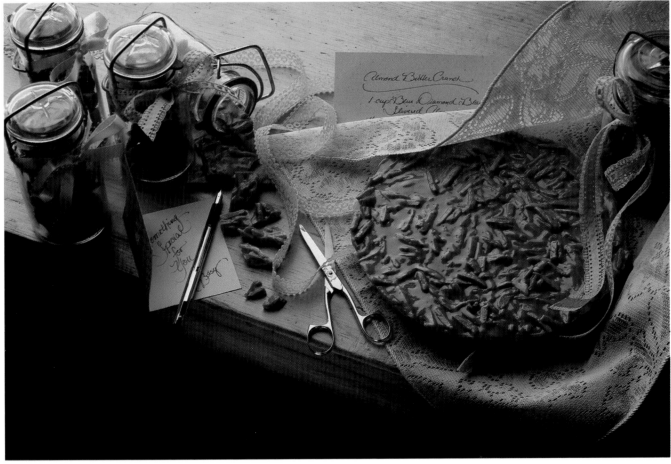

BUTTER ALMOND CRUNCH

1½ cups HERSHEY'S Semi-Sweet
    Chocolate Chips, divided
1¾ cups chopped almonds, divided
1½ cups butter or margarine
1¾ cups sugar
  3 tablespoons light corn syrup
  3 tablespoons water

Heat oven to 350°F. Line 13×9×2-inch pan with foil; butter foil. Sprinkle 1 cup chocolate chips into pan; set aside. In shallow baking pan spread chopped almonds. Bake about 7 minutes or until golden brown; set aside. In heavy 3-quart saucepan melt butter; blend in sugar, corn syrup and water. Cook over medium heat, stirring constantly, to 300°F on a candy thermometer (hard-crack stage) or until mixture separates into hard, brittle threads when dropped into very cold water. (Bulb of candy thermometer should not rest on bottom of saucepan.) Remove from heat; stir in 1½ cups toasted almonds. Immediately spread mixture evenly over chocolate chips in prepared pan; *do not disturb chips.* Sprinkle with remaining ¼ cup toasted almonds and remaining ½ cup chocolate chips; cool slightly. With sharp knife score candy into 1½-inch squares, wiping knife blade after drawing through candy. Cool completely; remove from pan. Remove foil; break candy into pieces. Store in airtight container in cool, dry place.

Makes about 2 pounds candy

STUFFED PECANS

½ cup semisweet chocolate chips
¼ cup sweetened condensed milk
½ teaspoon vanilla
  Powdered sugar (about ½ cup)
80 large pecan halves

Melt chips in very small saucepan over very low heat, stirring constantly. Remove from heat. Stir in sweetened condensed milk and vanilla until smooth. Stir in enough sugar to make stiff mixture. Refrigerate, if needed.

Place 1 rounded teaspoonful chocolate mixture on flat side of 1 pecan half. Top with another pecan half. Repeat with remaining pecans and chocolate mixture. Store in refrigerator.

Makes about 40 candies

CHERRY MERRY CHRISTMAS CRUNCH

2 cups walnut halves
1 cup candied red and green cherries,
    cut in half
2 tablespoons butter or margarine
1 teaspoon salt
1 teaspoon maple extract
¼ teaspoon cherry extract
2 cups sugar
¾ cup light corn syrup
¼ cup maple syrup

Generously grease baking sheet; set aside. Combine walnuts, cherries, butter, salt and extracts in medium bowl; set aside. Combine sugar, corn syrup and maple syrup in heavy, large saucepan. Bring to a boil. Carefully clip candy thermometer to side of pan (do not let bulb touch bottom of pan). Cook over medium heat until thermometer registers 300°F (hard-crack stage). Remove from heat; stir in walnut mixture. Quickly pour onto prepared baking sheet. Cool completely. Break into pieces.

Makes about 2 pounds candy

Butter Almond Crunch

CITRUS CANDIED NUTS

      1 egg white
1½ cups whole almonds
1½ cups pecan halves
      1 cup powdered sugar
      2 tablespoons lemon juice
      2 teaspoons grated orange peel
      1 teaspoon grated lemon peel
⅛ teaspoon ground nutmeg

Preheat oven to 300°F. Generously grease 15½×10½×1-inch jelly-roll pan. Beat egg white in medium bowl with electric mixer on high speed until soft peaks form. Add almonds and pecans; stir until coated. Stir in powdered sugar, lemon juice, orange peel, lemon peel and nutmeg. Turn out onto prepared pan, spreading nuts in single layer.

Bake 30 minutes, stirring after 20 minutes. *Turn off oven.* Let nuts stand in oven 15 minutes more. Immediately remove nuts from pan to sheet of foil. Cool completely. Store up to 2 weeks in airtight container.

Makes about 3 cups nuts

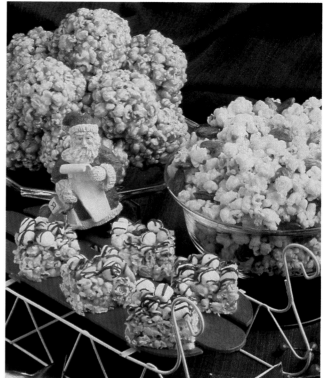

Clockwise from top left: Easy Caramel Pop Corn Balls, Almond Butter Crunch Pop Corn, Rocky Road Peanut Butter Pop Corn Bars

ORANGE–CANDIED WALNUTS

1½ cups sugar
½ cup corn syrup
      2 tablespoons butter
      4 cups California walnuts
      1 teaspoon orange extract

Melt sugar, corn syrup and butter in large, shallow pan over medium-high heat. Add walnuts. Cook and stir about 15 minutes or until sugar mixture begins to caramelize. Stir in extract. Spread walnut mixture evenly onto greased baking sheet, separating walnuts into small clusters. Cool completely.

Makes 4 cups

*Favorite recipe from **Walnut Marketing Board***

EASY CARAMEL POP CORN BALLS

2½ quarts popped JOLLY TIME® Pop Corn
      1 package (14 ounces) light caramels
¼ cup light corn syrup
      2 tablespoons water

Keep popped pop corn warm in deep pan in oven at 200°F. Melt caramels in heavy saucepan over low heat, stirring occasionally, about 15 minutes. Add corn syrup and water; mix until smooth. Slowly pour over pop corn in pan, mixing well. Shape into balls.

Makes 10 medium-sized pop corn balls

MICROWAVE DIRECTIONS: Microwave caramels and water in large microwave-safe bowl on HIGH for 2 to 3 minutes or until mixture is smooth. Stir every minute. Add corn syrup and mix until smooth. Proceed as directed.

ALMOND BUTTER CRUNCH POP CORN

½ cup butter or margarine
1 cup sugar
¼ cup light corn syrup
¼ teaspoon salt
¼ teaspoon baking soda
½ teaspoon vanilla
½ teaspoon butter extract
2½ quarts popped JOLLY TIME® Pop Corn
1½ cups whole almonds, toasted*

Melt butter in medium saucepan. Stir in sugar, corn syrup and salt. Heat to a boil, stirring constantly. Boil for 8 minutes, stirring only once, over lowest heat possible to maintain a boil. Remove from heat; stir in soda, vanilla and butter extract. Gradually pour over combined popped pop corn and nuts, mixing well. Turn into large, shallow baking pan. Bake at 250°F for 30 minutes, mixing well after 15 minutes. Allow to cool completely. Break apart and store in tightly covered container.

Makes about 3 quarts

*To toast almonds, spread on large cookie sheet and toast at 325°F for 15 to 20 minutes.

ROCKY ROAD PEANUT BUTTER POP CORN BARS

3 quarts popped JOLLY TIME® Pop Corn
½ cup raisins
1 cup light corn syrup
1 tablespoon butter or margarine
½ cup peanut butter pieces
⅓ cup chunky or creamy peanut butter
¾ cup miniature marshmallows
½ cup peanuts
½ cup semisweet chocolate pieces
1 teaspoon vegetable shortening

Place popped pop corn and raisins in large bowl. In saucepan, heat corn syrup and butter to boiling. Boil 3 minutes. Remove from heat. Stir in peanut butter pieces and peanut butter. Stir until smooth. Pour mixture over pop corn, tossing gently to coat all pieces. Press into buttered 9-inch square baking pan. Sprinkle marshmallows and peanuts over top, pressing lightly into pop corn mixture. Melt combined chocolate pieces and shortening over very low heat. Drizzle over top. Cool several hours before serving. Cut into 2¼×1-inch bars.

Makes 36 bars

FESTIVE POPCORN TREATS

6 cups popped popcorn
½ cup sugar
½ cup light corn syrup
¼ cup peanut butter
Green food color
¼ cup red cinnamon candies

Line baking sheet with waxed paper. Pour popcorn into large bowl. Combine sugar and corn syrup in medium saucepan. Bring to a boil over medium heat, stirring constantly; boil 1 minute. Remove from heat. Add peanut butter and green food color; stir until peanut butter is completely melted. Pour over popcorn; stir to coat well. Lightly butter hands and shape popcorn mixture into trees. While trees are still warm, press red cinnamon candies into trees. Place on prepared baking sheet; let stand until firm, about 30 minutes. *Makes 6 servings*

Sparkling
REFRESHERS

SPICED APPLE TEA

2 cups unsweetened apple juice
6 whole cloves
1 cinnamon stick
3 cups water
3 bags cinnamon herbal tea

Combine juice, cloves and cinnamon stick in medium saucepan. Bring to a boil over high heat. Reduce heat to low; simmer 10 minutes. Meanwhile, place water in another medium saucepan. Bring to a boil over high heat. Remove from heat; drop in tea bags and allow to steep for 6 minutes. Remove and discard tea bags.

Strain juice mixture; discard spices. Stir juice mixture into tea. Serve warm with additional cinnamon sticks, if desired *or* refrigerate and serve cold over ice. (Tea may be made ahead and reheated.) *Makes 4 servings*

HOT SPICED CIDER

2 quarts apple cider
⅔ cup KARO® Light or Dark Corn Syrup
3 cinnamon sticks
½ teaspoon whole cloves
1 lemon, sliced
    Cinnamon sticks and lemon slices
    (optional)

In medium saucepan combine cider, corn syrup, cinnamon sticks, cloves and lemon slices. Bring to boil over medium-high heat. Reduce heat; simmer 15 minutes. Remove spices. If desired, garnish each serving with a cinnamon stick and lemon slice.

Makes about 10 servings

PREP TIME: 20 minutes

CHRISTMAS CAROL PUNCH

2 medium red apples
2 quarts clear apple cider
½ cup SUN-MAID® Raisins
8 cinnamon sticks
2 teaspoons whole cloves
    Orange slices
    Lemon slices
¼ cup lemon juice

Core apples; slice into ½-inch rings. In Dutch oven, combine cider, apple rings, raisins, cinnamon and cloves. Bring to boil over high heat; reduce heat to low and simmer 5 to 8 minutes or until apples are just tender. Remove cloves; add orange and lemon slices and lemon juice. Pour into punch bowl. Ladle into large mugs, including an apple ring, some raisins and citrus slices in each serving. Serve with spoons. *Makes about 2 quarts*

COCONUT SNOWBALL COCOA

1 pint vanilla ice cream
1 cup flaked coconut
½ cup unsweetened cocoa
1 quart milk
½ cup dark rum (optional)
¾ to 1 cup cream of coconut
1 teaspoon coconut extract
½ cup chocolate-flavored ice cream sauce
    (optional)
8 maraschino cherries (optional)

Scoop ice cream into 8 small balls; immediately roll in coconut. Place on waxed-paper-lined baking sheet; freeze until ready to use.

Whisk cocoa into milk in large saucepan. Stir in rum, if desired, cream of coconut and coconut extract. Bring to a simmer over medium-high heat. Pour into 8 large heatproof mugs.

Float ice cream balls in cocoa. If desired, drizzle each ice cream ball with chocolate sauce and top with cherry. *Makes 8 servings*

Hot Spiced Cider

HOT HOLIDAY PUNCH

    4 cups apple cider
    1 cup granulated sugar
    ½ cup packed brown sugar
    1 cinnamon stick
   12 whole cloves
    2 cups Florida Grapefruit Juice
    2 cups Florida Orange Juice
       Orange slices (optional)
       Maraschino cherry halves (optional)
       Whole cloves (optional)

Combine apple cider and sugars in large saucepan. Heat over medium heat, stirring until sugars dissolve. Add cinnamon stick and cloves. Bring to a boil over medium heat. Reduce heat to low; simmer 5 minutes. Add grapefruit and orange juices. Heat, but do not boil. Strain into heatproof punch bowl. Garnish with orange slices decorated with maraschino cherry halves and whole cloves. Serve in heatproof punch cups.

Makes about 8 (8-ounce) servings

*Favorite recipe from **Florida Department of Citrus***

KAHLÚA® HOT SPICED APPLE CIDER

    1½ ounces KAHLÚA®
    1 cup hot apple cider or apple juice
    1 cinnamon stick

Pour Kahlúa® into hot cider. Stir with cinnamon stick.

Makes 1 serving

HOT MULLED PINEAPPLE JUICE

    6 cups DOLE® Pineapple Juice
    1 DOLE® Apple, cored and cut into
       chunks
    ½ cup DOLE® Raisins
    ½ cup packed brown sugar
       Grated peel of 1 DOLE® Orange
    2 cinnamon sticks, broken
    ½ teaspoon whole cloves

• Combine pineapple juice, apple, raisins, brown sugar, peel, cinnamon sticks and cloves in saucepan. Simmer 5 minutes.

• Remove and discard spices before serving.

Makes 6 servings

HOT BUTTERED PINEAPPLE SMOOTHIE

    5½ cups DOLE® Pineapple Juice
    ¼ cup packed brown sugar
    2 tablespoons butter or margarine
   10 whole cloves
    3 cinnamon sticks
    1 DOLE® Lemon, sliced

• In large saucepan, combine pineapple juice, brown sugar, butter, cloves and cinnamon sticks. Bring to a boil; simmer 5 minutes.

• Remove spices. Add lemon slices. Serve hot in mugs.

Makes 1½ quarts

FIRESIDE PUNCH

1½ cups cranberry juice cocktail
1½ cups cold water
  4 bags LIPTON® Cinnamon Apple or
      Gentle Orange Herbal Flo-Thru Tea
  2 tablespoons brown sugar
    Cinnamon sticks (optional)
    Fresh cranberries (optional)

In medium saucepan, bring cranberry juice and water to a boil. Add cinnamon apple herbal tea bags; cover and brew 5 minutes. Remove tea bags; stir in sugar. Pour into mugs and garnish with cinnamon sticks and fresh cranberries.

Makes about 5 servings

MICROWAVE HOT CHOCOLATE

1 quart milk
1 package (4-serving size) JELL-O®
    Chocolate or Chocolate Fudge Flavor
    Pudding & Pie Filling
  COOL WHIP® Whipped Topping,
    thawed

Pour milk into 2-quart microwavable bowl. Add pudding mix. Beat with wire whisk 20 to 30 seconds. Microwave on HIGH 5 minutes; whisk. Pour into mugs. Top with whipped topping and garnish with shaved chocolate, if desired.

Makes about 4 servings

Hot Pineapple Port Cup

HOT PINEAPPLE PORT CUP

6 cups DOLE® Pineapple Juice
1 bottle (750 mL) port wine
1 cup DOLE® Raisins
½ cup sugar
  Peel of 1 DOLE® Orange*

• Combine pineapple juice, wine, raisins, sugar and peel in Dutch oven. Heat to boiling. Remove from heat and steep 15 minutes.

• Remove and discard peel before serving. Serve warm.   *Makes 12 servings*

* Remove peel from orange with vegetable peeler.

"GLOGG"

3 cups boiling water
1 package (4-serving size) JELL-O®
    Brand Gelatin, any flavor
1 cinnamon stick (optional)
6 whole cloves (optional)
3 orange slices (optional)

Stir boiling water into gelatin in 4-cup measuring cup 2 minutes or until dissolved. Add cinnamon stick, cloves and orange slices. Cover and let stand 5 minutes. Remove spices. Serve with additional cinnamon sticks and clove-studded orange slices, if desired.

Makes about 3 servings

VARIATION: For single serving, use 2 tablespoons gelatin and 1 cup boiling water.

WISCONSIN SPICY APPLE EGGNOG

2 beaten eggs*
3 cups milk
2 cups light cream or half-and-half
⅓ cup sugar
½ teaspoon ground cinnamon
    Dash salt
¾ cup apple brandy
    Ground nutmeg

In large saucepan combine beaten eggs, milk, light cream, sugar, cinnamon and salt. Cook and stir over medium heat until mixture is slightly thickened and heated through, but *do not boil.* Remove from heat; stir in apple brandy. To serve, ladle mixture into 12 heatproof glasses or cups. Sprinkle each serving with nutmeg. Serve warm.

Makes 12 servings

*Use clean, uncracked eggs.

PREP TIME: 25 minutes

*Favorite recipe from **Wisconsin Milk Marketing Board***

PEACHY MEXICAN HOT CHOCOLATE

1 can (16 ounces) California cling peach
    halves or slices, undrained
¼ cup sugar
2 tablespoons unsweetened cocoa
2 cups milk
½ teaspoon ground cinnamon
1 teaspoon vanilla
¼ cup dark rum (optional)
    Whipped cream and additional ground
    cinnamon for garnish

Place peaches with syrup in food processor or blender; process until smooth. Set aside. Combine sugar and cocoa in heavy saucepan. Whisk in enough milk to make a paste, then whisk in remaining milk, peach mixture and ½ teaspoon cinnamon. Cook and stir until mixture comes to a boil. Stir in vanilla and dark rum. To serve, ladle hot chocolate into mugs or glasses. Garnish each with whipped cream and sprinkle with additional cinnamon.

Makes 8 servings

*Favorite recipe from **Canned Fruit Promotion Service, Inc.***

*Left to right: "Glogg", Microwave
Hot Chocolate (page 351)*

EASY COCOA MIX

2 cups nonfat dry milk powder
1 cup sugar
¾ cup powdered non-dairy creamer
½ cup unsweetened cocoa
¼ teaspoon salt

Combine all ingredients in 1-quart airtight container.
Makes about 4 cups mix or 16 servings

For single serving: Place rounded ¼ cup Easy Cocoa Mix in mug or cup; add ¾ cup boiling water. Stir until mix is dissolved. Top with sweetened whipped cream and marshmallows, if desired. Serve immediately.

COCOA MARSHMALLOW MIX: Prepare Easy Cocoa Mix in 2-quart airtight container as directed, adding 1 package (10½ ounces) miniature marshmallows.
Makes about 7 cups mix or 14 servings

For single serving: Place rounded ½ cup Cocoa Marshmallow Mix in mug or cup; add ¾ cup boiling water. Stir until mix is dissolved. Serve immediately.

HOT MAPLE TODDY

1 to 1¼ cups whiskey
1 cup CARY'S®, MAPLE ORCHARDS® or MACDONALD'S™ Pure Maple Syrup
¾ cup REALEMON® Lemon Juice from Concentrate
Butter and cinnamon sticks (optional)

In medium saucepan, combine all ingredients except butter and cinnamon sticks. Over low heat, simmer to blend flavors. Pour into mugs; dot with butter and stir with cinnamon sticks, if desired.
Makes about 3 cups

MICROWAVE DIRECTIONS: In 1-quart glass measure, combine ingredients as above. Microwave on HIGH (100% power) 4 to 5 minutes or until heated through. Serve as above.

HOT COCOA MIX

1 cup CREMORA® Non-Dairy Creamer*
1 cup nonfat dry milk
¼ to 1 cup sugar
½ cup unsweetened cocoa

In medium bowl, combine ingredients; mix well. Store in airtight container. To serve, spoon 3 heaping tablespoons mix into mug; add ¾ cup boiling water. Stir.
Makes about 3 cups

MOCHA: Add ¼ cup instant coffee.

MEXICAN: Add 1 teaspoon ground cinnamon.

LOW–CALORIE: Omit sugar. Add 15 envelopes low-calorie sweetener with NutraSweet® or 2 teaspoons (5 envelopes) low-calorie granulated sugar substitute. To serve, spoon 2 heaping tablespoons into mug; add ¾ cup boiling water. Stir.

*Cremora is a coffee whitener and should not be used as a milk replacement.

Easy Cocoa Mix

VIENNESE COFFEE

1 cup heavy cream, divided
1 teaspoon powdered sugar
1 bar (3 ounces) bittersweet or
   semisweet chocolate
3 cups strong freshly brewed hot coffee
¼ cup crème de cacao or Irish cream
   (optional)

Chill bowl, beaters and cream before whipping. Place ⅔ cup cream and sugar in chilled bowl. Beat with electric mixer at high speed until soft peaks form. *Do not overbeat.* Cover and refrigerate up to 8 hours. If mixture has separated slightly after refrigeration, whisk lightly with wire whisk.

To make chocolate shavings for garnish, make short, quick strokes across chocolate with vegetable peeler; set aside. Break remaining chocolate into pieces.

Place remaining ⅓ cup cream in heavy, small saucepan. Bring to a simmer over medium-low heat. Add chocolate pieces; cover and remove from heat. Let stand 5 minutes or until chocolate is melted; stir until smooth. Add hot coffee to chocolate mixture. Heat on low heat just until bubbles form around edge of pan and coffee is heated through, stirring frequently. Remove from heat; stir in crème de cacao. Pour into 4 warmed mugs. Top with whipped cream. Garnish with chocolate shavings.

Makes about 3½ cups, 4 servings

KAHLÚA® PARISIAN COFFEE

1 ounce cognac or brandy
½ ounce KAHLÚA®
½ ounce Grand Marnier
   Hot coffee
   Whipped cream
   Orange peel (optional)

Pour cognac, Kahlúa® and Grand Marnier into steaming cup of coffee. Top with whipped cream. Garnish with orange peel.

Makes 1 serving

SPIRITED COFFEE LOPEZ

4 cups hot coffee
½ cup COCO LOPEZ® Cream of Coconut
½ cup Irish whiskey
1 teaspoon vanilla extract
   Whipped cream

In heatproof pitcher, combine all ingredients except whipped cream; mix well. Pour into mugs; top with whipped cream. Serve immediately.   *Makes 5 cups*

KAHLÚA® & COFFEE

1½ ounces KAHLÚA®
   Hot coffee
   Whipped cream (optional)

Pour Kahlúa® into steaming cup of coffee. Top with whipped cream.   *Makes 1 serving*

Viennese Coffee

MOCHA COFFEE MIX

1 cup nonfat dry milk powder
¾ cup granulated sugar
⅔ cup powdered non-dairy creamer
½ cup unsweetened cocoa
⅓ cup instant coffee, pressed through fine sieve
¼ cup packed brown sugar
1 teaspoon ground cinnamon
¼ teaspoon salt
¼ teaspoon ground nutmeg

Combine all ingredients in 1-quart airtight container.
Makes about 3½ cups mix or 10 to 12 servings

FOR SINGLE SERVING: Place rounded ¼ cup Mocha Coffee Mix in mug or cup; add ¾ cup boiling water. Stir until mix is dissolved. Serve immediately.

MOCHA COOLER

1 quart DREYER'S or EDY'S GRAND Light Cafe Au Lait Ice Cream
½ cup chocolate milk or regular lowfat milk
Instant coffee granules or espresso powder to taste

• Place 2 scoops Dreyer's or Edy's Grand Light Cafe Au Lait Ice Cream in blender.

• Add chocolate milk and instant coffee granules. Blend until smooth and creamy.

• Pour into large drink glass. Garnish with sprinkle of coffee granules.
Makes 1 serving

NOTE: You may substitute DREYER'S or EDY'S Coffee Fudge Sundae Fat Free Frozen Yogurt for Light Cafe Au Lait Ice Cream.

ICED MOCHA

2 cups strongly brewed coffee
¾ cup skim milk
1 tablespoon packed brown sugar
½ teaspoon unsweetened cocoa powder
Ice

Add coffee, milk, sugar and cocoa to blender. Process until smooth. Pour over ice and serve immediately, or refrigerate, stir well and serve over ice.
Makes 2 servings

*Favorite recipe from **The Sugar Association, Inc.***

EGGNOG CHILL

½ gallon DREYER'S or EDY'S GRAND Eggnog Ice Cream
2 cups skim or lowfat milk
3 vanilla wafer cookies
Ground nutmeg

• Blend 2 cups Dreyer's or Edy's Grand Eggnog Ice Cream and milk in blender until smooth.

• While mixture is blending, use sharp knife to cut small slit in vanilla wafers so they will sit on side of glass.

• Pour shake into large drink glasses. Sprinkle with nutmeg. Garnish with vanilla wafers.
Makes 3 servings

Iced Mocha

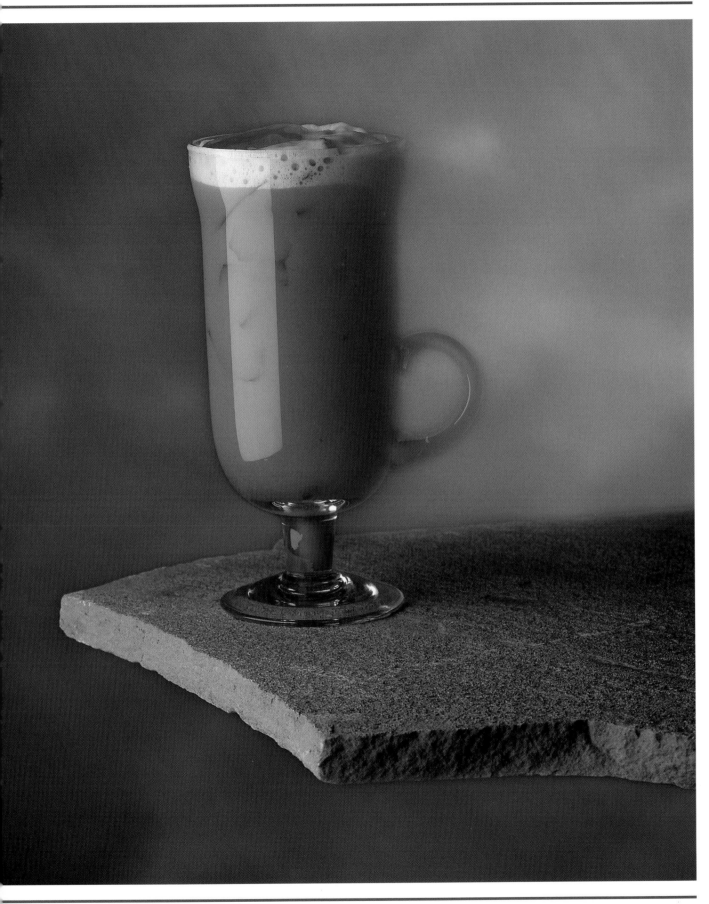

MAPLE EGG NOG

1 (32-ounce) can BORDEN® Egg Nog, chilled
½ cup CARY'S®, MAPLE ORCHARDS® or MACDONALD'S™ Pure Maple Syrup
Ground nutmeg (optional)

In large pitcher, combine egg nog and syrup. Chill. Stir before serving; garnish with nutmeg, if desired. Refrigerate leftovers.

Makes about 1 quart

APPLE SPICE EGG NOG

3 (32-ounce) cans BORDEN® Egg Nog, chilled
3 cups apple cider, chilled
½ teaspoon ground cinnamon

In large bowl, combine ingredients; mix well. Chill. Garnish as desired. Refrigerate leftovers.

Makes about 3½ quarts

KAHLÚA® & EGGNOG

1 quart dairy eggnog
¾ cup KAHLÚA®
Whipped cream
Ground nutmeg

Combine eggnog and Kahlúa® in 1½-quart pitcher. Pour into punch cups. Top with whipped cream. Sprinkle with nutmeg.

Makes about 8 servings

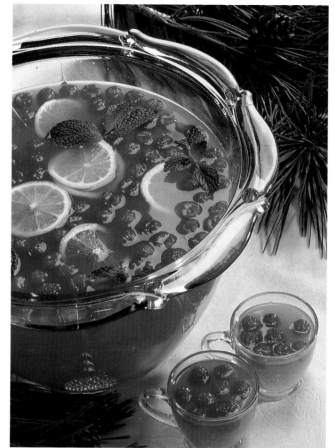

Pineapple Raspberry Punch

PINEAPPLE RASPBERRY PUNCH

5 cups DOLE® Pineapple Juice
1 quart raspberry-cranberry drink
1 pint fresh or frozen raspberries
1 lemon, thinly sliced
Ice

• Chill ingredients. Combine in punch bowl.

Makes 9 cups

CHAMPAGNE PUNCH

1 orange
1 lemon
¼ cup cranberry-flavored liqueur or cognac
¼ cup orange-flavored liqueur or triple sec
1 bottle (750 mL) pink or regular champagne or sparkling white wine, well chilled
Fresh cranberries (optional)
Citrus strips for garnish

Remove colored peel, not white pith, from orange and lemon in long thin strips with citrus peeler. Refrigerate orange and lemon for another use. Combine peels and cranberry- and orange-flavored liqueurs in glass pitcher. Cover and refrigerate 2 to 6 hours.

Just before serving, tilt pitcher to one side and slowly pour in champagne. Leave peels in pitcher for added flavor. Place a cranberry in bottom of each champagne glass. Pour punch into champagne glasses. Garnish with citrus strips tied in knots, if desired.

Makes 4 cups, 6 to 8 servings

NONALCOHOLIC CRANBERRY PUNCH:
Pour 3 cups well-chilled club soda into ⅔ cup (6 ounces) cranberry cocktail concentrate, thawed. Makes 3⅔ cups, 6 servings.

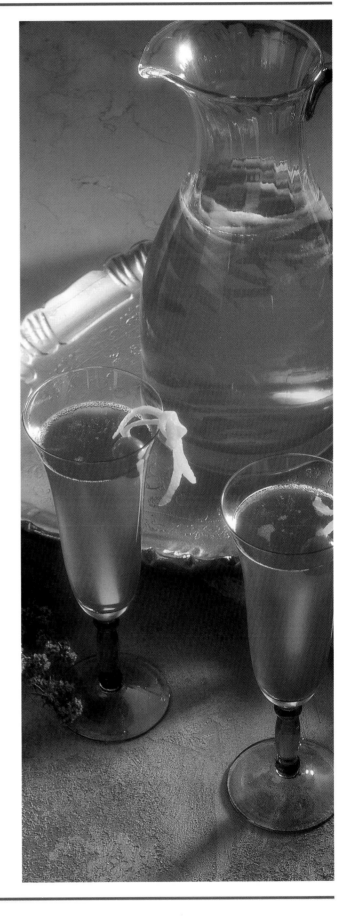

Champagne Punch

DOUBLE BERRY COCO PUNCH

Ice Ring (recipe follows, optional) or block of ice
2 (10-ounce) packages frozen strawberries in syrup, thawed
1 (15-ounce) can COCO LOPEZ® Cream of Coconut
1 (48-ounce) bottle cranberry juice cocktail, chilled
2 cups light rum (optional)
1 (32-ounce) bottle club soda, chilled

Prepare Ice Ring in advance if desired. In blender container, purée strawberries with cream of coconut until smooth. In large punch bowl, combine strawberry mixture, cranberry juice and rum. Just before serving, add club soda and Ice Ring.   *Makes about 4 quarts*

ICE RING: Fill ring mold with water to within 1 inch of top rim; freeze. Arrange strawberries, cranberries, mint leaves, lime slices or other fruits on top of ice. Gradually pour small amount of cold water over fruits; freeze.

CITRUS BERRY FROST

4 scoops or ¾ cup WYLER'S® Sugar Sweetened Lemonade Flavor Crystals
4 cups chilled cranberry juice cocktail
4 cups water
1 cup chilled orange juice
Ice

In large pitcher, combine all ingredients except ice. Serve over ice and garnish, if desired, with cranberries and orange slices.
Makes about 8 servings

CITRUS COOLER

2 cups fresh squeezed orange juice
2 cups unsweetened pineapple juice
1 teaspoon fresh lemon juice
¾ teaspoon vanilla extract
¾ teaspoon coconut extract
2 cups cold sparkling water
Ice
Lemon slices (optional)

Combine juices and extracts in large pitcher; refrigerate until cold. Stir in sparkling water; serve over ice. Garnish with lemon slices, if desired.   *Makes 8 servings*

CELEBRATION PUNCH

1 bottle (48 fluid ounces) DEL MONTE® Pineapple Orange Blended Juice Drink, chilled
1 can (46 fluid ounces) DEL MONTE® Apricot Nectar, chilled
1 cup orange juice
1 cup rum (optional)
¼ cup fresh lime juice
2 tablespoons grenadine
Ice cubes

In punch bowl, combine all ingredients. Garnish with pineapple wedges and lime slices, if desired.   *Makes 16 (6-ounce) servings*

Citrus Cooler

RASPBERRY WINE PUNCH

1 package (10 ounces) frozen red raspberries in syrup, thawed
1 bottle (750 mL) white zinfandel or blush wine
¼ cup raspberry-flavored liqueur
    Empty ½-gallon milk or juice carton
3 to 4 cups distilled water, divided
    Fresh cranberries
    Sprigs of pine and tinsel

Process raspberries with syrup in food processor or blender until smooth; press through strainer, discarding seeds. Combine wine, raspberry purée and liqueur in pitcher; refrigerate until serving time. Rinse out wine bottle and remove label.

Fully open top of carton. Place wine bottle in center of carton. Tape bottle securely to carton so bottle will not move when adding water. Pour 2 cups distilled water into carton. Carefully push cranberries, pine sprigs and tinsel into water between bottle and carton to form decorative design. Add remaining water to almost fill carton. Freeze until firm, 8 hours or overnight.

Just before serving, peel carton from ice block. Using funnel, pour punch back into wine bottle. Wrap bottom of ice block with white cotton napkin or towel to hold while serving.

Makes 8 servings

NOTE: Punch may also be served in a punch bowl, if desired.

Raspberry Wine Punch

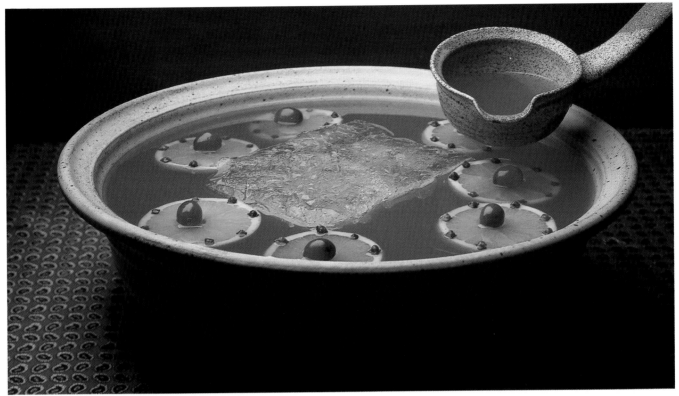

Cranberry Orange Punch

CRANBERRY ORANGE PUNCH

2 (32-ounce) bottles cranberry juice cocktail, chilled
1½ cups REALEMON® Lemon Juice from Concentrate
⅔ cup sugar
2 (12-ounce) cans orange soda, chilled
Ice

In large punch bowl, combine cranberry juice, REALEMON® brand and sugar; stir until sugar dissolves. Just before serving, add orange soda and ice. Garnish as desired.

Makes about 3½ quarts

EASY ORANGE FIZZ

Maraschino cherries
Mint leaves
1 (6-ounce) can frozen Florida Orange Juice Concentrate, thawed
Club soda or tonic water, chilled

Thoroughly drain maraschino cherries. Arrange mint leaves and cherries in compartments of ice cube trays; fill with water and freeze until firm to form decorative ice cubes. Prepare orange juice concentrate according to label directions, *except* substitute club soda or tonic water for the water. Pour into glasses over decorative ice cubes. Serve immediately.

Makes 4 (6-ounce) servings

Favorite recipe from **Florida Department of Citrus**

CRANBERRY SANGRÍA

1 bottle (750 ml) Beaujolais or dry red
    wine
1 cup cranberry juice cocktail
1 cup orange juice
½ cup cranberry-flavored liqueur
    (optional)
1 orange,* thinly sliced
1 lime,* thinly sliced

Combine wine, cranberry juice cocktail, orange juice, liqueur, orange slices and lime slices in large glass pitcher. Chill 2 to 8 hours before serving.

Pour into glasses; add orange and/or lime slices from sangría to each glass.
Makes about 7 cups, 10 to 12 servings

SPARKLING SANGRÍA: Just before serving, tilt pitcher and slowly add 2 cups well-chilled sparkling water or club soda. Pour into glasses; add orange and/or lime slices from sangría to each glass. Makes about 9 cups, 12 to 15 servings.

*Orange and lime may be scored before slicing to add a special touch. To score, make a lengthwise groove in fruit with citrus stripper. Continue to make grooves ¼ to ½ inch apart until entire fruit has been grooved.

KAHLÚA® PARTY PUNCH

2 cups KAHLÚA®
1 can (12 ounces) frozen apple juice
    concentrate, undiluted
½ cup lemon juice
1 small block of ice
1 bottle (25.4 ounces) sparkling apple
    juice
1 quart club soda or lemon-lime beverage
1 bottle (750 mL) dry champagne
    Thin lemon slices and small orange
      slices for garnish

Refrigerate ingredients until well chilled. Combine Kahlúa® with undiluted apple juice concentrate and lemon juice. Pour over small block of ice in punch bowl. Add sparkling apple juice, club soda and champagne; stir gently. Add lemon and orange slices.
Makes 30 (½-cup) servings (about 1 gallon)

NOTE: Kahlúa®, undiluted apple juice concentrate and lemon juice may be mixed and refrigerated the day before.

Cranberry Sangría

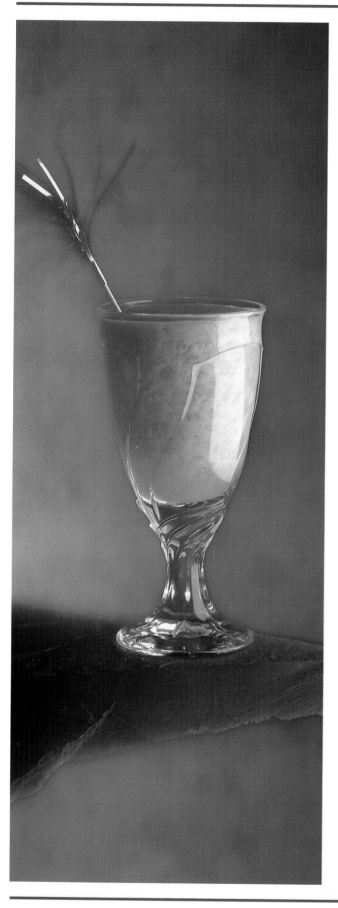

Peach Fizz

PEACH FIZZ

**3 fresh California peaches, peeled,
    halved, pitted and sliced
1 can (6 ounces) pineapple juice
¼ cup frozen limeade or lemonade
    concentrate
¼ teaspoon almond extract
    Finely crushed ice
3 cups club soda, chilled**

Add peaches to food processor or blender.
Process until smooth to measure 2 cups purée.
Stir in pineapple juice, limeade and almond
extract. Fill 12-ounce glasses ⅔ full with
crushed ice. Add ⅓ cup peach base to each.
Top with club soda. Stir gently. Serve
immediately.   *Makes 6 servings*

*Favorite recipe from **California Tree Fruit Agreement***

PIÑA COLADA PUNCH

**5 cups DOLE® Pineapple Juice, divided
1 can (15 ounces) cream of coconut
1 liter lemon-lime soda
2 limes, divided
1½ cups light rum (optional)
    Ice cubes
    Mint sprigs**

• Chill all ingredients.

• Blend 2 cups pineapple juice with cream of
coconut in blender. Combine puréed mixture
with remaining 3 cups pineapple juice, soda,
juice of 1 lime, rum and ice. Garnish with 1
lime, sliced and mint.   *Makes 15 servings*

LEMONY LIGHT COOLER

3 cups dry white wine or white grape juice, chilled
½ to ¾ cup sugar
½ cup REALEMON® Lemon Juice from Concentrate
1 (32-ounce) bottle club soda, chilled
Strawberries, plum, peach or orange slices or other fresh fruit
Ice

In pitcher, combine wine, sugar and ReaLemon® brand; stir until sugar dissolves. Chill. Just before serving, add club soda and fruit; serve over ice.   *Makes about 7 cups*

APPLE CINNAMON CREAM LIQUEUR

1 (14-ounce) can EAGLE® Brand Sweetened Condensed Milk (NOT evaporated milk)
1 cup apple schnapps
2 cups (1 pint) BORDEN® or MEADOW GOLD® Whipping Cream or Half-and-Half
½ teaspoon ground cinnamon
Ice

In blender container, combine all ingredients except ice; blend until smooth. Serve over ice. Garnish as desired. Store covered in refrigerator. Stir before serving.
Makes about 1 quart

FUZZY NAVEL CREAM LIQUEUR: Omit apple schnapps and cinnamon. Add 1 cup peach schnapps and ¼ cup frozen orange juice concentrate, thawed. Proceed as above.

Lemony Light Cooler

SPICED RED WINE

Grape Ice Ring (recipe follows)
½ cup sugar
½ cup water
**1 bottle (750 mL) Burgundy wine,
    chilled**
2 cups white grape juice, chilled
1 cup peach schnapps, chilled

Prepare Grape Ice Ring.

Combine sugar and water in small saucepan.
Bring to a boil. Boil, stirring constantly, until
sugar dissolves. Cool to room temperature.
Cover; refrigerate until chilled, about 2 hours.

Combine wine, grape juice, schnapps and
sugar syrup in punch bowl. Float Grape Ice
Ring in punch.   *Makes 14 servings*

GRAPE ICE RING

**2 pounds assorted seedless grapes
    (Thompson, Red Empress, etc.)**
Lemon leaves* (optional)

Fill 4-cup ring mold with water to within ¾ inch
of top. Freeze until firm, about 8 hours or
overnight. Arrange clusters of grapes and
leaves on ice; fill with water to top of mold.
Freeze until solid, about 6 hours. To unmold,
dip bottom of mold briefly in hot water.

*These nontoxic leaves are available in florist
shops.

BLOODY MARY MIX

1 quart vegetable juice cocktail
**2 tablespoons HEINZ® Worcestershire
    Sauce**
1 tablespoon fresh lime or lemon juice
¼ teaspoon granulated sugar
¼ teaspoon black pepper
¼ teaspoon hot pepper sauce
⅛ teaspoon garlic powder
Ice

In pitcher, thoroughly combine vegetable juice,
Worcestershire sauce, lime juice, sugar, black
pepper, hot pepper sauce and garlic powder;
cover and chill. Serve over ice. Garnish with
celery stalks and lime wedges, if desired.
                        Makes about 1 quart

NOTE: To prepare Bloody Mary Cocktail, add
3 or 4 parts Bloody Mary Mix to 1 part vodka.

HOMEMADE CREAM LIQUEURS

**1 (14-ounce) can EAGLE® Brand
    Sweetened Condensed Milk (NOT
    evaporated milk)**
**1¼ cups flavored liqueur (almond, coffee,
    orange or mint)**
**1 cup (½ pint) BORDEN® or MEADOW
    GOLD® Whipping Cream or Half-
    and-Half**
Ice

In blender container, combine all ingredients
except ice; blend until smooth. Serve over ice.
Garnish as desired. Store tightly covered in
refrigerator. Stir before serving.
                        Makes about 1 quart

Spiced Red Wine with Grape Ice Ring

Acknowledgments

The publishers would like to thank the companies and organizations listed below for the use of their recipes and photographs in this publication.

Alaska Seafood Marketing Institute
Almond Board of California
American Dairy Association
American Egg Board
American Lamb Council
Arm & Hammer Division, Church & Dwight Co., Inc.
American Spice Trade Association
BC-USA
Best Foods Division, CPC International Inc.
Bongrain Cheese U.S.A.
Blue Diamond Growers
Bob Evans Farms®
Borden Kitchens, Borden, Inc.
California Apricot Advisory Board
California Beef Council
California Kiwifruit Commission
California Raisin Advisory Board
California Table Grape Commission
California Tree Fruit Agreement
Canned Food Information Council
Canned Fruit Promotion Service, Inc.
Chef Paul Prudhomme's Magic Seasoning Blends®
Clear Springs Foods
The Dannon Company, Inc.
Del Monte Corporation
Delmarva Poultry Industry, Inc.
Dole Food Company, Inc.
Domino Sugar Corporation
Dreyer's Grand Ice Cream, Inc.

Farmhouse Foods Company
Filippo Berio Olive Oil
Florida Department of Agriculture and Consumer Services, Bureau of Seafood and Aquaculture
Florida Department of Citrus
Florida Tomato Committee
Grandma's Molasses, a division of Cadbury Beverages, Inc.
Heinz U.S.A.
Hershey Foods Corporation
The HVR Company
Illinois State Fair
Jolly Time® Pop Corn
Jones Dairy Farm
Kahlúa Liqueur
Keebler® Company
Kellogg Company
Kerr Group, Inc.®
Kikkoman International Inc.
Kraft Foods, Inc.
Lawry's® Foods, Inc.
Leaf®, Inc.
Lipton
McIlhenny Company
Michigan Apple Committee
MOTT'S® Inc., a division of Cadbury Beverages Inc.
Nabisco, Inc
National Cattlemen's Beef Association
National Cherry Foundation

National Dairy Board
National Fisheries Institute
National Honey Board
National Pasta Association
National Pork Producers Council
National Turkey Federation
Nestlé USA
Newman's Own, Inc.®
New York Apple Association, Inc.
Norseland, Inc.
North Dakota Barley Council
Ocean Spray Cranberries, Inc.
Oregon Washington California Pear Bureau
Perdue® Farms Incorporated
Pet Incorporated
The Procter & Gamble Company
Quaker® Kitchens
Ralston Foods, Inc.
Refined Sugars Incorporated
Chocolate Riesen® Caramels
Riviana Foods Inc.
Sargento Foods, Inc.®
The J. M. Smucker Company
StarKist Seafood Company
The Sugar Association, Inc.
Sun-Maid Growers of California
USA Dry Pea & Lentil Council
USA Rice Federation
Walnut Marketing Board
Washington Apple Commission
Wisconsin Milk Marketing Board

Index

METRIC CONVERSION CHART

VOLUME
MEASUREMENTS (dry)

¹/₈ teaspoon = 0.5 mL
¹/₄ teaspoon = 1 mL
¹/₂ teaspoon = 2 mL
³/₄ teaspoon = 4 mL
1 teaspoon = 5 mL
1 tablespoon = 15 mL
2 tablespoons = 30 mL
¹/₄ cup = 60 mL
¹/₃ cup = 75 mL
¹/₂ cup = 125 mL
²/₃ cup = 150 mL
³/₄ cup = 175 mL
1 cup = 250 mL
2 cups = 1 pint = 500 mL
3 cups = 750 mL
4 cups = 1 quart = 1 L

VOLUME MEASUREMENTS (fluid)

1 fluid ounce (2 tablespoons) = 30 mL
4 fluid ounces (¹/₂ cup) = 125 mL
8 fluid ounces (1 cup) = 250 mL
12 fluid ounces (1¹/₂ cups) = 375 mL
16 fluid ounces (2 cups) = 500 mL

WEIGHTS (mass)

¹/₂ ounce = 15 g
1 ounce = 30 g
3 ounces = 90 g
4 ounces = 120 g
8 ounces = 225 g
10 ounces = 285 g
12 ounces = 360 g
16 ounces = 1 pound = 450 g

DIMENSIONS

¹/₁₆ inch = 2 mm
¹/₈ inch = 3 mm
¹/₄ inch = 6 mm
¹/₂ inch = 1.5 cm
³/₄ inch = 2 cm
1 inch = 2.5 cm

OVEN
TEMPERATURES

250°F = 120°C
275°F = 140°C
300°F = 150°C
325°F = 160°C
350°F = 180°C
375°F = 190°C
400°F = 200°C
425°F = 220°C
450°F = 230°C

BAKING PAN SIZES

Utensil	Size in Inches/Quarts	Metric Volume	Size in Centimeters
Baking or Cake Pan (square or rectangular)	8×8×2	2 L	20×20×5
	9×9×2	2.5 L	22×22×5
	12×8×2	3 L	30×20×5
	13×9×2	3.5 L	33×23×5
Loaf Pan	8×4×3	1.5 L	20×10×7
	9×5×3	2 L	23×13×7
Round Layer Cake Pan	8×1½	1.2 L	20×4
	9×1½	1.5 L	23×4
Pie Plate	8×1¼	750 mL	20×3
	9×1¼	1 L	23×3
Baking Dish or Casserole	1 quart	1 L	—
	1½ quart	1.5 L	—
	2 quart	2 L	—